W9-CFU-492

POLITICS
AND
SOCIETY
IN
MODERN
ISRAEL

POLITICS AND SOCIETY IN MODERN ISRAEL

MYTHS AND REALITIES

SECOND EDITION

ADAM GARFINKLE

M.E.Sharpe
Armonk, New York
London, England

Library of Congress Cataloging-in-Publication Data

Garfinkle, Adam M., 1951– .
Politics and society in modern Israel : myths and realities / by Adam Garfinkle.—2nd ed.
   p. cm.
Includes bibliographical references and index.
ISBN 0-7656-0514-7 (c :alk. paper)—ISBN 0-7656-0515-5 (p :alk. paper)
  1. Israel—Politics and government. 2. Israel—Social conditions. 3. Israel—Foreign
relations. 4. National characteristics, Israeli—Anecdotes. I. Title.

DS126.5 .G357 1999
956.94—dc21   99-044578

CIP

Printed in the United States of America

BM (c) 10   9   8   7   6   5   4   3   2   1
BM (p) 10   9   8   7   6   5   4   3   2   1

This book is dedicated to Scilla,
my soul- and lifemate
(also my wife and mother of our children),
without whose uplifting love
nothing would get done or make ,sense.

Contents

Preface to
the Second Edition

The purpose of this book is to provide readers with a basic introduction to the society, politics, and foreign and security policies of the state of Israel. My aim has been to keep the book as short and clear as possible, as any introduction should be.[1] So it was when the first edition was published in early 1997; so it remains with this second edition in late 1999.

Such brevity and simplicity will not please everyone. Israel is a country that many Americans think they understand well, and some students sound sure that they do not need a basic introduction. This is partly because Israel is in the news more than most foreign countries—especially such small ones—and that, in turn, is because of several special connections between Israel and the United States. Israel is a Jewish state, and the European Christian origins of American society and political culture dictate that the reestablishment of a Jewish state on the soil of ancient Israel will bear historical and even theological interest to many Americans. Don't forget: the Puritans of seventeenth-century New England strove to create a "Biblical commonwealth" in America, the "wilderness Zion"—and they called their churches synagogues, too.

Israel is also a democracy, is important to most Jews who live in America, and is located in an area of strategic significance for the United States and its allies. Add to this the sheer drama of Israel's foreign policy and security predicament over the years, and it is obvious why Israel, despite being a small country very far away, has such a large news profile in America.

But just because Israel is often in the news does not mean that even reasonably attentive students have a comprehensive, balanced, or accurate grasp of Israeli society, politics, and foreign policy. Some may, but even many American Jews who visit Israel for the first time find, to their amazement and sometimes to their shock, that Israel is very different from what they imagined it would be. Even truly advanced students may find that reading a primer will not do them any harm, for an important kind of learning can sometimes flow from restating basic information in a new way.

It is hard to write an introductory text. When experts, scholars, and professors write for other experts, scholars, and professors, they can assume a certain base of knowledge, and on that base they can proceed to communicate whatever ideas, data, or interpretations happen to be on their minds. But when an author writes for beginners, he cannot assume much beyond basic comprehension of the English language. That makes it difficult to know how to start a discussion of complicated topics, and when to end it.

There are a few other reasons why this has been a hard book to write. First, most students are young—at least younger than their professors. By definition, young people have fewer life experiences than older people, and that includes simply having lived through events and, presumably at least, having paid some attention to them. I was sixteen years old, for example, at the time of the June 1967 War, a war that probably reshaped the region's politics and Israel itself like no other event since Israel's birth in 1948. I remember those six days well, but most students reading this book were not yet born. Little wonder, then, that their memories of those days are less sharp than mine.

Second, whatever life experiences students have had have probably not been in Israel, or else they would not need to read a primer in English, or in any language. So I had to figure out how to explain not only events my readers have never experienced but also the workings of a place in which they have never lived.

I should perhaps add something about my own experiences that led the publisher to think I was qualified to write this book. I have lived in Israel for various periods at different times in my life, but I am not an Israeli citizen. I first went to Israel in 1964, when I was thirteen years old. I spent four months working in a kibbutz orchard in 1971. I returned many times thereafter, including for a year spent working at Tel Aviv University (1992–93). During this year, I was accompanied by my wife and our three children, who attended Israeli schools (kindergarten, grade 2, and grade 5). We rented an apartment, had a car, got and paid bills, bought car and health insurance, watched TV and listened to the radio, went food shopping—in short, we did all the things that normal adults normally do wherever they live, and we did it in gradually more natural and effective Hebrew. In other words, while I am not a native Israeli or an Israeli citizen, personal experiences at different times in my life have made me reasonably familiar with how the country works.

Just as important, having been born, raised, and schooled in the United States provide me with two complementary benefits: I am distanced enough from Israel to facilitate a more balanced view of many topics than an Israeli citizen might be expected to have; and I know what Americans tend to assume about the relationships between society and politics, ideas and actions, domestic and foreign policy based on their socialization in the United States. The point of teaching is not to say what you know, but first to see what the student knows and then to enrich his or her understanding. This is what I've tried to do, partly by making many comparisons between Israel and the United States in an attempt to provide a baseline in the student's own experience from which to grasp the points I'm trying to make.

A third reason that writing this book was hard is that, as I explain in detail later on, Israel is not easy to explain in any event, even to older and more experienced readers, because it is not an ordinary country. Its history, demography, and political culture are atypical. It's also especially hard in the Israeli case to separate social from economic from political from ideological from historical factors; that's why I've done much cross-referencing from chapter to chapter to help tie the tale together.

Fourth, thanks in part to its unusual nature, its birth in war, and its survival ever since, Israel can be an emotional subject. Consider the fact that millions of people who are not citizens of the State of Israel—mainly Jews who live outside of Israel—love it devotedly, while a great many others hate it with similar energies. It's hard to think of any other country in the world, especially one the size of New Jersey and with a population of just six million, that generates such powerful passions in those who aren't even counted among its citizens! And as everybody knows, powerful emotions tend to distort objective analysis and description.

When it comes to Israel, I'm not a totally disinterested observer. But I'm also trained as a scholar, and I have tried to be as objective and fair as possible. Success at this is not best measured by making everyone happy, which is impossible, but by making Israel's most fervent friends and its most fervent enemies angry in roughly equal measure.

Fifth, the more introductory a book, the more generalizations and simplifications must be made—at least that is true if the book is to be less than a thousand pages long. But it is hard to generalize effectively and it can be irritating to simplify. People who like teaching and who love learning usually want to impart their own enthusiasm for the subject and their knowledge of it. So it is frustrating to have to leave things out in the interests of clarity and brevity.

A sixth reason why writing this book was hard is that Israel is changing fast. Between the time I was asked to write this book and the time I first finished it, dramatic developments in Israel's foreign and security policy took place. Peace between Israel and Jordan, the relative normalization of Israel's relations with several other Arab and Muslim countries, and the potential for peace between Israelis and Palestinians were all momentous developments whose full impact on the region and on Israeli society were not fully clear. Nor was the full impact of the Likud electoral victory on May 29, 1996, clear—an event that was only a little more than five months old when I completed the first edition.

Things have not slowed down since. As I write now, Israel has just passed another national election, one in which Labor Party leader Ehud Barak defeated Benyamin Netanyahu by a wide margin, 56 to 44 percent, on May 17, 1999. I discuss the implications of the new government and the nature of the election itself later on in the book. But suffice it to say for now that the May 1999 election showed several new trends and bears several significant implications for Israeli society, politics, and foreign relations—but all of them are still too new to more than guess at.

So it was hard. On the other hand, writing this book was both educational and in some ways even fun. It was educational because having to state basics for students requires a condensation that forces an economy of both thought and expression on the writer. Both are valuable exercises. It was fun partly because I tried to write the book in a way that would be fun to read. I have always believed that education and entertainment are kindred endeavors, and I've tried to make them so in this book. With the kind dispensation of the editors, I've applied a smattering of wit, told a joke or two, and related a few personal experiences in the form of vignettes interspersed throughout the text.

I've put them in boxes, just like this.

In short, I was asked to write an interpretive essay rather than a standard text filled with charts, facts, and statistics. (There are some statistics and facts, of course.) Accordingly, I've tried to style my prose not just to capture the information at hand but also to convey its feel. It was a challenge—but also fun—trying to do that. So I've gotten at least some enjoyment from writing this book, and from preparing its second edition, and I hope there's some enjoyment here for you, too, in the reading.

Finally, we come to the obligatory—but in this case freely given—expressions of gratitude. First of all I thank Howard Wiarda, without whom this book would never have been written. I also thank Harvey Sicherman, president of the Foreign Policy Research Institute, who allowed me the time to write much of the first edition at my office desk. My gratitude goes out, as well, to several students whose sharp eyes caught several ambiguities for me to clarify, among them Avi Alpert, David Friedenreich, and Yael Rosenberg. I also thank my cousin, Debbie Lincoln, who reviewed the text for me and helped me secure some elusive rainfall data and some of the maps used in this book. Special thanks go out to my good Israeli friends Asher Susser and Bruce Maddy-Weitzman, the former responsible for getting me to Israel for a year in 1992–93, much enhancing my knowledge of the subject, and the latter responsible for other kindnesses and aid too numerous to list. I also thank Geoffrey Wheatcroft, whose unexpected, and unexpectedly laudatory, review of a work intended mainly as a textbook in the (*London*) *Times Literary Supplement* on March 20, 1998 both helped advertise the book and subsequently made us corresponding colleagues.

Lastly—save for the dedication—I thank Patricia Kolb, Elizabeth Granda, and all the staff at M.E. Sharpe for their considerate, competent, and generous help in producing the book both the first time, and the second.

Adam Garfinkle
Bala Cynwyd, PA
June 6, 1999

POLITICS
AND
SOCIETY
IN
MODERN
ISRAEL

1

Introduction

Any book about the modern state of Israel must examine several areas of sociopolitical reality: the historical origins of the modern state; its main social and economic institutions; its general political culture; its electoral, judicial, and administrative bodies; its public policy agenda; and its foreign and national security policy. Key to all these topics, however, is understanding the process whereby Israeli experience is turning the Jewish historical mythos into modern Jewish reality.[1]

More than is the case with most countries, the origin of the present state of Israel is to be found in a set of ideas, not in the organic political evolution of a group of people living in a particular place over an extended period, which is how almost all other modern polities have developed. These ideas, which have roots in the ancient past but which speak to the modern (post-eighteenth-century) condition of the Jewish people, have a generative nature about them. Generative? I mean by generative only that, as in all other cases, beliefs about the past give rise to, or generate, expectations of the future.

In most cases, such expectations flow from historical continuity and resonate with extensive collective experience. For example, the United States has been a representative democracy within a large, ultimately continental-scale, state for the better part of two centuries; nearly all Americans expect that this will remain the case long into the future. This is certainly not an unreasonable belief, but that is not the point here. The point here is that the belief helps foster the ensuing reality. But understanding Israel means understanding the relationship between beliefs and expectations when the historical experience in question has been strikingly *discontinuous*. In such circumstances, reality is as likely to confound expectations as to confirm them. What happens then?

When reality delivers a rude shock to individuals, the response varies.

Some people adjust their expectations and beliefs in the light of reality, as in "Well, I'm not going to be a millionaire by the time I'm thirty after all, so I'd better adjust my way of living and learn to appreciate what I have." But others prefer to reinterpret reality to fit their beliefs and expectations, as in "I must become a millionaire by the time I'm thirty, so I'll make riskier investments, take legal shortcuts, and work against those 'conspiring' against me." The former strategy promises some short-term emotional pain but longer-term satisfaction. The latter strategy avoids short-term pain but risks long-term disaster.

Societies traffic in the same sorts of problems and basically employ the same sort of options for coping, although, obviously, societal beliefs present a far more complex phenomenon than individual ones. (An entire nation cannot lie on a psychiatrist's couch, for example.) The founders of the modern state of Israel expected certain realities to come to pass. Some of these have in fact come to pass, but others have not. How is Israel coping with its disappointments? For that matter, how is it coping with its achievements, which invariably raise the twin questions of every younger generation in any land: "So what?" and "What have you done for me lately?"

Israel the Exceptional

The beginning of wisdom in understanding the implications of the distance between mythos and reality in the modern Israeli experience is the recognition that Israel is not an ordinary country. At the base of its differences is the aforementioned discontinuity of its historical experience. Let us count some of the ways in which this is manifest.

In an ordinary country, most members of the main nationality that make up the country live inside it, not outside of it. But there are more Jews living outside of Israel than inside it. (There are more Jews just in the New York City metropolitan area than there are in Israel.) Such states are called *projection states*; there are not many in the world (Armenia, Botswana, Grenada, Greece before about 1850, maybe Lebanon but nobody knows for sure), but when they do exist it makes a big difference in the country's politics.

In no nation except Israel can the majority of people read and understand texts their forefathers wrote some four thousand years earlier. Israelis, whose native language is modern Hebrew, can.[2]

Most nations—and here we speak of like-minded groups of people, not territories, states, or governments—are bound together by a myth of tribal bloodlines, like that of Romulus for Italy and Russ for Russia; and it is literally true that most nations are extensions and elaborations of tribes or clan groups that expanded over time. Jews have the myth, for all Jews are supposedly descended from the Patriarchs and Matriarchs: Abraham, Isaac, and Jacob; Sarah, Rebecca, Leah, and Rachel. But they do not have the reality. Through centuries of diverse exiles and the intermarriages and conversions in and out of Judaism that took place in every generation, the genetic stuff of modern Jewry—and of modern Israel in particular, which is a modern Jewish genetic melting pot—is more diverse than just about any nation on earth.

In ordinary countries one can distinguish readily between ethnicity and religious affiliation among the people who live within it. There are French Catholics and French Protestants, and even French Muslims and French Jews. To be a Frenchman does not presuppose a religious identification. On the other hand, there are Muslims who are Arab and Muslims who are Turks, Indonesians, Bosnians, Albanians, and Malays. To be a Muslim does not presuppose a particular ethnic identification. But with Israelis and Jews it is not so simple. There are Israeli citizens who are not Jews—about 17 percent are Arabs, mostly Muslim but many Christian—but clearly Israel is a self-described Jewish state and was created as such. So the proper noun Jew can be set in distinction to Muslim, in which case one is contrasting religion; and Jew can just as readily be set in distinction to Arab, in which case one is contrasting ethnicity.

What this points to is that Jews are not just a religious group but also a people, and to become a Jew by religion is to become a member of the Jewish people as well. Obviously, therefore, Jews are not a race, although there are racial (that is to say, genetic) commonalities between large groups of Jews. Yet religion as such does not define a Jew, either. Not all Jews—and only a minority of Israelis—are religious, but they still consider themselves, and are, members of the Jewish people. Perhaps the best way to put it is this: Jews are people defined largely by possession of a common religious civilization, the longevity of which has produced racially identifiable clusters, and who today express that civilization in a variety of ways ranging from traditional observance to various forms of secularism, including secular nationalism.

This has created huge complications for Israeli law. Zionism stresses Jewish identity as a national group, not as a religious group. Yet there is no obvious way to define a Jew outside of at least basic religious criteria. A case in point is that of "Brother Daniel." In the early 1960s, a man named Daniel Rufeison, who was born a Jew but who later became a Catholic monk, petitioned Israeli courts to be declared a Jew and have that inscribed on his identity card. "Brother Daniel" wanted Israeli citizenship under the Law of Return, a law that enables Jews to become instant citizens of Israel upon immigration (others can also become citizens, but there is a standard waiting period just like in the United States). The Israeli High Court, in a split

decision, said no—that the common definition of a Jew was such that someone who actively professed another religion could not be considered a Jew.
While the Court did not dare elevate Jewish religious law (*halaka*) as the
binding authority in the decision, thus, in effect, making the state subordinate to religious law, its judgment certainly fuzzed the matter very thoroughly. And fuzzed it remains, as Israeli politicians and diaspora Jewish
leaders battle over the question of "Who is a Jew?" which often as not comes
down to "Who is a Rabbi?" But more of this later on.

To make matters even more complicated, most Jews who are not Israeli
citizens consider themselves members of the Jewish people, and this binds
them emotionally to Israel regardless of how they feel about religion. In the
American context, for example, we typically refer to Italian Americans, Irish
Americans, and African Americans, but to American Jews. Note which word
is the identifying noun and which the descriptive adjective. This is sugges-
tive of why Americans of Italian or Irish or Polish decent do not have the
same kind of relationship to Italy, Ireland, and Poland as most American
Jews have to Israel.

In an ordinary country, too, political sovereignty is based on typical historical relationships among territory (the country), people (the nation), and
government (the state). Most typically, the nation has long lived on the territory, and the state has evolved organically over time as an outgrowth of
authority relationships in society. The sense of nation as a conceptual unity
grows from people having lived together in more or less the same place for
a very long time, having intermarried, and having spoken the same living, if
evolving, daily language.

It follows from what has already been said that this is not so for Israel.
Ancient Israel developed in more or less such an ordinary way, but between
the years 135 and 1948, the great majority of Jews lived in what they conceived to be exile, their land ruled by a procession of foreigners: Romans,
Byzantine Greeks, Arabians, Crusaders, Seljuk Turks, Mamelukes, Egyptians, Ottoman Turks, and Britons. The Hebrew language became a language of liturgy and religious study as Jews adopted other languages for
daily life depending on where they lived. For a very long time, then, Jews
had no common spoken language and lived on no common territory.

During the exile, and despite the diversity of historical experiences within
it, the concept of a unitary Jewish peoplehood was maintained through the
power of an evolving portable religious civilization, rabbinic Judaism—in
other words, through the power of an idea. Jewish self-identification was
shaped not only by redacted memory of the ancient past and more recent
history, both as interpreted through this evolving civilization, but also by the
common experience of political powerlessness, more than occasional perse-

cution, and the varied and often highly creative synergies that developed between Jewish culture and the cultures in which Jews lived.

As a result of the experiences of these long years, the Jewish mythos evolved further. The initial fusion of monotheistic religion, a literary culture that expressed it, and a Land that concretized and sustained both, was changed to accommodate a new set of abstract attributes developed to define the essence of the Jewish spirit and the role of the Jewish people in exile. In this evolved formulation, the key element of the Land was not lost but abstracted. From the time of Abraham himself, Zion was always regarded as a representation of monotheistic culture, not just a place. The Land became a conceptual unity, instead of just a collection of valleys and hillocks, because the Jews saw God as a unity and the Jewish people as a unity as well. In exile, then, the representational nature of the Land was not as difficult to carry away from the Middle East as it might otherwise have been.

Nevertheless, Jewish thinkers clearly interpreted their post-exilic experience as an extension of the historical narrative contained in the Bible. The Zionist movement, which arose in the latter part of the nineteenth century in Europe, sought to express, condense, and reshape that mythos in quest of the rebirth of Jewish political sovereignty in the ancient Jewish homeland. The key aim was the reconcretizing of the idea of the Land, and in this Zionism succeeded. The restoration of Jewish sovereignty after an exile so diverse in its geographic and social manifestations, and so long in years, is unprecedented in human history. It is first the uniqueness of the Jewish historical experience and second the achievement of the Zionist movement that has given rise to virtually all of the out-of-the-ordinary circumstances we have just noted.

As a result of the Jewish self-consciousness of its own history, when the modern state of Israel came into being in May 1948, a new Jewish self-image wrought by Zionism came into being with it. As noted, it mingled ancient, exilic, and modern elements, sometimes deliberately, sometimes not. This image has shaped, and has itself been reshaped by, the Israeli experience ever since. To a lesser but still very significant extent, it has also changed the images and self-images of Jews still scattered throughout the world.

This mixture of images shows up today throughout Israeli culture, politics, and foreign policy. What is crucial, however, is that just as this mythos has shaped Jewish political culture in Israel, so the experience of independent Israel is reshaping the Jewish mythos itself. The relationships between Jewish religion and society, between Israel and the Jewish diaspora, and also between Israelis and Arabs in Israel and the Middle East generally, are all in flux thanks to more than half a century of independent, modern Israel.

In short, the story of Israel is to a considerable extent the story of an ongoing dialectic between mythos and reality. In this, Israel is no different from any other society, for the social world is everywhere autogenic—self-constructed—a collective projection of human intentionality. But owing to the peculiarities of Jewish history, perhaps nowhere on earth is this process so dramatically clear as it is in looking at modern Israel, a country that may be said to have willed itself back into existence from the ether of history. Having done so, however, Israelis now face the often unnerving task of reconciling myth with reality. Most of the major divisions in Israeli society and politics revolve around conflicting views and methods of how to do just that.

The Egg that Was a Golf Ball: Political Culture

So, the social world is full of autogenic dialectical relationships, is it? This is a mouthful, but it is an important mouthful, well worth a moment's reflection and unpacking.

It is the nature of social life that it freezes into itself the conceptions we have of it, or as I. W. Thomas once wrote: "If men define situations as real, they are real in their consequences." Another way of putting this is to recall the well-known notion of a "self-fulfilling prophecy," the observation that, for better or worse, people act on the basis of what they believe, and the actions taken very often work out to confirm the belief. For example, one's little sister at age fourteen thinks she's unpopular because she imagines herself to be unattractive, so she acts defensively and strange, thereby becoming unpopular and reinforcing her erroneous interpretation of why this is ("I'm unattractive"). The cycle is eventually broken when someone she cares for is persistently nice to her, or when she finally takes a serious look in the mirror.

The truth is that whole societies over time do roughly the same thing: they develop images of themselves against the mirror of their history, and then usually proceed to behave in ways that reflect the image. Sometimes the images are positive, sometimes not so positive. Peoples whose fate it has been to move from place to place over this planet—Jews, Gypsies, Armenians, groups of Africans, Chinese, Japanese, Germans, Gujaratis, Greeks, Lebanese, and others—have often carried these images with them, developing persisting and distinctive cultures of their own within larger social units.[3]

Sometimes the people and their images have "stayed home," so to speak. For example, Americans have tended to think of themselves as pragmatic, can-do, hardworking individualists who are fair-mindedly devoted to democratic processes and equality of opportunity. Americans have not always acted in accordance with such qualities, to be sure, but constant belief in them over more than two centuries has tended to drive our reality toward them. Certainly, American society is different from those in which greater value has been placed on communalism, racial or ethnic hierarchy, hereditary leadership, fatalism in the face of challenge, and passive subservience to authority.

Israeli society, the collective societies of Jews returned from exile, has its own set of images, its own character, its own signature so to speak. We will refer to it often in our discussion.

Of course, experience—and reflection upon it—ends up changing images, too, and sometimes groups of highly motivated people determine to act in ways that dramatically change both image and reality. That's one way to describe a social revolution, and, in this very sense, Zionism has been revolutionary in most respects for the majority of Jews both inside Israel and out.

The point is that ideas and beliefs matter, and that these ideas and beliefs come from the past, from history. Taken together, the ideas and beliefs about public life shared by most adult members of a society are called a *political culture*.[4] This is an important concept, one referred to several times in the pages ahead.

There is one other theoretical point to grasp before moving on. The reason ideas matter in social and political life is that human beings are fundamentally different from molecules, rocks, or rabbits. What distinguishes human beings from other features of the natural world is their consciousness, which is in turn a function of the brain's capacities for symbolic representation, foremost among them the capacity for language. We therefore must study human interaction in a way that differs from the way we study molecules, rocks, or rabbits. In the latter, we are interested principally in physical features. In the former, we are interested more in expressions of motive, intention, and interpretations given to physical actions. Let me give examples and explain why this is important.

Imagine someone walking in a field who at a distance spies what looks to be an egg. When he gets nearer to the object he discovers that it isn't an egg at all but a long lost golf ball. In this case, the golf ball is not interested in the error, nor would the egg have cared if the observer's first perception been the right one. But suppose upon entering a room our field walker mistakes a wake for a party. This mistake is liable to have very different consequences than the mistake about the golf ball. This is because what matters in the latter case is a mistaken symbolic definition of an event, not a literal error of observation.

Think of language itself. The physical noises our vocal chords make are called phonemes, and we literally hear phonemes in speech. But that's not what we care about. We care about the arbitrary symbolic meanings we have learned to attach to the phonemes.[5] The same is true in human interactions: there is a physical basis to everything, but what matters to most of us most of the time are the symbols attached to them.

The human use of symbols determines the different ways language works. The English word *rock* or *chair* refers to one of a class of actual objects. But there's the "Rock of Gibraltar" and the "Rock of Ages," and there are endowed "chairs" for famous, or fortunate, university professors—same words, different uses and meanings. In the first instances, we refer to actual objects while in the latter we refer to symbolic constructs. Despite the fact that adult humans live in an extraordinarily ornate and variegated symbolic universe, most of us never stop to think about the differences in the reality status of the nouns we use. But if we don't stop to think about it when studying societies and politics, we're apt to misunderstand the very nature of the subject.

It is important to understand this because symbolic exchanges can be subtle and very fluid and, unlike reactions in chemistry, they do not follow easily observed fixed rules. People can and do change what they mean by certain symbols, and in politics they can and often do lie about and in other ways try to hide their real intentions, which no self-respecting bromide compound confronting a group of O_2 molecules would ever do. Also, unlike chemical reactions, observers are inclined to care one way or another about the exchanges; emotions are involved. This is why the sum total of soldiers and weapons possessed by the Israeli Defense Force is not the Israeli Defense Force. This is why the territory and population of Israel does not subsume Israel. The Knesset (Israel's parliament) is not just a building.[6] The Israeli-Egyptian Peace Treaty is not just a piece of paper. *Hatikva* (the national anthem) is not just a song. The flag is not just a piece of material with a design on it for Israelis anymore than the Stars and Stripes is for Americans. The physical never exhausts the symbolic in politics, never captures it, never fully expresses it. That, in turn, is why the study of politics is not like the study of the natural sciences, and never can be.[7]

To understand another place or another time, we have to try to understand the mental universe of those who live, or lived, in it. Just accounting for observable behavior is not good enough. The fact that images, ideas, and symbols live a life dependent on but separate from the physical is why political reality is a dialectic between mythos and reality—and now we have come full circle on this point, having benefited, I hope, from the short journey.

Everyday Life in Israel: A Sketch

Before describing why Israel is the way it is, so that it can be compared to the way other places are—which is what comparative politics is all about— let us take a short, informal tour of Israel.

Modern Israel is not wholly inscrutable to the typical American. Israeli cities look much like American cities: they're crowded full of people and cars and taxis and smoke and noise, have hotels and other tall buildings with the usual accouterments—elevators, lobbies, awnings, and so forth—and there are buses for people who either don't have cars or who have them but are too smart to drive them downtown. Many signs are in English, and lots of the people a visitor would meet in Israeli cities speak a passable English nowadays. That visitor would recognize restaurants, movie houses, video rental shops, appliance stores, post offices, and banks, just as in the United States. The banks have ATM machines, and Israelis appear to use bank cards and credit cards just as we do.

A stroll down the street would reveal streetlights, public telephones, wastepaper baskets, used chewing gum stuck on the back of stop signs, advertising posters of various sorts, and many people who look as if they are in a hurry. There are places to play the lottery, called "Loto." Most of the people would be dressed more or less as an American dresses: men wear pants and shirts; women wear skirts, dresses, or pants suits; and young people wear jeans or shorts, T-shirts, and Chicago Bulls base-ball-style caps turned backwards.

The weather wouldn't be strange to a visiting American, either. If it's summer, it's hot. If it's winter, it's colder and can be rainy, and in some higher elevations there may be snow.

Inside a typical Israeli's urban living quarters, an American visitor would find familiar-looking furniture, bathrooms with all the usual fixtures as in the United States, beds, a dishwasher perhaps, a clothes washer, a micro-wave, and a television set—with cable.

In the countryside, too, a drive along the highway would also seem fairly normal. Israelis drive on the right side of the road as Americans do, not on the wrong side, as do the British and the Australians. The signs are symbols and are easily understood. All the cars have license plates, there are gas stations, and there are police cars hiding in the bushes, just like here. There are tractors and other farm equipment working the fields, and in the forests are little rodents, birds, a variety of trees, and a host of insects lusting after human blood—again, nothing obviously unusual here.

So if all this is true, then Israel must be much like the United States, right? Not exactly. If we retrace each of these steps on our tour and look closer, we will realize that, as a famous American personage once put it, "Toto, I don't think we're in Kansas anymore."

First, the city scene. There are English signs, yes, but there are mostly Hebrew signs, and Hebrew is written in another script. Is it the script of ancient Hebrew? No, it comes from ancient Babylonia. (You will learn how that happened, and why it is significant, in Chapter 2.) In some parts of some cities, many of the signs will be in Arabic, written in yet another script. The money has all three languages printed on it, but the Hebrew is most prominent. Why is that?

What accounts for the fact that so many urban Israelis speak decent English? Forty years ago, comparable people would have been almost as likely to know a passable French as a second language, and indeed, French was for a time Israel's second "official" language. Why?

If we look closely, we might see a concrete hole in the ground every so many blocks, with a Hebrew sign near it that would transliterate into English as *"bor bitahon."* There are also many signs that say *"miklat."* What is this all about?[8]

The public telephones do not take coins. They used to take little tokens called *asimonim*, and now they take phone cards. Why? Also, until November 1994, if an Israeli tried to call a place just nine miles to the east of Jerusalem, he couldn't get through. Why? Because Israel and Jordan were technically at war, and the Jordanians would not transmit the call.

If we were to buy an appliance from an Israeli appliance store and try to use it back in the United States, it would not work. Similarly, appliances taken to Israel from America do not work there unless the appropriate adapter is affixed. We use a fairly modest alternating current here, but in Israel, as in Europe, a considerably stronger direct current is used.

The digital readouts of the temperature on the bank building might confuse us momentarily, but not a European visitor. Israelis measure by Centigrade, not Fahrenheit.

Now the banks. If we are overdrawn on our account here in the States, our ATM machine will not dispense more cash. When Israelis overdraw their accounts, their ATMs will give them cash anyway. This is because almost everybody overdraws his or her account every month. Most banks let Israelis customers overdraw up to and sometimes beyond the amount of their next month's salary—with interest charges attached, of course. How does the bank know what any given person's next month's salary is? Because the customer has told the bank, and the majority of salaries in Israel are transferred electronically from employer to bank on the first of every month.

At the post office, as well, there are differences. Many of the customers will not be buying stamps or sending packages. They'll be paying utility bills, for Israeli post offices contain postal banks.[9] Almost no one pays utility bills by sending a check through the mail. In fact, Israelis do not use checks much, and when they do they certainly do not trust the mail service to deliver them. The joke that goes "The check is in the mail," to the extent that it is funny at all, is funny in a different way in Israel: virtually no check is ever in the mail.

Snail Mail

The mail in Israel is often sleepy. Americans complain when a letter takes four days to get from Washington to New York; Israelis seem happy when any letter arrives at all. In 1992–93 I lived on a new street in Ra'anana; amid much new construction, our apartment was in the only building on the street with a number. After living there about three weeks, it struck me that no mail had arrived. Nor had mail seemed to arrive at any of the other occupied apartments in the building. I asked some neighbors why this was; no one knew. So I went to the post office to ask if I needed to register to receive mail, for I had put my name on the mailbox in both Hebrew and English and figured that would be enough.

An older gentleman, originally from Morocco, smoking a pipe and wearing a skullcap, took my question in earnest. He led me to where the mail is sorted, sat me down, offered me coffee, and told me that the street is very new. I said I understood that it was new, but it was between two other streets that were not new, so, it seemed to me, it had to fit into some mail carrier's route, did it not? I was given to understand that it was not such a simple matter. It turned out that there was no wooden slat by the sorters' table that said "Netiv HaLamed Hey"—the street name—so all mail that had come for this street had been lying in a bag on the floor. Every so often, someone noticed the pile and sent a mail carrier on a special run—all of 300 yards from the post office. As for now, I was told, there was nothing for the Garfinkle family. I was not to worry; this would all be straightened out "before long."

"Before long" is a relative term in any language, maybe more so in Hebrew than in some others. Two days later we received eleven items in the mail on one Thursday. Then there was no mail until the next Thursday, when nine items appeared. "What an amazing statistical fluke," remarked my wife. I smiled and rolled my eyes.

I told a friend about this, and since one story deserves another, he told me that he had gone recently to a post office on a Friday morning (a foolhardy thing to do in any event) to conduct some business. He stood in line for a half hour, and just as he got to the window, the clerk decided it was time for a smoke (which had to be done outside). She did that little wiggle-waggle with the fingers that Israeli clerks do when they want to tell you to just keep your pants on—index finger touched to the thumb of the right hand, pointed upward, and then shook twice—and left. Being American born, this poor fellow flew into a rage and barged in on the branch director seething with complaint.

"Well, she's been working hard, and you don't expect her to work for two hours without a break, do you?" said the branch director.

"Let her have her break, but can't someone else take her place?"

(continued)

> "They need a break, too."
> "Well, can't you stagger the breaks so that at least one window is always open, or can't you fill in for her while she's gone? Look there; three dozen people are standing in two lines, neither of them moving at all."
> "Oh I absolutely couldn't do that."
> "Why not?"
> "Union rules."
> In Israel, there is nothing more to say upon hearing such a statement. Nothing useful, anyway.

Suppose an American visitor decided to go out at night in Tel Aviv looking for "professional company," let's call it. That person would find that a disproportionate number of the prostitutes these days—female and male—speak Russian, and that many are not even immigrants to Israel. There are also relatively few bars or taverns, but a seemingly inexplicable number of toy and candy stores. How come?

Also, Israel's big cities, especially Tel Aviv and Haifa, stay open virtually all night. Parties and get-togethers, even during the week, tend to start no earlier than 10 P.M. And yet, from all appearances, people are up and off to work early next morning. We've already discussed how Israelis finance their fun: they go into debt. A more difficult question, it sometimes seems, is: When do they sleep?

Israelis more or less dress like Americans, or perhaps a bit better—like west Europeans. But it is rare to find a man with a necktie on during the day. In a few cities, however, in certain sections, whole groups of people are dressed, even in summer, in long black coats and black hats (still no ties, however), with what look like strings hanging out of their shirts and long locks of hair curling down around both ears. Hippies from the fourteenth century? Not exactly.

Also, most Israeli men walk around bare-headed. But many don't. Aside from the black hats noted just above, some Israelis wear *kipot* (skullcaps). Some are black, some are colorful. Some are knitted, some are leather. Some are small, some are large. Do these differences signify anything? Yes, they do.[10]

It is, of course, normal that urban dwellers seem in a hurry. But in Israel most people hurry in the working world six days a week, not five. School is six days a week too, Sunday being a normal workday. But elementary schools, at least, are let out by 1 P.M. What do the children do then, since, like here, both parents tend to be at work until later (unless there's an infant or toddler to keep the mother in the house)?

Moreover, most male workers younger than age forty-seven are absent from their jobs for several weeks a year, and they're not on vacation. Where are they? On *miluim*, military reserve duty. Is *miluim* obligatory, or is it more like the National Guard in the United States? No, it isn't like the National Guard; they must go, unless they have a really terrific excuse.

As to the restaurants, they are plentiful and diverse. A typical American would recognize some of the food, but not all of it. Customers can get terrific fruit, great salads, wonderful chocolate bars, excellent beer, and even Ben & Jerry's ice cream. Israelis used to prefer frozen yogurt, but the local ice cream is improving and getting more popular.

Israelis also drink good coffee in several forms. American-style coffee is available, especially in city restaurants and places that cater to tourists, but few Israelis drink it. Turkish coffee, popularly called *botz* (mud), is more prevalent. Israelis also drink a more European concoction, *cafe hafookh* (upside-down coffee), when they want to relax, which is rich coffee with steamed milk and sugar. (This is called *cafe latte* in Europe and, increasingly, in America.) Israelis on the run also order *nes*, American-style instant coffee. *Nes* is short for Nescafe, a Swiss-French brand name, but it has a special twist in Hebrew; *nes* is also the word for "miracle." When it was introduced many years ago, instant coffee seemed a little like a miracle, so the name stuck. When Israelis drink tea, they often choose what Jews from the Arab world call *nana*, or mint tea. In recent years, various designer teas—mango flavor, orange spice, lemon tang, and so forth—have made inroads into local habits, just as in the United States and Europe.

But try finding soft white bread in Israel. Outside the most pandering tourist spots, there's little chance. Order a steak and prepare to be disappointed; red meat in Israel is "different" from what it is in the United States. Order an Israeli-made frankfurter and prepare to gag; it tastes like diesel fumes and glue with grease. Also, oddly enough to the mind of most Americans, until a few years ago there were no bagels in Israel—not until some American immigrants introduced them. Americans think of bagels as a Jewish food, but actually it is an East European food popularized in America by Jews who came from those lands. Zionist pioneers did not come to the land of Israel from Europe to eat like they did in exile.

On the other hand, there will be pita, shwarma, falafel, humus, tahina, and kabob, and eggplant prepared in at least a dozen different ways. These are mainly Arab foods adopted and adjusted to fit the Israeli palate. The usual flavors of soda and fruit juices are available, but so is peach nectar, pear juice, and mango juice.[11] As a rule, Middle Easterners eat less red meat, imbibe fewer calories, drink less alcohol, and eat more fruit, vegetables, and dairy products than the majority of Americans.

The movie houses and video parlors have a huge array of films to rent, in a dozen languages. (Woody Allen films, however, are not as plentiful or popular in Israel as one might think.) There is also every sort of American and European pop music to be heard, and most of the locally generated music in Hebrew generally sounds very Western. Some of it, however, sounds Yemenite. Many Israelis feel more or less at home listening to both.

Suppose we took a bus ride. One of the first things we might notice when the bus showed up is that Israelis do not form lines to get on a bus, or for any other purpose. They form human clots around the object of interest, whatever it is. Why?

As to weather, yes, it's hot in the summer as it is in most of the United States, but it very rarely rains from mid-April to mid-September. Few Americans or Europeans have ever experienced a five-month period without seeing a single drop of rainfall, have imagined the exhilarating feeling when it finally starts up again, or have anticipated how slippery streets get from clouds of oily exhaust when it does.

If we were in someone's living quarters, chances are it would be an apartment; individual private homes are still fairly rare in Israel. Even most Israeli prime ministers have lived in apartments—although Prime Minister Barak does live in a house in Kochav Ya'ir, an upscale Americanesque town not far from Tel Aviv. There will probably be a washing machine, but no drier. There'll be no standard water heater either; up on the roof, however, there will be an array of solar panels *(dudei shemesh)* doing the work. There aren't many gas appliances; stoves are mainly electric, although many people have cooking gas.

The TV set may well have cable, but with a difference. Since 1993, when cable was first widely introduced, the standard package has included Israeli-based channels with a mixed fare of Hebrew, Arabic, and other languages; four Arabic channels; three Russian; two Turkish; six English; and one each of French, German, and Catalan. Remote-surfing on Israeli cable TV is a very different sort of experience than it is here.

Also, there will be no centralized heating system, and the electrical outlets are not down near the floor as they usually are here, but several feet up the wall. Why?[12]

By the time a visitor to Israel gets out on the road, he will have noticed something else: guns and soldiers. There are what look like kids—including kids of the female variety—seemingly all over the place carrying submachine guns: on the street, on the bus, walking down the sidewalk, hitchhiking in groups on the roads, in cafes. There are few policeman on foot, but lots of soldiers. Imagine how it might feel to accidentally bump into a nineteen-year-old woman holding a submachine gun. There is a greater statistical probability, too, that she will be smoking a cigarette than would be the case with a typical ninete-year-old American female, with or without machine gun.

In smaller towns there are an inordinate number of what look like water towers, with ladders to get to the top. Are these really water towers?

Traveling around by bus, one may notice what looks like gray chaff all over the floor of the bus stations. These are the shells of sunflower seeds *(garinim)*, the chewing of which is a national addiction among the middle to lower middle classes—which is most of the country.

Another thing a visitor will notice out on the road is that distances between places are listed in kilometers, which is great for an American used to miles; one feels as if one is getting places incredibly fast. If one is in fact going incredibly fast in a rental car, it is good to know that the flashing lights on police cars are blue, not red.

License plates come in several different colors. This is not for decoration, but to distinguish private cars from various sorts of official cars, and also, until recently, from cars licensed in Israel (yellow) from those licensed to Arabs from Gaza and the West Bank (blue). All of the latter license plates had distinguishing letters and numbers allowing an informed observer to tell whether the vehicle's owner was from Gaza, Nablus, Jenin, Tulkarem, Qalqilya, Bethlehem, Jericho, or wherever. Why was this? Hint: The cops are not always hiding in the bushes to catch speeders. Now the license plates for such cars are prepared by the Palestinian Authority (PA). Sometimes, anyway.

An American visitor will also see an occasional area fenced off with barbed wire—lots of barbed wire. These are either military bases or prisons. A visitor will also see many soccer fields, tennis courts, and basketball hoops around schools and parks, but almost no baseball diamonds—and there's only one golf course in the whole country.

If we were to turn off into one of several hundred agricultural settlements, we would likely find people whose English is less proficient. The older they are, the less proficient it is likely to be. Until fairly recently, too, if we should just happen to turn off into certain settlements on any May 1st, we might have seen red flags flying over the administration building and water tower. Whatever for?

One of the main problems with traveling on Israeli highways is that the traffic is often terrible. A typical visitor in a rental car is likely to spend a lot of time going basically nowhere, just like every other Israeli in a car. Israelis cope with this by honking their horns. Another problem for most Americans, especially Midwesterners, is that as soon as one really gets going, a border appears and one has to stop. A driver starting out at Metullah in the farthest north near the Lebanese border can probably get to Eilat on the Red Sea before supper if he leaves right after breakfast—unless he gets stuck in traffic or accidentally hits a camel on the Arava Road.[13] Traveling long distance east-west, as opposed to north-south, is even harder. If our driver starts near the Syrian border north of Lake Tiberias and heads west for the Mediterranean, he can almost make the trip *during* lunch.

Israeli gas stations pump liters, not gallons, and Israelis pay sheqels, not dollars. This means that, unless a visitor is used to doing simultaneous equations in his head, he has no idea how much gas costs beyond the vague realization that it is very expensive. But most Israelis just put it on the credit card and let the bank deficit soar. Until recently, virtually none of the gas was unleaded; in the last few years, however, it has become available everywhere since all the new cars require it. But most cars still do not have emission control devices, and the haze during rush hour is dark and thick. Also, compared to most American highways nowadays, the sides of most Israeli roads are filthy with litter—except when Margaret Thatcher is in the country.[14] (Chapter 4 explains why.)

A lot of Israelis also drive recklessly. Far more people are killed and injured in car crashes than in war or by terrorism, and Israeli officials are at their wits' end trying to figure out how to stop it. Until about five years ago, however, there were virtually no cases of drunk driving; Israelis didn't need booze to drive poorly. Now there are cases of drunk driving, too. Why?

At the last stop on our tour, we are back in the woods with the rodents, birds, and insects. Suddenly it dawns upon us: *there are no squirrels.* There are, however, lots of cute little lizards, and an astonishing variety of birds.

The Chapters

This book contains seven chapters, of which this introduction is the first. As befits a book written for comparative politics purposes, each chapter begins with general statements about the themes addressed within. Each then gets down to specifics.

The next chapter attempts to tell the history of the Jewish people from the time of Abraham to the founding of the modern state of Israel in 1948. It makes no claim to inclusivity, of course, only to identifying the most pertinent historical themes, without which very little of what has happened since 1948 makes much sense. Chapter 3 is also historical: it describes Israel's basic institutions and situation as it began its journey as an independent state in 1948. It covers several different kinds of background, all necessary for what comes after.

Chapter 4 discusses Israeli society and economy, and Chapter 5 talks about Israeli political structures and parties. Together these chapters examine institutions and issues: what sorts of problems make up Israel's public policy agenda and how those problems are managed. The order of Chapters 4 and 5 is deliberate and meant to be generally instructive. In any society, politics

is like the tip of an iceberg, the visible, publicly available dimension of something larger and more basic—society itself. It is hard to really understand much of significance about the former without first understanding the latter. To take one example, unless one knows something about how Americans live—their standard of living, their education and attitudes, their values and expectations—how would it be possible to make sense of debates in the Congress over crime, health care, tax reform, or relations with Russia? Clearly, it wouldn't be possible at all.

Chapter 6 looks at a special, and specially important, case within the public policy debate: the problem of foreign and security policy. To many people outside Israel, it seems as if Israel's public policy debate is concerned exclusively with foreign and security policy. It is a very important component, true, which is why I devote an entire chapter to it. But Israel has domestic politics as well, and those politics are becoming more important in the Israeli environment as time passes.

Chapter 7 is about the future. It starts out discussing the Arab-Israeli peace process, an extension of Chapter 6 in many respects, and then moves on to other matters. I have tried to use this chapter to tie together the discussions of history, institutions, and issues that have gone before. I hope this discussion allows students to at least know what the right questions are for further study about Israel. It would be too much to expect very many answers.

2

In

the

Beginning

As suggested in the Introduction, Jews have a long collective memory as a people. The Jewish sense of self is deeply embedded in history, and history lives actively among Jews in the present tense in a way that many Americans find hard to understand. America is a society running from the past. America began as an experiment, a fresh start, an escape from the constraints and depredations of the Old World; immigrants to its shores often wanted to toss their Old World characteristics off the boat before they tossed their luggage onto the dock. American pragmatism has always been progressive, future-oriented, unfettered, and open to novelty. Maybe that's why American students tend not to like studying history, not to think it important, not to see its legacy as something sacred as well as instructive in the way that more ancient cultures usually do.

While Americans cannot easily remember the past, Jews cannot easily forget it. Writing in 1995, an Israeli public opinion analyst declared: "The traumatic recollection of the final days of the Second Temple—when internal strife and semi-civil war led to the fall of Jerusalem, the loss of national independence, and two thousand years of exile and suffering—is deeply embedded in the collective subconscious of the Jewish People."[1] The author was writing about divisions over foreign policy issues in Israeli politics in 1995, and yet he claimed that something that happened in the year 70 c.e., more than nineteen centuries before, actually mattered in the here and now.[2]

He was absolutely right, too. No one who really understands Israel would think to doubt it. Opponents of Prime Minister Yitzhak Rabin's peace policies in the 1992–95 period, for example, sometimes accused him of having a *galut* mentality, a shorthand phrase for the obsequious mental posture of the passive, fearful exile Jew. More liberal elements liked to turn the tables, arguing that right-wing Jews who opposed conciliation and peace were really the ones acting like Jews in *galut* in their obsessive, paranoid fear of everything gentile. Contemporary Israeli politics, when discussed by serious Israelis, is sometimes discussed in terms of events that happened centuries ago—indeed, in terms of events some of which are so old as to be mentioned in the Hebrew Bible.[3] Try to imagine an issue in American politics or foreign policy seriously being discussed in reference to anything that happened more than five or six decades ago. It's very, very hard.

History always matters in political life, and the more self-conscious people are of their history (or of their mythic images of it), the more it matters. In Israel, it matters a lot; Israelis are constantly hurling their historical mythos at recalcitrant present-day realities. So before we can talk about the modern state of Israel that came into existence in May 1948, we must dwell for a while in the past.

Ancient Jewish Commonwealths

The Jewish version of early Jewish history isn't hard to find. It's in the Five Books of Moses, called by Jews the Torah, or the law-scroll.

According to the Torah, God created the world, created man, and ten generations later, brought the flood in the generation of Noah. Ten generations after that came Abram (later renamed Abraham), the first Jew because he was the first man to recognize God as the sole, unitary creator of the world. Abraham's journey is not only spiritual, it is also literal. Born in Ur Kasdim (in Sumer, present-day Iraq), he moved with his family to Harun (in present-day Syria) and from there, with wife Sarai (later renamed Sarah), into Canaan (present-day Israel), the land, according to the Bible, that God showed him.

The partnership between Abraham and God led to a contract, a covenant. Because Abraham proved his faith, God promised to multiply his descendants and to give them the land of Canaan. What exactly was Abraham's achievement that he deserved such a gift? As noted in passing in Chapter 1, Abraham recognized the unity of God as creator, and this enabled him to see his descendants as a single people, and the land as a conceptual unity wherein the people would acclaim and serve God. The unity of these abstractions also gave rise to another, binding element: literary culture, for without a form of symbolic literacy such abstract ideas cannot be communicated, socially shared, and maintained through the generations.

This combination gave rise to the first idea of a nation, for a nation is more than just a collection of tribes. Tribes have farms and pastures, but a nation has a Land. Tribes are based on concrete social relations, but a nation is based on abstracted ones. Tribes do not self-reflect; they do not mean, represent, or signify anything beyond themselves, and they do not wish to do so. But nations stand for ideas; they have purposes and ambitions that transcend just living. Abraham was therefore not only the first monotheist but also the first nationalist.[4]

Abraham's covenant is renewed with Isaac, Abraham's son by Sarah. (Abraham's first-born son, Ishmael, by Sarah's handmaid Hagar, is also to father a great nation, the Arabs.) The covenant is renewed again with Isaac's son Jacob, rather than with Jacob's twin brother Esau. Jacob had twelve sons—later to become twelve tribes—from two wives (Leah and Rachel) and their two handmaids (Zilpah and Bilhah). The first eleven of these sons and one daughter were born in the Harun during the years Jacob worked for his father-in-law, Laban. The evening before he was about to cross back over into Canaan with his family and flocks, Jacob wrestled with an angel. The angel did not prevail, and in this mystical encounter Jacob's name is changed to Israel—literally, "he who contends with God."

The twelfth son, Benjamin, was born to mother Rachel inside the land God promised to Abraham's descendants, near Hebron. Rachel died in childbirth, and, according to tradition, her tomb is still there, on the roadside. But Jacob's family did not stay long in Canaan; famine forced Jacob to send his sons to Egypt to buy food. Meanwhile, the eleventh son, Joseph, sold into slavery by his jealous brothers and thought dead by his father, had risen to become viceroy of Egypt. Through Joseph, Jacob and all his family—numbering seventy souls—went down to Egypt to live in an area called Goshen.

But the old pharaoh died and a new one arose who enslaved the children of Israel *(b'nei Israel)*—called, logically enough in English, Israelites, not yet Jews or Israelis. From the time Jacob went down to Egypt, the period of slavery *and exile* was 400 years. Then Moses entered the scene, chosen by God to be the human instrument of Israel's liberation from slavery and its return to its own land. The Exodus from Egypt, dated by tradition to correspond to about 1220 B.C.E., is the first of a pair of closely linked epochal events in Jewish history, and is marked as the date of the creation of the Jewish people, now risen from seventy souls to a multitude during their time in Egypt. Seven weeks later came the revelation at Mount Sinai, the giving of the Ten Commandments, and subsequently the rest of the Torah, and, according to the rabbinical tradition, an oral law to be used to interpret the written law. The children of Israel were chosen specifically to be "a light unto the nations" and "a kingdom of priests" to spread the message of the oneness of God, and therefore of humanity, the crown of his creation, to the entire world.

The people were awestruck by these events, but insufficiently so for the purposes at hand. They failed the test of faith while Moses was on the mountain for forty days receiving the Torah from God. For sinning by building and worshipping a golden calf, and particularly by showing a lack of faith in God's ability to deliver the land over to them in the incident of the twelve spies, they were punished, sentenced to wander in the wilderness for forty years until the adult generation of former slaves was dead. Their free-born progeny would enter the land. Literally on the edge of this event, and the end of Moses's life, the Five Books of Moses come to an end, the historical narrative subsequently taken up mainly in the books of Joshua, Judges, Samuel, Kings, and Chronicles.

Why belabor this well-known story, the historical verification of which is impossible? Because the Jewish sensibility, and the Israeli sensibility, is suffused with the metaphors of chosenness, slavery, exile *(galut)*, wandering in the wilderness, liberation, a covenant over the land of Israel, and the redemption of it, that resound from the Biblical narrative. There is no way to understand modern Zionism, and its broad and deep emotional appeal to Jews, without understanding what the power of the Biblical narrative of Jewish history has meant to Jews for more than 3,000 years.

From the book of Joshua onward, the Biblical narrative finds increasing confirmation in available historical evidence. Between roughly 1180 and 1100 B.C.E. was the time of the Judges, and the gradual conquest of Canaan from its aboriginal inhabitants. Eventually, the Israelite tribes moved toward unity, and a kingdom under Saul was established, soon followed by the reign of King David from 1004 to 965 B.C.E. David's reign saw the capture of Jerusalem from the Jebusites and the subsequent unification and territorial expansion of Israelite power. In 965 B.C.E. Solomon succeeded his father David as king, and under his reign ancient Israel reached the height of its power and splendor with the construction of the First Temple in Jerusalem. After Solomon's death in 933 B.C.E., the more or less unified kingdom of Israel split in half. The southern part became known as the kingdom of Judea, the northern part as the kingdom of Israel. In Judea was the land of the tribes of Judah, some of Benjamin, and the major part of the tribe of Levi serving in the temple. The other ten tribes were in the north, where they existed until the kingdom of Israel was devastated by an Assyrian army in the year 722 B.C.E., and the population carried off into an exile from which it never returned, and thus the ten "lost tribes."

Meanwhile, the kingdom of Judea—hence the name Jews—continued on under a succession of kings counseled and scolded by a succession of prophets. Judea fell, however, to Babylon in 586 B.C.E. The temple in Jerusalem, the preeminent symbol of both Jewish political sovereignty and Judaism as a religion, was destroyed and most of the population exiled to Babylonia—present-day Iraq. Thus did what is called in Jewish history the First Commonwealth come to an end.

This is not the place to detail ancient history, but what matters is this: Whether in unified form before Solomon's death or in divided form thereafter, the Israelite tribes formed a government, collected taxes, formed alliances; conducted trade and diplomacy near and far, mustered an army, went to war, and made peace as a normal, integrated part of that region for more than four hundred years. The United States of America, by contrast, is just a bit more than half that old.

The story isn't over yet. Babylon fell soon to Persia, and under Cyrus the Great the Jews were restored to their homeland in 538 B.C.E., and the temple was rebuilt. Not all Jews immediately returned to Judea, however; a substantial community remained on the banks of the Euphrates River and thrived. Indeed, the period of the Babylonian exile—the first exile—greatly transformed Jewish theology and practice, and began to make it portable. Without this experience, and the symbolic national literature generated during it (many scholars believe that the Torah was edited into something like its present form in Babylonia), it is doubtful that the Jews could have survived a second, far more devastating exile.

Persian rule gave way to Greek rule under Alexander the Great in 331 B.C.E. During all this time, however, the Second Temple stood and a Jewish monarchy ruled with considerable local autonomy most of the time. Greek culture came to have a powerful if divisive influence on Jews and Judaism, as had the Babylonian experience before it. Religious conflict, political intrigue, regional diplomacy, and personal ambition eventually led to an attempt by a Selucid Greek ruler, Antiochus IV, to undermine Jewish autonomy and attack Jewish religious practices. In 169 B.C.E., Antiochus entered Jerusalem, laid waste to much of the city, butchered many of its inhabitants, and defiled the temple with the acquiescence of a corrupt Jewish priesthood.

A small group of Jewish zealots resisted Antiochus, his army, and his local allies. Led by Judah Maccabee and his five sons, Jews mounted a guerrilla war from the countryside and eventually succeeded in taking back Jerusalem in 165 B.C.E. They rededicated the temple and established their own independent political dynasty, known as the Hasmonean. These events are celebrated every year by Jews in the holiday known as Hanukkah, a word meaning "rededication."

Bear in mind what this holiday is really about: a military victory, the regaining of national independence, and principled resistance to assimilation into a wider, more cosmopolitan, and generally attractive culture. This becomes of utmost importance in Jewish history, right up to the beginning of the Zionist movement in the nineteenth century, and even in Israel today. In America the usual near coincidence of Hanukkah and Christmas has led some uneducated Jews and many Christians to think that Hanukkah is some sort of Jewish Christmas. It is a time for much casual ecumenicism wherein Christians and Jews celebrate a generic "holiday season" festooned with decorated trees and multicolored lights. From the Jewish point of view, however, this is precisely the opposite of what Hanukkah is all about.

In any event, Hasmonean independence did not last very long by historical standards. By the year 4 B.C.E., Roman power was bearing down on the eastern Mediterranean. Just as important, Hasmonean rule had collapsed into periods of civil war and internecine chaos. These divisions were accompanied by and contributed to sharp divisions among Jews over theological issues and issues of religious practice. This was the time of King Herod and, according to Christian tradition, the birth of Jesus. Herod expanded the temple complex and built up Jerusalem, but he could do nothing about the divisions within that led to further subjugation and collapse. In the year 66, the Jews rose up against Rome in rebellion, but they were soon defeated. In the year 70, a Roman army sacked Jerusalem and burned the temple down, thus ending the Second Commonwealth. Taken together, the periods of the First and Second Temples totaled almost a thousand years of independent and semi-independent Jewish governance in the land Jews believed had been given to them by God. If one counts the period of the Judges, and the early kingdom under Saul and David, one is talking about a 1,400–year experience with political sovereignty in what is today Israel.

After the destruction of the Second Temple, Jews still lived in the land, but Roman rule was harsh. It was not of the "live-and-let-live" sort of previous conquerors, Antiochus IV excepted. Moreover, the destruction of the temple and the government simultaneously threw the sharp debates about theology and religious practice into a new and superheated context. As had been the case after Antiochus defiled the temple, a Jewish rebellion with strong religious overtones broke out against Roman rule. It was led by Shimon Bar-Kochba ("son of a star"), and for a ragtag force it scored some notable successes against the Roman Empire—for a while. The revolt's successes added to its very heady religious significance, with some very famous sages, including Rabbi Akiva, seeing in Bar-Kochba the messiah predicted by the Prophets.

It must immediately be pointed out that, in contrast to Christian notions of the messiah, the Jewish notion, then and now, is quite different. Classical Christianity posits that Jesus was born of Mary as a virgin, that God made

Himself incarnate in Jesus as a man, and that Jesus was physically resurrected from death.[5] To both Jews and Muslims, such ideas are heretical. According to Jewish thinking, the messiah is someone—a person by tradition from the House of David—who will save the people from oppression, erect a righteous government, and bring peace and justice not only to Israel but to the world.[6]

This is what Rabbi Akiva thought Bar-Kochba would achieve, but he failed. First the northern fortress of Gamla fell, and finally the southern fortress of Masada fell; the revolt was crushed, and the Romans celebrated *Judea capta*— "Judea is captured"—in the year 135 C.E. As punishment for the revolt, well in excess of half the Jewish population was exiled from their land, and the country was renamed Palestina, a term taken from the Philistines, the Jews' long-time adversaries, who inhabited the southwestern part of the country.[7]

Thereafter, Palestine fell under Christian (Roman and then Byzantine) control until the Arab conquest in the year 638. The Seljuk Turks then became the Muslim masters of the region, and then came the Crusaders, who established domination over part of Palestine between 1099 and 1291. The Mameluke dynasty recovered Palestine for the Muslims and ruled until 1516, when Ottoman rule commenced. Ottoman Turkish rule lasted almost exactly four hundred years, until the end of World War I and the subsequent establishment of the British Mandate.

The Varieties and Significance of Exile

What happened to the Jews after the destruction of the Second Temple is of utmost importance in understanding both the survival and the historical mindset of the Jewish people, and the underlying political culture of modern Israel. The Babylonian experience notwithstanding, most peoples who are conquered and despoiled by greater powers usually disappear—if not literally, then culturally. Had this happened after the Roman conquest, there would have been no modern state of Israel and no Jews. But it didn't happen, and it is important to understand why.

Thanks to the generation of rabbis that arose during and following the Roman expulsion of the Jews from Israel, Judaism and the Jewish people found a way to continue without the temple, without the priesthood, without political sovereignty, and even without living in the land. Exactly how this happened is not of concern here except to say that both the writing of the Talmud[8] and the subsequent dependence on it for law and cultural orientation were the keys to this process. What matters to the subject at hand is how the rabbis interpreted the national calamity, and how they and their successors used that interpretation to ensure the continuation of the nation.

The rabbis interpreted the national tragedy within the context of the Biblical and especially the Prophetic tradition. The covenant described after the Exodus from Egypt is not an unconditional promise but a conditional one. The text is clear: God gives the land to the children of Israel, but only if they obey God's commandments. Many passages in the Torah and in the Prophets warn that if the people stray from the path of truth and righteousness, God will expel them from the land as punishment—for example, Deuteronomy 8:19–20, and 28:49–50, 64–65. That is how the Prophets interpreted the first exile, and how the sages saw the second exile: that the weight of sin grew so large as to bring calamity upon the nation.

Over the years, Jewish theology developed the conclusion that from the second exile there would be a final redemption, a return to the land, the rebuilding of the temple, and the coming of the messiah. Drawing on Isaiah, this time would also bring global harmony through universal recognition of the oneness of God. The Jews' gift for playing this role would be the land of Israel in perpetuity, along with universal acceptance of that gift.

The early centuries of the second exile also led the rabbis to some very definite conclusions about the nexus between politics and religion. Their view was that the Bar-Kochba revolt and the rabbis' support for it were both disastrous. Had Bar-Kochba not futilely opposed the power of Rome, the people would have remained on the land, the temple might well have been rebuilt, and Jewish autonomy, if not full independence, might in time have been restored. The temptation to seek redemption, to bring about the messianic era by taking up arms, struck them as a dangerous folly that belied too little faith in God. The way to redemption was through piety, charity, and righteousness, and when God concluded that the people had paid the price of their transgressions, He would restore them to their land.

As a result of this attitude, the rabbis sought to change the image of the Maccabean revolt, then the primary symbol of Jewish politico-military glory. The books that tell its story, Maccabees I and II, were deliberately left out of the Hebrew Bible, but are part of lesser literature known as the Apocrypha. The Prophetic reading associated with the Sabbath of Hanukkah is from the prophet Zachariah, where the dramatic emphasis is on this verse: "Not by power and not by might, but by My spirit says the Lord of Hosts." And of course there was the emphasis on the miracle of the temple oil at the rededication, which lasted eight days when it should have sufficed for only one— an event about which there is no recorded reference in the previous six centuries after the incident supposedly took place.

Although it happened a very long time ago, the redrawing of the Maccabbean myth, and indeed, the entire attitude of rabbinic Judaism toward political action, is still important. In relatively modern times, the same attitude was sharply reinforced by the Shabbtai Tzvi episode of the seventeenth century, in which a charismatic figure claiming to be the messiah led a segment of European Jewry to disaster.[9] We will return to the redrawing of the Maccabbean myth later because what Zionism did, in essence, was to attempt to return Jewish attitudes on this count to pre-rabbinic ones. Unnerving though it may be to those with little patience for history, it is just not possible to understand what Zionists were up to in the twentieth century without knowing at least a little about what the rabbis who wrote the Talmud were up to in the fifth century.

Not all Jews who were exiled stayed exiled. In time, groups returned to what was now called Palestine. Jews lived particularly in the cities of Jerusalem, Hebron, Tiberias, and Safad. They also lived in rural communities elsewhere in the Galilee, in Bashan (today's Golan Heights), and along the Mediterranean coastal plain. Still other groups of Jews were to be found at the time of the Arab conquest of the Middle East in the seventh century living in Egypt, Mesopotamia, Syria, North Africa, Anatolia, Persia, and Central Asia. From there some even wandered along the fabled Silk Road into China where, at Kaifeng, a Jewish community thrived from the sixth century to the sixteenth. Thanks to the Arab empires, in which Jews had found several niches useful to the Muslim rulers, Jews occupied a special place in Moorish Spain. And from Spain and elsewhere, Jewish communities moved in the early Middle Ages into France, Italy, and the Germanic princedoms—typically along the river valleys that were the main trading routes of those times.

The reconquest of Spain by the Catholic Kings, completed with the fall of Granada in 1492, was a disaster for Jews as well as Muslims in Spain. Many Jews likened it to the fall of Jerusalem to the Romans some 1,400 years earlier. Jews were expelled, and from Iberia they wandered in all directions: into Europe and England, into Turkey and North Africa, back to the Middle East and Palestine. A few followed Christopher Columbus to the New World as well, along with his mapmaker and navigator, Avraham Maputo, a Spanish Jew.

By the beginning of the sixteenth century, then, there were Jewish communities spread over most of the world. Over time, their specifically Jewish customs and attitudes mixed with and adapted to a great extent to the conditions in society in general, with respect to language, dress, philosophy, literary style, and so forth. Jews also contributed much to the societies in which they lived. Also, some Jews broke off from the Jewish community and assimilated into the larger society, while others intermarried with the local populations, bringing into the Jewish people new blood. In time, over many centuries, Jewish communities in North Africa and the Middle East began to resemble superficially those communities in general, and the same was true of Jewish communities in Europe.

Nevertheless, Jews remained distinctive everywhere within the broader community, both because they wished to do so and because society before modern times was defined either by faith or ethnicity in such a way that those who were different were excluded. Before the end of the eighteenth century there was no concept of general citizenship, or equal rights, or pluralist political communities constructed by consent. Jewish distinctiveness within the general population was sometimes benign on balance—the Golden Age of Spain was golden for both Muslims and Jews—sometimes not, for Jews suffered much persecution in almost all the places they lived, mainly on religious grounds.

Contrary to what many think nowadays—largely, it must be said, on account of the popularity of the modern Zionist characterization of it—Jewish life in exile turned brutish, impoverished, and subject to systematic physical attack and decimation only in fairly recent times. Many scholars link the end of feudalism and the rise of capitalism in western Europe with the growth of systematic anti-Semitism based not only or mainly on religious prejudice but also on economic competition. Jews and other minorities (Armenians, Greeks) had been the entrepreneurial grease in the creaky wheels of late feudalism. When economic changes drew native populations from the countryside to urban areas, and as indigenous middle classes arose, Jews stood in places that native Christians wished themselves to stand. Jews were expelled from one European country after another—England, France, Germany— and gradually moved east by necessity and sometimes at the invitation of Polish barons who wanted *kulturvolk* (peoples of culture)—Germans and Jews mainly—to bring their skills and connections to enrich their lands.

By the seventeenth century, probably the majority of European Jewry lived in the Austro-Hungarian and the Russian empires of Central and Eastern Europe. But this turned out not to be a long respite from difficulty, at least not by historical standards. As both new technologies and the national idea penetrated Central and Eastern Europe from farther west, the same combination of ideology and interest put Jewish communities at risk. Many communities became impoverished and were periodically subject to murderous attack—the Chmielnicki massacres (1648–55) in what is today the Ukraine and Poland being a notable case in point.

As a result of both sources of Jewish distinctiveness, the internally chosen and the externally imposed, Jews tended to adapt distinctive ways of making a living—cloth making and dyeing, for example. And because of contacts maintained with Jews in other lands, Jews became instrumental in international trade and finance—the import-export business, so to speak.

For this reason, too, a few select Jews often served the court of the country in which they lived as translators, financial advisers, ambassadors and emissaries, economic pioneers in imperial borderlands, and so forth. In the fourteenth century, for example, Jewish customs officials working for the Ottoman Empire wrote to Jewish customs officials in Italian city-states using the Hebrew script.

Even nineteenth- and twentieth-century America featured "court Jews" specialized in matters financial and diplomatic. Judah P. Benjamin became Treasurer of the Confederacy. Not so long thereafter, Henry Morgenthau, of German Jewish descent, became U.S. Secretary of the Treasury. The financier Bernard Baruch was a close adviser to every U.S. president from Woodrow Wilson to Harry Truman. Examples from throughout European and also Middle Eastern history could be multiplied by the thousands. This is neither coincidence nor conspiracy but culture: the outflow of a legacy of adaptation in exile almost two millennia in the making.

This is not *just* history, however. Cultural roles like these amounted to survival traits in exile, and traits that a people develop over nearly two thousand years do not disappear just because some Jews found a modern state, write an anthem, and hoist up a flag. When we noted earlier that the Zionist mythos today contained elements of the past, these traits, honed during centuries of exile, serve as good examples. They are also examples of what scholars like Thomas Sowell and Frances Fukuyama rightly call cultural or social capital.

The relationship of the Jewish community in exile to the society at large mightily shaped Jewish attitudes toward political power and its discontents. Certain archetypal roles emerged that still find resonance in modern Israel. For example, there was the *poritz*, a Yiddish word for the local potentate or baron. Historically, the Jewish relationship with the *poritz* was ambiguous. On the one hand, the Jews, as an alien minority, were beholden to the baron, their well-being resting on his goodwill. On the other hand, should he withdraw his protection, disaster loomed. So the *poritz* was simultaneously benefactor and potential tormentor.

Hence, from the Middle Ages forward, Jewish communities appealed to the *hofjuden*—talented court Jews usually responsible for administering the financial affairs of the realm—to plead their case in times of distress before the *poritz*. The *hofjude* had no power in the conventional sense; his success depended on native wit, eloquence, and good connections at court. Relatedly, there was the *shtadlan* (literally, "one who intercedes"). The *shtadlan* was a broker, modeled on a figure familiar from Jewish commercial activity, who sought to cultivate influential intermediaries in contacts with the *poritz*. The *shtadlan*, complementing the *hofjude*, might be a well-connected, assimilated Jew or a well-disposed gentile. Anyone who thinks such archetypes are mere relics of history has never spent more than five minutes thinking hard about U.S.-Israeli relations over the last several decades.

As noted, the exile was quite diverse. In general, European Jewish communities came to be known as Ashkenaz (after the ancient Hebrew word for a people living in what is today Germany; see Genesis 10:3), and those that came from Spain as Sepharad (the Hebrew word for Spain). The former spoke German dialects as a daily language, which evolved into Yiddish, a Germanic language with some Hebrew vocabulary and written in the Hebrew script. The latter had spoken Ladino (a Spanish dialect mixed with Hebrew) in Spain. After the expulsion, some maintained Ladino for centuries—and some Turkish Jews still speak it today. But after Spain, Sefaradim (plural form) eventually came to speak the language of their community, be it Arabic, Italian, Persian, or whatever.

This isn't "just history" either; Jewish Israelis alive today come from more than sixty countries speaking several dozen native languages. And while acculturation to Hebrew is usually rapid, Israel has traditionally published more newspapers in more different languages per capita than any country in history. Unless the nature of the exile is understood, this cannot be explained.

Despite the long years and the increasing diversity of exilic experiences, Jews everywhere maintained several basic commonalities. First, everyone understood that they were in exile, and they experienced exile not as individuals but as members of a more or less self-governing community that related to the larger society as a corporate entity.

Second, these communities were traditionally religious—secularism had not been invented before the sixteenth century—and that meant that the theology of exile for punishment, and redemption at the time of the messiah, was a near universal assumption within the communities far and wide. It also meant that many customs remained shared because of religious obligations. So, for example, Persian Jews might stew their fowl with apricots while Hungarian Jews would roast theirs with paprika and garlic, but no one would cook an animal that was not slaughtered according to kosher slaughtering laws, and no one would cook a chicken with cheese or cream. Differences between different rabbinical groups—say, in Egypt and in France—did arise, but they were relatively minor: the main corpus of Jewish law had been detailed by the sixth century in the Talmud, and this bound together the communities thereafter no matter where they were.

Third, Jews everywhere referred in their prayers to the land of Israel, daily asking God to "rebuild Jerusalem, speedily in our days." They followed the liturgical calendar in accord with the seasons as they fell in Israel and not where they lived (praying for rain and for dew, for example).

Fourth, relatedly, because Hebrew and Aramaic remained the language of prayer and study, at least the leaders of the communities were capable of communicating with each other—and often did so despite having adopted different daily tongues. This allowed Jews to share not only local news but also bits and pieces of new knowledge—medical, scientific, mechanical, commercial, and philosophical. This gained them much, but also generated them a great deal of envy and resentment among the general population, which led to much hardship and persecution.

Fifth, all the communities were within, but not of, the general communities in which they lived. Jews lived a life of sometimes creative and happy, sometimes stressful and dangerous marginality. But it was marginality just the same, and that was an experience Jews everywhere shared even if the specific contents of the experience differed substantively from place to place, and from time to time.

Sixth, most of the communities at one time or another experienced severe persecution and expulsions (far more in Europe than in Muslim domains), and so were not only in exile but often in exile from a previous exile. Seventh and finally, thanks largely to all of the above, Jews wherever they were never stopped feeling that all other Jews were their brothers and sisters, their extended family: "All of Israel is responsible one to the other," says a famous line from the Talmud, and most Jews took it both literally and seriously. The experiences of exile counseled that Jews could rely only on other Jews in times of distress—a historical "lesson" that Jews of the twentieth century have still not forgotten.

The Emancipation and the Birth of Zionism

By many measures, Jews have been the most successful transterritorial civilization in human history. Despite the countless incidents of discrimination and depredation experienced since 135 C.E., Jews not only survived but often excelled in the professions, business, and intellectual life. But in the late eighteenth century there occurred an event, at once intellectual and historical, that transformed the Jewish condition, and nothing has ever been the same since. That event was the French Revolution.

What do the exploits of Robespierre and his associates have to do with the Jews and with modern Israel? Just this: the Revolution let loose on the world a set of ideas that made the traditional relationship between Jewish communities and the non-Jewish societies in which they lived untenable. To put it simply, two ideas mattered most.

First was the idea that *individuals* as opposed to communities had political rights. Second was the idea of *secularism*, that society could be governed by the spirit of reason and according to natural law that could be understood through science, and that religious doctrine and religious institutions should not dominate or even play a major role in political life. The Declaration of the Rights of Man, by enshrining the universal validity and applicability of these two principles of revolution, led in due course (February 9, 1807, to be exact) to the formal Emancipation of the Jews. This meant that Jews as individuals could be citizens of France on an equal basis under a government in which Christianity and Christian clergy played no formal role. This was unprecedented in 1,700 years of Jewish experience in exile.

It was also an unprecedented challenge to the Jewish community. Jewish communal leaders had learned well over time how to deal with non-Jewish power on a community-to-community level, but they had no experience with such novel ideas as universal individualism and secularism. Moreover, it should come as no surprise that the shift in attitudes that accompanied the Renaissance, and which ultimately lay behind the political upheavals of the French and American revolutions, had also affected Jews. Jews, who were mainly urban dwellers, knew of and contributed much to the development of its science and, with it, the enshrinement of human reason as the font of the new social and political order.

French Jews reacted enthusiastically to the Emancipation, for it promised relief from persecution and second-class social status. But it also made massive voluntary assimilation a prospect for the first time in post-exilic Jewish life. As Napoleon's army spread the ideas of the rights of man across Europe, Jewish emancipation spread with it. So did new problems of Jewish accommodation with society without and individual choice within.

The philosophers of the French Revolution thought of their creed as a universal one. Neither parochial religion nor narrow ethnicity, they believed, should dominate political life. According to the *philosophes*, science and reason composed the path to social justice and international peace. Such ideas were very attractive to many Jews, so much so that many left Judaism and assimilated into what they took to be a new and progressive, optimistically minded liberal Europe.

Additionally, a variety of efforts were undertaken to find halfway houses between traditional Jewish identity and the attractions of the new European society at large. Reform Judaism, which was founded in Germany in the 1850s, tried to do to Judaism what European Protestants had done to Christianity: extract and emphasize general moral principles as opposed to ritual or law, privatize religion as a matter of personal faith rather than communal observance, eliminate all aspects of Jewish peoplehood from Jewish civilization, and jettison all religious obligations (dietary laws and Sabbath observance, for example) that resulted in observable distinctions between Jews and non-Jews. Other reactions, extensions of Moses Mendelsohn's prerevolutionary *Haskalah* (Enlightenment), sought to preserve the spirit of Jewish law and peoplehood by modernizing Jewish attitudes according to the progressive aura of the period.

Such was the intellectual environment of Jews west of the czarist empire a half-century after the French Revolution. But the revolution generated a strong reaction in Europe. The *philosophes'* ideas and Napoleon's armies has discomfited the crown heads of the rest of Europe. First Napoleon was stopped and then defeated by 1814; but it took a while for the intellectual reaction to gel. The revolutions of 1848, and their general failure, mark this reaction. As opposed to the idealistic, rational universalism of the French Revolution, the conservative reaction highlighted nationalism, at the center of which was a belief in the "natural" community of those with similar culture. Similar culture referred to language, a common historical mythology (myth of tribal bloodline), and, often, a common Christianity.

The rise of modern European nationalism, beginning in western Europe and year by year, decade by decade, moving ever more strongly into the Hapsburg and then the Russian empires, generally bode ill for Jews. Before 1848, the sense among most Jews was that despite the new political tumult all about them, there was a fair chance that they would inherit a stable and safe role in the future of a liberal Europe. Increasingly after 1848, pessimism became the order of the day, and the farther east one was, the more pessimistic one generally became. There, the new nationalisms were not as much tempered by the spirit of the Renaissance, which had never reached that far, nor chastened by the Wars of the Reformation, which took place farther west. Central and Eastern Europe were less Protestant, more Catholic and Eastern Orthodox, and the attitudinal differences between the former and the latter were real.

The soul of Europe was split after mid-century between those who clung to the legacy of universalism, secularism, and reason and those who advocated nationalism, faith, and the romantic sensibility. Jews found themselves in a quandary. The victory of the former promised to protect the rights of Jews to citizenship and legal equality, but it risked assimilation and the destruction of Jewish solidarity and even identity. The victory of the latter would make it easier to marshal Jewish distinctiveness, but the return of government-sanctioned persecution directed by ardent, chauvinistic nationalists threatened to reverse decades of progress and, possibly, to bring additional horrors almost beyond imagination.

In the Russian Empire, the impact of the French Revolution and the reaction against it was played out in microcosm in a single country. Czar Alexander

II (1855–81) instituted sweeping reforms that greatly benefited the Jews and other minorities of the Russian Empire. For Russian Jewish subjects of the czar, Alexander's reforms were comparable to the emancipation that had taken place in western Europe half a century earlier. But here, too, reaction set in; after Alexander II was assassinated in 1881, his successors turned the clock back. The May Laws of 1882 undid all of what Alexander II had done and more besides. The new nationalism in Russia expressed itself as pan-Slavism and in cultural Russification campaigns throughout its territory. Government-inspired anti-Jewish riots, called *pogroms*, proliferated. Times got very, very bad for the roughly 3.2 million Jews of the Russian Empire, then nearly 70 percent of the world total of Jews.[10]

By 1882, Jews faced deeply unsettling prospects across Europe, the exact nature of their problem and the range of alternatives open to them differing by degree on account of the uneven political developments across Europe during the previous eighty years. In places such as France, Britain, Germany, Holland, and Belgium the choice was among traditional communalism, Reformism, or assimilation. The latter two choices implied, as well, that Jews would support liberal-progressive, anti-nationalist political forces to the extent possible.

In the Russian Empire, the main choices for Jews were traditional communalism, emigration, and assimilation. The former, adopted by the majority, requires little explanation: Jews saw themselves in exile as Jews had seen themselves for more than 1,000 years, paying for the sins of their ancestors and waiting patiently for God to redeem them to their land with the coming of the messiah. Those who chose to emigrate also acted as Jews in exile had acted before: they pulled up their tents and looked around for the most hospitable shelter until God would come and redeem them. For the overwhelming majority who decided to emigrate, their destination was America. By far the overwhelming majority of American Jews are descended from those who left the Russian Empire between 1882 and 1924. The third choice, assimilation, implied more often than not a political vocation dedicated to revolution against the czarist empire, for liberal-progressive political movements either did not exist or were not promising in the Russian environment.

Then another choice, another option, arose for European Jewry: Zionism.

All of the choices before European Jewry described above have in common one sort of continuity or another. Those who left Europe did so in accordance with an age-old pattern of exilic nomadism. All the rest tried to figure out a solution to the Jews' European problem *in Europe*. Zionists were the most pessimistic of all observers of the "Jewish problem," as it was almost universally called by Jews and non-Jews alike, as it existed at the end of the nineteenth century: they believed that there was no solution to the Jewish problem within Europe.

The problem, as the Zionists saw it, was not just to survive, nor the survival of individual Jews, but the survival of the Jewish people as a people. That ruled out assimilation of all sorts, whether to the life of a liberal bourgeoisie in western Europe or a furtive revolutionist in Eastern Europe. Moreover, they wanted to survive as Jews in the modern world, and that ruled out what seemed to them the increasingly obscurantist forms of orthodoxy that dominated eastern Europe. As for a Haskalah-like modern orthodoxy developing in western Europe, or Reformism, the Zionists believed that European society was headed in a dark, anti-liberal direction that would make such solutions impossible. One Zionist, Bernard Lazare, writing in 1899, seems even to have virtually predicted the Jewish Holocaust[11] in Europe between 1939 and 1945: "Today the Jewish question is raised more powerfully than ever. From every side a solution is sought for it. Truly it is no longer a matter of knowing whether anti-Semitism is or is not going to win seats in Parliament; *it is a matter of knowing what is to be the fate of millions of Jews.*"[12]

So if emigration was just running from the problem, and no solution was to be found in assimilation or Reformism, or in revolutionism either, then what was left? What was left was an act of historical discontinuity: breaking the shackles of Jewish dependency by ending the exile and returning to the land. What was left, as Zionists saw it, was a second exodus from slavery to freedom. What was left was Zionism, thought of as the national liberation movement of the Jewish people.

It was almost by a process of elimination, therefore, pushed forth by an increasing sense of desperation, that a handful of Jews in different parts of Europe—who were unknown to one another—hit upon an idea that evoked radical discontinuity: the establishment of a Jewish homeland, and in time a sovereign state, on the territory of ancient Israel, called Palestine since 135 C.E. Of course, this idea, to come independently to different individuals around the same period, did not fall out of the sky. There were reasons for its evocation, as a brief description of the men who were its founders make clear.

There is no doubt about who the first two Zionists were. They were both rabbis—one Sepharadic, one Ashkenazic—and both lived in central Europe in places where traditional religiosity was still strong (unlike the west) but where the ideas of the Renaissance and French Revolution were known (unlike the east). The first was Judah Alkalai, the rabbi of Semlin (near Belgrade), who in 1839 astonished his congregants by calling for the establishment of new Jewish colonies in Palestine to hasten the coming of the messiah. Alkalai cited the *Zohar*, the book of Jewish mysticism, in arguing that only the efforts of every individual Jew would convince God to begin the process of redemption. Then, independently of Alkalai in 1843, Rabbi Tzvi Hirsh Kalischer of Thorn, in East Prussia, argued similarly that Jewish salvation could take place by natural, as opposed to supernatural, means and did not require the advent of the messiah in its early stages. Prayers were not enough, he argued—just as Rabbi Akiba had said at the time of Bar-Kochba—and he urged the formation of a colonization society, settlement in Palestine, the training of young Jews in self-defense, and the establishment of a Jewish agricultural school in Palestine.[13]

Both Alkalai and Kalischer were ahead of their time. When they wrote and preached, optimism still clung to Jewish souls in western Europe, passivity to the masses in eastern Europe. Religious authorities attacked their impiety, while those Jews who were more secularly minded thought they were quaintly mad.

A dozen years thereafter, the Zionist idea received its first systematic treatment and, for the first time, was expressed in non-religious terms by someone who was not a rabbi. Moses Hess, from Bonn, Germany, stumbled across the writings of Rabbi Kalischer in 1857 at a time when he was becoming increasingly aware of cosmopolitan anti-Semitism in western Europe, and when he became engrossed in the works of the great Italian nationalist Giuseppe Mazzini. The result, in 1862, was the first modern Zionist tract, called *Rome and Jerusalem*. Hess uncannily prefigured the themes of secular, socialist Zionism, but in 1862 his book was ignored. Hess's convoluted writing style discouraged readers and translators alike, and he was thus mostly unknown to the other Zionist intellectual pioneers who followed him.

Meanwhile in Russia, the liberalization of society after 1855 led to a Jewish cultural revival. Borrowing from themes in the culture at large that extolled beauty and nature, productivity and strength, some young Jews moved away from traditional religion toward a cultural Judaism that saw Zion as an idyllic land of muses. This was the specifically Russian *haskalah* of Moshe Lilienblum and Judah Leib Gordon, and it too saw a merger of Jewish culture and Russian social inclusion. As part of their efforts, they sought a revival of Hebrew as a living language with which to write essays and poetry. Peretz Smolenskin founded a Hebrew literary journal called *HaShahar* (The Dawn), which stimulated Eliezer Perlman (who later changed his name to Ben-Yehuda) to an extraordinary task: the systematic revitalization of Hebrew from a liturgical and written exegetical language to a living, spoken one.

As time passed, the shadow of pan-Slavism lengthened, and the optimism of the Russian Haskalah gave way to pessimism. Moreover, the Russian Jews involved in the cultural revival gradually got political. Watching new nationalisms sweep the Balkans and Eastern Europe, Ben-Yehuda said: "Why should we be any less worthy than other peoples? What about our nation, our language, our land?" Lilienblum, Smolenskin, and most of the others, who had started out optimists, ended up advocating massive emigration to Palestine. But it took another man to put the case in writing for the masses of Russian Jews.

Leo Pinsker, from Odessa in the Ukraine, wrote *Autoemancipation* in September 1882. It was by far the most systematic analysis of the insolubility of the Jewish problem in Europe, and Pinsker instantly became a celebrity. Thanks to his book, the Haskalah changed from a cultural into a political movement and expanded its base from a few hundred to tens of thousands of activists. It soon spread from Russia into Poland and Romania as well.

As important, between 1882 and 1891, more than 22,000 Jews—some socialist, many not—came to Palestine in a movement called in Israeli history the First Aliyah (Ascent).[14] This nearly doubled the Jewish population of the land, estimated to have been about 25,000 in 1880, much of that, in turn, the direct consequence of the extraordinary efforts of Sir Moses Montefiore, a British Jew whose practical efforts to plant Jewish settlements in Palestine paralleled and exceeded the efforts of Alkalai and Kalischer. (The Jewish population of Palestine in 1800 was only about 6,000, most of that in Jerusalem, and the rest in Hebron to the south, Safed and Tiberias in the north.)

The Jews of Palestine, however, had a hard time of it. The new arrivals, mostly secular, socialist, and political, clashed with the older *Yishuv* (resettlement), who were religious and not very political. Moreover, their settlements were not economically successful. These problems were noted by Asher Ginsburg, known better by his pen name, Ahad Ha'am (meaning "One the People"), who urged his fellow Zionists to mobilize the help of Jews in western Europe to negotiate a charter of Jewish settlement with the then rulers of the land, the Ottoman Empire. Ahad Ha'am thus anticipated the main effort of the final figure we deal with here, the man credited with being the father of Zionism: Theodore Herzl.

Like Hess, Herzl was a German-speaking Jew and, like Hess, had been assimilated and estranged from traditional Judaism. The Zionist idea hit him suddenly one day in 1894; when it did, he had never even heard of Alkalai or Kalischer, Hess or Pinsker.

Herzl was a journalist, a political liberal, a writer of popularity and style on cultural and social trends. In 1891, Herzl became Paris correspondent for the *Neue Freie Presse*, Austria's leading newspaper. In Paris, Herzl encountered a politicized anti-Semitism he had never known in the Hapsburg Empire. This politicized anti-Semitism reached a crescendo in 1894 with the infamous Dreyfus trial, wherein a Jewish army captain was accused of espionage for Germany. Dreyfus was framed, but the trial was the occasion for rabid outbursts of French anti-Semitism. Listening to the mobs shout "death to the Jews" transformed Herzl; he later described his idea of establishing a Jewish state in Palestine as dreamlike, totally transformative, and intoxicating.

Just as Ahad Ha'am had advocated, Herzl formed a plan to go to the wealthy Jewish families of Europe to gain support for his venture. His plan, which they rejected, became in 1895 a book called *Der Judenstaat* (literally The Jew State).[15] Whereas Hess had been ignored writing in German in 1862, Herzl was not completely ignored in 1895. He gathered a few devotees, and thanks to his dedication and his belief that Jews everywhere were one people, Herzl had the organizational drive and practical-mindedness to do something Hess never could: create an organization that represented and bound together German-speaking, French-speaking, Yiddish-speaking, Russian-speaking, Polish-speaking, Romanian-speaking, and Hungarian-speaking Jews throughout continental Europe, as well as the English-speaking Jews of Britain and North America. The First Zionist Congress, consisting of 204 representatives, began on August 29, 1897, in Basel, Switzerland. Herzl's genius for organization and public relations assured that this would be an event to make a worldwide splash, and it did. After the first day of the congress, Herzl wrote in his diary: "In Basel I create the Jewish State."

It wasn't really all that easy to do, however. The main tactical goal of the Zionist organization was straightforward: to muster all means—and particularly the friendly assistance of Western governments through *hofjuden* and *shtadlen*—to persuade the Ottoman government to provide a charter for Jews to settle Palestine. Herzl's plan was laid out along the lines of a colonial company similar to those that other Europeans had designed for India, Mozambique, and the Gold Coast.

Getting the charter did not happen as Herzl had hoped. In western Europe, wealthy Jews turned him away, looking upon Zionism as a threat to their hard-won if still endangered citizenship rights. The Jewish masses of central and eastern Europe, however, increasingly flocked to the Zionist banner. Thus, when by 1902 a disappointed and fatigued Herzl favored accepting a Jewish homeland in East Africa (commonly referred to as the Uganda proposal, but present-day Kenya was meant), which the British government had offered, the tide of east European Zionism made this impossible: only in Palestine could the idea of a Jewish homeland evoke sufficiently broad support to make the project practical. This was true particularly for the Zionists of the Russian Empire. Even though they were the most ostensibly socialist and anti-religious of the group, they were in truth more culturally insular than west European Jews. They were consequently more tightly bound to traditional Jewish religious images than they themselves understood or admitted.

Meanwhile, Russian Zionists argued for continued emigration and settlement along socialist organizing schema. In line with this project they established the Jewish National Fund in 1901 to raise money to buy land and support
Jewish settlement in Palestine. The top-down approach of Herzl became known
as *political* Zionism and the bottom-up approach of the Russian Jews as *practical* Zionism. The two branches competed, but competed more or less cooperatively, until 1904, when Herzl died at the age of forty-four.

After Herzl's death the Zionist movement faced many problems. It was
considered heretical by the religious establishments of traditional Judaism:
the rabbis saw Herzl as another Bar-Kochba, another Shabbtai Tzvi, another
dreamer tempted by the lure of redemption before its time, whose efforts
they were sure would surely bring disaster of one kind or another. Assimilated Jews of western Europe thought they knew the shape of that disaster:
proclamations emphasizing unitary Jewish peoplehood and declaiming
against the health of European civilization would feed the forces of nationalist reaction, jeopardize hard-won Jewish legal rights, and stir up the mobs
against them whenever times turned bad. Zionism was therefore a small
movement; the majority of Jews, both religious and assimilated, declared
their enmity and opposition to it.

As a small movement, Zionism was also a poor movement. And as a poor
movement, it lacked funds to build settlements in Palestine and support networks of activists in Europe simultaneously. This, in turn, aggravated the
differences within the movement between political Zionists and practical
Zionists. And to top it off, the Ottoman government obstructed whatever
efforts the Zionists made in Palestine, refused to grant a charter, and ignored
Zionist arguments that Jewish settlement would benefit the empire.

Nevertheless, the rapidly worsening situation of Russian Jewry and the
growth of "scientific" and populist anti-Semitism amid the ever more strident nationalisms of Europe persuaded increasing numbers of Jews that Zionism, however fanciful and even crazy it seemed, might be the only answer.
Zionism's survival as a unified movement in the decade between 1904 and
1914 also owed much to the extraordinary efforts of two men: Max Nordau
(1849–1923) and Haim Weizmann (1874–1952).

During this period, too, Zionist ideology congealed, and it did so in the
direction of socialist, or Labor, Zionism. It borrowed heavily from the socialist ideologies then most popular among intellectual classes in Europe.
The elements of this ideology are extremely important to grasp, for they
have carved out a deep legacy in modern Israel.

First, Labor Zionists basically agreed with Marx that religion was the
opiate of the masses. They saw traditional Jewish views as laden with superstition, as being anti-modern and anti-scientific, and as inculcating a disas-

trous political passivity in their adherents. Taken together, Labor Zionists believed that orthodox religion was regressive and accounted for what we would call today the obsessive-compulsive traits of many of its adherents.

Second, Labor Zionists reasoned that these abnormalities, and incidences of self-hatred, were a function of the abnormal social structure of the Jews in exile. In exile, Jews were forced into particular professions and social niches, as well as physical ghettos. The class structure of the people was distorted, and it therefore followed from the Marxian concepts of substructure and super-structure that Jewish attitudes would be distorted, too. The only way to fix this problem was to create a Jewish society with a normal social structure, with Jewish owners and managers and also Jewish workers and peasants—and, as some Zionists even put it, only partly in jest, with Jewish cops and Jewish robbers, Jewish prostitutes and Jewish johns. And this, they were sure, could never happen in Europe. A well-known Hebrew song of the Zionist pioneers expressed the basic idea well: "*Anu banu artza, banot u'lehibanot ba*" ("We are going to the land to build it and be built by it").

It followed, too, that exile was exile, no matter where it was. Zionist ideology asserted that Jews would never be more than second-class citizens in practice, vulnerable to anti-Semitism anywhere outside of Israel. There was no diaspora, a gentle, almost politically neutral term; there was only exile. The aim of Zionism, it followed logically, was not just to save European Jews in trouble, to create a shelter for the oppressed, but to gather in all the Jewish people into Israel—or as many as possible—because only in that way could Jewish history itself be normalized and the Jews returned to their proper place in history.

Third, Labor Zionists thought in terms of the group, not the individual. Like all socialist revolutionaries, they believed that things got done only by movements, not by individuals. That required a certain amount of conformity, selflessness, and lack of ostentation.

Fourth, relatedly, Labor Zionists of this age believed in rational planning, the social ownership of the means of production, and collectivism in agriculture. It was, in short, anti-capitalist, either a little or a lot depending on the person and the twist of ideology.

Fifth, speaking of agriculture, Labor Zionists, virtually none of whom had been farmers in Europe, waxed almost mystical about the land and about farming it.[16] The key to normalizing the Jewish social structure was agriculture, and the soil of Eretz Israel seemed to most to have almost magical powers of healing and spiritual renewal. Here, clearly, the traditional religious devotion to the land merged, usually unconsciously, with Labor Zionist ideology. It is also worth noting that Labor Zionists could get much more enthusiastic about agriculture than industry because lots of Jews had personal experience as temporary members of the industrial proletariat in Europe and knew from personal experience that there was nothing romantic or glorious about it. They had little or no experience with farming, so about it they could think whatever they liked.

Sixth, Labor Zionism was egalitarian-minded. It brooked no distinctions based on accidents of birth, including sexual distinctions, and regarded talent and hard work as superior to family pedigree and abstract intellectual pursuits. It saw social justice and equality as the highest moral nobility.

Seventh, Labor Zionism believed in internal democracy; as long as one accepted the basic tenants of the creed, arguments over tactics would be decided by majority rule. And they were.

In short, pre-state Labor Zionists saw themselves as revolutionaries trying to remake and thereby save the Jewish people through political organization and action. Just as Marxism aimed to create the new man, free of pettiness and false consciousness, Labor Zionism aimed to create the new Jew. They had a very specific sense of what this meant. In Europe, Jews were dependent, beholden to others; in Israel, they would be free and independent. In Europe, Jews spoke the languages of other peoples; in Israel they would speak their own language, Hebrew. In Europe, Jews were passive in the face of physical threats; in Israel, Jews would defend themselves and their rights. In Europe, Jews were bookish, pale, and pasty; in Israel, Jews would thrive in the world of real work, their skin bronzed and tawny from it as in days of old. In Europe, Jews were never really at ease, never really felt at home; in Israel, and only in Israel, Jews could and would find real peace of mind and the satisfaction of having real roots.

There were some ideological difficulties and disputes within Labor Zionism, as seems always to be the case in highly ideological movements of the Left. As the successor to the ideals of the French Revolution, Zionism as a form of nationalism ran against the grain of the internationalism, or universalism, of the socialist ideal. Some sought to reconcile the problem by adjusting their understanding of socialism, others to broaden the definition of the nation by including Arabs, with whom some Jewish Marxists felt a shared class identification. Lev Borochov, for example, argued that Arab peasants shared class interests with the Jewish farmers and proletariat, and therefore had more in common with Jews than with their fellow Arab landowners. Radical socialism always overestimated class solidarity and underestimated ethnic or cultural-national ties, and this was just another example of that error.

Another philosophical problem concerned Judaism itself. Many Labor Zionists saw their own movement as the logical next stage of Judaism brought into the modern world. They brought with it notions of a chosen people, too, believing that the Jewish role as a light unto the nations would be manifest in the purity and quality of socialism that Jews would be able to create in Palestine. Jews remained special, only in a modern way. Other Labor Zionists rejected such notions, seeing the future homeland as fully normal, "just like the other nations," with no claims to special status and with no concern for modernized religion.

And they argued, too, over socialist ideology itself. Some were radical and in their *kibbutzim*, their agricultural collectives, allowed no private possessions and mandated that children from the age of six weeks sleep apart from their parents in a children's house. Others were less extreme, and in time formal divisions occurred over such issues. Some *kibbutzim* split down the middle, literally erecting fences between radical and less radical camps. This is important because when normal Israeli political life began in earnest in 1949, the Labor Zionist camp was split into factions whose origins dated from often arcane disputes thirty years old and older.

It is on account of such problems and divisions that Zionism produced an extensive literature dealing with cultural, ideological, historical, and personal facets of the movement.[17] The Zionist founders talked and wrote so much that one wonders sometimes when they had a chance to do anything else. But Labor Zionists did not just sit around in Europe and talk. Many came to Palestine and worked. The Second Aliyah, as it is called, between 1905 and 1914, brought another 30,000 Jews to Palestine, bringing the total Jewish population to about 85,000 (compared to roughly half a million Arabs). In 1909, the Yishuv—the name for the Jewish resettlement of the land—started the first socialist-inspired collective settlement, or *kibbutz* (from the Hebrew word for group, *k'vutzah*): Deganya, near Lake Tiberias.[18] By 1914, there were fourteen such settlements; about 12,000 Jews lived in rural areas, either in *kibbutzim* or in small cooperatively run villages called *moshavim*, the first of these being Nahalal, established in 1921.[19] A new Jewish city, Tel Aviv, had taken root as well on the Mediterranean coast just north of the Arab city of Jaffa.

The success of the Second Aliyah gave confidence to the Jews of Palestine and to their brethren still outside contemplating immigration. It also implanted in the governments of Europe the idea that Jewish resettlement in Palestine was serious and economically viable, for the settlements of the Second Aliyah, as opposed to the First, were self-sufficient. They also remained highly ideological; for socialist ideological reasons, the *halutzim* (pioneers) of the collective settlements did not use Arab labor for fear of becoming capitalist exploiters. This was bound to be misunderstood by the local Arabs, who knew little or nothing of European Jews and even less of secular socialist theory. And it was misunderstood.

Toward Statehood: War, Mandate, War, and War Again

Ironically, although "practical" Labor Zionism came to dominate the Zionist movement after Herzl's death, it was an unexpected success of Herzlian political Zionism that put the movement on the road to eventual success. The success of the Second Aliyah was a necessary precondition for the breakthrough, but not a sufficient one. It took a world war to bring that about.

When war erupted in 1914, Britain found itself with Ottoman Turkey for an enemy, which was ironic because British diplomacy had long tried to support Turkey for balance-of-power reasons. Early in the war the British government sought any means, fair or foul, to undermine Turkish control over its far-flung domains, especially the Arab ones where European powers—notably Britain, France, and Germany—had growing economic and political interests. The Arabs had been near rebellion against Istanbul even before the war began, and weaning some of them over to the Allied side was not all that difficult. The British promised the Arabs an independent state after the war under the domain of the Hashemite family, then of Mecca in the Hejaz. This involves the fascinating story of the Arab Revolt, the Sykes-Picot accord, the British-Hashemite relationship, British double-dealing with Abdel Aziz ibn Saud of Nejd, and the latter-day telegenic exploits of British Arabists like T. E. Lawrence—"Lawrence of Arabia."

For our purposes, however, another British promise is more germane, and its story just as fascinating.[20] Just as London tried to rile up the Arabs against the Turks, creating a fifth column within the enemy camp, it tried to enlist Jewish help against both Turkey in the Middle East and Germany in Europe. How? By promising the Zionists that, after the war, the British government would look favorably upon the creation of a Jewish homeland in Palestine, sanctioned by the international community and, presumably, protected by Great Britain itself.[21] This became known as the Balfour Declaration, promulgated on November 2, 1917, in the form of a letter to Lord Rothschild, head of the British Zionist Federation, from the British Foreign Minister, James Arthur Balfour. It read, in part:

> His Majesty's government views with favor the establishment in Palestine of a national home for the Jewish people . . . it being clearly understood that nothing shall be done which may prejudice the civil and religious rights of existing non-Jewish communities in Palestine, or the rights and political status enjoyed by Jews in any other country.

The final phrasing of the declaration, which went through several drafts before being finalized, deserves careful examination. The notion of a national home did not explicitly mean an independent state, but it strongly implied one.

Conversely, the rights of the existing non-Jewish community are described as civil and religious, *not* as political. And while everyone knew that these communities referred overwhelmingly to Arabs, Arabs are not explicitly mentioned, while the Jewish people is mentioned. The last phrase, about the rights "enjoyed" by Jews in other countries, is also notable. It is not a very Zionist remark, because ideological Zionism did not recognize the stability of Jews' "rights" in exile. But it was insisted upon by the one Jewish member of the British War Cabinet, Edwin Montagu, whose anti-Zionism stemmed from his fear that the status of assimilated British Jews like himself would be jeopardized by the Zionist idea.

The Balfour Declaration was not merely a function of Britain's wartime needs. Nor did it have anything to do with money. Two other factors contributed much to its coming into being: Christian Zionism, and the power of personality.

The Anglican Church was inclined to a Judeophilic view of history, and some of its theologians had long argued that an ingathering of the Jews was necessary before the Second Coming of Christ. Anglican Bibles almost invariably featured maps showing the distribution of the tribes of Israel in ancient Palestine. Some of its lay leaders were particularly enthralled by the idea of the return of the Jews to Palestine, the most notable perhaps being Anthony Ashley-Cooper, the seventh Earl of Shaftesbury, who from the 1830s onward devoted much effort to promoting Jewish return to Palestine. It was Lord Shaftesbury, a close associate of Lord Palmerston, the British Foreign Secretary, who agitated for Palmerston's placement of a British Consul in Jerusalem (Mr. William Young arrived in 1838). It was also Shaftesbury, not a Jew or a Jewish Zionist of later vintage, who invented in 1851 the famous slogan "For a people without a land, a land without a people," later picked up and popularized for a time by Israel Zangwill.[22] Forms of Christian Zionism persisted in British upper-class education into the twentieth century. It is a theme in English literature of that era, as in George Eliot's famous novel *Daniel Deronda.* Balfour was affected by it, and so was Winston Churchill, General Lord Allenby, then Prime Minister David Lloyd George, and most of the British aristocracy.

As to the power of personality, we must turn to Dr. Haim Weizmann. Weizmann was a chemist by training, a diplomat by nature, and an optimist by temperament. Though born in eastern Europe, his education and work had taken him west to Germany and also to England. He had worked with Herzl and with Nordau, and had been responsible for cultivating British Jewry and the British government. Given his prior experiences and contacts among the British, when the war broke out Weizmann put himself at the service of the British government. It happens that he soon fell upon a remarkable discovery: nitroglycerin, and how to make usable munitions from it. Weizmann used his service to the British war effort and his extensive access to British leaders to lobby for the Balfour Declaration. His ministrations fell on sympathetic ears, and he was successful. Weizmann was the ultimate *shtadlan.*

To many religious Zionists nowadays, the series of events that led Zionism from a poor, failing, divided, and bedraggled movement in 1907 to the Balfour Declaration breakthrough just a decade later suggests the miraculous. The unexpected outbreak of World War I, the eccentrically helpful attitudes of the British elite, the appearance of Weizmann at exactly the right time, in exactly the right place, with exactly the right discovery, all seems too much for coincidence. Weizmann himself was not a believer in miracles, but he was not entirely oblivious to the way things seemed to fall into place. He once said, half-jokingly one supposes, that it wasn't necessary to be crazy to be a Zionist, but it helped. Of course, he wasn't crazy— just successful in ways he could not explain.

The Balfour Declaration truly was an enormous windfall for the Zionist movement, and the movement was grateful. A Jewish brigade fought alongside the British army, and fought well.[23] Aaron Aaronsohn and some of his friends also spied successfully against the Turks for the British. Of course, Jews never mounted a fifth column inside Germany as some British planners had hoped; as Weizmann knew, very few assimilated German Jews had any sympathy for the Zionist idea for exactly the same reason that Edwin Montagu had opposed the Balfour Declaration.

The declaration cemented a relationship between Zionism and the greatest of the victorious Allied powers. The British Mandate for Palestine that came officially into being in 1924, but was functioning more or less from April 1920, made emigration to Palestine easier and more attractive because it was much safer, and it eliminated the multiple barriers of Ottoman days. The Jewish population of Palestine had declined between 1914 and 1919 from 55,000 to 35,000 owing to emigration, starvation, deportation by the Turks, disease, and combat fatalities. But by 1922 the Jewish population had reached 84,000, an obvious indication of the influence of British control over Palestine on the progress of the Zionist movement.

Two years later, another event took place that aided greatly the Zionist ingathering of Jews to Palestine: the United States shut its doors to Jewish immigrants. From 1920 to 1923, annual Jewish immigration to Palestine had averaged about 8,000; in 1924 it jumped to 13,000, and in 1925 to 33,000. Palestine had become not just a place for idealist Zionists to go but a place—increasingly the *only* place—for Jews in trouble to go, whatever their politics.

There was plenty of trouble, no doubt about that. By the 1920s, Europe's two fundamental ideological camps—the successors to the French Revolution and the reaction to it—had spawned extreme varieties: communism and fascism. Both were anti-democratic, both claimed to be socialist, and both claimed to be scientific—Marxism as the "master science" and scientific racism that reached its extreme in Nazi racial and eugenics theories. The result was polarized politics in most of Europe, at one end the Bolshevik regime in the Soviet Union and at the other an array of fascist nationalisms, the first and most notable in Benito Mussolini's Italy. In the new central and eastern European states created out of the fallen Austro-Hungarian Empire and the geopolitical spillover of the Russian Revolution—Poland, Hungary, Austria, Czechoslovakia, Yugoslavia, Lithuania, Latvia, and Estonia—ideological rivalry put Jews in a vice. The nationalist Right saw all Jews as alien within the new ethnoculturally defined state, and the Left tended to see them as class enemies. There was less and less of a liberal political middle ground for Jews to hold to as time passed.

Thus, much of the immigration to Palestine between 1924 and 1932—the Third Aliyah—came from these areas. Most of these immigrants were not Zionist idealists. They had no intention of becoming farmers. They did not share a sense of mystique in the land. And they were not socialists for the most part. They were, it is fair to say, economic refugees with relatively few choices of where to go. The character of this group is important, for it is from the Third Aliyah, from the shopkeepers and other petit bourgeois who came in the 1920s, that Israel's burgeoning urban population was drawn to Tel Aviv, Haifa, and Jerusalem, and that the seeds of Israel's non-socialist political parties that came into being after 1948 were sown.

For at least the first ten years of the British Mandate, government policies greatly favored the Zionist enterprise. Thanks to Arab refusal to have anything to do with the Mandatory government—for the Arabs vehemently denied the legitimacy of the Balfour Declaration and the Mandate based upon it—Zionists populated the British administration at nearly every level. The country's infrastructure improved markedly, which helped the Zionists who were building a nationwide movement, and hurt the Arabs, whose political and economic institutions remained highly local for the most part. The Zionists and the British did not agree on everything, of course, the ideal northeastern and eastern borders of Palestine being a case in point.[24] But for the most part, the Zionists continued to have good working relations with the British and the British continued to affirm their support for the Zionist program.

This allowed many institutions of the Zionist movement to form in a relatively benign environment. Founded in 1920 was the *Haganah*, the Jewish self-defense force, which later became the Israeli Defense Force (IDF). The Jewish Labor Federation, the *Histadrut*, was also founded in 1920 and began to function on a nationwide basis in the years that followed. The Histadrut

became a very important wing of the Jewish Agency, the institutional em-
bodiment of the Zionist movement under the Mandate. Obviously, a Labor
movement needs a union, and in many respects, the Histadrut and the Jewish Agency were two sides of the same organization, the former responsible
for organizing the economy, the latter for taking care of relations with the
Mandatory authority and the supportive movement outside Palestine.

The Jewish Agency did not come about until 1929, however. Early in the
Mandate period, all Jewish groups (except Agudah Israel[25]) organized a proto-
government called *Asefat Hanivharim* (Assembly of the Elected), made up of
a kind of mini-parliament elected by secret ballot. The Asefat Hanivharim,
which met only once a year, in turn elected a kind of executive authority called
the *Vaad Leumi* (National Council) and this council in turn was run by a smaller
executive. It was this executive that did business with the British Mandatory
authority. Meanwhile, the World Zionist Organization—the same one created
by Herzl in 1897—became the Jewish Agency, as called for under Article 4 of
the Mandate. The Vaad Leumi and the Jewish Agency thus cooperated as the
internal and international dimensions of the Zionist movement until 1948.

While the first decade of the Mandate went well for the Zionists, things
began to go badly starting in the late 1920s. The year 1929 was particularly
troubled.

First, as more Jews came to Palestine, the local Arab population became
more fretful that their status, expectations, and rights were being jeopardized. The first Arab violence directed against Zionists took place in Jerusalem in 1920, and was followed by riots in Jaffa the next year. But things
calmed down thereafter for a number of years. In 1929, however, major
outbursts of violence occurred in Jerusalem and Hebron that killed 133 Jews
and caused Jews to abandon their settlement in Hebron.[26]

Zionist attitudes toward the Arabs varied widely. Some argued for a binational state, believing that without Arab cooperation the Zionist future could
never be fulfilled, but such individuals, including Martin Buber and Judah
Magnes, got far too little support and sympathy from the Arab side to make
their positions practical. Others hoped the Arabs would emigrate, whereas
in fact the economic progress of the Yishuv as well as British infrastructural
investments were actually attracting Arabs to Palestine from neighboring
countries. Still others, like a young David Ben-Gurion, believed that a future Jewish state would manage to live with an Arab minority, and even that
such a minority would furnish a link to the rest of the Arab world, with
which the Zionists hoped to live in peace. But most Zionists, especially those
still in Europe and those living in cities in Palestine, simply did not think
much about the Arabs one way or the other. To them, the Jewish problem
was a European problem, and their concerns were focused closely on that.

Second, after 1927, immigration rates fell off, and when the worldwide depression hit Palestine in late 1929, economic activity slowed with it. It was as if virtually all those Jews who were going to come to Palestine had already come, and the Jewish population was nowhere near a majority. Zionist leaders in those days believed that they could not declare a state until they formed a majority, and the decline in immigration suggested that Zionism, as a movement, was not going to become the majority movement of the Jewish people—a catastrophe from both organizational and programmatic perspectives.

Third, the British government changed in July 1929, and the new Labor cabinet under Prime Minister Ramsey MacDonald was much less sympathetic to Zionism than its Conservative predecessors had been. They had not been schooled as had the Anglican elite of the previous generation, they saw British economic and strategic interests as lying more with the Arabs than with the Jews, and they soon instituted new policies in Palestine that restricted Jewish immigration, Jewish land purchases, and Zionist access to the Mandate bureaucracy. The change in British policy threatened to worsen the other two problems of the year: it would, it was feared, encourage Arab opposition and violence and make the attainment of a Jewish demographic majority all the more difficult to achieve.

The rise of Nazism in Germany in 1933 changed Zionist circumstances once again. From 1933 to 1936, Jewish immigration to Palestine rose sharply as the shadow of anti-Semitism darkened over Europe. The Fourth Aliyah, as it became known, brought about 190,000 Jews to Palestine from Germany and Central Europe. These Jews tended to be well educated and skilled, and many were able to bring their savings and family wealth with them. This aliyah greatly enriched and strengthened the Yishuv.

Partly as a result of this influx, and partly because Arab leaders were emboldened by the rise of Hitler and Mussolini, an Arab general strike broke out in 1936, accompanied by much violence against both the British and the Jews. It did not end until 1939, by which time the British government, looking toward the clouds of a new world war, had repudiated virtually all of the principles of the Mandate. The British issued a White Paper that virtually ended Jewish immigration into Palestine at the worst possible moment from the Jewish point of view.

The Palestinian Arab leadership, led by the Mufti of Jerusalem, Haj Amin al-Husseini, allied with the Axis powers against Britain, just as the Hashemite Arabs had allied with the British against the Turks in World War I. They expected an Axis victory to drive Britain and the Jews from Palestine, and give rise to an independent Arab state under German patronage.

As for the Zionists, the onset of Nazism and World War II posed agonizing problems. On the one hand, the rise of Nazi Germany seemed to validate the Zionist analysis of European political and intellectual trends: there was no solution to the Jewish problem in Europe, at least not one that left many Jews alive. Both the Nazis and the Zionists, in their very different ways, agreed on this, and in the late 1930s there occurred what Israeli historians refer to as the *Ha'avara*—the transfer of Jews and Jewish property out of Germany to Palestine. Some of these transfers were negotiated directly between Nazi authorities and representatives of the Jewish Agency, which both Palestinian Arabs and the British Mandatory authorities opposed. It was not easy—to put it mildly—for Zionists to sit with Nazis, but they feared the alternative was even worse. It is important to note that in the late 1930s, before the outbreak of war and the subsequent downturn in German war fortunes, the Nazi government expressed an interest in getting rid of its Jews, not in murdering them. Had the British supported the Ha'avara process instead of trying to stop it to mollify the Arabs, tens and perhaps hundreds of thousands of Jews murdered in the Holocaust might have made it alive to Palestine.

On the other hand, the coming war sharpened the British strategic sense that its interests lay in making allies of the Arabs in the Middle East as a whole to blunt German and Italian entreaties to them. To the Zionists, this meant that the benign environment of the Mandate would likely not return under British rule. The Jewish Agency decided, therefore, as David Ben-Gurion put it, to fight the war as if there were no White Paper, and to fight the White Paper as if there were no war. And indeed, a Jewish legion fought along side the British army in the Middle East and Europe, while at the same time the Jewish Agency tried to sneak as many Jewish refugees into Palestine as it possibly could. This was called Aliyah Bet, and it succeeded in bringing around 200,000 Jews into Palestine between 1936 and 1940.

The war also resulted in a far greater sense of urgency among Zionists for the need to achieve statehood. While Weizmann and the older generation wanted to wait for a Jewish majority in all of Palestine, Ben-Gurion argued for statehood as soon as possible, even in only part of the land, or even if there were a Jewish minority, and his position won out. Adopted in 1942, this view became known as the Biltmore Platform (after the hotel in which the crucial meeting was held).

When the war in Europe ended in 1945, the extent of the destruction of the Jewish population of Europe soon became known. About 6 million Jews—one-third of the entire Jewish population of the world—had perished in Germany and all the lands under German occupation. The Nazis, in the throes of racial hatred in the final three years of the supposed "Thousand Year Reich," were clearly set on genocide. While they worked able-bodied men (often to death), they systematically concentrated on murdering women and particularly children. Of the 6 million Jewish dead, over 1.5 million are estimated to have been age twelve and under.

Nor did it escape attention that not only had Germans engaged in the horror but so did substantial numbers of anti-Semitic sympathizers elsewhere. Many non-Germans were downright enthusiastic about shipping their Jewish citizens to the death camps, most notably in Latvia, the Ukraine, France, Romania, and the Nazi-puppet state of Croatia.

Not even the Zionists, pessimists though they always were about Europeans, could easily assimilate the enormity of what had happened. The point of recounting these events here is not to test the human ability to hold back tears at the realization of what unspeakable things human beings are capable of doing to one another. The point is to emphasize the impact of the Holocaust on the very soul of modern Jewry, which is so great that it truly surpasses calculation. Perhaps the best way to describe the impact is to return to sources.

In the Bible, the story is told of how Balak hired Balaam to curse the Jewish people, but God prevented him from doing so. In one of his perorations, Balaam declared that Israel is a people destined to dwell alone, that Israel was not to be reckoned among the nations (Numbers 23:9). Jews had taken this prophecy to heart during their long exile, whose vicissitudes of living *among* but not really *with* other peoples deepened its essential truth. The modern era, for a brief moment, seemed to hold forth the possibility that this was no longer true, as Jews became active parts of a new European civilization. Simply put, the Holocaust reconfirmed Balaam's words; after Auschwitz, Jews had never felt so alone. At the least, then, the Holocaust finally convinced Jews and Jewish survivors the world over of the need for a Jewish state. It was Hitler who finally made Zionism a majority movement among world Jewry.

The Holocaust also had a major intellectual impact, and not just on Jews: it deeply shadowed, if not ended altogether, the pervasive sense of optimism that the European civilization which emerged from the Enlightenment and the Renaissance—the hallmarks of the modern era itself—was really any different, any better morally, than any age that had gone before. The faith in reason, the faith in science, the faith that the material and moral progress of mankind went hand in hand—an article of faith of the French *philosophes* and their successors—were all badly battered by the war. What had been done had been done not by loin-clothed "savages" in the jungles of Africa or Southeast Asia but by Germans—the descendants of Goethe, Mozart, and Leibnitz. If Enlightenment rationalism could produce fully dressed savages who used science instead of spears to murder by the millions, what was it worth after all?

As a result, the Holocaust did much to sweep away the optimism of socialist idealism from the Zionist movement. The movement remained socialist by program, but its spirit had changed irrevocably. It took mountains of corpses and ashes to sharpen the movement's sense of Jewish exceptionalism, to link the sufferings of past exiles to those of the twentieth century, to blunt the sense that Zionists could really create a qualitative discontinuity in Jewish history for the better, to prove that divisions between cultures were real and perhaps ineradicable. Reduced was the impulse to normalize the Jewish social structure, heightened was the determination to create an independent state where Jews in distress could come. If they died there fighting for their own land, at least they would die as free men—like the sons of Judah Maccabee, and like Bar-Kochba and his followers.

Also, the non-socialist Zionists of the Third Aliyah had by now come into their own as an organized political force. Led by Vladimir Ze'ev Jabotinsky, the Revisionists established the New Zionist Organization and, in 1925, the Revisionist party. The Revisionists called for *Shelemut Ha-moledet* (the entirety of the homeland), which meant for them both banks of the Jordan for the Jewish state. Jabotinsky recognized the distinct character of the Palestinian Arabs, but denied that they had any national rights in Palestine. Over these and other issues the Revisionist Zionists had mighty arguments with their socialist colleagues, and the movement formally split in the interwar years.

The Revisionists were small in number before World War II, and had rather different attitudes from the socialists. They had little interest in the spirit of the Prophets of Israel or in dreams of social justice. They wanted a normal state that could defend Jews and fight for Jews everywhere. Jabotinsky admired Mussolini, and the spirit that motivated many of his followers was quite simple: revenge against the gentile world for centuries of persecution and humiliation. For obvious reasons, the Holocaust strengthened the Revisionist movement within Zionism, but it still remained far short of majority support.

The end of the war, and the revelation of the Holocaust, changed not only the spirit of Zionism but also world attitudes toward the Jewish plight. Whether it arose from guilt or sympathy, there was soon massive support for a Jewish state in Palestine. The support was sharpened by the fact that, in 1946, tens of thousands of Jewish survivors languished in displaced-persons camps all over Europe; despite what had happened, the British government still refused Jewish emigration to Palestine. The U.S. government under President Harry S. Truman took the lead in trying to defuse the problem, and ran afoul of its British ally in so doing.

By the middle of 1946, the Jewish Agency had virtually given up trying to change British attitudes by persuasion. It now looked for American help; sought to bolster its military capabilities, building on the experience of fighting in World War II; and tried to secure its far-flung agricultural settlements in preparation for renewed violence with the Arabs and, possibly, the British. The Jewish Agency and its defense force, the Haganah, were soon outflanked tactically by the Revisionists, who had their own paramilitary units. Etzel (or the Irgun[27]), which had been founded in 1937, and the even more extreme Stern Gang, began a campaign of shootings and bombings against British military personnel and buildings.[28] By October 1947, Jewish attacks had killed 127 British soldiers and wounded 331 others. The Jewish Agency opposed such actions but could not stop them. The British engaged in reprisals, which had the effect of rallying virtually all Jews in support of the violence and against the British. Mixed in to this violence was substantial British-Arab violence, and some between Jews and Arabs although, ironically, this was the least of the trouble at the time.

By early 1947, the British wanted out of Palestine. This was not only because the Mandatory authority could not stem the violence, and not only because British policy was roundly unpopular in most of the world, but also because Palestine was quickly loosing its strategic significance for the British. The British had wanted Palestine in the first place, after World War I, as a link in the imperial route to the Persian Gulf and, ultimately, India, the pearl of the empire. With the significance of an overland route through Palestine from the Mediterranean to Iraq now overtaken by technology, and with Britain clearly in the process of losing India, the costs of hanging on to Palestine seemed clearly to outweigh the benefits. So in February 1947, the British turned the problem over to the United Nations, which promptly empowered an eleven-nation special commission to study the matter.

As UNSCOP (United Nations Special Commission on Palestine) was deliberating, an astonishing event took place that riveted the world's attention. In early July, 4,500 Jewish DPs (displaced persons), the majority of them concentration-camp survivors, set out from France to Palestine on a rickety Chesapeake Bay ferry. As expected, the British Navy intercepted the ship, "escorting" it toward a full British armada twelve miles off the coast of Palestine. The British intended to then board the ship, as they had done others before, and send its hapless passengers to a DP camp on the island of Cyprus to join some 26,000 other Jews. But suddenly the ship unfurled a banner, *The Exodus*, and refused British permission to come aboard. Hand-to-hand fighting broke out as the British tried to seize control of the ship. The British then resorted first to tear gas and then to machine guns: three Jews were killed, scores injured, but still the British were fought back. Meanwhile, the ship's radio had been broadcasting a frenzied account of the events to Haganah radio receivers on shore, which in turn broadcast it live around the world. The British then threatened to ram and sink *The Exodus* with all hands. Only at this point did the ship surrender.

Prime Minister Ernest Bevin then decided that the passengers of *The Exodus* would not go to Cyprus but back to DP camps in Europe, first France and then, ultimately, Germany. This in fact occurred, and as it did the world press followed the story.[29] Sending bedraggled Jews to Germany, of all places, seemed the height of British heartlessness. Half in anger, half in compassion, UNSCOP decided to send an investigative committee to refugee camps in Germany and Austria to interview the DPs. There committee members found wretched survivors of the concentration camps living literally in the ashes of a war that had wanted to consume them all, and all of them measuring their lives against the day of departure for Palestine.

The Exodus event and its aftermath clearly influenced the committee, whose majority soon recommended the partition of Palestine into a Jewish and an Arab state.[30] In drawing borders, the committee was in certain respects generous to the Zionists, placing the vast stretches of the Negev Desert within Israel, partly out of general sympathy and partly owing to the success of a few experimental Jewish settlements there, notably Revivim. But the map it suggested, based on demographic factors, was not viable strategically, and a war appeared inevitable. The British would leave, and the Palestinian Arabs, along with all but one of their Arab allies (Transjordan), would try to destroy the new state of Israel.

Nevertheless, the Zionist movement decided to accept partition even though almost all Zionists believed that all of Palestine west of the Jordan River belonged to the Jewish people by right of history and the principles of the Mandate. Why compromise? Because independence would allow the immediate ingathering of the Jewish DPs, and would allow the Haganah to operate freely in defense of Jewish settlements either under attack or soon to be under attack. Some members of the Jewish Agency did not feel as though accepting partition meant forswearing a claim to the territory set aside for an Arab state, but many thought this inevitable. Since there were not yet enough Jews in Palestine to populate all the land, and time was of the essence, there was no other choice. Additionally, the Haganah had done well fighting the Arabs thus far in minor skirmishes, and with world sympathy and especially American support, the Zionist executive's private assessment was that it could survive a fight, however difficult it might be.

The Arabs rejected partition, completely and utterly, vowing a war to the death—the Jews' death. Nevertheless, on November 29, 1947, the U.N. General Assembly voted for the partition resolution, 35–13, with both the United States and the Soviet Union (for very different reasons) voting in favor. The date of implementation was established as August 1, 1948, moved up subsequently by the British to May 14. On that day, late in the afternoon on the 5th of the Hebrew month of Iyar in the year 5708—1,878 years after the destruction of the Second Commonwealth and just over fifty years after Herzl convened the First Zionist Congress in Basel—David Ben-Gurion proclaimed the independence of the state of Israel. The very next day, a half dozen Arab countries declared war.

3

Society and Polity
at Independence

Beginnings are notoriously important because divergences that are small at the start of a journey become ever greater as time passes. Decisions made in molten times soon harden and, after they do, it can be hard to change established patterns. That's why it is important to get a sense of Israel in its first year or two: the impact of the war, the lay of the land itself within new borders, the human material, the institutions inherited from the Mandate period, and Israel's early foreign policy. Despite the fact that Jewish civilization and history were already very old in 1948, and that the core institutions of the state had time to mature during the Mandate, the actual establishment and administration of a state still required making many important decisions under great time pressures. Nothing can really be adequate preparation for that.

When we remember, too, that these decisions upon independence all took place in the context of a war on the one hand and relatively huge inflows of immigrants on the other, we begin to understand how frenetic the experiences of Israel's first few years as an independent state truly were. These times, this accelerated experience, set the basic tone for the state as it existed before the epochal June 1967 War, even though, naturally enough, after a few years a sense of normalcy gradually replaced the emergency mentality of the first few years. While the comparison should not be taken too literally, Israel in the nineteen years between 1948 and 1967 felt a little like America between Cornwallis's surrender at Yorktown in 1781 and the War of 1812: new, exhilarated, and successful, but worried about how fragile everything still seemed, and conscious of the fact that history was being made beneath the very soles of one's shoes.

The War for Independence and Its Impact

The war that Israelis refer to as the War for Independence was really two wars more or less in succession, and it is a good thing for Israel that they did not overlap very much. The first of the wars began and was already virtually over before the British left Palestine in May 1948. That was the war between the Jews and the Palestinian Arabs inside the Mandate area, led on the Palestinian side, as before, by Haj Amin al-Husseini and his cohorts.

Haj Amin al-Husseini had spent much of World War II in Berlin hosted by the Nazi regime, in return for which he broadcast pro-Nazi propaganda in Arabic. But now he and his family and aides were back in the Middle East and, with the crucial exception of King Abdallah of Jordan, all of the surrounding Arab countries supported Haj Amin's aim of first seizing and then ruling over Palestine. After November 1947, the British government dealt with Haj Amin as de facto Palestinian Arab leader. Most British officials and military officers in the region believed that, together with the Arab states, the Arabs would win the coming war and the al-Husseinis would become the rulers of Palestine. Hoping to preserve residual British interests in Palestine and bolster those interests in the Arab world generally, where the British position was still dominant, many British guns found their way into Arab hands and many British positions were turned over to Arab troops between November 1947 and May 1948.

By March 1948, two months before the end of the Mandate, fighting was in full gear, but the war was neither conventional nor particularly well organized on either side. There were atrocities against civilians, and counter-atrocities, such as the massacre of Jewish doctors and nurses on the road to Hadassah hospital in Jerusalem on Mount Scopus, and the subsequent Lehi-Etzel massacre at the Arab village of Deir Yassin.[1] Neither side operated under a unified command; neither could control all the forces dedicated to its own side. As the level of violence and confusion rose, much of the wealthy but politically divided Arab elite began to send capital and family outside Palestine for safety's sake. First slowly, and then with increasing intensity, this flight wrecked the local Arab economy and contributed greatly to the growing flight of Arabs from Palestine.[2] Some Arabs expected to return soon and in triumph, some did not.

By the same token, Arab-Jewish violence was not limited to Palestine. As political tensions and fighting spread in Palestine, Jewish communities found themselves attacked in Aleppo, Syria, and also in Aden, Egypt, and Iraq. This tension also set these communities to flight, most of them in the direction of Palestine.

The Zionist Provisional National Council, under the direction of David

Ben-Gurion, at first adopted a defensive posture against Arab attacks, which were aided by Arab volunteers from Syria and elsewhere prior to May 1948. Ben-Gurion decided to defend all of the far-flung Jewish settlements in the country, rather than concentrate Jewish forces in contiguous areas along the coast and between the coastal plain and Jerusalem, and rather than attack the Arabs (which he believed remaining British forces would try to prevent anyway). This worked in part because of the notorious ineptitude of the Arab forces. Meanwhile, the Zionist leadership in both the Vaad Leumi and the Jewish Agency did all it could to avoid all-out war with the Arab states after May, and to acquire weapons and support from outside in case that war occurred anyway.

Also, before May, the Zionist attitude toward Arabs living in areas set aside for the Jewish state was ambiguous. On the one hand, all Arabs were seen as potential security threats. On the other hand, in hopes of eventually gaining peaceful relations with the Arabs, and wanting to avoid a politically damaging refugee issue after the war, Ben-Gurion pleaded with Arab populations to stay where they were, assuring them that no harm would befall them. Also, even if the Zionist leadership had wanted to drive out the Arabs against their will, it lacked the means to do so. There was no formal, official, or accepted plan to do so, either.

Nevertheless, again, what was going on locally, place by place, took on a dynamic that no one controlled. Virtually all of the Arab population of Safad, for example, fled after the killing of a dozen Arab villagers by a Jewish militia in April 1948. In Zionist mythology, the tale of the Davidka—a noise-making mortar cannon that supposedly convinced the Arabs that the Jews had some superweapon ready to use against them—"explains" the Arabs decision to leave. But that was not the main reason.

By May, when the state was proclaimed and the second war began, the refugee flight was in full force. By the time it was over in 1949, as the dust of war was settling, around 750,000 Arabs had left Palestine and about 165,000 had stayed.

The second war began the day after Israel's independence was proclaimed, on May 15, 1948. For nearly all Jews everywhere, the proclamation of independence was a very happy occasion; Jerusalem, Israel's largest city then and now, was established as Israel's capital, and the first thing the provisional National Council did was make void all restrictions on Jewish immigration into Palestine. But Ben-Gurion wrote in his dairy that day that he felt no joy because he knew war with the Arab states was inevitable.

This war seemed at first sight to be an unwinnable proposition for Israel. Rhetorically, the Arab world was united against Israel. On paper, their armies outnumbered that of the Haganah in every category, especially manpower, and again, on paper, the Arabs had organized themselves into a single unified force under the formal command of King Abdallah of Transjordan. The map itself was such that Jewish territory was easily cut both in the north and in the south, where the country's contiguity depended on indefensible thin belts of land. Moreover, the United States, upon whom the Jews depended for support, slapped an arms embargo on both sides, which clearly disadvantaged the Jews. That is how it seemed, even to most Jews in Israel and out, but that is not how it really was.

The Arabs were not united. King Abdallah, an enemy of the al-Husseinis, had agreed secretly with the Jewish Agency—specifically, with Golda Meir—that his troops would occupy only those parts of Palestine set aside for the Arab state. While interpretations differ as to how explicit these arrangements were, and how reliable they were in the tumult of war, Ben-Gurion relied on King Abdallah's honor. So it is not accurate to say, as many Zionist versions do, that on May 15 Transjordan invaded Israel with the other Arab armies; rather, it invaded Arab Palestine.

Meir and King Abdallah could not agree about Jerusalem, however. The partition resolution had said that Jerusalem was to be internationalized, but both sides claimed it and brutal fighting took place there. When the war ended, the city was divided, and the Old City, with the shrines holy to Judaism, Christianity, and Islam, fell into Jordanian hands. But otherwise, Ben-Gurion trusted King Abdallah, and this allowed him to deploy what forces he had to deal with Syrian, Egyptian, Iraqi, and Lebanese troops—the Egyptian forces being by far the most formidable. Doing so left most of the midsection of the country open to easy penetration from the east, but Abdallah, who thought of the Jews as future allies against his Arab competitors, kept his promises.

Moreover, recall that Abdallah was the unified commander of the Arab forces attacking Palestine. Obviously, his double-dealing showed that he was not really interested in unifying anything. So the individual Arab armies did whatever they wished; there was little coordination on the Arab side, as each Arab regime vied with the others as much or more than they aimed their sights at Israel. These divisions showed on the battlefield, and the young Israeli army took advantage of them.[3]

Also, the Arabs were not well armed, not well trained, not well led, and did not fight well at all (except the Jordanian Arab Legion in Jerusalem). It must be recalled that the British and French still essentially controlled the arms supplies to Egypt and Syria, and all these Arab countries were either newly independent (in the case of Syria) or very much dependent on Britain (as with Egypt and Jordan).

Moreover, the Arab forces were expeditionary forces fighting in terrain

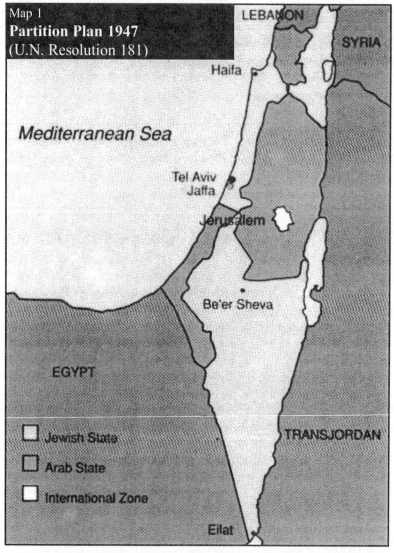

Map 1
Partition Plan 1947
(U.N. Resolution 181)

they had never before seen. Had they had local Palestinian military allies to help and coordinate them, it would have been a different matter, but, as noted, the Palestinian forces led by the Mufti were already defeated by May 15. The Arab armies' supply lines were long, but Israel's were short. The Arabs did not have the support of an organized local population; the Israelis clearly did.

Also it is important to note that rural Jewish settlements were accustomed to the necessity of self-defense, something that had become imperative during the 1936–39 Arab Revolt. Also important was the experience gained by Jews fighting alongside the British in World War II, especially compared to the Arabs, whose reluctance to fight with the British during that war left them without any serious combat experiences. And there had been some sympathetic British officers, most notably Orde Wingate, who had helped train the Jews during the 1930s.

Additionally, despite the U.S. embargo, the Israelis managed to get their hands on weapons from outside far more easily than could the Arabs. Thanks to Jewish veterans from World War II and sympathetic Jews in many countries, as well as to a Soviet government anxious to ensure the exit of the British from the Middle East, the Haganah was buoyed from a flow of weapons, including a few airplanes, that gave them important advantages over the Arab expeditionary forces.

Most important perhaps, Jewish society in Palestine stuck together and worked cooperatively. This was a life-or-death battle; Jews were under no illusions about what would likely happen to them if they lost. Many people hadn't believed Hitler's ravings in the 1930s; what were Jews to think now, so soon after the Holocaust, when enemies threatened loudly and boastfully to exterminate them? Clearly, morale counts a lot in a war whose technical sophistication is modest, and morale was a factor that weighed on the Jews's side in 1948.

Not that the war was easy for Israel. At one point early in the war Egyptian armies advanced toward Tel Aviv, and the Israeli redoubt at Yad Mordekhai fell with heavy losses. Egyptian planes bombed Tel Aviv, causing civilian casualties. Israeli forces were also never able to control the areas around Jerusalem they believed vital, not to speak of losing the Jewish quarter in the Old City to the Jordanians. And the war was very costly in human life: Israel suffered more than 6,000 dead (about 4,000 soldiers and 2,000 civilians), which was about 1 percent of the entire population. Given the interlocked nature of the Yishuv community, everyone knew someone who had either died or sustained the loss of a loved one.

When the war was over in February 1949—after a series of truces and finally the signing not of peace treaties but of military armistices—Israel was the clear victor. It had augmented its territory some 21 percent (about 2,500 square miles) compared to the partition resolution boundaries, and it had relieved the strategic liabilities of that map to some extent. A Palestinian Arab state never came into existence; instead, most of what was left of its territory was occupied and in 1950 annexed by Jordan, the one Arab country with which Israel had been able to negotiate and reach some limited understanding during the 1947–49 period. The rest—Gaza—was occupied by Egypt. The United Nations set up the United Nations Truce Supervision

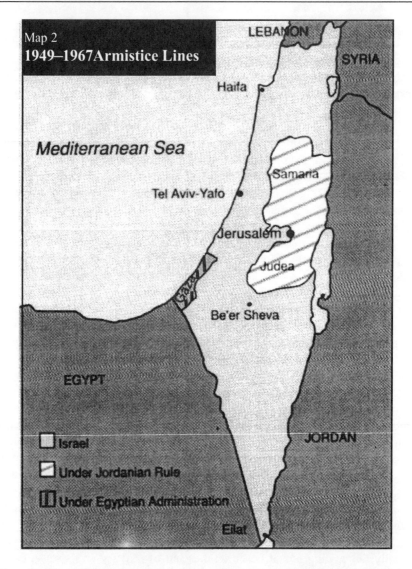

Map 2
1949–1967Armistice Lines

LEBANON

SYRIA

Haifa

Mediterranean Sea

Samaria

Tel Aviv-Yafo

Jerusalem

Judea

Gaza

Be'er Sheva

EGYPT

☐ Israel

▨ Under Jordanian Rule

▥ Under Egyptian Administration

JORDAN

Eilat

Organization (UNTSO) to oversee the armistices, and from the UNTSO there evolved what became known as the Mixed Armistice Commission to hear complaints from the various sides about the activities of the other.

Israel won the war, and its immediate postwar situation was such that it did not have to worry about imminent existential military threats. But it had not won the peace, which is to say that military success could not be translated into a political settlement with its neighbors. A Palestine Conciliation Committee was also established under U.N. auspices, and it gave birth to a peace conference convened at Lausanne in 1949. But the conference failed over Arab demands that Israel accept back all the Arab refugees who had left what became Israel as a precondition to any negotiations. Israel offered to take back 100,000 refugees (out of roughly 600,000 to 750,000 who left), but only in the context of a negotiation that would aim to establish peace. The Arab states all refused to consider the proposal, and the Lausanne talks ended in failure.

The War for Independence had major impacts on Israel. Three are especially noteworthy. First, the events of 1948 truly and fully turned the Palestinian-Zionist conflict of the Mandate period into the Arab-Israeli conflict of the independence period. The Arab world as a whole, trying to come to terms with its own divisions, its own problems, and the legacy of its own difficulties with European power and ideas, now saw Palestine as the quintessential issue of Arab nationalism. For domestic and Arab regional purposes, Israel had become a convenient enemy throughout nearly all of the Arab world. The Arab states had been weak and divided in the "first round," the war of 1948, but it was by no means clear that they would remain so forever. With huge manpower advantages, oil wealth, and increasing foreign-policy options with the receding of British and French power, a "second round"—which almost all Israelis expected sooner or later—might not go like the first.

Second, the war and the regionalization of the conflict it caused made Zionists out of the sizable Jewish populations living in the Arab world—in Egypt, Syria, Iraq, Libya, Yemen, Morocco, Algeria, Tunisia, and Lebanon. It also affected Jews living in Iran and Turkey, Muslim but not Arab countries. Most of these Jewish communities, in existence for centuries or even millennia, suddenly found their circumstances untenable. Some came to Israel enthusiastically out of newly kindled religious motive, some came reluctantly; some did not come at all, but preferred a new exile in France, the United States, Canada, or Latin America. Some came quickly, like 45,000 Yemeni Jews in 1949 in Operation Magic Carpet, and 123,000 Iraqi Jews in 1950 in Operation Ali Baba. These people were housed in tent cities, called *ma'abarot,* for lack of housing. Other communities came later in the 1950s. The *aliyah* from the Arab world swelled the population of Israel by the end of the decade, and this massive, historically unprecedented movement was clearly stimulated by the 1948 war.

Third, the political implications of the Arab refugee flight in particular have been enormous for the state and for Zionism ever since. Ever since the War for Independence, the origins of the refugee problem have been at the philosophical core of the Arab-Israeli dispute. The Palestinians and the Arabs in general have typically believed that the Jews stole Palestine from its

Basra to Beersheba

Yehudit was six years old when she was flown with her parents and sisters and brothers from Basra to Israel in a plane that, she remembers, landed in Jordan for refueling on its way to Israel. All their friends were with them—almost all the Jews of their town—but they could take only what they could carry. "One day we were in Basra, living in a palace, with fountains and servants, and the next we were living in the desert near Beersheba in a tent with nothing but the clothes on our back, and a few personal trifles. I remember my parents often being speechless after that, as though they were happy and sad at the same time. Thus they remained until they died."

Arab owners, and that in the war Jews drove Arabs from their homes by force of arms, after which their villages were razed and all evidence of their existence extirpated. Zionism has thus been accused of cultural genocide and "ethnic cleansing."

Contrarily, Zionists note that most of the land obtained before the 1948 war was purchased, not "stolen," and historical records show that there was always more land offered for sale by Arabs than there was Jewish National Fund resources to buy it. Zionist propaganda, too, has claimed that in 1947–48 Arab leaders told Arab villagers to leave their homes so that Arab soldiers could kill the Jews and drive them into the sea, after which the villagers would return and claim the Jews's property for their own.

Both of these versions of 1948 events are essentially false. There were cases of Arabs being driven from their homes at bayonet point, notably in the strategic areas of Ramle and Lod, and there were examples of Arab calls for villagers to leave, but taken together this does not explain more than about 15 percent of the refugee phenomenon. Rather, the fears and confusion created by irregular warfare, the flight of the Palestinian aristocracy and the destruction of the local economy it caused, and the failure of Palestinian Arab society to cohere in the face of a threat were all more important factors. This is proved by looking at those Arabs who left—who were mainly urban, more educated, and often connected to family outside Palestine—and those who stayed—who tended to be the least sophisticated, least literate, least wealthy, most rural echelon of the population, those without the money to flee or a family member and a place to flee to.[4]

But it is what people believe that often matters the most, and people under emotional stress tend to believe simple explanations with clear-cut good guys and bad guys rather than more complex ones that require detachment and serious study. The 1948 war is called by the Arabs *al-nakba*, the disaster, and they consider it the Zionist version of "original sin." Israelis, on the other hand, consider their victory akin to a miracle given the on-paper odds against them. Most Arabs still believe that Israel purposely did something unspeakable to the native Arab population. Most Israelis still believe that the Arabs would have done something unspeakable to them had they not successfully defended themselves in a war they had not wanted and they had not started. Moreover, it is clear to them that throughout the Mandate period the Jews were willing to compromise with the Arabs, but that the Arab political leadership refused all conciliation, all compromise, even all negotiation. And the Zionists accepted partition, while the Arabs did not.

Given the continuing, unabating Arab hostility after the war, now compounded by the humiliation of military failure, Israel lost little time in planning a future without the refugees. Abandoned lands became state lands, adding greatly to the land Jews had purchased through the Jewish National Fund during Mandate times and the state lands it inherited. For a time, as noted, Israel offered to let 100,000 Arabs return, but the Arabs rejected the offer. As positions hardened and memories burned, the refugee issue became a painful reminder of the costs of historical change and the wars that usually come with it. But building the state of Israel went on anyway; as new towns and villages arose, new roads were built, new fields were put to the plow as new immigrants came to settle the land, and the character of the countryside, economic and demographic, changed dramatically.

Israeli attitudes toward the Arabs also changed as a result of the war. Hoping against hope, many Labor Zionist idealists continued to believe right into 1947 that a war with the Arabs could be avoided, and that some sort of cooperative future was still not out of the question. But the war dashed such dreams. The viciousness of irregular warfare left bad memories on all sides and throughout all strata of society.

Instead, areas of Arab habitation were placed under military government after the armistices. This meant that they could not leave those areas without permission. Military courts meted out justice in secret. Under military rules, army commanders could search and seize anyone or anything at will. They could also take land, deport law offenders, and detain anyone indefinitely if suspected of some act of treason or violence.

Conversely, the universal hostility of Arab states from afar, with whom Zionists had never had any dealings, confirmed the sense that Arab antipathy was broad-based, culturally deep-rooted, and likely impossible to conciliate. This is why victory in war did not bring on a sense of euphoria in Israel, but seemed instead only to signify a breathing space between rounds in a conflict more bitter and intractable than anyone earlier had wanted to admit.

Nevertheless, Israel proved to itself and the world in 1948 that Jews could fight. The image of Jews being led passively to the gas chambers during World War II was one Zionists longing to create the new Jew could not bear. The vanquishing of the Arabs went a long way toward allowing the deeply wounded Jewish generation of the 1940s to recover its dignity, its sense of pride, its hope for a respectable future. And Israel's victory not only performed this task for Israelis, it did so vicariously for Jews throughout the world.

The sad thing was that Israelis did not hate Arabs or want to hurt them before the War for Independence. When they girded for battle in 1948, they would have much rather been fighting Nazis and their European anti-Semitic tormentors over the centuries. And emotionally, in a way, they were. And yet they did hurt the Arabs. Most Israelis, still deeply seized by their generations-long conflict with Christian Europe, knew that it was too much to expect Arabs to understand, and certainly to sympathize with, their special Jewish problems. As Israeli novelist Amos Oz has put it, both Jews and Arabs were really struggling with the legacy of Europe in the first half of the twentieth century, and it was almost an accident that, each in coming to terms with European power, they collided with each other in Palestine. But collide they did.

Many Israelis realized this at the time, and most sense it one way or another today. Many if not most Israelis regret what happened to the Arab population of Palestine in 1948, and while it seems odd to those unfamiliar with the conflict, many Israelis sympathize with the Arab dilemma. Only an unvarnished minority have ever taken any pleasure in exercising military dominance over the years. For most Israelis, it is enough to remember that 1948 was a time of desperation, of fear, of do to or be done to, and under such circumstances, where efforts to reason and to compromise have already failed, one does what one must do to survive. Until recently, most Israelis have felt that the mold cast in 1948 has never really changed.

The events of 1948 represent a morally ambiguous way to start one's modern history, and that ambiguity has become part of the very fabric of Israel's existence. This is one reason Israelis are, on balance, so interested in making peace with the Arabs. It isn't that they fear losing a war; Israel's relative conventional military advantages today are probably greater than ever. Israel is not pressed to sue for peace on account of literal security concerns. It is that peace with the Arabs, and especially with the Palestinians, is the only way to a normal existence, and for some, the only way to lift the burden of psychological ambiguity about their own early history. Peace with the Arabs is often referred to as an issue of legitimacy, and what this usually means is that Israel can only really feel fully secure in the Middle East when the events surrounding its establishment are put aside by its neighbors as truly in the past. That is one meaning of legitimacy, but an even deeper one is that Israelis can look back on those events without any sense of guilt, that what happened was not only a historical necessity but also that the losers then need not feel like losers forever.

Political Geography and the Zionist Zeitgeist

Quite aside from the psychological implications of the 1948 war, there were important physical realities that set the scene for independence. It is impossible to speak both separately and intelligently about history, politics, war, geography, and demography in the eastern Mediterranean, and especially in Israel. They are all bound up together, and the connections require some explanation.

The 1947 partition boundaries were such that Israel was to consist of 5,600 square miles. The 1949 armistice lines left Israel about 8,000 square miles. This is a very small area compared to the United States. Israel in its pre-1967 borders was about the size of New Jersey. Moreover, about half the country's land area consisted then, and still consists now, of the Negev Desert—the entire south of the country—which cannot support a large population. The habitable parts of the country in 1948, then, were more like the size of Vermont, one of the smaller states of the United States. Only about a third of the land was cultivable. (This helps explain the rarity of golf courses in Israel; using scarce water on precious land for sport is something Israel cannot afford.)

Small countries have the distinct disadvantage of offering little strategic depth. Small countries with population concentrated in areas that are habitable are even more vulnerable to disaster should military defeat loom. Small countries with small populations, moreover, when surrounded by larger countries with much larger populations, can ill-afford to make too great a distinction between strategic areas and marginal ones, and between military personnel and the rest of the adult population. There are several good historical reasons why Israel would have considered virtually every inch of its sovereign territory to be unalienable and why Israel's military would become a citizens' army. But added to these reasons were the exigencies of geography: there just wasn't any choice.

Geography too, it is easy to see, greatly influenced the development of Israeli military doctrine. We will return to this matter later, but Israel's strategic depth was so minimal that it adopted an offensively minded deterrent strategy of hitting the enemy on his turf whenever possible rather than allow a war to be fought within Israel. That, in turn, is why Israel focused on developing its air force and on conceiving a land forces concept emphasizing highly mobile armored units, for these are the best tools for power projection. Also, Israel determined that a small professional army could defend the borders in peacetime, but that in war a full national mobilization would be necessary. Therefore, every adult had to have military training and be organized in reserve units *(miluim)*.

Moreover, because of Israel's tight space and small population compared to likely enemy assets, every aspect of the national infrastructure had to be designed in such a way that it could quickly support a national mobilization during an emergency. The country's men, by and large, would drop their jobs, pick up a gun, and get to the border; and the country's women, by and large, would pick up the jobs left by the men to keep the entire economy from collapsing. Every bus, every truck, every railcar, every plane, every boat was given a role to play in an emergency. Such a mobilization *(konninoot)* is obviously extremely disruptive of social normalcy and the economy.

And this is why Israeli mobilizations cannot be realistically maintained for very long. This fact also contributes to a strategy inclined to preemption in crisis, which is a handmaiden to offense-mindedness. Indeed, the combination of Israel's geographical and demographical constraints, and the military orientation they dictate, go far to explain why Israel did what it did in June 1967. (See Chapter 6 for details.) Unfortunately, many accounts of that war, written by people who do not live in the Middle East, have failed to appreciate the importance of such factors.

Despite its small size, there is within Israel a tremendous diversity of climate and topography so that, in a way, it seems like a bigger country than it really is. In the north is the Upper and Lower Galilee, a fairly hilly area that gets more rain than the rest of the country. The land is hard to farm except in small parcels, and has a never-ending supply of jagged rocks large and small. So it is that the best-watered region does not lend itself easily to modern agriculture.

Going south and west, below the port city of Haifa, one comes to the coastal plain of Sharon. Here the land is easier to farm, but there is less rain. In between, south of the Galilee but to the east, between Mount Tabor and Mount Gilboa, is the Valley of Jezreel, which is one of Israel's most verdant and agriculturally productive regions, and a region where many of Israel's oldest agricultural settlements are located. Going north along the Jordan River in the Jordan Valley toward Lake Tiberias was an area known as the Hula Valley, after the swampy Lake Hula, its most prominent geological feature. The Jordan Valley itself is subtropical, and in many places it is too hot for comfort. Some of it is below sea level, and in certain seasons used to breed plagues of malarial mosquitoes. The valley itself, on both sides of the river, tended to have native residents much darker in skin color than surrounding areas; these were Nubian and other slaves who escaped their masters and fled to the valley in hopes that no one would pursue them there. The Hula area was even more malarial by reputation than the Jordan Valley, and for good reason.

South and east of Tel Aviv, heading toward Beersheba, the country is even drier and generally less densely populated. Directly east is the salient of territory that leads up to Jerusalem, and steeply up. From sea level near Ashdod on the Mediterranean the land begins slowly to climb until reaching Latrun. From there, the land rises sharply, and the road to Jerusalem is a steep one up to 2,700 feet at Mount Scopus. To get from the bottom of the mountain to the top is only about thirty miles as the crow flies, so this gives some idea how abruptly the terrain changes. Given the undulating lay of the land, there are not many roads, and in certain areas of the climb, there is only one road for wheeled vehicles.

This is why, in the battle for Jerusalem in 1948, keeping the road open was both an essential and a very difficult task. The road today is littered—this time deliberately—with destroyed Israeli vehicles, memorials to the costly battle for Jerusalem.

East and east-northeast of Beersheba are the southern parts of the Judean Desert and the Dead Sea, the lowest point on earth (1,300 feet below sea level). From the Dead Sea south along Wadi Arava,[5] the border with Jordan, there are a few springs (oases, they're sometimes called) to support some settlement, but mainly the area is very hot, infested with black flies or mosquitoes depending on the time of the year and quite inhospitable. West of Beersheba is Gaza, an area of about 135 square miles, occupied by Egypt after the 1948 war.

The major parts left of Arab Palestine after the 1948 war that were conquered and then annexed by Jordan form what became known as the West Bank, an area encompassing about 2,200 square miles. (Jordan's King Abdallah called it this instead of Palestine, because he wanted to erase the name—and with it the Palestine national movement—from consciousness. He failed.) For Israel, the two regions of the West Bank under Arab control—Samaria to the north of Jerusalem and Judea to the south—created a 330–mile border with Jordan. Aside from security difficulties created by such a frontier, it made communication and transportation within the country rather awkward. Both regions of the West Bank are hilly but, even so, it was much easier before 1948 to get from Jerusalem to Tiberias along the Jordan River route than to have to travel west nearly to the coast, then north past Hadera, then around the Wadi Ar'a going just north of the Jezreel Valley to Afula, and then up and east toward the Jordan River to get to the lake. Geography was diverse enough; political geography made things even more complicated. Similarly, to get from Jerusalem down to Ein Gedi near the Dead Sea is a forty-minute drive traveling directly southeast. But given the way the border ran, it was necessary to go back down the Jerusalem corridor to the southeast, then swing around outside the Hebron district of the West Bank, and then head northeast to get to Ein Gedi and the Dead Sea.

Clearly, borders that are circuitous and irregular are literally longer than ones that follow straight lines. Israel's security perimeter after the 1949 armistices was therefore very long and required constant patrolling. Even with the patrolling, given the nature of the landscape and the irregularity of the border, it was impossible to keep intruders and terrorists out completely. Israel resorted to very liberal use of barbed wire, both at the border and in other strategic spots inside the country, over the years on account of such difficulties, and the legacy can still be seen today; much wire is to be found hither and yon, and can be a nuisance on nature walks and at impromptu picnic soccer games in the fields.

The diversity of the landscape gives rise to the phenomenon of microclimates, where it can be 25 degrees Fahrenheit and snowing in Jerusalem, and 65 degrees Fahrenheit and stone dry at the Dead Sea just thirty-five miles away.[6] Amman, east of the river, is comparable to Jerusalem in this respect, and there are some places in central California where more or less similar phenomenon take place. But Israel's range of diversity in such a small place is virtually without equal on the entire globe. Israel has the mountains and the sea, a vast desert and subtropical river valleys, rich agricultural land and rock-strewn hills.

Going hand in hand with climate diversity, of course, is the diversity of the indigenous plant and animal life, which is also remarkable. Israel is at a meeting place of continents—Africa, Asia, and Europe in a way—and it is part of the Great Rift Valley, a huge tectonic-induced trough running from East Africa up into Southwest Asia. As a result, its geology is extremely varied, and the area is also active geologically, which explains the many hot springs in the region. It also explains some of the area's topology; the Golan Heights, for example (the area Israel took from Syria in the June 1967 war) is volcanic soil, and the cones of extinct volcanoes (*tilim* in Hebrew) are strategic high ground still today. Historically, devastating earthquakes have rocked the area, laying waste to cities and civilizations. There has not been a major earthquake in modern times; many seismologists think the region is due.

Israel also happens to be on a major migratory bird path between Europe and Africa. Between native species of birds and species that travel through,

Israel has an astonishing assortment of bird life for such a relatively arid place. So even if Israel had no history and no people, it would still be interesting and beautiful.

But of course it does have people, and always has. The relationship between land and people is so old that the two merge in ways that are sometimes subtle enough that the untutored do not even see them. Walking along the paths and trails of the Galilee, for example, one can see flattened grooves worn into the sides of hillocks almost as though they were terraces. They look almost natural to the hill, but they are not natural, and they are not exactly terraces either. They are the results of literally thousands of years of goats and sheep being led back and forth by their shepherds—Canaanite, Israelite, Samarian, Arab, Circassian, what-have-you. The sight is breathtaking, but only if the viewer knows what he is looking at.

Another very important natural feature of the land concerns water. Water is what has determined which lands have been sown, which used for pastureland, and which areas have been the abode only of nomads. Water distribution has in turn determined in large part where habitation has been established longest and large populations sustained, where roads have run, and where internal borders have arisen.

One of the first things that strikes North Americans when they come to the Middle East is how arid the area is. Indeed, Israelis visiting North America or Europe for the first time are prone to remark that green things here are deeper green than green things in the Middle East—and indeed they are. Contrarily, Americans and Europeans who set up housekeeping in Israel are quick to notice the amazing levels of dust that accumulate (thanks to proximity to the desert and the prevailing winds).[7]

Israel is known as a land flowing with milk and honey, and not without reason for, compared to much of the surrounding region, it is relatively well off. But it is still very dry compared to North America. Average rainfall for eastern Pennsylvania, where I live, is about 111 centimeters (44 inches) per year. In Israel, on average, it's about half that—60 centimeters (24 inches)— in the northern part of the country, which receives by far the most rainfall. It is 50 centimeters (19–20 inches) in the Tel Aviv-Jerusalem central area, 20 centimeters (8 inches) in the northern Negev near Beersheba, and 2.3 centimeters (about 1 inch) moving toward Eilat in the far south.[8]

Moreover, as the foregoing discussion suggests, rainfall is extremely irregular in its distribution over the land as a whole. About 80 percent of Israel's rain falls in the north, where only 30 percent of the cultivable land lies; it is for this reason that Israel built its National Water Carrier integrated irrigation system, inaugurated in 1964, to capture the water and bring it to where the better land is. Some areas to the south are almost always dry, and when it does rain in the south, it rains hard and much of the water—about 80 percent—runs off to the sea before the land can absorb it.[9] The standard yearly deviation from the statistical averages in wet areas can be extreme. On average, the overall yearly deviation is 20–30 percent.[10]

Besides rain, the land depends on dew. Some mornings it looks as though it has rained because the dew can be very heavy wherever the daily temperature gradient is high. Israeli meteorologists and weather statisticians measure dew and count it in the precipitation figures because it is so important relative to the whole. Dew is so important that, as with rain, there is a special seasonal prayer for it (at Passover time), and many Israelis are named Tal, the Hebrew word for dew.

The rain patterns seem irregular, but plotted as a fractal, the wet and dry periods seem to come in dual cycles of seven years within forty years. When dry cycles coincide, it's drought time, as the Bible itself records. When wet cycles coincide, there are what are sometimes referred to as "century floods." These floods can be as dangerous as droughts.

The rainy season is also quite short: from December to February about three-fourths of all rain falls, and from late April to early September it virtually never rains, except the occasional freak thunderstorm resulting from the end of a *sharav*, or *hamsin* (Arabic), as it is often called.[11] Now consider what this means: in most of the rest of the world, winter is when nature is more or less dormant and late spring, summer, and early autumn are the growing seasons. It is exactly the reverse in the eastern Mediterranean. Over the centuries, this has affected work schedules, plans, and habits a great deal. Unless it rains when it is supposed to rain, and unless farmers work very hard at the beginning and the end of the growing season, agriculture can be a risky proposition. That's why animal husbandry, which is less vulnerable to yearly fluctuations in rainfall, and limited nomadism in the areas around Beersheba have been traditional over extensive areas, while sedentary agriculture has been more limited historically. Even today, the pattern of rainfall explains why Israel grows vegetables in the Jordan Valley, grapes higher up near Mount Carmel, and citrus in the Sharon plain.

Water availability and the irregularity of winter weather patterns have always been constraints on population size in the eastern Mediterranean, and this has always had political implications. During the Mandate period, for example, the British tried to limit Jewish immigration on the basis that the absorptive capacities of the land were too modest to support large populations, and that calculation in turn revolved around estimates of water availability. Zionists were from the very start aware of the problem, and their response took two forms: designing their ideal borders to bring within the homeland the sources of all major surface streams and aquifers; and bringing to bear modern hydrological science and technology to overcome natural constraints to the extent possible.

Before it is possible to make sense of these two aspects of Zionist thinking—*neither of which is passé*—one has to have the basic water facts in mind. Hydrologically speaking, Israel sits mainly within the Jordan Valley catchment basin. The Jordan River is the main surface stream. Its basic source is the snows of Mount Hermon in the Golan Heights, by far the largest mountain in the area. The waters of Hermon flow down and, while sometimes above ground, forming striking waterfalls, the waters eventually percolate underground through massive limestone formations and emerge as three springs to the southwest: the Dan, the Hasbani, and the Banias. The Dan is the largest of the three, and arises in Israel proper. The Hasbani is the smallest; it emerges in southern Lebanon and flows southward into Israel. The Banias emerges in the northeast corner of Israel, in an area bearing a complex history.[12] Before June 1967, however, the Banias was in Syrian-controlled territory a few hundred yards from the Israeli border.

The three tributaries meet up inside Israel to form the northern Jordan River. The waters used to converge on Lake Hula (since drained), and after making their way out of the muck, pour into Lake Tiberias, Israel's crucial freshwater reservoir. The river flows south out of Lake Tiberias, where it is soon joined by the Yarmuk, which flows into the Jordan at Naharayim from the east. Just south, the land begins to drop off precipitously, and the river hurls itself down below sea level into the Jordan Valley. There, joined by several seasonal streams, mainly from the eastern side, the Jordan flows south into the Dead Sea.[13] Thanks to evaporation and the salt content of the side wadis mentioned above, the river becomes increasingly saline as it flows south. (This was true when the Jordan was a wild river; it is even more the case today now that the river is channeled, dammed, and diverted.) The Dead Sea has no outlet and is the saltiest body of water in the world. Virtually nothing can grow in it. It is so salty that bathers cannot sink in it.

The entire Jordan River system generates only about 1,800 million cubic meters (mcm) of water per year. That's about 1 percent of the annual flow of the Nile. While the upper Jordan can be pretty wild and rapid in the rainy season, and while the dropoff south of Naharayim is pretty dramatic too, to the point that the river is totally unnavigable there, most of the river most of the time is neither deep nor wide, gospel lyrics notwithstanding. There are several spots near Jericho where it is possible to wade across in the summer without getting wet above the knees.

In addition to the Jordan, there are a few minor streams that flow west into the Mediterranean from the Carmel range, near Haifa. In Israel they're called rivers (like the Kidron, the Alexandroni, and the Yarkon near Tel Aviv). In Tennessee and West Virginia there are creeks that carry more water.

Beyond surface flows there are aquifers. An aquifer is an underground cavern that holds water. When it rains, water percolates into the ground and fills the cavern. When there is enough water, it finds a way to pop out the side of some hill and form a spring. Some springs, like those at Ein Gedi, Rosh Ha'ayin, Sahne (renamed *Gan Hashlosha* in Hebrew), and Ma'yan Harod, are perennial; others are intermittent. Where the topography is right, the aquifers have been tapped by wells. For the most part, the higher lands of Judea and Samaria (the West Bank) catch the rain as the clouds move off the Mediterranean and head east. The water then rolls back down the grade below the surface from east to west. There are three main aquifers in the region: a large one in the center that flows west (Yarkon-Taninim), a small one that flows east toward the Jordan Valley, and a small one that flows north into the Valley of Jezreel out of the foot of Mount Gilboa.

Because of this hydrological circumstance, the Zionist movement formed a view of borders that accorded with its desire that the land absorb millions of exiled Jews. That meant both having the water sources inside the borders and employing the latest irrigation and hydrological technology to move the water around. Zionist efforts to get hydrologically efficient borders—and the British effort to achieve this for the Zionist movement for which Britain was sponsor and protector—were only partly successful.[14]

But the motives for the borders that were sought, it must be emphasized, had much less to do with sentimental Biblical or historical criteria than with practical concerns of economic development. Labor Zionists were secularists and scientific rationalists who believed in progress through engineering back in the days before environmentalists and ecologists even existed. They had detailed pre– and post–World War I plans, many of them the brainchild of Pinhas Rutenberg, to join Lebanon's Litani River to Palestine's hydrological equation, in return for which Lebanon could gain more electrical power than its people had ever dreamed of. They had plans to drain the Hula swamp, channel the Jordan, generate electricity from it, and run railroad and trolley cars from its power. They had plans to divert the Jordan from its course to irrigate the fertile but dry coastal plane, where the majority of Jews in the land lived.

Zionism's sense of its being progressive combined ideology, social theory, and development engineering into a single package. Foremost among the latter was the determination to make the desert bloom through modern hydrological science and technology. Without understanding the natural features and limitations of the land's geography and hydrological situation, it is impossible to understand what kinds of motivations drove Zionist settlement, land purchase, defense, and development policies during Mandate times and after into the period of Israeli independence.

Political Demography and Origins of the Israeli System

Geography and history are important, but people remain the most important factor in political life. When the War for Independence ended, Israel had a majority Jewish population. By the end of 1948, there were about 716,700 Jews in the country and about 165,000 Arabs. Of the Arab population, about 19 percent was Christian, living mainly in Jerusalem and Nazareth. Another 10 percent consisted of Druze, Circassians, and other smaller minorities.[15] Of the Jewish population, 591,400 out of 716,700 were of European (Ashkenazic) origin, and of those, 393,000 were born in Israel. Only 105,000 of the 716,700 were of Asian or North African origin (Sepharadic), and of those only 35,000 were born in Israel.

It is also important to note that the great majority of the Jewish population was secular in orientation and committed to Zionism. But not all of it was. Remember that Palestine had never been empty of Jews. From the second century, and throughout the exile, Jews had lived especially in Jerusalem, Safad, Tiberias, and Hebron. Except for Hebron, these Jewish communities existed continuously into the nineteenth and twentieth centuries; for the most part, these were communities whose main ambition was theological study, and who sent emissaries from time to time into the diaspora to raise funds *(haluka)* for the pious of the land. (The support of scholars is a time-honored tradition in Judaism.) Some of the community was Sepharadic, some was Ashkenazic, and some was *hasidic.*

The *hasidim* were followers of Rabbi Israel Bal Shem Tov, and they arose as a movement in late-seventeenth-century Europe in opposition to the rigid scholasticism they believed had overtaken European Jewry. The *hasidim* emphasized the mystical over the rational, the musical over the ascetic, the spirit of the law over the letter. They also tended to invest great powers in their spiritual leaders, which led to *hasidism* splitting into subsects (Lubavitch, Satmar, Kotzker, and others) that, over time, occasionally became antagonistic to one another. Those who opposed *hasidism* became known as *misnagdim* (those who oppose).

These divisions among Sepharadim, *misnagdim,* and *hasidim* in the religious community in Israel are not academic. They still exist and they still matter socially and politically, as we'll see later on. For now what is important is this: until the 1930s, all the existing religious communities of Eretz Israel, like those in exile in Poland, tended to see Zionism as anathema, something reminiscent of the disaster of Shabbtai Tzvi, only worse for its total disdain for religion.[16] But two men, a father and his son, changed this forever.

In Mandate times, religious Jews were organized politically in a system inherited from the Ottomans, where each confessional grouping had its own courts and local legal autonomy. The British Mandatory authority in 1921 accepted as second-nature the idea that there should be a chief rabbi for Palestine. There was one for England, one for Ireland, one for Italy and France for that matter—as had been the European custom since Emancipation—so it stood to reason that Palestine, of all places, should have one, too. This idea of officially sanctioned rabbinical authority surprised the Labor Zionist leadership who, as secularists, were a bit nervous about the notion. But the religious communities were not about to give up their rights and status by being subsumed under the Zionists, whom they generally distrusted and disdained.

Two compromises were eventually reached. A chief rabbi was chosen, but clearly it had to be someone at least willing to talk to the secular Zionists: Rabbi Avraham Yitzhak Kook. This compromise was reached thanks to the existence of the Mizrahi organization, which had decided tactically to fight for Torah within the general Zionist organization rather than oppose it altogether.

The Mizrahi organization was the brainchild of Rabbi Samuel Mohilever, who was in essence a spiritual descendent of Rabbis Alkalai and Kalischer. Mohilever believed that the revival of Eretz Israel was an obligation of the Torah, and in 1893 he organized a faction within Russian proto-Zionism he called *Merkaz Ruhani* (Spiritual Center), which got shortened via acronym to Mizrahi—a word meaning "Eastern" or "Oriental" but which, in this case, has nothing to do with Sepharadim. Mohilever supported Herzl's work, trying all the while to make the movement more religious. His work was carried on by Rabbi Isaac Jacob Reines, who made Mizrahi into a major organization. Mizrahi was always a small faction at Zionist congresses before 1917, but the secularists, though in deep disagreement with them, were wary of expelling them because of the tempting link they represented to the religious masses of Jews in Eastern Europe.

By 1921, religious Zionists in Mizrahi constituted nearly 20 percent of the rank-and-file of the movement as a whole, although not that large a percentage of Jews within Palestine. (Once Zionism had been catapulted by the Balfour Declaration and the Mandate, the movement's support broadened notably.) Religious Jews who decided against joining the Zionists, mainly *hasidim,* meanwhile decided to organize themselves into Agudah Israel, which insisted on and eventually got in 1927 a separate status from the Mandatory authorities. So when it came time to choose a chief rabbi, the movement naturally turned to those with whom it had already been dealing, and that meant Rabbi Kook. That, in turn, deepened the split within the Orthodox community into religious Zionists and the anti-Zionist Orthodox, which in turn remained split in *hasidic* and *misnaged* factions.

Rabbi Kook, and his son Tzvi Yehuda Kook, did not just carry on the Mizrahi perspective. Rather, they elaborated it theologically in such a way that—it is not too much to say—they overturned 1,500 years of thinking in rabbinic Judaism on the relationship between political action to rebuild the land and the theology of the messianic era. Rabbi Kook, the elder, did not just tolerate the secular Zionists or try to make them better Jews. Rather, he believed that they were unwitting instruments of God in preparing the re- demption and, for that reason, he wasn't greatly bothered by their some- times boastful dismissal of religion. Indeed, some aspects of Zionist pioneering were believed fully positive, as with the *kibbutz*—and a religious *kibbutz* movement was started that still exists today.[17]

Understand the importance of this: Kook, for the first time, ascribed to actions undertaken by avowed enemies of traditional religion a transcen- dental meaning rooted in the divine plan of Jewish history. He believed that Orthodox religious authorities should not scoff at secular Zionists, for these secularists were motivated sincerely by what they thought was best for the Jewish people. To Kook, that meant that the "inner essence of holiness" remained within their souls, and that being the case, there was every reason to believe that, in time, they or their descendants would return to the Torah. He saw redemption and messianic times coming, and understood Zionism in those terms. He described the state of Israel as "the beginning of the dawn of our redemption" *[raysheet tzmihat g'ulatanu]* and with this language he wrote the prayer for the state of Israel still in use today in Jewish prayer books everywhere.

Because Rabbi Kook was unquestionably a great scholar and a pious man, his attitude toward Zionism represented a practical revolution within the religious Jewish world and within the Zionist movement. His views autho- rized religious Jews to play a full role in Zionist society and political organi- zations. He died in 1935, but by then Mizrahi had, like the Labor Zionists and the General (Revisionist) Zionists, transformed itself into an organiza- tion with schools, a labor wing, property, boards of directors, fund-raising apparatuses, and the whole panoply of organizational features. American Jews who reached adulthood before 1948 remember the little *pushkes* (blue and white tin charity boxes) everywhere in Jewish homes, synagogues, clubs, and business establishments. Some of the tins were for the Jewish National Fund to buy land in Palestine, but at least as many were to raise money for Mizrahi—*haluka* in a new, politicized, Zionized form.

The changes wrought by Rabbi Kook the elder (we will return to his son later on) made their mark at a crucial time, and Israeli political history is inexplicable unless one understands why. The majority of Orthodox Jews in Europe were murdered in the Holocaust. But large numbers of survivors came to Palestine after the war, swelling the religious population among the Jews. This included *hasidim,* who were attracted to Agudah Israel, and non-*hasidim,* who were attracted more to Mizrahi—for lack of any suitable alternative. In their straitened circumstances, they became Zionists by default. Many, however, saw in the scale of the Holocaust the prophetic war of Gog and Magog that would precede the coming of the messiah, and they were therefore far better prepared to see Zionism in the way that Rabbi Kook did than in the way their rabbis in Europe had.

The slowly increasing ideological affinity between at least some secular and religious Jews in Palestine was accelerated by the 1948 War. The Orthodox had not prepared themselves for war as the Zionists had, and yet the Haganah fought for the safety of all Jews, no matter who they were or where they were. The battle over Jerusalem, the most costly of the war, was waged because Jerusalem was and remains the heart and soul of the Jewish nation. But Jerusalem was populated disproportionately by Orthodox Jews, and the Haganah's efforts on their behalf were not wholly lost on them.

In short, as a result of the novel circumstances of independence, war, and the arrival of so many Orthodox Jews in Palestine in the few years before 1948, the Labor Zionist and both main camps of religious Jews—the Zionist Mizrahi and the anti-Zionist Agudah Israel—came to terms. They made a basic deal: Labor Zionists, now constituted in the Mapai party organization, agreed to accept the status quo in religious affairs until a written constitution could establish the relationship of religion to the Zionist state, and the religious entities agreed to participate in the governing coalitions of the state, or in Agudah Israel's case at least to support them less formally. That meant, on the one hand, that rabbinical courts would continue to hold sway over issues like marriage, divorce, adoption, and conversion, and it meant that the state in all its administrative bodies would publicly observe the Sabbath and Jewish holidays. The religious calendar became, more or less, the state calendar as well. On the other hand, to the secularists it meant that there would be no fundamental split between Jews in Israel and that meant, in turn, that diaspora Jewish support for the new state would not be limited or compromised by such internal divisions. This, in a nutshell, is the Israeli system of political demography created in 1948, and voted into being by the first Knesset election in 1949.

This compromise also meant, pragmatically speaking, that Mizrahi—later renamed the National Religious party—and to a lesser extent Agudah Israel, would be politically dependent on the majority Labor grouping, and would help Labor stay in power over the General Zionists. In return for their support for Labor, the religious parties expected—and got—Labor's support for their own agendas: financial help for religious schools, military exemptions for religious women and *yeshiva* students,[18] and general support for the Orthodox interpretation of the religious status quo.

This deal did not please everyone. The General Zionists and the Herut party felt that they had been outflanked. They were right. Neither came into any share of effective power until May 1977. Some Labor Zionists felt that too much power had been given to the religious establishment, and this contributed to the establishment of parties further to the left, such as Mapam (although it was not the only reason for Mapam's existence). It also drove one or two Labor Zionists into the Israel Communist party.[19] On the other hand, some *hasidim*— mainly from the Satmar sect—refused to have anything to do with the state of Israel, and they thought that Agudah Israel's agreement to deal with the government legitimated an entity that deserved no legitimation. Some joined a group called *Neturei Karta* (Guardians of the City, in Aramaic, the language of the Gemorrah) that first formed in 1935 (see Chapter 5). Neturei Karta still exists, and still opposes the Jewish state, even to the extent that it furnished advisers to the Palestine Liberation Organization in times before the PLO agreed to recognize Israel's right to exist. Outside Israel, the Satmar sect is also known for its rejection of the state of Israel.

While the bargain did not please everyone, it pleased most well enough to last for almost thirty years. And when it shifted, it shifted because the religious "swing vote," usually around 12 percent in Israeli elections over the years, deserted Labor and joined the Revisionist Likud bloc over ideological issues that developed after the June 1967 War (explained in Chapter 5).

Clearly, then, the character of the state at its beginning was predominantly Ashkenazic. The relatively large number of those born in the land is testimony to the influence of especially the Second, Third, and Fourth Aliyot (plural for *aliyah*); the community was deeply rooted and speaking Hebrew as its first language, even though its highest leadership continued for many years to be composed mainly of those born abroad.[20] And it represented a compromise among dominant Labor Zionism, General or Revisionist Zionism, and Religious Zionism, all of which were legitimated within the democratic system.

A word about Israeli democracy is in order before moving on. As we already know, Israel's population was swelled by immigration from non-European areas in the 1950s and thereafter. Demographically speaking, Israel has become less and less European as time has passed. But its political culture has remained more European than its demography would indicate. There are several reasons for this.

The basic institutions of the Zionist movement and the state were European in origin, and, as noted at the very beginning of this chapter, beginnings are notoriously important. The patterns laid down were European, and the absorption of immigrants socialized them into these patterns. Jews from Morocco, Yemen, Iraq, and elsewhere did not all of a sudden stop thinking like Oriental Jews and start thinking like Ashkenazim. Over time, however, they became more Europeanized, and their children, products of the Israeli school system and the army, came out as a hybrid—as real Israelis. Moreover, Israel's best allies, first France and then the United States, were Western countries and their cultures were often attractive to Israelis living in somewhat austere conditions by comparison.

At the same time, Israeli popular culture—in arts, literature, music, food, fashion—became less European and more Oriental. Again, a mix emerged that is today truly Israeli. Zionism's original ambition to create the new Jew did not have in mind the reintegration of the Jewish world culturally between East and West, but that is exactly what has happened in Israel over the years.

But Israeli *political* culture has remained European for the most part—despite there being a Sepharadic majority today—and that means, in Israel's case, a democratic political culture. Oriental Jews were quick to appreciate democratic culture. While most of them were not equals to Ashkenazic Jews in terms of economic power or political access, many realized that in time they could be. Back in Iraq or Yemen, such notions would have been fantasies. Besides, whatever their problems in Israel, Oriental Jews certainly did not yearn for the type of authoritarianism and corruption as that which existed in the states they had left.

But that still does not explain Israeli democracy. After all, the majority of the founders of Zionism did not come from democracies. The Russian Empire? The Hapsburg monarchy? Not a chance. All that most early Zionists knew about democracy they had read in books. Moreover, none of the three traditions of political Zionism borrowed from general currents that were democratic, not socialism of the Marxian variety, not Revisionist nationalism of the imitative Central European variety, and not Orthodox Judaism of any variety. Not even Herzl seemed very interested in the form of government a Jewish state would take. So why did Israel become a democracy in 1948?

Three reasons stand forth. One was the inherent pluralism of the movement as it developed; it was diverse in terms of physical distribution, personality, and ideology. The only way to keep the movement together was to compromise, and majority rule—the hallmark of democracy—was the only way to ensure fair compromise.

A second reason was the power of the British and American examples, and the deep admiration that the two preeminent leaders of Zionism after Herzl—Weizmann and Ben-Gurion—had for them. Clearly, the Mandate experience deepened the appreciation for and experience of British democracy despite growing tensions between Britain and the Zionist movement.

The third reason is that Israel came to associate itself with the West in the Cold War, and the Cold War for the most part pitted the democracies against totalitarianism. Israel's association with the strongest wings of diaspora Judaism, in America and Western Europe, also strengthened the hold of the democratic ethos. Israeli democracy, too, however improbable its origins, is part of the Israeli system.

Legacies: *Yishuv* to State

As mentioned earlier, many institutions of the state developed during the Mandate period. In essence, the Vaad Leumi became the government, and its executive the cabinet. The Haganah became the Israel Defense Force *(Tzvah Haganah L'Israel,* or *Tzahal)*. Certain institutions, like the Jewish National Fund and the World Zionist Organization component of the Jewish Agency, remained technically separate from the institutions of the state because of diaspora Jewry's role in them, but as a practical matter they became mainly arms of state policy. The incubation period of the Mandate was extremely important in the process of creating a mature social and administrative fabric, such that the transition to statehood and independence was eased by convention, experience, and common expectation.

The colonial experience of the United States comes to mind as a vaguely similar experience: American society existed before the end of British rule, and its experiences led to the government's being structured in certain ways and not others. In both cases, civil society existed before the state. This may seem a trivial remark, for is it not always that way? Actually no, it isn't. Look at Kazakhstan and Uzbekistan in Central Asia, or at several heterogeneous states in sub-Saharan Africa whose borders were drawn by Europeans for their own imperial convenience. In these cases, the state existed before civil society, before nationalism as a conscious doctrine, and before the development of a sense of unified nationhood. Such conditions often make political and social stability hard rows to hoe.

But in the Israeli case, what was special was the extraordinary role played by ideology and explicitly political organizing. The Pilgrims didn't know they wanted their own independent country in 1620 when they landed at Plymouth Rock. But the Zionists pretty much knew what they wanted from the start in 1897. And the Labor Zionists knew what they wanted it to look like in social and political dimensions, too. As a result, all during the Mandate, Labor Zionists deliberately tried to build up all the institutions of a state, and they subordinated those institutions for both practical and ideological reasons to the incubus of a party, which was in every respect socialist.

The Jewish Agency and its Zionist executive leadership clearly allowed and even sought the participation of religious and Revisionist Zionists, but there was never any doubt about who was in charge from the late 1920s onward. Partly for this reason, the Revisionists formally split off in the 1930s and tried to develop competing institutions; so whereas the main Zionist organization had the Haganah, the Revisionists had the Irgun as of 1937. Similarly, while the Jewish Agency had its schools and technical institutes, religious and Revisionist Zionists developed their own educational institutions.

But Labor Zionists went much further and were much more successful at laying down basic institutions, largely because they focused overwhelmingly on economics. The *kibbutz* movement was at the core of the party ideology in the beginning. Buying, owning collectively, and working the land mattered, while most other Zionists were mainly city folk. By the late 1920s, however, a Jewish proletariat had developed in the cities, largely in the construction industry, and the Labor Zionists paid careful attention to their role in shaping the new Jewish society. As noted, the Histadrut, the labor union, was an arm of the party formed in 1920; when one joined the union for all its benefits, one joined the party as well.

Technically, the Histadrut was not a union but a union federation. It was made up of two socialist factions, the more moderate *Ahdut HaAvodah* (Workers' Unity) and the more doctrinaire *HaPoel HaTza'ir* (Young Worker). These factions within Labor Zionism persisted for many decades, but clearly, the Zionist movement as a whole was Labor Zionist in orientation and the Histadrut reflected this majority impulse.

Because the Histadrut was an expression of the movement as a whole, its function was not limited to collective bargaining for workers. Rather, its aim, and the aim of its factions, was to establish a Jewish workers' *society* in Palestine. To do this, it established in 1923 the *Hevrat Ovdim* (Workers' Brotherhood), which was essentially a corporation for creating, buying, owning, and operating businesses and industries. At first it functioned predominantly as a holding company for several independent initiatives, but it clearly laid the seeds for the idea of an economy basically owned by the union, which is to say, owned by the dominant party, which is to say, owned by the state.

The key initiative with which the Hevrat Ovdim worked was a cooperative wholesale business that bought and marketed the produce of *kibbutzim* and *moshavim*[21] in a group of retail stores mainly in the cities. This was called *HaMashbir HaMerkazi* (The Central Supplier). (Again, this is not just history: in Israel today, the largest department store chain is called *HaMashbir LaTzarkhan,* and this is no coincidence.) In 1926, Hevrat Ovdim founded a bank: *Bank HaPoalim* (Laborers' Bank), which is still one of Israel's largest. In 1926, it organized a marketing outlet for dairy products,

T'nuva. The same year it started a housing business (which got low-cost credit from Bank HaPoalim) called *Shikun Ovdim* (Workers' Housing). It also created the *Kupat Holim* (Sick Fund), the origins of Israel's national health system. In 1925, it created its own newspaper, *Davar,* and even its own theater company, *Ohel* ("tent" in Hebrew), the forerunner of Israel's national theater, *HaBimah* (the Stage). It had its own school system and system of adult education and vocational training schools. It also began industrial companies, the most important of which was *Solel Boneh* (Paving and Building), which contracted itself to the British government. By 1935, more than three-fourths of the entire Jewish working population of Palestine was within the fold of the Histadrut.

Now, consider: What became of the relationship between Shikun, the Histadrut's housing company, and Solel Boneh, its construction company, and the Israeli Ministry of Housing and Construction formed in the government in 1949? The former companies had histories, had workers, had managers, and had money in the bank. The ministry had a minister, an office, and a small staff. Most likely, the minister and his staff came from Shikun, the building was built by Solel Boneh, and probably was financed by Bank HaPoalim. What was the relationship? Pretty chummy.

Even sports clubs and youth movements were organized and run by the party and party factions. Even today in Israel, most soccer clubs that compete in the national league and most youth groups are not sponsored by businesses or municipal governments; rather, they are mainly offshoots of political or social organizations.

In Mandate times, the Revisionists copied aspects of this system, creating their own youth groups, such as Betar, and their own schools. The point was to create loyal cadres of followers and to indoctrinate them with their own version of Zionist ideology. But again, they were unable to compete with Labor Zionists in the economic sphere, and when it came to building the state, that's what mattered most.

In other words, through the Histadrut the Yishuv managed to generate indigenous economic growth—at high rates, too—and to build an economy all under the hand of managers who were party members, and whose ambition it was ultimately to create a state to go with the society and the economy. Keeping everything under one roof, so to speak, made complete sense at the time: the Histadrut functioned as something akin to a central planning agency for the economy. It moved money around where it was needed, taking from profitable businesses and subsidizing infant enterprises, schools, and food staples for the population. It became self-sufficient, excluding the Arabs and the British (except as customers for Solel Boneh and so on). Obviously, then, when the state came into existence in 1948, the economy and the so-

cial structure it supported were already going concerns, and they were organized along lines that conformed to socialist formulas.

One can say, then, that in 1948 the dominant Zionist party became the
state, but at the same time the state was beholden to the union, which was an
arm of the party. In other words, the lines dividing the three entities were
pretty thin. Ben-Gurion was such a dominating personality in the early years
of Israeli statehood that his position as the head of Mapai (acronym for
Mifleget Poalei Eretz Israel, Land of Israel Laborers party) and also prime
minister overwhelmed all else. So did the state own most of the means of
production and operate the economy through its ministries? No, not exactly,
because the union owned and ran most of them instead. But the union in turn
was an arm of the party that dominated the state.

It is hard for most Americans to understand such a thing. Try to imagine
a situation in which the main union, the AFL-CIO, owns three-quarters of
the U.S. economy, has its own daily mass-circulation paper, and runs its
own health care system that covers the majority of American workers. Now
imagine that this union is inextricably connected to a political party—the
Democrats, say—whose ideology justifies this situation and that therefore is
always in power because nearly all union members would nearly always
vote for it. Now what would be left for the government to do except take
care of foreign policy and national defense? In domestic policy, the state as
such would be almost superfluous, or, put differently, it would be an emana-
tion of other social forces. And so it was in Israel.

Moreover, thanks to the small size of the state and its population, and to
the strong sense of community that pervaded it, the system worked. It generated growth without excessive bureaucracy or corruption, and it generated a
level of basic equality that conformed to norms of social justice held by the
majority of the population. It has become popular nowadays, after the collapse and discrediting of European socialism, to argue that socialism doesn't
work and can't work as an economic system. Not so; what it proves is that
socialism can't work when it is imposed involuntarily on a mass society. But
if the society is small enough and the population is positively oriented to a
sense of community, it can work well enough. The Zionist concept of a state-
centered polity was called *mamlakhtiyut,* or statism. In Israel, it had a very
positive connotation for most people.

Besides, why would the new Israeli government want to change the system it inherited and helped to foster in 1948? It wouldn't, and it didn't. What
it needed to do was consolidate, formalize, and partially restructure the system. On balance, this turned out to be fairly easy, but it was not without
incident. As noted, the Revisionists bolted from the unified Zionist movement in the 1930s and tried to develop parallel arms to Labor Zionism. We

have already noted, too, that their paramilitary forces, Etzel and Lehi, did not obey Haganah orders in 1947–48. Even during the war itself, after May 15, Etzel continued to operate as a semi-independent force. Though technically under Haganah command, Etzel didn't always act like it. This was illustrated vividly by the famous *Altalena* incident.

Etzel was active in the 1948 War in bringing recruits and weapons to Israel. In early May 1948, Etzel bought an American LST ship and sailed it to France, where it was loaded with arms, ammunition, and about 500 recruits. It sailed on May 29. Ben-Gurion had given permission for it to land on June 20, despite the fact that the first cease-fire had been reached and the *Altalena*'s landing would be a violation. When the ship was about to land, Etzel suddenly demanded that 20 percent of the arms go exclusively to its own units. Ben-Gurion refused. Shooting broke out near the landing area north of Tel Aviv. The ship caught fire, somewhere between seventeen and eighty-two people were killed (accounts differ!), and some of the cargo was lost. As a result, Ben-Gurion determined to abolish all remaining Etzel units and unify the armed forces under state command. This he did in short order.

The split between Labor Zionists and Revisionists was always sharp. Under the press of emergency in 1948, the divisions were softened. But the *Altalena* incident made them bitter once more. Things got personal as well as ideological. The Revisionists requested after 1948 that Jabotinsky's body be brought to Israel for burial. Ben-Gurion absolutely refused, saying that as long as he could prevent it, he would. And he did.[22]

In any event, since the unity and control of the union-party-state was consolidated within months of independence, the relationship of the Israeli government to the economy and society was mediated through the Histadrut long after 1948, and in many ways it still is. For example, the prices for many food staples in Israel today are determined by a conjunction of union and government officials. The market does not determine the price except in broad parameters. The economy has only begun to change qualitatively in recent years from the system institutionalized after 1948.

Of course, human nature being what it is, the circumstances under which socialism works well as an economic system are very few. And even in Israel, the party-state symbiosis has had its downside. For example, employment came to be politicized. If someone wanted to get a job in a Histadrut enterprise, he had to join the union and that meant becoming a party member. Jobs were often given out as patronage, and party members from prominent families often got the best jobs. One had to work one's way up in the union and in the party to increase one's economic prospects, and that was a function of hard work but also of personal and political loyalties. But suppose someone wasn't a socialist and didn't want to get involved in that sort of subculture? That person was just out of luck, and had to turn to the non-Histadrut, fully private economy as an alternative.

Both before 1948 and after there was, of course, a private and a non-Histadrut sector of the economy. Labor Zionism was socialist, not communist. It favored social, union control of the main means of production, but it never contemplated forced collectivization, the banning of private property, or the use of coercion to force all the people to tow the party line. But the environment of the private economy was not especially favorable to its growth. The socialist ethos was such that state policy discouraged the development of a class of fat cats. Socialist Zionists were suspicious of the unfettered market; they did not like capitalists.

As long as the private economy was small, it was fine. But if it rose to compete with Histadrut functions, that spelled trouble. It not only compromised ideological desiderata but undermined Labor Zionism's political constituency and the organizing principle of *mamlakhtiyut*. It is quite simple really: people who depend on the state party and its union auxiliaries for their livelihoods don't vote against the party. Those who are not dependent just might. The larger the private economy not beholden to the state, the more votes would be cast for the opposition—in this case, the group of parties or factions among the Revisionists.

As a consequence, the Israeli state has never made it easy for fully private enterprise to flourish. As long as it was under Labor control, the state always made its major purchases from Histadrut corporations wherever possible. Taxes on private business were very high, almost extortionist. One needed licenses and had to undergo inspections for practically everything. One had to pay fees to the state in order to get them, and even with the fees one couldn't always get them. If one wanted to import something to sell privately, one paid a customs levy so high as to make the item virtually unaffordable, which left the market to often inferior union-produced goods.

There have been exceptions here and there, but even these are political in nature. The diamond trade, for example, flourishes in Israel and the government tends to leave it more or less alone. This is partly because it is a province of Orthodox Jews, and the religious parties have won special privileges over the years in this regard. Secularists have often reasoned that it is better to let *hasidim* (called in Israel *haredim*, "those who fear God") make a living this way—with less rather than more government interference—because the alternative might be to have these people become a burden on the state by filling the ranks of those on the public dole.

Israel has paid an economic price over the years by discouraging private entrepreneurship. Economic growth would have been even higher than it has been and, more important, many thousands of business-minded Israelis who have left Israel for Europe and the Americas because they simply could not function in their business in Israel might have stayed. Also, Israel's dealings in the economy have frustrated foreign investment, including foreign investment by sympathetic diaspora Jews.

At the same time, Israel has tried to sell state bonds to diaspora Jewry and to attract direct contributions, both efforts meeting with much success. American and other diaspora Jews mostly do not realize it, but the money they've sent to Israel over the years, while "helping Israel" in a general sense, has probably reinforced and made less politically costly the state's attitude toward private enterprise. Though the latter effort was not directly connected to state policy regarding private business, the capital it has attracted from diaspora Jewry for the direct use of the state made up in some part for the shortfall in tax revenues caused by the systematic frustration of entrepreneurial endeavor.

In the last twenty years, the Israeli economy has undergone significant reform (see Chapter 4), but it is still highly socialized. Thus, long after Israeli socialism lost its ideological fervor, the state has remained largely socialist in structure, even during the tenure of non-socialist governments after 1977. That, too, is part of the Israeli system.

Immigration, Security, and Settlement

By the time the 1948 war was over and Israelis started to look around, two hard facts became clear. First, their security situation, while fairly safe for the time being, was uncertain for the future. Second, Israel was a very small country, and to become firmly rooted it needed to have more people. Security and immigration, therefore, were closely linked in the Israeli mind from the start, both to be encouraged and directed by the state.

Settlement was a priority—the hypotenuse, so to speak, between security and immigration. Just because the state now existed was no reason to stop settling the land. The land in all of its extent had to be settled for security reasons. Establishing a presence had the effect of bringing the country under better and better control. And the only way to do that was to have a larger population to distribute around. This was how the Zionist executive had always seen things in the Mandate period, when the idea of the paramilitary settlement—the *nahal*—was conceived. After 1948 the only things that had changed were that there were fewer Arabs in the country[23]—hence more opportunity for settlement—and no British soldiers to help keep order—hence proportionately more responsibility for the state. Between 1952 and 1962, eighteen entirely new "development towns" were founded—more or less planned communities founded specifically for immigrant populations. Between 1950 and 1960, too, eighty-four new agricultural settlements were established in nearly every corner of the country.

It was not just practical considerations that linked security, immigration, and settlement, however. This triad went right to the heart of Zionist ideology. After what had happened in World War II, it was clearer than ever that Jews needed to look out for their own security, for no one else would. Settlement still carried with it the mystique of the land, of agriculture, and that mystique in turn nurtured a concept: *moledet*. *Moledet* means literally "birthplace," but in the Zionist tense it meant homeland, a devotion to being rooted in a place, and schools and youth groups avidly developed naturalism as a form of virtual land worship. Young people were encouraged—indeed, almost forced—to walk the land, to learn it, to know every hill, every outcropping, every stand of trees, a knowledge that simultaneously conveyed a sense of purposefulness and bequeathed useful data in case one ever had to fight on the terrain. Immigration, in turn, was the fulfillment of the Zionist enterprise itself, the ingathering of the exiles and the virtual re-creation of a genuine, normal Jewish national history from where it left off in the year 135 C.E. Immigration was the bestowing of *moledet* on those who would reach out and take it.

It is important to understand just what this was all about. In Chapter 1 we learned that the theologically correct reading of Jewish history after the destruction of the Second Temple held within it an expectation of a Third Commonwealth and, with it, some fairly heady developments: the rebuilding of the temple and the coming of the messianic age. Zionism was not a consciously premillennarian movement in this sense; it sought a transformation of Jewish history, but not by supernatural means. And yet in a way Zionism simply secularized Jewish expectations of redemption rather than dismissed them altogether. The warnings of the rabbis of the nineteenth century, that Zionism was like Bar-Kochba and Shabbtai Tzvi, a giving in to the redemptive temptation, were not entirely without foundation.

In any case, the state of Israel devoted itself to attracting *aliyah* for both practical and ideological reasons. One of the first laws passed by the Knesset was the Law of Return. It says, basically, that any Jew anywhere in the world can come to Israel and, upon declaration that he or she wishes to become a citizen of the state, becomes one, just like that.[24] If there's an election the following week, that person can vote. If, on the other hand, that person is of military age, that person has to go into the army or be trained for reserve duty.

If someone who is not Jewish wishes to become a citizen of the state of Israel, it is possible, but a naturalization period must elapse first, as is the case in virtually every other country. But for a Jew, it was the Zionists' belief that waiting almost 2,000 years "to come home" was waiting long enough. (There are only a few examples of such a situation elsewhere; Germany, for example, has a similar law of return for ethnic Germans who lived previously in places such as Poland, the Czech Republic, and Russia.[25] And the Palestinian Authority says it plans such a law, too.)

In addition to the Law of Return, immigrants to Israel had, and still have, a series of special rights. They could defer military service. They were given a temporary place to live and a stipend to live on. They were taught the language by the state. They could maintain bank accounts in hard currencies for a specified time period, which native Israelis were generally not allowed to do until recently. They were allowed to bring certain items into the country without paying the usual duties and fees. In short, the country tried to make immigration to Israel as attractive as possible by offering special incentives, and Israeli emissaries *(shelihim)* actively tried to attract immigration from Europe and North America.

Interestingly, some of these efforts strained relations in the early 1950s between Israel and diaspora communities. Most self-styled Zionists outside Israel thought of themselves as Zionists because they supported Israel's right to exist *for those Jews who needed it.* Israel was a point of pride, and a geographical form of charity for Jews needing a refuge from anti-Semitism. They might even need that refuge themselves some day, but not likely, and certainly not now. Ben-Gurion didn't see things this way. He believed that all Jews should come to Israel because that was where they belonged. A Zionist was a Jew who lived in Israel or who was planning to live in Israel. There *was* a difference. Frankly, a lot of diaspora Jews felt that Israel was fine for those Jews who needed it, but it should not compromise their status in the United States, or Britain, or France, or wherever. A tension arose that has been variously managed, overlooked, accepted, and lied about, but never resolved. Nor is it likely to be resolved. (We return to this later, without resolving it.)

Israeli emissaries also propagandized widely in the Arab world. While believing that it was for the good of the communities as well as Israel's good, representatives of the Israeli government used almost every means, fair and foul, to persuade the Jews of Iraq, Morocco, and elsewhere to come to Israel. Each community is a different case, and it is not easy to generalize about these efforts, but clearly, in some cases, as with the Iraqi Jewish community, the state operated subterfugically against the lay and rabbinical leadership of that Jewish community. In all likelihood, it was for their own good, as later events showed. Still, it was at least a bit presumptuous. It showed, however, how important the concept of gathering the exiles was, not just in practical but in ideological terms. It also shows that, contrary to some recent

Sepharadic propaganda, the state did not discriminate against non-European Jews in the sense of not wanting them to come to Israel. On the contrary, it pursued their immigration to Israel most actively—even though they were generally not treated as equals once they arrived.

But what to *do* with such people once they arrived? By and large, Jews from the Arab world were less educated, less technically oriented, and less modern than the Ashkenazic Jews in Israel. And the government's official view notwithstanding, there was prejudice against them on cultural grounds. One way the Israeli government decided to deal with the matter was with the notion of a development town.

As mentioned, developing the entire area of the state and populating it with Jews was an urgent matter following the War for Independence. A development town was a planned settlement, complete with Histadrut buildings, roads, agricultural support systems, health care, schools—the works. And these towns were often in underpopulated parts of the country—the northern Negev, the upper Galilee—and along the border in places like Afula, Beit Shean, and Qiryat Shmona. For cultural reasons poorly understood at the time, immigrants from the Arab world, and from Turkey and Iran, did not generate the sorts of economically vibrant communities that European Jews did, and a certain amount of frustration and hostility arose as a result. Many Ashkenazim thought of the Sepharadim as inferior and lazy; many Sepharadim thought the government was using them as economic guinea pigs and cannon fodder.

Divisions between European and Oriental Jews in Israel have not disappeared—and in some ways, as in the political party system, they are becoming more overt—but they have certainly been muted over the years. Not that many places that started out as development towns remain homogeneously "Moroccan," for example, and socialization into the schools and the army has led to a level of integration and intermarriage that is dispatching the problem quite fast, at least by historical standards. One can see this in the slow but steady rise in the percentage of Sepharadim who attend college after leaving the army; in the 1950s and 1960s, the number was under 5 percent, but today it is closer to 17 percent in a country where the national average is 38 percent. Remember that only forty years have passed since the possibility of the problem arose in the first place. By most world standards, that is fast work.

As should be clear from the foregoing, the Israeli government believed in economic planning. It did not trust the market or the private sector for this purpose, for the simple reason that the former wasn't trusted to accord with security requirements and the latter was too small. Businessmen would not invest in an area where people didn't want to live, but security policy was determined to put people everywhere it could.

Relatedly, planning settlements implied planning roads and irrigation systems, both major infrastructural investments. For the former, there was Solel Boneh. For the latter, however, institutions were yet to be created, but they soon were. *Tahal* came into being as a "private" company, associated with the union, to plan water projects, but this company's client was almost exclusively the government.[26] Similarly created was *Mekorot,*[27] a water engineering, construction, and maintenance firm. Together, Tahal and Mekorot planned and built the National Water Carrier that started operation in 1964, and they still manage Israel's water system today.[28]

Early Foreign Relations

Israel was accepted quickly as a member of the international community. It was admitted to the United Nations on May 11, 1949, and soon won recognition from fifty states, at that time the vast majority of U.N. membership. The first two were the superpowers: the United States and the Soviet Union.

Not surprisingly, Israel's foreign relations at the beginning of the state were devoted to promoting security and immigration. Israel needed weapons and people. It naturally became most interested in those countries that could supply them. It also needed money—foreign aid. In 1948, Israel could not feed itself. So many people were coming so fast that production could not keep pace, and the war, of course, led to sharp drops in production as manpower wielded weapons instead of plows.

As for weapons, Israel could turn to few countries: Britain, the United States, the Soviet Union, and France. Hostility over the British role at the end of the Mandate made going to London out of the question. The Americans maintained their embargo after the war. France was willing, but did not have a great deal to offer. The Soviet Union seemed to many Israelis the best bet, but Soviet policy was to court the Arabs.

One of Israel's best friends in the early years turned out to be West Germany. The new German government, mortified over the legacy of World War II, wanted to make amends with Israel insofar as it could. A public agreement on German reparations to Israel was reached in September 1952, and called for payment to Israel of $715 million (in 1952 dollars). Some of this money went to the state, some directly to Israeli nationals who had suffered at the hands of the Nazis. Other private state-to-state arrangements also helped Israel secure small arms, ammunition, communications equipment, and other military-related supplies. A small-scale arms relationship also began with France.

The United States, a supporter of the Zionist movement under President Truman, provided no weapons but did give much needed economic and food aid. Also, contributions from diaspora Jewry helped a great deal. Today, such contributions amount to less than 1 percent of Israel's GNP. Back in the late 1940s it was nearly 10 percent.

As for people, the desire for Jewish immigration also led Israel to take an interest in places that otherwise would have evoked little concern. One such place was South Africa; another was Argentina; still another was Romania.

Israeli foreign relations also contained a broader ideological element. Labor Zionists remained more or less serious socialists. Ben-Gurion, who had spent some of the World War II years in the United States, was fond of America and suspicious of the USSR, but had been further to the Left as a young man even than most Labor Zionists, and he too wondered what lay ahead for Israeli-Soviet relations. It must be recalled that Israel's political images were shaped by World War II and the European political constellation that preceded it. Europe was split between fascism and communism, and since the enemy of one's enemy is one's friend, many Zionists embraced the Soviet Union as a kindred spirit. Moreover, had not the communists displaced the hated czar? They could not be all bad, could they?

The extent to which certain elite groups in the Haganah, particularly elements of the special forces Palmah group, were pro-Soviet is undeniable. During and just after World War II, the Palmah endeavored to bring in and hide from the British as many weapons as it could. One place that weapons were stored was a limestone cave south of Beersheba, at the time more than two miles from the nearest road and accessible only by foot with pack animals. In the cave, which can still be visited today, there are carved in the white limestone walls hammers and sickles along with names and Palmah symbols and slogans. This is not particularly surprising since, by 1942, almost half of Palmah members came from left-wing *kibbutzim,* which have always supplied Israeli political and military leaders way out of proportion to their demographic weight in society.[29]

The Soviet Union was also an intriguing place for Israeli statesmen because there, and in North America, were the only large Ashkenazic Jewish communities that had escaped the Nazis. Israeli policy toward the Soviet Union, from 1949 through 1991, had at the top of its agenda the prospects that as many as three million Jews might somehow be brought to Israel. The problem with American Jews was that they *wouldn't* come; the problem with Soviet Jews was that they *couldn't* come.

On balance, Ben-Gurion preferred a policy of neutrality after the 1948 war. The reason was not principle but common sense. Israel wanted something from the United States and something from the Soviet Union: weapons, aid, and people. Ally with one, and antagonize the other, so better to stay friends with both as long as possible. This turned out not to be very long. The relationship with the United States became increasingly important to Israel for diplomatic reasons, for the United States soon became both Israel's largest aid donor and simultaneously the state most active in trying to forge Arab-Israeli conciliation. In the latter domain, American diplomacy inclined to ask Israel to do things—with regard to refugee repatriation, for example—that Israel felt it could not safely do.

In 1950, Washington put the screws to Israel. It asked Ben-Gurion to vote for the U.S.-led United Nations "police action" in Korea and against the U.N. admission request of mainland China, just as Israel had almost completed negotiations for mutual recognition with Peking, as Beijing was then called in English. Israel resisted but eventually complied. Meanwhile, Stalin had grown bizarre in his old age, and increasingly paranoid and anti-Semitic. By 1951, it had become clear that Israel could not expect to have normal or friendly relations with the Soviet Union.

Otherwise, Israel developed a regional strategy after 1948 that lasted for many years, and in some respects still lasts today. It was called the peripheral strategy, and was in essence a very simple idea. The Arabs were the problem, so Israel's aim was to make friends with countries on the Arabs' periphery for whom the Arabs also represented a problem. Specifically, that meant trying to forge good ties with Iran, Turkey, and Ethiopia. Since all three of these countries were pro-Western in the 1950s, and specifically tied up with the United States in military and economic aid relationships, this was yet another element leading Israel increasingly to cast its lot with the West in the Cold War.

One of Israel's main failures in foreign relations in the early years was to cement good relations with India, which became independent at roughly the same time as Israel. Ben-Gurion and Moshe Sharett, as foreign minister, saw India as another great ancient civilization come back to the world stage—just like Israel—and they believed that the two countries, as democracies and neutralists in the Cold War, would have a lot in common. But India spurned Israel; its leaders sympathized with the Palestinian Arabs and did not wish to antagonize the Arabs in order to blunt expected Arab sympathy for Muslim Pakistan. In due course, India also allied itself with the Soviet Union. Israeli-Indian diplomatic relations were not established until 1992.

A final note about foreign policy. Israel was blessed with a multilingual population owing to the nature of its founding. Also owing to its founding, it had contacts in more places than one would expect a small Asian state of only 1 million inhabitants to have had. And, given its interest in the welfare of Jews everywhere, its desire to collect information also exceeded that of most small Asian states. In short, Israel had certain special reasons to emphasize intelligence work, and certain special assets with which to do it. A small, vulnerable state also needs big ears for early warning if it is to defend itself effectively.

So after independence Israel created three kinds of intelligence agencies: the *Shin Bet* (short for *Shirut Bitahon,* Security Service)[30] for domestic matters, comparable to the FBI; *Aman,* for military intelligence, comparable to the Defense Intelligence Agency (DIA); and the *Mossad* (short for *HaMossad Le Modein V'Tafkedim Meyuhadim,* the Institute for Intelligence and Special Tasks) for foreign intelligence gathering and special operations, comparable to the Central Intelligence Agency (CIA).

Within a few years, Israel scored some dramatic successes in intelligence work. Almost from the start it was reading sensitive Egyptian cable traffic, and sometimes saw Arab League meeting memoranda before Arab governments saw them. At one point, one of its spies, Eli Cohen, had become part of the inner circle of the Syrian leadership for quite a long time before he was discovered and hanged. Israel reportedly knew about the coming abdication of Jordan's King Talal in 1952 before his son, Hussein, knew about it. Israel was the first country to get a copy of Nikita Khrushchev's famous speech denouncing Stalin to the 23rd Party Congress in 1956, quickly communicating it to the CIA. Thanks to all this, Israel acquired a reputation for efficiency and skill in intelligence work. It is a reputation it retains still, despite hatching some spectacular screw-ups in recent years. To all this we will return as well.

4

Society and

Political Economy

in Contemporary Israel

As we have seen, Israeli political culture at the outset in 1948 combined several elements into a systemic whole: the combination of diaspora cultural traits with the self-willed character of the new Jew or Zionist; the union-party-state symbiosis; the social and political compromise between secularists and religious traditionalists, nearly all of European origin; and the democratic infrastructure that allowed all of the aforementioned factors the flexibility to adjust to challenges with the passage of time. Since 1948, Israel has undergone a great many changes, but the essential elements of this systemic whole remain, albeit with some significant amendments.

First, the mix of diaspora ("old Jew") as opposed to Zionist ("new Jew") traits and attitudes remains; nearly 2,000 years of history are not overturned in half a century of independence. No matter how strong the new nationalist myth, the old cultural reality endures.

Second, the union-party-state symbiosis has undergone extensive change—unraveling, really—on the formal level. The Histadrut is no longer an exclusive wing of the Labor party and its kindred ideological affiliates. Indeed, in 1994, Haim Ramon resigned his position as minister of health in the Rabin government, bolted from Labor, formed his own party, and won majority control of the union. As important, the rise of non-Labor-led governments under the Likud bloc after May 1977 put ever more distance between the party of the founders and the operations of the state. But this symbiosis existed for so long that most institutions of the state still reflect it to one degree or another.

Third, the secularist-religious compromise remains; a written constitution is still to be written. But it has been changed by the religious bloc's ideological shift to the right after 1967, and strained more generally by an increasing lack of mutual toleration between secular and religious views of public policy. In the last few years, the impetus to upset the 1948 compromise came not mainly from Orthodox Jews in Israel trying to increase their influence over the secular majority, but from non-Orthodox Jewish movements in the United States trying to alter Israeli arrangements and practices for their own ideological reasons.

This has led, in turn, to new strains on Israeli democracy. There is no question that Israel remains a democracy and a vibrant one. But in recent years there has been a surge of extra-parliamentary political activity, which is usually a sign in any democracy that the system of representation is not channeling public sentiment within institutional boundaries as well as it might. The public has become increasingly skeptical of government capabilities to solve pressing problems, and regularly bemoans the lack of creative and effective leadership. Moreover, as noted earlier, while Jewish Israeli society is ever more integrated, the political system is still tempted to party formation along intra-Jewish ethnic lines. The May 1999 election campaign showed this vividly. Finally, the Arab population of the state has become more adept at using democratic procedures to advance its own interests, but in some respects this has worsened Jewish perceptions of its Arab citizens, a trend that, in the longer run, could also undermine democracy if mutual fears and suspicions are mishandled.

This chapter and the next explore these continuities and changes from various angles. In this chapter we focus on the society and the economy, and in the next we concentrate more directly on the political system and the public policy agenda. As the narrative proceeds, as before, I introduce basic vocabulary, information, background, and make several other assorted observations so as to give a better feel for the subject.

The New Demography and Its Implications

One of the most dramatic changes between the Israel of 1948 and the Israel of today is the distribution and nature of its people—its demography. Let's look at the numbers.

In 1948, to repeat, there were about 880,000 people, of whom about 717,000 were Jews. By 1961, there were 2.18 million citizens of the state, of whom 1.93 million were Jews. That's more than a doubling in thirteen years, a statistic that indicates a very extensive absorption of immigrants, as well as a high rate of natural increase.

By 1972, the state's population had reached 3.15 million, of whom 2.69 million were Jewish. By 1982, there were 4.06 million people, of whom 3.37 million were Jews. In 1995, the population was 5.47 million, of whom 4.43 million were Jews. Overall, the population has continued to grow rapidly, but not as rapidly as during Israel's first decade. The net growth rate from 1993 to 1994, for example, was 2.5 percent, of which 60 percent was due to natural increase, the rest to immigration. The same general trends have been present in the latter half of the 1990s, with Israel's population in 1999 reaching six million.

Population growth of this magnitude had obvious implications for the state, the society, and the economy. As far as the state was concerned, the growth of population showed everyone, Jew and Arab alike, that Israel was very likely here to stay. Israel's capacity to absorb refugees and develop economically made Arab pretenses of destroying the state by siege rather than direct attack sound increasingly implausible. Israel's growth was sobering to the Arabs; it was also a factor in changing the psychology of Israel's neighbors, for it slowly but surely convinced most that, eventually, some way had to be found to live in a Middle East that included Israel.

As far as economic development was concerned, clearly it is people who work that make wealth, and the more working people there are, all else being equal, the more wealth they will produce. Israel's economic growth over the years tracks well with population increase. By and large, too, immigrants to any country tend to be younger than the mean population group from which they come, and younger people work longer and often harder than older people. This has also affected Israel's economic development.

More people also meant that more of the country could be settled and thus secured from attack and terror. A larger population provided a general sense of increased security as time passed, and this was important to a population that, in general terms, felt as though it was isolated in the region and constantly under threat of renewed warfare.

Just as important as the numbers of immigrants is where they came from. As mentioned in Chapter 3, the great waves of immigration have made Israel less and less demographically European over time. Let's revisit some figures. In 1948, there were 591,400 Jews of Ashkenazic origin and only 105,000 of Sepharadic origin.[1] In 1961, there were 1.01 million Ashkenazic Jews and 818,330 Sepharadic Jews. By 1972, the scale had tilted; there were 1.19 million Ashkenazim and 1.27 million Sepharadim. And by 1982, there were 1.34 million Ashkenazim and 1.50 million Sepharadim.

Also noteworthy is the data on Jews of mixed Ashkenazic-Sepharadic

---

Salah!

The cultural differences between European and Oriental Jews in Israel were and remain significant, but Israelis from all origins have learned to laugh at these differences at least some of the time. A famous Israeli movie from the early 1960s, called *Salah Shabbati,* is about a Moroccan immigrant who ends up living in a temporary tent city. At one point, Salah is given a job planting trees in a Jewish National Fund forest. As he and his fellows are planting, an Israeli official rides up and sticks a Jewish National Fund sign in the ground reading "Isaac Greenberg Forest." A few minutes later a limousine drives up and out steps a wealthy American Jewish couple, the Greenbergs, along with their Israeli hosts. The Greenbergs see the sign, are delighted, look around for a few minutes, and are soon on their way. Then the Israeli official returns, takes away the sign reading "Isaac Greenberg Forest" and puts in another saying "Morris Goldberg Forest." Salah reads the sign, and starts carefully pulling out the saplings he has spent all morning planting. When the JNF official sees him uprooting saplings, he goes over to him and excoriates him saying: "What are you doing, you fool? Why are you uprooting these trees?" Salah replies: "Because these are Isaac Greenberg's trees, and I am going to save them for him."

---

background. In 1948, there were only 20,300 such people. In 1961, there were 106,900. In 1972, there were 461,000, and in 1982, there were 690,400. Now there are so many that the existence of the Ashkenazic-Sepharadic divide is demographically suspect, even though its political salience, for reasons discussed in the next chapter, has not subsided and in some ways has grown.

The Arab population of the country also increased rapidly, particularly the Muslim population. In 1948, 1961, 1972, and 1982 the figures were 165,000, 247,100, 461,000, and 690,400, respectively. The Arab population of the state in 1995 was above 800,000, roughly 17–18 percent of the population. (Because the population is young, Arabs make up only 12 percent of the voting age population.) The Arab population of Jerusalem, mainly of those not citizens of the state, is also substantial and rising faster than the Jewish population. By the year 2010, about 31 percent of the city's inhabitants will likely be Arab—about 250,000 out of 818,000—if demographic considerations alone are left to determine the numbers

Among Israeli Arabs, Muslims increased from 170,800 in 1961 to 530,800 in 1982—more than a tripling. Over the same years, the Christian Arab population increased from 50,500 to only 94,000, less than a doubling in twenty-one years. This was caused by higher rates of natural increase among Muslim Arabs and by higher emigration rates on the part of Christian Arabs. Christian Arabs are about 12 percent of the non-Jewish population, and the Druze have made up roughly 9 percent of the non-Jewish total throughout.

Perhaps most important of all in the demographic statistics we are reviewing, the Jewish immigrant population in 1948 was about 463,000 and the home-born population about 254,000, a ratio of roughly 65 percent to 35 percent. By 1961, that ratio of immigrant to home born was about 62 percent to 38 percent, not much of a change, and the reason is clear: the huge influx of Jews mainly from the Arab world. By 1982, however, that ratio was 41 percent to 59 percent. Immigration had slackened, and of course, older age cohorts die faster than younger ones.

A native-born Israeli is colloquially called a *sabra*, a local cactus that is tough on the outside but sweet and soft on the inside, a combination Israelis believe fits their nature. In any event, by the early 1970s, Jewish *sabra*s outnumbered immigrants. This was an important milestone psychologically and politically. It meant that Israeli society was literally organic to the Middle East. It also complicated Arab political positions, which usually held that any Jew in Israel born after 1917 (the Balfour Declaration) had to return to his or her country of origin after the state of Israel was destroyed. How much sense did it make to tell a nineteen-year-old *sabra* in the middle 1970s that he had to return to where his parents came from, Poland or Romania? It made no sense, and all but the least sophisticated Arab statesmen and politicians knew it.

Another key datum from the Zionist point of view was that as Israel grew in population, it also grew in terms of the percentage of world Jewry that lived in Israel. Israel was a projection state in 1948, when less than 10 percent of world Jewry lived in Israel. By the 1960s, the number climbed to 13 percent, 20 percent in the 1970s, 25 percent in the 1980s, and, thanks largely to the substantial immigration of "Soviet" Jews to Israel, to about 36 percent today. (Some time in the first quarter of the twenty-first century, the lines will cross thanks to a relatively youthful Israel society, the advancing assimilation of North American Jewry, and further immigration. When it does, Israel will house the majority of world Jewry for the first time since the second century of the common era.)

What else do these demographic data tell us? They suggest that the Israeli population developed a capacity to grow increasingly youthful over time. Immigrants, as noted, tend to be young and young people have children. The state's mean population grew older until 1981, but thereafter, because of a demographic ripple effect, it got younger. With the Ethiopian and Russian Jewish immigration, the trend was again reversed, but only temporarily. All along too, the government has encouraged women to have large families in an effort to populate the country, build the state, and—everyone knew it in their hearts—replace the more than a million and a half Jewish children murdered by the Nazis.

The data also tell us that Ashkenazim as a group earn more and hold positions of leadership more frequently than do Sepharadim. There are many exceptions, but statistics are statistics. Even crime data bear out the divide: there are more Sepharadim in jail than Ashkenazim, obviously a function of socioeconomic statuses, not moral differences. Ashkenazim excel at white-collar crime, while Sepharadim tend to predominate in petty theft, domestic violence, and nonpayment of debts. Obviously, Israel is still not a fully integrated society, but forty years is not a long time to achieve full integration. Many countries with heterogeneous populations less diverse than Israel's are less well-integrated societies than is Israel, and most have had lots more time to work at it.

The differences between the groups, however, may get worse instead of better on account of economic changes afoot in the country. In general, Israel is becoming less a patronage-based public-sector-dominated economy and more a private enterprise, one based on a meritocracy. What this implies is that the relatively modest skewing of income distribution historically in Israel may give way to a greater skewing; indeed, in the last eight or so years it has already done so. If such skewing assumes clear lines between a vast majority of fast-tracked Ashkenazim on the cyberhighway of the future and a majority of slower-tracked Sepharadim stuck in the more stagnant traditional economy—or worse, dependent on the state—then intercommunal harmony could deteriorate, reversing the general trend of the past four decades. Those, especially outside Israel, who advocate the rapid economic rationalization and privatization of the Israeli system sometimes do not contemplate the social implications. It's cute to sport bumper stickers that proclaim: "It isn't whether you win or lose . . . it's whether *I* win or lose," but it isn't necessarily wise for government policy to adopt that sort of thinking.

The Netanyahu government, however, had precisely this view, and aggressively sought privatization. It also cut the budget and began reducing the size of the public sector, which made political sense since that sector is mainly a pro-Labor constituency. But many, even some in the Likud, have feared that the combination of rapid privatization and budget cutting will not lead to a kinder and gentler economy, but to a greater gap between rich and poor, and more social conflict as a result. Unfortunately, too, the educational philosophy of the largest Sepharadic social movement and political party, Shas, is retrograde; it stresses religious education and not the sort of skills that could enable young Sepharadim to ascend the socioeconomic ladder.

In this regard, it is worth mentioning that in addition to *aliyah* to Israel, there has been Jewish emigration (*yerida*, from the Hebrew for "going down") from it. Since 1948, roughly 255,000 Jewish citizens of the state have left Israel permanently, and another 200,000 or so are living outside of Israel temporarily at any given time. Of the total of nearly half a million, about 300,000 Israelis are resident in the United States; indeed, far more Israelis have moved to the United States than American Jews have moved to Israel since 1948. The remainder of those Israelis abroad has gone to Europe, Australia, Latin America, Canada and, lately, a small number have gone back to Russia or other former republics of the Soviet Union for family or business reasons.

Yerida was becoming a serious problem in the mid-1980s, and it was affecting national morale for, obviously, the Jewish state was supposed to attract, not repel, Jews from their land. For a few years, emigration from Israel almost equaled immigration to Israel. But the *aliyah* of Ethiopian and Soviet Jewry in the mid-1980s and early 1990s changed that, at least for the time being.

The reasons for Jewish emigration from Israel have varied. Before 1948, many Jews who had come to Palestine left because of considerations of safety, standard of living, and family reunification. After 1948, some of the reasons stayed the same, but others changed. Some rejoined displaced family members from World War II who settled elsewhere, some fled the pressure of living in a small place under constant security threat, and some went abroad to study and found employment or married non-Israeli spouses who kept them away. But the reason given most often is economic opportunity— either to be freer to wheel and deal in business or to practice one's profession free of constraint or at a higher level. Few left easily, or stayed away without some remorse.

Since the early 1980s, immigration rates to Israel have picked up sharply because of two extraordinary events: the collapse of the Soviet Union and the rescue of Ethiopian Jewry in Operation Moses. In the Zionist imagination, these events affirmed with renewed strength the state's mission and its necessity.

Soviet Jews began to get permission to leave in the 1970s, thanks to political and economic pressures brought by the United States and enabled mainly by Senator Henry M. "Scoop" Jackson, who lobbied tirelessly for a law (the Jackson-Vanik amendment) linking Soviet behavior toward its own people—including the right to leave—with improvement in U.S.-Soviet relations.[2] The Soviet Jews who came to Israel in those years—about 100,000— were for the most part self-conscious Jews and Zionists. They were also European in culture, generally well educated, and highly motivated. The even larger numbers of Soviet Jews—around 300,000—who came in the 1989–92 period as the Soviet Union collapsed, were less enthusiastic about *aliyah* or knowledgeable about Judaism or Zionism. They came because they had nowhere else to go, thanks to President George Bush's decision to restrict the number of Soviet Jews coming to the United States so that they would go to Israel instead, as the Israeli government wished and had requested.[3]

The new generation of Soviet Jews in Israel had the older generation to help them out: to teach them Hebrew, help them get jobs, instruct them in Jewish culture, and so forth. The combination is interesting for other reasons, too. The first wave of Soviet Jews came for idealistic reasons, and they had suffered a great deal as *refusniks*—those who refused to submit to Soviet pressures—in trying to get out of the USSR, as the famous case of Natan (Anatoli) Sharansky illustrates. These were, let us call them, Ben-Gurion immigrants—immigrants of idealism. The second wave came for practical reasons: desperation, fear, and panic. For them, Israel was not an ideological or a personal quest, it was a *nachtasyl*, a night shelter, as the notion of a refuge was traditionally put in Yiddish. These were, let us call them, Herzl immigrants.

The rescue of Ethiopian Jews is really an extraordinary tale. Ethiopian Jews used to be called *falashas* until it became better known that *falasha* was a deprecatory name, meaning stranger, given this community by other Ethiopians. For a long time, European and Oriental Jews knew that there were people in Ethiopia who thought of themselves as Jews, and whose internal myth held that they were descendants of King Solomon and the Queen of Sheba. They didn't know very much about the community, however, nor how many members of it there were. In the 1980s, owing to extreme instability and civil war in Ethiopia on account of the weakening and subsequent fall of the Marxist regime there, this community became endangered and some of its members managed to make their way to Israel, where they were generally accepted as authentic Jews.

While scholarship has cast doubt on the authenticity of Ethiopian Jews' claims about their origins and even their Jewishness, the state, accommodated in this case by the rabbinate, nevertheless ruled that they were indeed Jews. This made a certain sense: the Ethiopian Jews believed they were Jews, felt a kinship with other Jews, and retained what seemed to be unmistakably Jewish facets of religious practice, language, and even occupational patterns in their culture. And they were clearly in trouble. So the Israeli government worked in secret with the Sudanese and Ethiopian governments to airlift them to Israel. Some emigration occurred between late 1984 and mid-1985, and then the major exodus took place in 1991. Altogether, about 33,000 Ethiopian Jews were brought to Israel.

Make no mistake: Ethiopian Jews look far more like other Ethiopians than they do like most other Israelis. While some came from urban areas and were relatively literate technically—at least by Ethiopian standards— the majority had never enjoyed such household amenities as electricity and running water—rather like the Yemeni Jews airlifted to Israel in 1949. Educating and training such people to live in a relatively advanced society would obviously be difficult. Moreover, by the early 1990s, Israel was not underpopulated anymore, and it was already struggling to absorb huge numbers of Russian Jews. So why did Israel go out of its way to bring the Ethiopians to Israel?

It is because Israel is still an ideological state whose main raison d'être is the ingathering of the exiles and the protection of Jews wherever they may be. Israel behaves in the region and in the world most of the time according to the dictates of *realpolitik*—hard-nosed realism; a small state in a dangerous neighborhood cannot afford to do otherwise and expect to survive. But that has to do with tactics, with "how" questions. When it comes to values, when it comes to the "why" questions, Israel often acts on the basis of what most neutral observers would have to say are unrealistic premises. Zionism still behaves as a form of secular messianism, its main goal being the historical redemption of the Jewish people and the reversal of the effects of thousands of years of exile. This is not the sort of aim to which the word realist easily applies.

One sees the effects of this idealism where it is absolutely most central: the makeup of the people themselves, Israel's changing demography. Recall we talked about mythos and reality, and about self-fulfilling behavior. The Zionist myth is that the Jewish people are a unity, no matter where they are or what they look like. Israel has acted consistently on the basis of that belief for more than fifty years, and as a result has literally created a new reality: the most unified, integrated, intermarrying, mixed-complected, DNA-diffused Jewish society in the world—or for that matter, in Jewish history.

The ingathering of Ethiopian Jewry raises another point that cannot be avoided: racism. Israel was stigmatized by the U.N. General Assembly in 1975, which equated Zionism with racism. (The measure was repealed in 1992.) What the enemies of Israel meant was that Israel was a state based on an ethnic criterion, and that if a person did not fit that criterion (being Jewish), then that person—say, an Israeli Arab—was necessarily a second-class citizen, and that was racism.[4] Why Israel was singled out in this regard, when several dozen ethnically heterogeneous states in the United Nations actively discriminate against ethnic minorities within their midst, was never explained.

The more common meaning of racism to most Americans, however, is unwarranted prejudice against others who are different, particularly whose skin color is different. In this more practicable and common sense, is Israel racist? Can a country whose people look far more Caucasian than Negroid go out of its way, and against the dictates of narrow rationality, to gather in Ethiopian Jews—and grant them immediate citizenship under the Law of Return—be racist? It's hard to see how.

On the other hand, no society is without its prejudices and its tensions, especially an objectively heterogeneous one like Israel. Who tends to dislike whom, however, depends on who one is.

For a long time, many Ashkenazim looked down upon immigrants from Morocco, Yemen, and elsewhere. Some still do, but as indicated, as Israeli society becomes more integrated these prejudices are eroding, even though some politicians try to play on them for personal reasons. Often overlooked is that some of the Oriental communities, the *Edot Hamizrah*, looked down on each other. Many Iraqi Jews thought of themselves as the aristocrats of the *Edot Hamizrah*, for example, and sometimes had unpleasant things to say about Egyptian, Moroccan, or Yemeni Jews. By the same token, years ago, some European Jews in Israel—German Jews, say—looked down their noses at those they thought less refined—Polish Jews, say. Over time, these kinds of antipathies have virtually disappeared.

To some extent, these attitudes were imported from the Arabs or the Europeans themselves, who, Jews aside, sometimes have had unpleasant things to say about one another.[5] Thus, too, Russian Jews, especially members of the more recent group to arrive, appear to be the only group of Israelis who dislike the Ethiopians. This they appear to have picked up in part from anti-black prejudice in the Soviet Union, a subject about which any African student who studied in Moscow can deliver an earful. Also, as immigrants, Russians have more contact with Ethiopian Jews than the average Israeli, and that may contribute to the tension.

Most Israelis seem to like the Ethiopians, who have made a reputation of being industrious, gentle, intelligent, and eager to integrate into Israeli society. Contrarily, many Israelis see the more recent waves of Russian immigrants as ignorant of Jewish culture and sometimes hostile to it, as haughty, dishonest, and inclined to drunkenness. Several Israeli newspaper commentators have remarked that the gentility of the Ethiopians is a welcome antidote to the brashness and hard-edginess of Israeli culture. When they speak of the Russians, they speak usually of their many skills and the sheer weight of their numbers.

Unfortunately, there have been signs of growing problems with the Ethiopians. Not all have been absorbed into the economy, the Orthodox rabbinate has not recognized Ethiopian clergy as equals, and a very hurtful incident occurred in early 1996 that has made relations very sensitive. Blood donated by Ethiopians, especially those in the army, was being systematically dumped because Ethiopians had a much higher incidence of AIDS than the rest of the population (although AIDS cases in Israel are very few compared to the United States). When this medical precaution became known, it caused an outpouring of anger from the Ethiopians (in Amharic, "blood" also means "soul") and a deep embarrassment among many Israelis. Prime Minister Peres apologized to the community publicly, but the damage was done.

If one goes to Israel (or has been there already), one sees skin hues from deep black on the one hand (the Ethiopians) to blond and blue-eyed on the other. To put it into an American context, most Israelis are somewhere in between, darker than most American whites, but lighter than most American blacks. In general, as in the Arab world, this makes blondes relatively rare. It also makes red-heads stand out; Israelis sometimes refer to them as *jinjees*. But it makes prejudice predicated on skin color alone virtually nonexistent.

Israeli Arabs

There is, however, much Jewish prejudice against Arabs, including Israeli Arab citizens of the state. Though it has nothing to do with skin color, at times this prejudice borders on racism.

It is unclear how widespread such attitudes are. Their source, however, is no mystery. Unlike racism toward blacks in America, who clearly are not responsible for most of their ancestors' having been dragged to North America as slaves, Israeli attitudes toward Arabs are not based on thin air. For whatever reasons, Arabs have been mainly hostile to Jews in this century, and Jews are bothered by such hostility and fear it. Prejudice is an all too human response in such circumstances. Imagine how most white Americans would feel about the black minority if America was a tiny state surrounded by several generally hostile countries with almost entirely black populations.

Unlike the case in America, however, there is little pressure to integrate Jewish and Arab populations. Neither side wants it; both prefer to maintain separate cultures. While many Israeli Arabs have learned Hebrew just to get along (partly because they find it so easy), few Israelis thus far have learned Arabic (partly because they find it so hard). There are not all that many points of contact between the two groups, certainly not many where they meet as equals. But again, that's how both groups prefer it, for the most part. Arabs want their own schools with the language of instruction being Arabic, and Jewish teachers in a secular school would feel strange teaching the Hebrew Bible as literature to Muslims.

Israelis do distinguish differences among Arabs. For example, Palestin-

---

Uri, Ibrahim, and Me

In 1971, I worked in a citrus orchard with two others, Uri, a "problem child" of Yemeni immigrants sent to the *kibbutz* for social therapy, and an Israeli Arab named Ibrahim, from a nearby village. The three of us got along well despite having three different native languages; we used Hebrew. One day when we came into the dining hall for lunch, we sat down together, joined by two of Ibrahim's friends. After the meal was over, a female *kibbutznik* came over to Uri and me—Yemeni delinquent and North American imbecile in her mind, no doubt—and criticized us for eating with "filthy Arabs." Since Uri was darker complected than Ibrahim, this obviously wasn't about skin color. It was very disturbing just the same.

---

ian Arabs who are not citizens of Israel, but who live in territories occupied by Israel, are distinguished by most Israelis from "our" Arabs—Arab citizens of the state who live inside the Green Line.[6] Israelis know that the Arab citizens of Israel have rarely if ever posed an active threat to Israeli security. Incidents of terrorism or violence or subversion perpetrated by Arab citizens of Israel have been very rare since the early 1950s.

Nevertheless, even Israelis who are in no way racist worry about the high birthrates among the Arabs, and their increasing identification with Palestinian nationalism in the occupied territories. They also know that if Israeli Arabs acted in unison, they could place perhaps sixteen of their community in the Knesset instead of the usual six or eight, making them a major non-Jewish political force in the Jewish state. In the 1999 election, they placed ten seats in Knesset, perhaps a sign of even more political clout to come. Israelis also worry about the growing Islamization of the Israeli Arabs—as evidenced lately by the rapidly growing Islamic schools and what they teach—and some think that it is only a matter of time before a few Israeli Arabs decide to become terrorists and suicide bombers. (It happened for the first time im September 1999.) The 1999 election also showed that Islamists and nationalists among the Arabs did somewhat better than the more traditional Arab parties. Nevertheless, as of mid-1995, the police ministry established armed civil guard units in Arab towns and villages to enable Arab citizens to better control crime in their own neighborhoods. And in 1999 three other milestones were reached: the first Arab "Miss Israel" was crowned (Rana Raslan, from Haifa); the first female Arab members of Knesset took her seat; and the first Arab High Court Justice was swore in, Abdel Rahman Zuabi, from Nazareth.

Since December 1966, Israeli Arabs have not lived under emergency regulations, but while some volunteers are accepted, most have not been allowed to serve in the Israeli army. But few wish to do so, in any event. This is important because army service is a major gateway to rights and privileges in Israel, and as a result, Israeli Arabs are saddled with major disadvantages despite their technically equal citizenship rights. They are indeed second-class citizens in many practical, but not legal, respects, which gives rise to a paradox: Israeli Arabs as second-class citizens within Israeli democracy have more civil liberties but less sense of dignity than Arabs who are first-class citizens of Arab states that are authoritarian dictatorships or military governments.

Also, Arabs cannot carry a political veto—even a small or occasional one—because there is no district representation in Israel; as we'll see in the next chapter, the entire country is one electoral district. Thus, areas of predominately Arab habitation are not represented nationally. And Arab areas have also come up with the short end of municipal budget subventions from the central government. Part of the reason for this is plain prejudice—why should Jewish taxes pay for Arab villages?—and part has to do with the formula by which the central government provides municipal subventions. The fewer the services the municipal government provides and the lower its local tax base, the less matching money will come from Jerusalem. Since Arab municipal government tends to be minimalist and Arab towns tend to be poorer, they are entitled to less. In recent years, the Israeli government has committed itself to rectify discriminatory budget allocations, and in 1993 a five-year equalization plan was begun. It made progress but did not achieve full equalization. The program will resume under the Barak government.

Israelis similarly distinguish Israeli Arab citizens who are townspeople—in places like Acre, Haifa, and Nazareth—from the bedouin mainly in the south of the country in the northern Negev (though there are some in the Galilee as well), whom they define as "bedouin" rather than "Palestinian." On the one hand, the bedouin are widely viewed as a kind of Arab gypsy—semi-nomadic, illiterate, dirty, poor, and prone to feuding among themselves, but honest, friendly, interesting, and generally harmless. More than that, some bedouin serve ably in the Israeli military as trackers and border police. Unfortunately, despite such service, the army has sometimes been brusque and arbitrary in appropriating bedouin pasture areas in the Negev for use by the army for training purposes, and in some cases also for housing developments around an expanding Beersheba.

Israelis also distinguish between Muslim and Christian Arabs. Muslims are generally considered more problematic, all else being equal, because Islam, understood in certain political ways, tends to inflame conflicts of interests and links Muslim Arabs to a wider, hostile Muslim world. The Christian community, on the other hand, is on balance more urban, more cosmopolitan, more multilingual, and better educated—that is to say, more like Jewish Israelis. On the other hand, because Arab Christians are somewhat marginalized in a majority Islamic culture, they have often gone out of their way to act more Arab than the Arabs, and that has sometimes meant taking the lead in anti-Western and anti-Israel advocacy.

Israelis also know the difference between Arabs in general and the Druze. The Druze speak Arabic, but as noted earlier, they have a heterodox interpretation of Islam that sets them apart from other Israeli Arabs.[7] Druze in Israel have traditionally been friendly to Jews and to the state. They serve in the Israeli army and they have served over the years with distinction. Most Israelis respect and even have affection for the Druze.

Israelis also distinguish between other Arabs: Egyptians, whom they have always respected, and Jordanians, whom they have respected as much or more, as opposed to Syrians and Iraqis, for example, whom Israelis tend to think of as vicious, fanatical, and primitive compared to their co-nationalists.

Hatred of Arabs tends to increase directly as one moves from the Left to the Right of the political spectrum, which in Israel has been defined mainly by views on security issues, not economics. The Israeli extreme Right, which we discuss in more detail later, tends to believe that Arab hostility to Israel is limitless, endless, and ubiquitous. One cannot make peace with such people, they believe, and they sometimes speak in terms that dehumanize the enemy—a common phenomenon in all places and at all times, it would seem.[8] One Israeli politician, a former general named Rafael Eytan, once spoke of the Arabs as drugged cockroaches in a bottle, for example—a remark that disgusted most Israelis. But on the Israeli far Right such attitudes are common and in the ultranationalist settler movement in the West Bank and Gaza, they are more common still.

This settler movement, it is worth noting, has a disproportionate number of religiously observant American Jews in it. Most are idealistic and oblivious to the social history of the area and of the Arabs who live there. But some, especially followers of the late Rabbi Meir Kahane who are members of now outlawed organizations such as Kach and Kahane Hai, are outright racists. They characterize Arabs as the Canaanites that the Torah ordered the children of Israel to extirpate. The question is: Where did they get such extreme attitudes, attitudes that almost no *sabras* share? While it is impossible to prove, such attitudes were probably born in places like Crown Heights and Brooklyn, New York, where black-Jewish relations have long been extremely tense. It seems that some of these individuals have transferred their anti-black bias in America to an anti-Arab bias in Israel.

There are, admittedly, only a few hundred people in this category. But it takes only a few—like Baruch Goldstein, who murdered twenty-nine Arabs in a Hebron mosque in February 1994 and set the peace process on its heels for months—to do a great deal of damage. For some reason, some people more than others need enemies to define themselves. These appear to be such people.

So much for what a range of Israeli Jews think of Arabs. What do Israeli Arabs think of Israeli Jews and the state of Israel? The best answer is: it varies.

Most Israeli Arabs are naturally ambivalent about Israel. On the one hand, deep in their hearts they see the country as Palestine and believe that it ought to belong to them. In one recent poll, some 25 percent of Israeli Arabs said they did not think Israel had a right to exist. They see the Jews as usurpers, and they resent the de facto second-class treatment they have received over the years. They understand perfectly well that Israel is a Jewish state, and that this forever excludes them from full integration in the community. Israeli democracy can never work fully for them, and they know it. They feel a kindred spirit with other Palestinians, and with Arabs in general, and the Muslims among them, who are the large majority, increasingly feel fellowship for other Muslims—as noted, religiosity is spreading rapidly among Israeli Arabs.

On the other hand, Israeli Arabs know Israeli Jews face-to-face, and they therefore have never been able to accept the fantastic stereotypes that the leaders of the Arab states have perpetrated among their own people. They also appreciate the standard of living they enjoy; remember, the Arabs who became citizens of Israel in 1948 were at the lowest socioeconomic rung of Palestinian Arab society, and the relative rise in their living standard has been meteoric. They have running water, paved roads, decent housing, schools for their children, health care, abundant food, electrical service, telephones, modern agricultural equipment—all are revolutionary compared to their situation before 1948. Some Israeli Arabs are, in fact, quite wealthy.

Israeli Arabs have also come to appreciate the benefits of democracy. Since 1949 there have been Arab members of Knesset, and Arab municipalities have been able to run their affairs according to democratic procedure. This has not been universally true within the Arab world, to put it mildly, and most Israeli Arabs know it.

Arabs have also retained their cultural autonomy for the most part; they have their own schools in Arabic, and have not been forced to conform to Hebrew texts or culture. They do get a moderate dose of Hebrew literature and culture, however, which has had the paradoxical effect of helping the community learn to articulate its interests within the predominate Jewish culture.

Additionally, although they will not often say so in public, some Christian Arabs see Israel as protection against the rising sea of Islam in which they live. Israel lets Christian Arabs use their own school books, something they would probably not be allowed to do in a Muslim-dominated environment. Christian Arab citizens of Israel thus feel even more ambivalent about Israel than most.[9]

So it is not just a matter of Ashkenazim against Sepharadim, and Arabs against Jews in some simple way. Nothing in Israel is that simple.

The Role of External Threat and the IDF

It is hard to exaggerate the role of Israeli threat perception in the development of Israeli society. The Yishuv encountered conflict with the Arabs almost from the start, developed its strength during Mandate times in the shadow of near constant challenge, and began independence in war. Ever since, whether realistically or not, Israelis have lived with a sense of siege, believing that if they lost just one war, that would be the end of the state and the end of them all. This is a tough way to live even after people "get used to it." But there was no choice. As one Israeli wit put it: "The Zionist founders, in their great wisdom, decided to plop the country down in the midst of 100 million mostly hostile Arabs. So what did they expect to happen?"

There have been three major implications of the sense of protracted siege, and several minor ones.

First, the military establishment, the Israeli Defense Force (IDF), has been an extremely important social institution. Being a professional soldier in Israel is a very high-status profession. Being a member of an elite battalion, such as the Golani Brigade, is the dream of thousands of boys. Far more Israeli youngsters want to be air force pilots than wealthy businessmen or movie stars or sports heroes. Israel's best and brightest have traditionally been attracted to the military, and the status it has afforded them has often worked as a wedge to enter politics and academia, too. Prime Minister Yitzhak Rabin was an army general, a veteran of the *Palmah*, and was chief of staff during the June 1967 War. Ehud Barak, the current prime minister, was also chief-of-staff and is the most decorated Israeli soldier ever.

Rabin and Barak are the only two Israeli prime ministers who were also military heroes, but many other generals have served in high political positions over the years: Moshe Dayan, Yigal Allon, Ezer Weizmann, Haim Herzog, Ariel Sharon, and many others. Right-wing political parties tend to attract generals as heads, too. Rafael Eytan heads the now out-of-Knesset Tzomet party, but Tzomet was in Knesset for several consecutive sessions. Rehavam Ze'evi heads the far right, pro-transfer, Moledet party. The outer left wing attracts them as well, however: for example, the late Matityahu Peled served on the general staff, and Colonel Meir Pa'il remains active in various left-wing groups. It is not uncommon in security debates in Israel for opposing sides to marshal "their" generals to support their views, and there are plenty of generals and colonels with opposing viewpoints to go around.

As a result of pressing security concerns, the military has always had a large claim on the state budget, and with budgetary clout usually comes power and influence. Israel is no different. This is also why, in Israel, the Ministry of Defense is usually thought of as the key civilian cabinet post, even more prestigious than the foreign minister much of the time, depending on the personalities and their relationship to the prime minister.

And because the military has been so important, and because the military elite have tended to come disproportionately from Labor Zionist institutions—particularly the *kibbutzim* (including Prime Minister Barak)—the political views of the upper echelon of the Israeli military have tended to be left of center. This contrasts sharply with many countries, where the military tends to be a focus of conservative and "hawkish" opinion. Traditionally, the opposite has been the case in Israel.

Second, because the population is small and a standing regular army could not suffice in an emergency, Israel had to have a people's army. Israel has mandatory, nearly universal conscription. After high school at age eighteen, everyone goes into the army, men for three years and women for two years. Everyone, male and female, is trained in weapons and tactics. Every male, too, has obligations for years beyond obligatory service to serve in reserve battalions. This involves retraining from time to time. Since threats to Israel have come in the form of irregular warfare and terrorism, Israelis believe it is important for everyone to know how to take care of himself—and herself—in a security emergency.

This sensitivity starts young. Even kindergarten children are taught how to react in case of a security emergency. American kids get fire drills and lectures about not taking candy from strangers—all very important. But in Israel, parents and teachers manage to communicate to children a level of gravity in such matters that is at least an order of magnitude or two more serious than is the case here. Kids grow up fast in Israel; there really hasn't been much choice.

In the United States, children are recombined as they go through school from year to year, assuming that there are enough kids to make up more than one class per grade level. Not in Israel, and this is deliberate. In Israel, children generally stay in the same groups all the way through school and go into the army together. There is thus from the start an effort to create a sense

---

Hit Him Back?!

When my youngest son, Nate, was five years old, he went to what is called *gan hovah* (the obligatory year of kindergarten before first grade). At first, it took him a while to get used to the roughness of the play. Boys would often greet each other in the morning by kicking and jumping on each other with glee. Nate's previous experience at day care in the United States had been a lot more genteel. One day I saw two boys square off in the playground, and one give the other a good pop to the chin. The victim ran to the teacher complaining that Yossi had hit him. The teacher said, quite typically: "Well, go hit him back." By the time this child gets to first grade, he knows not to embarrass himself by going to the teacher over such matters.

When Nate entered first grade back in the United States the next year, we were not surprised to learn that he was "a bit rough" with his friends.

---

of mutual obligation, a sense of community, a sense of camaraderie, and a sense of general equality. Israeli education also tends to stress bringing everyone along together in the class; far more attention is given to remediation for those students who need it than in stimulating or fast-tracking the very bright. By the time eighteen-year-old Israelis get to the army, they already know intimately those who go in with them, and they already know by second nature how to function and think as a unit.

Moreover, by the time Israelis are teenagers, they know about and think about going into the army, and they have to consider psychologically that they personally may have to go to war and either kill someone, risk being killed themselves, or watch their best friends get killed—which for most is even worse. American high school and college students have circles of friends and often think of them as being very tight. No doubt they are, but when American kids talk about being ready to die for a friend, they are almost invariably speaking figuratively. When Israelis talk about it, they mean it literally.

This strong sense of mutual obligation explains why the country as a whole is exhilarated when Israel displays its military prowess effectively. It's because nearly everyone can genuinely feel a part in and pride in the success. It's why the pain of a military failure or screw up is widely shared. It explains the anger against a reservist who in 1994 made a wrong turn into an Arab village, and was beaten and stabbed rather than use his weapon to defend himself, as he was trained. It explains the extraordinary interest in

---

Speaking of Emergencies

A friend of mine named Jan—a recent American immigrant to Israel—was terribly flustered at her job. She told us how coworkers would come to her near the end of the day, begging her to work overtime because of this or that *herum* (emergency). As an American, she took this seriously until her boss noticed and took pity on her: "In America, an emergency at work is a real emergency to people, but in Israel we use the word all the time. We live in an atmosphere of constant emergency. But an emergency in an office isn't really an emergency. Don't let people take advantage of you; just go home, and have a nice supper."

---

the fate of Israeli prisoners-of-war such as Ron Arad. The army command in essence tells its soldiers: do your best, put yourself out, take initiative, and if you get into trouble, we'll move heaven and earth to get you out of trouble. That bargain is sacred to Israelis, and that is why soldiers in captivity make national news daily, even if years have gone by since they've been taken or heard from.

It also explains Memorial Day, the fourth of Iyar. Israelis have designed an exquisite emotional roller-coaster. Memorial Day is the most solemn day of the year for most Israelis, even more important than Yom Kippur for secularists. At 11 A.M., Israel (at least all Jewish Israel) simply stops. Wailing sirens go off all over the country, and everyone observes a moment of absolute silence. Traffic stops. People get out of cars and buses and stand perfectly still. Many cry for the more than 17,000 Israeli soldiers who have died in action since 1948. And then as soon as night falls, Independence Day starts, which is filled with wild festivity, joy, fireworks, and celebration.

The contrast is stunning, and really is a fitting microcosm for Israel as a whole—from the depths of tragedy and grief to victory and celebration. This is nothing if not modern life imitating historic myth: Israeli war dead, Holocaust dead, and the Jewish dead from ages of exile and persecution merge into one, while the first independence day and every other independence day merge into one as well.

By and large, by the time they're done with obligatory army service, Israelis have internalized this formula wherein Israeli life recontains Jewish history and emerges triumphant. More practically speaking, they also know how to react quickly and effectively in emergencies, and most of them know what a real emergency looks and feels like. Most Israelis have been to war too, sometimes more than once, and that certainly qualifies as a personal emergency.

There are many other subtle effects of such experiences on Israeli society. One is a tolerance for government secrecy and selected abridgment of human rights. Most Israelis accept it as natural that some things should not be made public—what happens to citizens recruited to spy against Israel, for example. Until quite recently, no information was ever available about such individuals, the argument being that even the acknowledgment that such people existed harmed state security.

Also, most Israelis realize, and accept as necessary, that the security services use physical and sometimes very harsh interrogation methods against Arabs in the occupied territories who have been arrested for security violations. Why is this accepted? Because the information extracted from prisoners can be, and in fact has been, used to prevent other attacks that threaten the lives of Israeli civilian and military personnel. The general view is that the security of Israeli society, especially when it comes to matters of life and death, overrides the individual rights of Arab suspects. Many civil liberties advocates in America and Europe have difficulty with this view, but Israelis point out that they have little experience of the security dilemmas with which Israelis have lived for many long years.

Israelis long to relax, to be and feel normal, just like everyone else. And they do it whenever they can, and do it hard. Israelis have a reputation for fighting hard, playing hard, and relaxing hard. War and tension, absorbed from childhood, has given the entire society a hard edge. It's not that every male is a Rambo and every female, a Batwoman—not at all—but most Israelis understand the difference between what is really serious and what isn't. The army and security are serious, a lot more serious even than going to work, and certainly more serious than what's on TV.

It's so serious that politics, which can be very emotional and divisive in Israel, is not allowed in the army. The professional army is strictly enjoined to be professional; no partisanship is allowed. This is why so many Israelis were upset when some young recruits and some reservists refused to serve in the occupied territories. Even many of those with similar political views thought it wrong and dangerous to bring politics into the matter of national service; the majority view was that one does one's duty in the army, and exercises one's democratic rights outside of it. This parallels the theme of *taharat neshek* (purity of arms), where force is always used within the rules and in self- or national defense, never for personal emotional, political, or imperial purposes.[10]

It's so serious that Israelis try to cordon off the IDF from the foibles of normal life. Like anybody else, Israelis know how to goof off and kick back— even, lately, take drugs. But they don't do it in the army, don't want their children to do it when they go into the army, and when they hear of such things going on in the army, alarm bells go off big time.

Israelis do seem to live as if either in, or ready for, or waiting for, an emergency. They have gotten so used to it that it's almost a way of life. Relatedly, Israelis are addicted to the news, and the news comes on the radio every half hour. This habit primes people to expect excitement, usually of the unpleasant kind. People thus like to say things to the effect: "We have our problems, but at least it's never boring here." In short, Israelis have tried to make the best, culturally speaking, of a difficult situation, and in doing so have formed a part of their own national character. (That is, they have acted autogenically; remember from Chapter 1?)

To have a center of something indisputably serious in one's life is to change that life. When the whole society more or less has the same center, it creates a collective purposefulness that only certain types of hardship seem to be able to supply. One of the reasons that Israeli society coheres as well as it does is the common experience of army service and even war, and the common assumption that all individuals owe it to society to do their part. Mass societies that lack the immediacy of threat and the common experience of military service—like the United States—really are different kinds of communities. The sense of community is less intense. This is also why poor neighborhoods anywhere in the world, for all their problems, sometimes have a stronger sense of community than affluent ones.

Not surprisingly, perhaps, Israelis tend to have less tolerance for chit-chat and small talk than many Americans. It's hard to generalize, but they also tend not to like speaking of theories, generalities, or abstractions. This may not be a military attitude exactly, but it does seem related to one. Most Israelis like to come to and keep on the point when they're involved in something of importance to them. Americans are often said to be too brash, direct, and frank when they sit down to do business with Japanese, Chinese, Arabs, and Latin Americans. But Americans often find *Israelis* relatively brash, direct, and frank. Israelis, then, clearly cling to the far end of the scale as far as such traits are concerned.

Israelis are sometimes rude to an extent that it even bothers other Israelis. In 1995, Bezek, the telecommunications company, instituted a program to get people to be more polite on the telephone.[11] Few thought it had much chance of success. Besides, the curt nature of many Israelis is not a function of army experience and discipline alone. Several other reasons are often cited: histories of individual hardship; the sense of kindredness ("How polite are you to your brother?"); the revolt against Jewish diaspora meekness; the styles of socialism, and others beside. No one doubts that the tensions of everyday life, however, of which the sense of being part of a national army is key, play the largest role.

The third major impact is that army service and the sense of its supreme importance is a common experience. Sepharadic and Ashkenazic, secular and modern Orthodox—all experience the same basic system. With the exception of most, but not all, *haredim*—the non-Zionist Orthodox—everyone who is bodily able goes into the army. More important, immigrants to Israel, or surely their children if the immigrants are too old, go through it as well. Army service for immigrants or their children has traditionally been the critical means of integrating into the society, of learning the language, and of apprehending the zeitgeist of the country. Israeli leaders over the years understood this well; they knew the army (as well as the school system) was the key agent of socialization in a largely immigrant and very heterogeneous society, and they used it accordingly.

Indeed, had it not been for sharp Arab hostility in the early decades of the state, the army would not have become such an important institution, and Israeli society would not have congealed so quickly or so well. Arab political bombast after 1949, combined with Arab failure ever to mount a serious conventional military threat to Israel before 1967, played an important role in the strengthening Israeli society, which has always been the ultimate backbone of the state's security. To Israelis it was never clear that the Arabs would not again attack, and their threats had to be taken seriously despite their never having been implemented before the spring of 1967.

Quite aside from its social role, the IDF holds high status in the country for another, simple reason: its success. Every Jew in Israel is proud of what the Jewish army has been able to do. Not only did it defeat the Arabs in 1948, it deterred any major Arab threat until 1967. As we will examine in more detail in Chapter 6, in 1956 Israel invaded Egypt, seizing the Sinai Peninsula and moving to the banks of the Suez Canal, decimating the Egyptian army with astonishing quickness. Then, in 1967, an Arab alliance led by Egypt threatened Israel again. But Israel waged a preemptive war, stunning the Arabs and capturing the entire West Bank from Jordan—including the Old City of Jerusalem—the Golan Heights from Syria, and Gaza and the Sinai (again) from Egypt. In October 1973, after an initially successful attack by Egypt and Syria, Israel counterattacked, driving onto the African side of the Suez Canal and pushing the Syrians back toward Damascus. The roads to both Cairo and Damascus were open to the IDF.

Then on July 4, 1976, Israel pulled off the most spectacular in a series of stunning commando-style operations, freeing a hijacked airliner and its passengers at Entebbe, Uganda. (The commander was Ehud Barak.) In June 1981, the Israeli air force destroyed the Iraqi nuclear program by bombing the Osirak reactor in a surprise lightning strike. In 1982, Israel invaded Lebanon, defeated the Syrian army once more, and set siege to an Arab capital,

Beirut. In 1985, the air force bombed PLO headquarters in Tunis, 1,500 kilometers away. Israelis have lost faith in their leaders and their allies from time to time, but they have never lost faith in *Tzahal*.

Never lost faith, but in recent years the image of the IDF has been somewhat eroded. Several reasons may be proffered. First, as the security situation improves overall, the psychological need for the army recedes with it. Second, the budget has been reduced—from about 45 percent of the whole budget in 1984 to about 22 percent in 1995—and whenever in politics money flees, so eventually does status. Third, having to serve in the occupied territories, whether as regular army or reserve soldier, has reduced the luster of service. Fourth, there has been an increase in training accidents—including two disastrous and deadly ones in successive years at a camp in the Negev called Tze'elim—and this has reduced the confidence of parents who entrust the army to take care of their children. Fifth, there have been occasional lapses of professionalism and discipline as when, in 1994, a platoon of Israeli soldiers in southern Lebanon essentially ran away from its post before a small-scale Hizballah attack. And finally, drugs have gotten into the army, at least on a small scale, and this has knocked the army off its pedestal in the eyes of many older war veterans. Withal, the status of the IDF remains high.

The Managed Economy

We have already spoken of some of the basic predicates of the Israeli economy, especially *mamlakhtiyut*. The economy has been driven and shaped largely by the state, and before 1948 by the Vaad Leumi of the Jewish Agency and its associated organs such as the Jewish National Fund. This tendency has been a function of both ideology and the circumstances of Arab hostility and military siege. In 1999, about half of Israel's $98.5 billion GDP still flowed from central government expenditures, and that figure does not include vast parastatal economic activities vouchsafed within the Histadrut. We have also noted that the country is small and relatively arid, but it also happens to have few natural resources: scant forests for lumber, no significant deposits of valuable minerals aside from copper and potash, potassium, and magnesium within the salts of the Dead Sea. Also, Israel has virtually no oil or natural gas, making it dependent on external sources of energy.

The state also controls imports and exports fairly closely. While a free trade zone exists with the United States, based on an American decision of 1984, and a special arrangement short of that has existed between Israel and the European Community (now the European Union), import duties (called *mekhes*) are high on many goods—on automobiles, the *mekhes* rate is 95 percent, for example. This makes many imports extremely expensive, douses demand for many of them, and allows Israeli products to predominate in many areas through the strategy of import substitution.

Moreover, the country is populated by a diverse group whose mean population has been fairly young since 1948. Israel has had to spend high percentages of its resources on defense-related activities (25–45 percent of GNP compared to 5–8 percent in the United States), and it has repeatedly undertaken the costly job of integrating hundreds of thousands of immigrants into the society.

Under such circumstances, the general experience of other states would suggest that the Israeli economy has not been a success story. But that suggestion would be wrong. And this is not just because of high population growth rates on account of immigration, which will always swell GNP. Per capita income has increased as impressively as absolute GNP. Since 1948, Israel has consistently demonstrated high rates of economic growth (with the exception of the 1966–67 period). In forty years—that is to say, by 1988— Israel's GNP increased by a factor of 10 and the standard of living nearly quadrupled. For twenty years, between 1953 and 1973, Israel averaged gross domestic product (GDP) growth of nearly 10 percent—an amazing achievement. Equally amazing, during this period of high sustained growth the average inflation rate was only about 7 percent.

What this means in specific terms is that the Israeli population experienced fairly dramatic increases in the standard of living. For example, households with telephones increased from about 30 percent at the time of the June 1967 War to about 80 percent by 1990. The number of households with electric refrigerators increased from only about 30 percent in 1955 to 99 percent in 1980. Those owning washing machines increased from 9 percent in 1958 to 88 percent in 1990. Those households with private automobiles increased from 4 percent in 1962 to about 50 percent in 1990. The raw numbers are also impressive. For example, in 1965 there were about 68,000 telephone subscribers; today there are 2,656,000, and a huge proliferation of cell phones. In 1965 there were 24,000 private automobiles; today there are 1,229,000. In 1965, Israel shipped 3,520 tons of freight; today it ships 270,000 tons. In 1965, 110,000 tourists arrived in Israel; in 1999 the number will be about 2,300,000.

During this period Israel also managed to transform its economy from a mainly agrarian one to an economy with diversified agricultural, industrial, and service sectors and still maintain high levels of growth all along. Today, agriculture employs only 3 percent of the work force, contributes only 2 percent to GNP, only about 5 percent of exports, and only 2 percent of capital investment—all orders of magnitude decreases from Israel's first twenty years of independence. By the mid-1990s, Israelis enjoyed a standard of living comparable to that of Great Britain or Italy, with income distribution less widely skewed than either Britain or Italy. Life expectancy for woman was nearly 80 years by 1999, 75.5 years for men, rates that compare favorably with the most advanced countries.

By mid-1995, too, the unemployment rate was down to 6.9 percent, whereas the yearly rate for 1994 was 8.1 percent—but by mid-1999 it was back up to almost 9 percent. For a country that has absorbed 560,000 Soviet Jews in the last four or five years—nearly a tenth of the population—such generally low unemployment rates show the vitality of the economy more clearly than any other statistic.

Additionally, thanks to the collapse of the Arab boycott with the advance of the peace process in the early 1990s, and selected privatization measures undertaken by the government, most observers believe that Israel stands on the cusp of a huge economic boom. This boom is believed to be based on Israel's strategic location, and especially on its possession of a well-educated, talented, and competitively priced workforce suited perfectly to the requirements of the information age. By the mid-1990s, despite the fitful progress of privatization, that promise was in the midst of fulfillment.[12] Israel's economy in the 1991–96 period grew faster than any other industrial economy—averaging over 5.2 percent per year—with the lowest levels of unemployment in the country's history, and with modest rates of inflation.

What explains Israel's economic record? Three things really: a growing, diversely talented, ambitious, and patriotic workforce; massive capital subventions from abroad; and uncharacteristically efficient public-sector management. Let us speak briefly of each of these elements in turn.

As noted earlier, immigrant populations tend to be young and eager to achieve for themselves and their children. Immigrants to Israel were no exception and, if anything, their eagerness to work and work hard was sharpened by the cultural environment in which they found themselves. Labor Zionism has always had a strong work ethic, a belief that labor was noble and ennobling of the worker. That's mainly why the work week is six days long instead of five.[13] New citizens, who had often lived under economically straitened conditions as well as persecution, generally reacted to their new opportunity with enthusiasm even though, in the case of the Sepharadic immigrants of the 1950s, they lacked experience in the areas in which most became employed, such as agriculture and construction.

This enthusiasm was partly idealistic. While it may sound corny today, Jews who immigrated to Israel were encouraged to feel that they had finally "come home" and that they were home to stay. Through their work they built their own land, not that of someone else. A strong sense of community also encouraged people to pull their weight in their work as they did in their military obligations. In short, working hard was patriotic as well as self-interested. For an assortment of reasons, then, attitudes toward work were positive, and attitude counts for a lot in economic development.

The working population was overwhelmingly oriented toward "development," toward a rapid expansion of the economy in order to defend the state, encourage immigration, and generate higher standards of living. The fact that socialist ideology venerated work—even of Stakhanovite dimensions[14]—and disparaged soft living also helped. It is also important to remember that most of the people who came to Palestine, and then to Israel after 1948, were not particularly refined socially or genteel people. There were such Jews in Europe and in the East—court Jews, parlor Jews, Jewish capitalists and burghers—but they were usually not attracted by Zionist revolutionary asceticism and the prospect of scraping out a life in a hostile environment. Those who came were not predominantly Jews of the upper classes, but of the middle and working classes. They were used to labor, albeit not always of the same sort, even if they had never heard it praised as an ideological imperative. Such experience counted for a good deal in terms of morale.

The social origins of the majority of Israelis also explains a few traits that persist generally in Israeli society even today. We noted earlier that Israelis seem to outsiders somewhat gruff, and we noted that the pressures of living in a semi-mobilized, semi-militarized society over many years has contributed to this. But there is another reason for it. Most Israelis do not descend from genteel society, and their general cast of manners shows it. Other cultural factors aside for the moment, this unscrubbed demeanor is not different in essence from what would be found in the working-class neighborhoods of Manchester, Munich, Moscow, or Milwaukee.

Another spinoff of the "development" point of view and the social origins of the bulk of the Israeli population is the Israeli attitude toward the environment. As noted in Chapter 1, Israel seems dirty to most Americans. The landfills are overflowing. Garbage mounts up; there is a huge pile near the road to the airport—the Hiriya dump—that, some fear, may collapse in heavy winter rains and block the highway. The air and water do not meet American standards; indeed, as cars have proliferated, air quality has gotten worse, with Tel Aviv sometimes approaching Mexico City as the city with the worst air quality in the world. And while the environment has in recent years become a major concern, old attitudes—that such concerns are unaffordable bourgeois luxuries—are still prevalent. Many observers like to say that Israel is just twenty years or so behind the United States, which experienced its first Earth Day, after all, only in 1970. But it's more than that. It has to do with class status and class consciousness. To get the general point, compare what the streets look like in many urban working-class neighborhoods in North America with those in middle- and upper-middle-class suburbs. There's no time warp here; there's a socioeconomic class warp.

While the Israeli economy was primarily state-controlled in terms of the ownership of large industries, land (nearly 90 percent is still state-owned!), development planning, and pricing policies, the element of coercion typical of authoritarian socialism was largely missing from it in Israel. People had choices as to whether to live in the city or the country, to engage in agriculture or industry. They could start their own businesses if they really wished, and many did.

The relative openness of the economy is very important because immigrants came to Israel with diverse skills. Because the economy was relatively open, labor could pour itself into activities for which its experience and training were generally appropriate. This made the economic integration of immigrants easier than would otherwise have been the case.

Over the years, Israel has developed a reputation for having a well-educated workforce, and one adept at the key principle of economic modernization: adapting science to maximize a country's natural factor endowments of labor, capital, and resources. Israeli achievements in basic and applied science over the years have been extremely impressive. The Weizmann Institute in Rehovot and the Technion in Haifa are two of the most productive scientific research organizations in the world. The quality of graduate science education at Hebrew University, Tel Aviv University, Haifa University, and Ben-Gurion University is very good. Israel graduates more top-rate scientists than it can employ; large numbers of Israeli scientists and engineers end up living abroad for professional reasons.

Israel's success at science education and engineering—mainstays of a growing and diversifying economy—is both ironic and a little mysterious. Jews in exile had developed a reputation for bookishness. The scholarly achievements of religious Jews in religious endeavors, and subsequently their achievements in other endeavors, has always been something of a wonder to many people. This has led some (including some Jews) to believe simply that Jews are smarter than most other people, and this belief over the ages has led to no little amount of suspicion and hostility. Wiser people have explained this achievement by recourse to culture: education was seen as the key to both piety and worldly success, and generation after generation of Jews in exile impressed its importance on their children. In generational time, that which is esteemed and valued in any culture develops itself into a shared trait.

Early Labor Zionists, however, saw in Jewish bookishness a distorted personality and a general unhealthiness. They held that excessive intellectu-

---

A Five-Day Work Week?
A story is told that back in the early 1960s a young aide came to Prime Minister David Ben-Gurion and said to him: "Now that Israel is an established fact, with a growing economy and a more normal life, would you consider moving the country to a five-day work week?" To which Ben-Gurion reportedly answered: "A five-day work week, you say? Yes, I'll consider that. But first let's start with a one-day work week, then we'll move to a two-day work week, and then at that point we will make an evaluation of the situation. . . ."

---

alism was bad and needed to be balanced with manual labor and vigorous sport.[15] Indeed, many saw Jewish intellectualism as a form of escapism. The Israeli educational system has reflected this attitude by and large, eschewing—as noted above—fast-tracking superior students and teaching the superiority of strength, valor, and community instead. Indeed, until recently Israel did not spend that much money on elementary and secondary education. Teacher salaries have been low, leading to frequent strikes. Amazingly (to a typical American), the average Israeli tends to get angry at the teachers for inconveniencing them by striking rather than angry at the government for exploiting the teachers—which is why the strikes rarely achieve their goals. Schools are crowded and poorly maintained, hours are short, discipline is a problem, noise levels are excruciating, and standards are not high in many fields. The Israeli secular school system, it appears, has tried hard indeed to undo the exilic image of the bookish Jew.

And yet Israel still somehow turns out a highly literate, technically proficient and educated workforce—and, as noted, an impressive cadre of high-caliber scientists and engineers. Exactly how it does this isn't clear, even to Israelis. The most likely explanation is that a century of Zionism—and a far shorter time for many families living in Israel—has not even come close to eradicating Jewish exilic intellectual traditions, whose strength persists where intellectual habits are most strongly formed—by the family hearth.

There is also a puzzling debate within Israel about how hard Israelis work. The data show that Israelis do produce; their labor productivity per capita is among the highest in the world in certain selected categories, although it is on average at or near the bottom of the OECD countries. Hence, over the years many Israeli leaders have spoken despairingly about how lazy Israelis are.

In the late 1980s, an Israeli cabinet minister quipped that Israelis wanted to earn like Americans, live like Europeans, and work like Africans. This unfortunate remark was scored and the minister apologized, but the basic point is nevertheless clear: Israelis want the good life but don't want to work for it. (Why Israelis should be different from anyone else in this regard was never asked or explained.) Also, many employers in Israel in the 1980s used to remark that if it came to hiring Jews or Arabs to do manual labor, most employers would rather hire Arabs, not just because they were less expensive to hire but because they worked harder, complained less, and took fewer sick days.

What explains the divergence between the data and the "common knowledge" attitudes about Jewish labor in Israel? For one thing, the generation of founders did work extraordinarily hard, for the reasons given earlier. They were patriots and idealists exuding the sheen of freedom and the exhilarating sense of a historical homecoming. The second and third home-born generations simply could not keep up that kind of pace; they simply didn't have the same fire in the belly. So Israelis became "lazy" by Ben-Gurion's standards, he being a man who rarely slept more than three or four hours per night and whose appetite for work well into his seventies was legendary.

Also, Israelis have got somewhat softer with the coming of higher standards of living. This is a universal phenomenon. Just as one gets progressively less hungry as one's stomach fills up, people get less eager to work as their basic needs are satisfied. This is as true of the United States or Sweden as it is of Israel. Most Israelis don't even really work a six-day week anymore. Friday was always a shortened day because of the coming of the Sabbath at sundown, and there are chores and preparations to do: cleaning, shopping, cooking, and so forth. But whereas thirty years ago Israelis were accustomed to knocking off work two hours before sundown, now they knock off work four or five hours before sundown, which is the middle of the day most of the year.

Work patterns have changed, too, as Israel's economy has changed. In Israel's early years—and of course during pre-state times—agricultural work dominated the country and the towns and villages took their cues from the agricultural pattern that, in the eastern Mediterranean, follows the climate just as it does in other parts of the world with similar weather. In rural areas—on a *kibbutz* or *moshav*, for example—workers rise with the dawn and get in an hour or two of work before breakfast, which is a much larger meal than most Americans take in the morning.[16] Then it's back to work until around 1 P.M., after which the main meal of the day is taken. Then, because it's so hot, workers do not return to work but go home to rest, and most people get in a few hours sleep. By 4 or 5 in the afternoon, when the heat of the day dissipates, workers return to their chores and work usually until around 7 or 8 P.M. Then there's supper, a lighter meal, and afterward people socialize usually until quite late by American standards. As a result, most Israelis who live on agricultural settlements split their sleep into two shifts.

To accommodate this, stores would close after the midday meal and re-open in the afternoon and stay open into the evening. This pattern even dominated in large cities. So this is why schools go six days but let out early, and why Israelis start their socializing so late in the evening.

Life in the countryside has not changed very much, but in recent years, city life has adopted patterns resembling the kind of typical work schedule we have in North America—and more than 90 percent of Israelis live in cities. There are several reasons for this. First, increasingly less of the popu-lation is engaged in work out of doors, so the weather is less a factor in fatigue. Thirty years ago, too, there was little air-conditioning; now nearly everything is air-conditioned. Second, more people drive to a workplace away from where they live. It's very inconvenient and wasteful to go back and forth from home to work twice each day, especially with traffic being the way it is. And third, most of Europe and America do not operate on such a split schedule, so business suffers if it is connected to or dependent on relations abroad.

Despite the work pattern changes, social patterns have not all adapted. Parties still start late, stores are still open late. This is probably why more Israelis complain of being tired these days. Attitudes remain the same to a considerable extent, for better and for worse.

Israelis as a group may work less hard and also in different patterns than they did thirty years ago, but they still work hard compared to many other societies. Moreover, immigrants still have the taste for income and con-sumption. Most important perhaps, productivity has stayed relatively high largely because technological innovation has picked up where individual motivation may have gone down. As the economy became more technically sophisticated, it became more important to work smart than to work hard, and Israelis seem to be getting the hang of it.

One of the factors that has enabled the transformation of the economy, and that has augured for the generally increasing importance of capital to labor, is the steady inflow of capital from abroad. Israel has imported capital since 1948. During Israel's first thirty years, inflows of capital were a very large percentage of domestic capital formation, and most of this capital was used for investment in industry. Where did it all come from? It came from wealthy Jews abroad, from immigrants bringing their assets with them, from loans and grants from the U.S. government and German reparations, and from the sale of bonds. From all these sources, capital inputs in the form of unilateral transfers to Israel amounted to about $7 billion between 1948 and 1967.

What? Me Do It?

The collectivist mind-set of socialist Zionism, reinforced by the IDF experience, has had multiple effects on Israeli society, not all of them benign. For example, people will not generally take the initiative to, say, clean up the garbage and broken glass in a children's playground because they assume it's someone else's job. When my wife took it upon herself to do a little general maintenance at the new *gan* down the street, one woman came over and asked: "Why are you doing this?"

"Because it's filthy and unsafe here," my wife answered. "Want to help me?"

"It is not necessary for us to do this; the city pays people to do it."

"But this place has been a mess for months and it gets worse every day. Come on; it'll only take ten minutes to make a difference."

Confronted with such alien but irrefutable logic, the woman had no choice but to agree. "She had a strange look on her face the whole time," my wife reported to me, "like she had just discovered something, but couldn't figure out exactly what it was."

That may not sound like much to U.S. citizens, who are used to figures that fit with a population in the hundreds of millions, but in Israeli terms it's a lot of money. If the U.S. population was, very roughly, fifty times the size of Israel's during this period (4 million to 200 million), then on a rough per capita basis, $7 billion in Israeli standards translates to $350 billion (over about nineteen years) by our standards. That's a lot of money.

Since the early 1970s, German reparations and transfers from individuals have become relatively less significant, and aid from the United States relatively more important. Also, since 1986, all U.S. aid to Israel has been in the form of grants, as opposed to long-term low-interest loans. (We return to discuss the U.S. aid package to Israel in Chapter 6.)

Another change is that Israelis save less than they used to; this applies both to individuals and to the government. In the earlier years of the state, most capital was invested, little consumed. As the economy grew, so did attitudes toward consumption. Early in the life of the state, austerity was a necessity reinforced by ideology and patriotism. Over time, austerity eased and attitudes changed; people earned more, spent more, wanted more. This put individual attitudes in conflict with government priorities from time to time. Over time, Israel developed a chronic trade deficit, and the government also was burdened by relatively large debt service in the late 1960s, 1970s, and much of the 1980s. By 1983, Israel's foreign debt per capita was said to be the highest in the world; things have improved since then. Israel's main exports have been diamonds (industrial and jewel quality), citrus, flowers, textiles, chemicals, and industrial products and components. Imports have included food and a whole host of industrial and consumer goods.

Israelis also love to travel abroad, but when they do, they spend hard currency, so the government imposed a stiff travel tax (since rescinded). Until recently, it was also illegal for the average Israeli to buy, own, or keep hard currency for purposes of speculation. To buy hard currency for a trip abroad, a citizen had to bring valid tickets and a valid passport to the bank, where all transactions were recorded and certified in triplicate. This was partly because the government wanted to keep hard currency earned from imports so that it could pay its debts. It was also to maintain the currency; if everyone sold sheqels to buy more stable dollars or deutschmark, then the Israeli currency would become close to worthless, as many currencies in the world really are. This was a matter not only of economic policy but of national pride. Now restrictions on foreign accounts and holding foreign currencies have been liberalized. This has eliminated a black market for foreign currencies, and in a way, is also a sign of pride that the sheqel can compete, at least among Israelis, with other hard currencies.

Israelis also wanted increasingly to import items; the government kept duties high so that domestically produced goods would prevail, and with them the jobs of Labor party-voting Histadrut-member workers. But this also kept the trade balance manageable, and helped stabilize the value of the currency to some degree. On the other hand, a little inflation, as long as it was predictable and more or less under control, was of use to the government because a gradually eroding currency made Israeli goods cheaper abroad and imports more expensive. All else being equal, that's good for balance-of-payments purposes.

The system worked fairly well most of the time. To meet its own financial obligations and take care of political constituencies—especially in an economic system that is highly public-sector oriented—the Israeli government usually elected to print more money, especially just before an election. More money chasing a stable supply of goods will always produce inflation, but as noted, this can be controlled and a government often has incentives to generate some inflation, as explained just above.[17] Moreover, in Israel salaries are indexed to inflation so inflation does not produce sharp reductions in living standards or gross inequalities between those who depend on salaries for a living and those who don't.

Israel nevertheless has dealt with bouts of out-of-control inflation since 1948. Before the early 1970s, inflation was single digit and manageable. It hit 12.0 percent in 1970, was at 39.7 percent by 1974, 50.6 percent by 1978,

131.0 percent by 1981, and 145.6 percent by 1983. At the time of the 1984 election, the yearly rate of inflation was estimated to be about 400 percent.

How did this happen? Before the October 1973 War, Israeli economists were worried about a superheated economy pushing inflation rates higher. Relatedly, imports grew too fast, leading to a worsening balance-of-payments problem and a sharp increase in foreign debt. So the government of Golda Meir deliberately tried to slow growth, largely by raising taxes. Then came the war, which made all the economic problems worse. Tourism declined, replacing lost military equipment was expensive, and production sagged. So by 1977 Israel ended up with low real growth rates and high inflation simultaneously.

The sharp inflation of the 1980s occurred for several additional reasons. One was that the high rate of economic growth, resumed after the 1967 War, fell off after 1972 and did not recover, while government expenditures remained high and new capital imports did not make up for the shortfall. Things got out of hand, too, for reasons of sheer mismanagement. Likud finance ministers, as representatives of a right-of-center, non-socialist party, tried to desocialize Israel's economy, but Likud was not about to end the patronage system that had always proved to be so politically potent. So it didn't reduce the public sector; indeed, under Likud, the percentage of Israel's economy that was government dominated actually grew: the percentage of Israelis working in the public sector grew from 26.1 percent in 1976 to 31.0 in 1991. Instead, Likud ministers tampered with the economy around the margins, reducing subsidies, freezing some government wages, and limiting civil service employment growth. Most foreign currency regulations were abandoned, the currency was left to float against the dollar, and depreciation was expected to restrain imports and help exports. To reduce inflation, still more taxes (this time a 12 percent value added tax, or VAT) were imposed to reduce consumption.

It didn't work. The fact that salaries were indexed to inflation fed the spiral and inflation worsened. With imports reduced too and less import duty collection, a government deficit emerged. It was financed by selling bonds to Israel's Central Bank (since no one else would buy them). This made tight monetary policy hard to implement and, worse, in advance of the 1981 election, the government printed way, way too much money.

The sharp inflation of the 1980s was solved by the Labor government led by Shimon Peres between 1984 and 1986. In a remarkable demonstration of social coherence very hard to come by in larger societies, a social compact was made in which everyone agreed to tighten their belts and share the pain of adjustment. Both wages and prices were frozen, the money supply was restricted, and certain imports were banned by fiat. The government spent

---

Another Zionist Success Story . . .
The mismanaging of the economy resulted in several philosophical jokes, one of which, for our purposes, is illuminating. Zionism, in its effort to make the new Jew, wanted to overturn traits Jews picked up in exile. In exile, Jews didn't speak Hebrew; in Israel, they would. In exile, Jews didn't fight for their rights; in Israel, they would. In exile, Jews were scrawny and bookish; in Israel, they'd be healthy and strong. In exile, it was said, Jews grew to be masters managing other people's money; in Israel, they'd show that they couldn't even manage their own, and a 400 percent inflation rate proved that beyond all doubt!

---

less, people spent less, inflation was broken, and for about a decade the rate of inflation was back down to single digits.[18]

The inflationary experience, however, was long lasting. Remember we noted earlier that Israelis tend to run deficits in their personal bank accounts? One of the reason is the experience of the 1980s. If someone's money will buy more today than it will next week, and even less than that next month, why save it? Heck, spend it; and ever since that's what many Israelis have done.

The inflation debacle was especially important because, more than any other single phenomenon, it convinced Israelis that they should reduce the scope of the public sector and privatize the economy to a considerable degree. Given the political obstacles, the need for public resources to spend money on defense, and the legacy of Labor Zionist economics, it has not been easy to do this, but progress has been made. In 1998 and 1999, the government even undertook to sell 49 percent of the national airline, El Al, one of the symbols of state achievement.

Ironically, however, the inflation debacle virtually wrecked the Israeli banking system, and the government decided to buy most of the banks in order to prevent their collapse. The government, however, has been slow to sell off its shares, largely because, upon economic recovery, banking turned out to be a lucrative business—as it usually is. This is so despite government regulations preventing banks from investing in real estate, insurance, and certain other business activities.

So crosscutting incentives, some favoring privatization and some retarding it, are still at work in Israel. Favoring privatization are most businessmen and professional economists; opposing it are the unions, the Labor party apparatus associated with the unions, and those who fear that unbridled capitalism will undermine social cohesion by undermining the welfare system and creating too much disparity in income and private wealth. Let two examples suffice here.

Bezek is the government-controlled company that runs the telephones, television connections, and virtually everything else bearing on communications. It was decided some years ago to limit Bezek's monopoly power; cable television and international telephone service would be opened for competition, for example. But Bezek workers are unionized under the Histadrut—which has 750 thousand members out of a total work force of 1.9 million—and in October 1992 they went on a campaign of disruption and strikes to overturn the considered policy of both a Likud and a Labor government. Everyone knows that privatizing at least some of what Bezek does will create jobs—and better-paying jobs than Bezek workers have now—in response to a vibrant Israeli private market for communications technology services and products. It will benefit consumers and provide more revenue to government. Such knowledge, however, does not always move the Histadrut.

An even better example of how money, bureaucracy, and inbred patronage work in Israel is provided by the storm over the financing and organization of *Kupat Holim Klalit*. Kupat Holim Klalit is the far-flung institution that takes care of the health needs of about 80 percent of Israelis. It is part of the Histadrut. It is worse than broke, and everyone knows that the reason owes much to its subordinate relationship to the Histadrut. Put simply, the Histadrut draws from the hefty salary deductions people pay for Kupat Holim in order to support and succor its administrative staffs.

The Histadrut has solemnly made repeated promises of internal reform to benefit Kupat Holim, and broken every one. From 1992 to 1995, the Israeli Labor government struggled to find a way to free Kupat Holim from the clutches of the Histadrut. Thanks to the efforts of the first health minister, Haim Ramon, something started to happen in February 1993. The prime minister pronounced himself in favor of Ramon's plan, the doctors liked it, and even the relevant Knesset committee was dragged along. Then it died. Why?

For one thing, workers everywhere try to save their jobs and benefits even if what they are doing is not efficient for the economy as a whole. They can be boisterous and effective despite the fact that Israelis have yet to discover the picket line, or any other straight line for that matter. (Strike days usually signal extra time to shop and run errands, which is why members of the inconvenienced public tend to snigger when it rains on a strike day.) But the real Israeli difference remains this: the Histadrut is part of the labor movement, and any Labor party government in effect comes from the same place. Thus, the then newly elected chairman of the party, Nissim Zvilli, publicly excoriated Ramon when he dared suggest that Kupat Holim Klalit be made independent of the Histadrut. Soon thereafter, the Labor Party Central Committee forbade Ramon—who was, it bears repeating, a party mem-

ber and the government's health minister—from introducing his bill into
Knesset. This would be, in American terms, like the head of the AFL-CIO
ordering a cabinet member in a Democratic administration to do or not do
his bidding.

In 1995, the image of the Histadrut dove further with revelations of corruption of various sorts. Evidence arose that some politicians whose base
was the Histadrut illegally used union money to finance their campaigns.
That included Israel Kesser, former head of the union, who became transportation minister in the Rabin government. Then, in April 1995, a Magistrate Court in Tel Aviv approved an extension of the detention of Arthur
Yisraelovich, treasurer of the Histadrut for the last twenty years, for funnel-
ing money to several political campaigns.[19]

The Histadrut is only one bureaucracy in Israel, however. There are many
others. Individuals tend to interact with the public sphere in Israel in a predictable way. Basically, government bureaucrats build a wall of You Can'ts
by requiring signatures and stamps. The structure is so brittle that citizens
then proceed to find ways around the official channels. This sometimes takes
longer and costs more than doing things the ordinary way, but since there's
always the chance of beating the system, most people find it irresistible to
try. The same goes for obeying traffic signals and speed limits, which leads
to carnage on the highways nearly every Friday and Saturday night.

One shouldn't exaggerate Israel's bureaucratic problem, however. For
the ordinary person, red tape in Israel isn't more bothersome than it is in the
United States. Many procedures seem to have no rationale whatsoever, but
Israel is small enough that people can usually find a human being who more
or less knows what's going on. Most bureaucrats won't go out of their way
to be helpful—many believe that the public exists to serve them rather than
the other way around—but if citizens put the right question to them, they
will give the right answer. If, additionally, citizens do the most amazingly
unexpected thing of all—smile at them—some bureaucrats are actually
friendly.

As always, it seems, it's the businessman, especially the small businessman, who is most plagued by bureaucracy—and with him the
would-be foreign investor. But foreign investment is not impossible in
Israel, and on paper Israel has liberal rules concerning it. Unlike the
case with many governments, Israel permits 100 percent foreign ownership of businesses and sometimes allows tax holidays as investment
incentives. It also applies its regulatory laws evenly and consistently,
and there is no danger of sudden nationalization, as has been the case
elsewhere. Besides, to again compare with matters in the United States,
ask a small U.S. businessman tabout how helpful the U.S. federal gov-

ernment is and prepare to be sent from the room shrieking in horror from tales of bureaucratic sabotage and hernias caused by the weight of accumulated paper and dried clotted ink. In short, bureaucracy could be a lot worse in Israel. It could be Russia.

Without doubt, Israeli bureaucratic routines raise the cost of doing business and hurt the economy. A group of wealthy American Jews began trying in 1992 to establish a free trade zone (FTZ) in Israel, which they claimed would create 20,000 jobs without costing the taxpayers or the government a single sheqel. From the looks of free trade zones elsewhere, there was no reason to doubt them. The Knesset had to pass a law for the zone to come into being, and after a good deal of difficulty it finally did in 1994. Opponents argued that if manufacturers in the FTZ were exempt from government taxes and benefits, then all manufacturers in Israel would demand similar treatment and the government would be out billions of sheqels. Those in favor of the FTZ showed that actually the government would not be out a single agarah because government subsidies to exporters exceed revenues collected therefrom as it is. But even if this claim were true, note the presumption in this argument: that the business sector exists to provide money to the government rather than that the government exists to provide basic services to the economy. This, in a nutshell, is what's the matter with the Israeli economy. The zone, if it is ever allowed to work as advertised, could be helpful generally as well as beneficial economically simply by demonstrating that there are other ways to do things.

Finally, we come to the third factor in Israel's economic success: public-sector management. We have mentioned the government role in the economy several times in various contexts, and that is because it is unavoidable at every turn. Socialist ideology, the nature of the Yishuv as a largely immigrant community in a hostile environment, the security burden, the mammoth job of integrating huge numbers of immigrants and refugees all augured for a large government role at the outset in society as a whole, including the economy. So did the fact that, as noted earlier, economic planning was never wholly separate from security planning, and the market could not be trusted to result in a population efficiently dispersed from a security perspective.

As time passed too, the fact that capital inputs arrived to Israel less through private investment and more in subventions directly to government helped maintain the government's central role. Wise investment of capital in science and technology paid off handsomely, and there is general recognition that without government input this would probably not have occurred. Given these necessities and benefits, Israelis have gotten used to and have mainly accepted the costs of government management of the economy.

The Israeli economy, for example, has always lived with price controls on basic food staples, and it still does. In the beginning, this arose from literal scarcity, the need to feed yet-to-be-employed immigrants, and the willingness of food producers to accept social responsibility over profit motives—after all, *kibbutzim*, as socialist collectives, did not see maximizing profit as their raison d'être. Price controls still have the effect of smoothing out income disparities in a country still unwilling to accept very sharp socioeconomic class divisions. Basic foods are cheap and of high quality. Mainly however, price controls nowadays benefit local producers by guaranteeing them a certain market and a certain income. In many cases, competitive imports are simply banned. A true story about a potato makes the point well.

In February 1993, as McDonald's pursued its ambition to set up shop in Israel to vie with the local Burger Ranch chain, as well as Burger King, in the burgeoning fast-food industry, a problem arose: the kind of potatoes McDonald's uses to make its fries are not grown in Israel. Since McDonald's insists with an energy bordering on obsession that its meals taste uniformly the same from Moscow to Minneapolis, it wished to import the spuds. Moreover, since Israel is not set up to cut and process the potatoes according to the McDonald's system, McDonald's executives planned to import the potatoes already cut and frozen. The Israeli government said no; use local potatoes and processing facilities or no deal. The Agriculture Ministry, wishing to protect local farmers' interests, agreed to subsidize Kibbutz Sa'ad to grow the right crop.

The economic stupidity of this decision was transparent to anyone who had passed Economics 101. If McDonald's set up shop and imported its potatoes, it would not take long before Israeli farmers and food processors would seek to penetrate that lucrative market, with or without government encouragement, and they could easily compete with imports because they don't need to worry about import duty or significant transportation costs. But the Israeli Agriculture Ministry chose instead to subsidize potato farming, restrict imports, and in effect support a production cartel. As a result, the Israeli taxpayer stood to get fingers stuck in both eyes: one from the cost of the subsidies their taxes support and the other from the higher prices for the product that inevitably result from a production cartel. (In the end a compromise was worked out: the Israeli factory was modernized and new strains of potatoes grown to suit McDonald's specifications.)

We have already related how well the Israeli system worked in the Yishuv and during the early years of the state. We have also mentioned the cost: driving many entrepreneurs away and depressing private investment in the economy in favor of public investment. Public investment and industry ownership by government, especially when conjoined with centrally planned development programs and price controls, has usually resulted in economic disaster elsewhere. The countries that once formed the Soviet Union are a dramatic case in point, but so is Cuba, Tanzania, Nicaragua under the Sandinistas, and dozens more cases. This is basically because people, no matter how clever, cannot be smarter than the market in distributing information about the rational employment of economic assets. This isn't a very idealistic or romantic sort of truth, but it's the truth just the same and every attempt to evade it provokes one kind of expense (economic) or another (political), or both. But if this is true, why didn't Israel become an economic disaster by the early 1960s?

Several reasons have already been mentioned: ideological consensus, a dominant agricultural sector *not* motivated by profit maximization, a lack of coercion with regard to the labor force, a highly motivated work-oriented growing population, and large infusions of capital from abroad. Another reason, however, is Israel's small size.

The transactional (bureaucratic) costs of centralized economic planning increase geometrically—not arithmetically—with the scale of the economy. Just as larger animals have to have proportionally larger bones to support their mass, larger economic systems engage more people, more resources, and more diversified transactions over greater physical space. Learning about it, monitoring it, ordering and implementing changes in it, collecting taxes in it, and providing services for it are all absolutely and relatively harder as scale increases, which is to say: economic management costs more and takes longer. When bureaucracy, which never produces anything, consumes relatively more resources it leaves less for the rest of the economy. In other words, while planning is never as smart as the market, its gets relatively stupider compared to the market as the absolute size of the economy grows. Israel is small, so costs have been relatively low.

Israelis still complain about bureaucracy, however. But everyone complains about bureaucracy. If we need government at all—and we do—there is going to be *some* bureaucracy. In the Israeli case, too, much public-sector bureaucracy is patronage based, although less than in the past. As we note again in Chapter 5, Israeli political parties are awarded control of various ministries in accord with the web of loyalties and exchanges that are integral to the political system. It is natural, therefore, that if a certain party maintains the portfolio for the postal system for several years, its supporters will come to hold public service jobs in post offices. (Any American who doesn't understand this has never left the suburbs.) In such circumstances, keeping one's job does not depend foremostly on job performance but on what we call connections—what Israelis call *protexia*. Whenever there is a situation like this anywhere in the world, there will be surly and undermotivated public servants. Israel has its share.

However, in the core economic sectors of the bureaucracy, despite the systematic distortions caused by price controls, professionals have done a relatively good job over the years in limiting the damage. One of the reasons is that many are drawn from the industries they come to control, so they understand how these industries work. In the Soviet Union, contrarily, there were "economic engineers" in the central planning ministries who generally knew nothing about the industries they were regulating. This makes a big difference.

And again, Israel is small and socially informal. If a planning mechanism isn't working and it's irritating the workers it affects, chances are that someone will complain and explain. Compare this to a situation where a mechanical engineer in, say, Yakutsk wanted to make a point to a faceless bureaucrat thousands of miles away in Moscow. This makes a bigger difference. Indeed, the American economic bureaucracy (vested in the Agriculture Department, the Commerce Department, parts of the Justice Department, parts of Housing and Urban Development, the Interstate Commerce Commission, the Food and Drug Administration, the Federal Communications Commission, and several other agencies that intervene in and distort the market), because it operates on a much larger scale economy, is probably more "expensive" and distortive of the American "capitalist" economy than Israel's bureaucracy is of the "socialist" Israeli economy.

A final point about the government role in the economy: Israeli security has depended, among other factors, on having a higher-quality military since it could not have a larger one than that of its combined adversaries. Quality is a function of many things—training, morale, experience, and tactical skill— but high-quality weapons help, too. A country as small as Israel cannot achieve full independence in the manufacture of sophisticated weaponry. It relies on the United States today, France in the past, for many high-tech items. But Israel has sought to make itself as independent as possible, and part of the reason is economic: it adds high-technology jobs in Israel.

In some areas, military electronics and avionics, for example, Israel has excelled in building military technology. On April 5, 1995, for example, Israel successfully launched an *Ofek-3* satellite on its own Shavit missile. For a country of less than 6 million people, this was quite a feat. But the capital costs involved in developing high-technology military systems are usually very high, and sometimes the only way to recoup such costs is to plan on an export market. Israel has developed such markets, and exports of weapons and related equipment have become a significant source of earnings. For various reasons, the government owns and manages Israel's defense industry, and invests in it as well. Since 1989, demand for Israel's defense-industry products has dropped, both because domestic needs are less and, after the Cold War, external demand is less as well. The market as a whole is more competitive, and Israel's government-owned defense industries were thrown into financial crisis.

In addition, the economic imperative to export has sometimes driven Israel's foreign policy and image into places the Israeli Foreign Ministry would rather not have seen it go. When Israeli munitions show up in places like Guatemala and Rwanda, it causes diplomatic heartburn. The problem, however, is just a manifestation of the continuing connection between economic management and security concerns, and the central role of the government in both.

While the basic principles of Israeli statism have not changed much, the economy has nevertheless changed within its strictures. It has grown tremendously in both absolute and per capita terms. It has diversified, moving from an agricultural to a mixed agricultural-industrial-service based economy. With these changes have come attitudinal shifts as well, especially as regard the role of ideology in society.

Ideology, as the term is usually used, refers to an explicit program of social and political policies based on a set of core values or principles. Ideology is not a blueprint exactly, more like a schematic or a template used to interpret reality and inform social and political change with positive meaning. It is no accident that the term ideology is associated with revolution, for it is during molten times that the intellectual and moral frameworks underpinning society come to the surface; the old values have become visible because they have become problematic, and new ones become explicit as a result. In normal societies, political and moral values usually flow smoothly into day-to-day affairs, become absorbed by them, and remain more or less transparent as long as they work to organize things well enough.

Zionism was very ideological in its early days; it was, after all, explicitly presiding over a social revolution whose necessity arose from the collapse of the old social and moral order in the diaspora. The revolution succeeded and then, like all such revolutions, it wound down and became normalized. Ideology, once explicit, became implicit, inhering in institutions and the orderliness of everyday life. Young Israelis, therefore, simply do not want to hear about Zionism cum ideology. When they are taught it in school by their elders, they usually express supreme boredom and sometimes ridicule the indoctrination-like methods some teachers use (because that's how it was taught to them).

But Zionism and socialism are inseparable in their origins, and so along with the casting aside of interest in heroic, mythipoetical versions of Zionist history, most Israelis have also cast away any interest in socialism as an ideology. This has given rise to a paradox: Israel is organized as a socialist system, but it is socialism without ideology. For reasons explained earlier, it is socialism that for the most part works, so it is socialism that is forgotten, so to speak. Contrast this with the situation in Eastern Europe and the Soviet Union between the 1950s and the 1980s. There one had the reverse: socialist ideology, but not socialism. The Communist elite—the *nomenclatura*—was the ruling class, enjoying all the perquisites of wealth, status, and privilege, and to the extent that social leveling took place in the rest of society, it was achieved by making everyone poor. The Communists talked all the time about socialism but never achieved it; Israelis more or less achieved it and now almost never talk about it.

One can see these changes, economic and attitudinal, in the example of the *kibbutz*. Gone are the days when microscopic ideological differences resulted in great arguments that ended up dividing *kibbutzim* with fences right down the middle of the settlement—as happened with Heftzi-Ba and Beit Alpha in the Jezreel Valley. Gone are the days when *kibbutzim* were mainly agricultural. And while *kibbutzim* never held within them a large percentage of Israelis, today they are home for only about 2 percent of the population in some 250 communities, while about 400 *moshavim* house about 135,000 Israelis.[20] *Kibbutzim* also care a lot more about profit—even though it's collective profit rather than individual profit—than they used to; it has become an economic necessity. And they function less and less as a true collective.

Take kibbutz Revivim in the northern Negev, for example. It used to be totally agricultural, children all lived in children's houses, and members' dwellings were deliberately modest and ascetic as befitting the revolutionary personality. They also used to take pride in rotating most jobs so that subclasses would not develop on the *kibbutz*, and so that the least pleasant work—like cleaning out chicken coops in 112 degree weather—would not have to be done by the same people all the time.

Today Revivim is at least half engaged in industry. While most other *kibbutzim* specialize in agriculture-related manufacturing, such as irrigation systems, processed food and food-processing equipment, and so forth, at Revivim there's a state-of-the-art specialized plastics fabrication factory, where precision parts are molded by computer design for medical, industrial, and other high-tech products. The *kibbutz* has paid to educate its members and their offspring in the necessary skills—engineering, design, computers, finance, marketing—and the labor structure of the *kibbutz* is very specialized; most jobs don't rotate anymore. The *kibbutz* also prides itself on having American and Australian *olim* (immigrants) whose excellent English skills have been put to work nurturing and managing the factory's expanding international business connections. The members' homes are increasingly elegant; they look a lot like the sort of low-rise condominium and garden apartments to be found in nicer suburbs in the United States. They have kitchens, so people can eat their evening meal at home instead of in the communal dining hall, and the kids are around a lot after school and most sleep at home, too. There are still regular meetings, but they concern budget, planning, jobs, and the distribution of new perquisites; *not* the lofty teachings of Marx, Borochov, or Ben-Gurion.

Kibbutzim are also in business together. The Kibbutz Hotel Chain is the largest chain in Israel, with thirty hotels and thirty more bed-and-breakfast hostels. It caters to tourists and does very well. Relatedly, the *kibbutzim* also run water parks—with giant slides, wave machines, and children's amuse-ments—like the one at Shfayim near Herzliyya, which are profitable. Of course, all of this is a far cry from what socialist communalism was like in the 1950s.

Also, while society at large used to idealize the *kibbutzim* and their brave and idealistic members, many Israelis today think of the *kibbutz* as a curios-ity, and would have even a lower opinion of it than they do if it were not for the fact that Israel's best professional soldiers are often still of *kibbutz* back-ground. The typical city- or town-dwelling Israeli thinks of *kibbutz* life as incredibly boring and insular, and would never put up with the intense peer pressures and gossip cauldron that characterize a *kibbutz*. Many also believe that if someone is not born to a *kibbutz*, the only people who would want to join one are social misfits who can't "make it" in the real world, or starry-eyed idealists from abroad who are dumb enough to think that it's actually great fun to work in a chicken coop in 112 degree heat.

Religion

Just as the Israeli state has been heavily involved in the economy, it has been heavily involved in religion. Given the Zionist movement's origin and inter-nal development, there was no choice in the matter. To explain how and why the relationship between religion and state in Israel came about, let me first describe the basic features of the parallel situation in America.

In America we speak of the separation of church and state. What this used to mean is that the state should not provide advantage to any one de-nomination over any other, not that the state should be anti-religion. The principle of state neutrality in religious disputes was learned the hard way from the Wars of the Reformation and the discrimination against heterodox Christian sects by the Church of England, the members of which made up the American colonies' earliest European population. Separation of church and state never meant the elimination of religious sensibilities and precepts from public life, nor that the government should not support religion so long as it did not unfairly empower or advantage one sect over another. Since virtually everyone was Christian in late eighteenth-century America, the idea of supporting religion without supporting a church was not a banal notion. All forms of Christianity shared certain principles that the state could recognize and promote. Certainly that's what Thomas Jefferson, who wrote Virginia's law of religious toleration, had in mind. He meant that whatever people couldn't agree on theologically should be kept private or inside their church, but that whatever they did agree upon would be, and should be, a natural and benign part of the public weal.

What has this got to do with Israel? The principle of there being a role for religion in Israel's public life is beyond debate because almost everyone accepts it; but the principle of toleration for diversity of beliefs and practices is also "beyond debate" in a different sense because the Orthodox religious establishment exerts itself to snuff it out. In short, the situation in Israel in this regard is nearly the exact opposite of the situation in the United States today. Here, official toleration of diverse beliefs and practices is accepted but public association with religion is not. In Israel, public association with religion is accepted but official toleration of diverse belief and practice is not.

There are three other crucial differences, too.

First, in America, whose origins are largely Protestant and whose political culture has been shaped by Protestant attitudes, religion has always been conceived as mainly a matter of private belief. This is enabled by the fact that, unlike both Judaism and Islam, Christianity has no canon of religious law whose expression and enforcement necessarily intrude into the public sphere.[21] Jewish thinking about these matters is very different: Judaism is oriented toward deeds more than beliefs, toward the social more than the individual. Religious law, whether dietary restriction, Sabbath observance, or even the prohibition against idolatry, does intrude into the public sphere.[22]

Second, ethnicity and religion are separate in America; there are Irish, Italian, Polish, German, Croatian, and Hispanic Catholics, and Protestants of English, Scottish, Welsh, French, German, and Scandinavian origins. But Jewishness combines peoplehood and faith. Moreover, Jews as an ethnic group did not possess a religion; in a way the religion possessed them, preserving and unifying the group throughout its exile. Without the binding, unifying force of Jewish religious law, Jews would not have survived their long and diverse exile as a single nation.

Third, in America, the religious identification of non-Jews is generally not linked in any important way to specific political histories. Lutherans or Methodists may have originated in a specific time and place in Germany during the sixteenth century, but that is not especially significant to Lutherans or Methodists in America today. That history and that place lack any sacred dimension; they have little or no connection to theology. Moreover, one could be a Lutheran or a Methodist in the Netherlands, or Zimbabwe, or Denmark, and it would make no difference theologically. But the religious identification of Jews in Israel is linked to the memory of the First and Second Commonwealths; it is history with a sacred dimension, and it is integral to the theological interpretation of Jewish history. As important, virtually all Jews know that Israel is the place that is most integral to Jews, and that Jerusalem is the place that is most integral to Israel. One can be a Jew anywhere, but there are some commandments that can be performed only in Israel. There is a sharp and indissoluble theological distinction between the land of Israel and everywhere else.

The fact that Jewish law by nature intrudes on the public domain in Israel, and is seen by the overwhelming majority of Jews as having a right to do so, begs the question of who is to be the agency of that intrusion. As we have seen, Zionism was on balance a secular movement whose relationship with traditional religion was always somewhat strained. Nevertheless, the great compromise institutionalized in 1948 between Labor Zionism and religious Zionism remains more or less intact today, and the reason it has is not just one of political convenience or ideological gridlock.

Few secular Zionists have ever been content to base Israel's claim to the land of Israel solely on pragmatic criteria such as acute need. Even Ben-Gurion, a very irreligious person by conventional standards, looked upon the Bible as the ultimate Jewish claim to the land of Israel. He saw that claim as more historic in nature than theological, to be sure, but even Ben-Gurion could not bring himself to see the Bible as just an ordinary book of history and literature. Ben-Gurion took a Hegelian view of history, seeing in it the transcendent patterns of human destiny, and the Bible was the key Jewish document of that history. This is hardly an attitude one would describe as pragmatic.

Besides, because of its deep historical sensibility, secular Zionism was, and is, fated to honor the religious civilization that preserved the Jewish people in exile, the twentieth-century disagreements between the two notwithstanding. Even for secularists, therefore, it was unthinkable that a Jewish state would have no Judaic content. And who besides rabbis could say authoritatively what that content ought to be? These are the questions and the problems that have kept the 1948 compromise alive. And it's a good thing for Israel that it is still alive.

We have already described in brief the general attitudes of secular Zionists, religious Zionists, and religious non-Zionists toward each other. Before we can move this analysis ahead, we need to describe the actual reality of religion in Israel.

Orthodox rabbis have a virtual monopoly on interpreting Judaism and Jewish law in Israel insofar as public policy is concerned. Two rabbis are of specific importance at any given time: the chief Ashkenazic rabbi and the chief Sepharadic rabbi.[23] They head the religious establishment, which consists of courts that adjudicate all matters having to do with marriage, divorce, abortion, adoption, and conversion. If they could, the rabbis would assume responsibility for the determination of who is a Jew for the purpose of defining who is eligible for citizenship under the Law of Return. This issue has come up repeatedly over the years, with the government always taking a more lenient position, and the rabbis almost always arguing for a stricter one—an argument that derives from the absence of any definition of a Jew in Israel's declaration of independence and from the basic compromise wrought in 1948. The decision concerning who is a Jew is vouchsafed in the Ministry of Absorption, not the Ministry of the Interior or the Religious Affairs Ministry, and this ministry has always been held by a non-religious party.

There are also rabbinical boards responsible for *kashrut* (dietary law) standards, public enforcement of the Sabbath, and the limits of archeological digs. (Chapter 5 tells more about this.) Most important perhaps, the rabbis oversee the religious school system, and they have curriculum input in textbooks used in non-religious schools.

These same concerns are handled for Muslims by Muslim clerics and for Christians by Christian clerics, as was the case in the *millet* system during the four centuries of the Ottoman Empire as well as during the British Mandate. Indeed, Israel's current system is inherited directly from the Ottoman method, as passed through the administrative prism of the British mandate. So this is nothing new; to the contrary, this system is very, very old.

The point is, there is no civil law pertaining to such matters in Israel. If a man and a woman who happen to be atheists want to get married, there are no justices of the peace to seek out. There are religious ceremonies, or there are no ceremonies. The only way to get around this is to leave the country temporarily; the rabbinical courts do recognize civil marriages performed outside of Israel. Israelis who insist on this, or who want to get a divorce without encountering the religious courts, often go to Cyprus. In Israel, Cyprus has roughly the same reputation and function as Elkton, Maryland, and Las Vegas, Nevada—locales known for their very casual attitude toward such ceremonies.

Because of this system, public functions in Israel do not take place on the Sabbath. No one is allowed to go to work in the government, say, on a religious holiday. The national airline, El Al, does not fly on the Sabbath or Jewish holidays and serves only kosher food. Non-kosher food cannot be sold in government buildings, either. Israeli diplomats and statesmen, when they travel abroad, are expected to honor these conditions in public functions, and most of the time they do.

But the rabbis don't get their way on everything. There have been huge arguments about public transportation on the Sabbath. The rabbis would like it all halted. Secularists refuse, so the compromise reached is that municipalities can decide based on their own local wishes. So in Jerusalem, there is no public transportation on the Sabbath, except Arab buses. Some neighborhoods close down their streets so outsiders cannot pass through, and if they do anyway, local residents have been known to pitch stones at them. In Haifa, however, there is public transportation on the Sabbath.

There has also been an argument over *kashrut*. Israeli secularists want to be able to import meat from anywhere they choose; the rabbis insist that all imported meat be kosher. If they had their way, the rabbis would also insist that all restaurants owned by Jews be kosher, but they don't have their way on these matters. Restaurants that want a kosher certification have to get it from the government rabbis, but if a restaurant doesn't want a certificate of *kashrut*, and wants to serve non-kosher meat raised, say, on a *kibbutz*, no one can stop it. Some anti-religious *kibbutzim* even raise and slaughter pigs. The rabbis got a law passed saying that pigs could not be raised on Israeli soil, so the pigs are raised on platforms so that their hoofs don't actually touch the ground.[24]

The rabbis can't even stop the Conservative and Reform movements, based mainly in the United States, from buying real estate, establishing synagogues and even private schools, running seminaries, and publishing books in Israel. All these institutions do exist on a small scale, but clergy from these movements cannot perform marriages or engage in any other official functions.[25]

This gets complicated when it comes to particulars. Suppose a Conservative rabbi marries a Jewish couple in, say, Hartford, Connecticut, and they have a son who later makes *aliyah* to Israel. Is he considered a Jew and eligible for citizenship? Yes. Are his parents recognized as being married so that he is not technically a bastard? Yes, but not because a Conservative rabbi performed the ceremony. They're married according to what we can term the Jewish version of common law marriage. Now suppose a Conservative or a Reform rabbi performs a conversion to Judaism in Hartford, and suppose it's the conversion of a woman.[26] If *her* son, raised all his life as a Jew, came to Israel at age twenty-two to make *aliyah*, would the Israeli rabbinate recognize him as a Jew?

For purposes of the Law of Return, current practice is to ignore the issue. But if that young man wants to marry a Jewish woman in Israel, he must first undergo a ritual conversion process accompanied by what is sometimes not an entirely hands-off circumcision ritual.[27] On several occasions, the religious parties in Israel have tried to pass a law on "who is a Jew," which comes down really to "who is a rabbi," which in turn comes down to the question of who can authorize a conversion, with all that implies for future generations. If such a law passed, then the answer to the above question—Is he Jewish?—would clearly be no. Many American Jews—those who affiliate with the Conservative or Reform movement—were appalled at this prospect because the personal status of many of them as Jews would have been called into question. This is still a divisive issue. It is the kind of problem that explains why a written constitution does not exist in Israel, for all such matters would have to be definitively settled first.

Now, it so happens that the majority of Jewish Israelis are not religious. This doesn't mean they don't believe in God; it just means that do not observe Jewish religious law (*halakha*) as interpreted through the tradition. It doesn't mean that they are ideological Labor Zionists who reject religious observance as a matter of principle, although some do. It's just that they live in a modern secular environment and religion is of limited importance to them. They learn Jewish history, traditions, culture, philosophy, and literature in public school. They get born, circumcised, *Bar Mitzvahed*, married, divorced, and buried according to Jewish religious law, and most are perfectly content with that most of the time.[28] They are not content, however, with rabbis trying to enforce their standards of observance on others with regard to what they do on their day off, where and what they can eat, and what the weekend bus schedules are going to be.

Indeed, there is much hostility to the Orthodox rabbinate among the majority (more than 70 percent of the Jewish population) of secular Israeli Jews. They see the rabbis as coercive and intolerant. They're not particularly agitated at the enforced second-class status of Conservative and Reform Jews in Israel because most wouldn't attend such services or use such schools anyway—they see this as an "American Jewish problem"—but they do tend to see it as a symptom of the rabbis' general intolerance and their appetite for power. They also see the Orthodox rabbis as excessively political and unspiritual, concerned with ritual and legal minutiae, but seeming never to have a word to say about kindness, humility, or God's love for humanity. Secular Israelis who are familiar with the situation in America sometimes remark that although Israel is full of rabbis, the average person doesn't "have a rabbi" like congregants have rabbis (or ministers or priests) here.

Relatedly, most secular Israelis resent the power of the religious political parties (discussed in Chapter 5) and especially their claim to huge chunks of the state budget for their own institutions. They distinguish, however, among religious groups.

Religious Zionists of the Rabbi Kook school of thinking are generally modern Orthodox. Making up 10 to 15 percent of the Jewish population, they dress normally—the men and boys wear knitted *kipot*, most married women cover their hair in public but few wear wigs—and they live all over the country, integrated with secular Israelis in the sense that, in any given apartment building in any given town, one will frequently find both religious and non-religious families. The women work outside the home. Most important, male and female alike go into the army and do reserve duty like everyone else. They're patriotic and they pull their weight. Nor do they vote as a solid block; many modern Orthodox vote for Labor or Likud instead.

The *haredim*, the non-Zionist Orthodox who wear the black hats and long coats, truly exasperate most secular Israelis. Making up perhaps 6 percent of the Jewish population, they are concentrated in and around Jerusalem and in B'nei Brak near Tel Aviv. They always live in their own neighborhoods and vote in block for Agudah Israel. Most speak Yiddish among themselves instead of Hebrew, although they all know Hebrew and use it when speaking with non-*haredim*.[29] *Haredi* women generally do not work outside their home community, and the majority of married women shave their heads and wear wigs.[30] Neither men nor women serve in the army—although in recent years some men have gone into army service. To be blunt, some secular Israelis see the *haredim* as fanatical atavistic freeloaders who have yet to discover modern hygiene. Divisions along similar lines between modern Orthodox and *haredim* are far milder, but not entirely absent.

The distaste that many secular Israelis—and again, they are the large majority—have for the Orthodox rabbinate and the *haredi* groups in the society has given rise to an odd phenomenon—odd to Americans, anyway. In Israel, the division between those who think of themselves as secular and those who think of themselves as religious is very stark. This is caused to a great extent by the division of the school system into secular and religious systems, so that through peer pressure the sense of distinction is built up from childhood. In the American Jewish community, there is a range of observances between strict Orthodoxy and secularism or assimilation. For example, many Conservative Jews attend synagogue fairly regularly and observe Jewish holidays, but do not keep *kashrut* (or keep it inside their homes but not outside them). Many avoid going to work on the Sabbath, but they do not follow strictly the prohibitions against driving a car, cooking, and so forth according to the religious law. Such in-between behavior is rarer in Israel—though not as rare as many think[31]—and many Israelis have a hard time understanding it.

So much for how secularists see the religious. Now, how do the religious see the secularists?

What's in a Name?

Some social divisions in Israel are evident even in the names people give their children. Orthodox Jews generally use names from the Bible: Avraham (Abraham), Itzhaq (Isaac), Ya'acov (Jacob), Yosef (Joseph), Moshe (Moses), Sara (Sarah), Rivkah (Rebecca), Rahel (Rachel), Hana (Hannah), Leah (Leah), Yehudit (Judith), Root (Ruth), Shmuel (Samuel), Natan (Nathan), Daveed (David), and so forth. *Haredim* use the same names but often say them with an old-fashioned European, Yiddish-like pronunciation, as with Avrom, Yankel, Moishe, Dovid, Shloimi, Sora, and so forth. Secular Israelis also pick Biblical names, but oftentimes somewhat less common ones, such as Itamar, Asher, Nimrod, and Boaz. But they also choose names after animals, flowers, and other natural phenomena: Tzvi (hart), Dov (bear), Tal (dew), Vered (rose), Shoshana (lily), Tikvah (hope), and Na'ava (comely). Often enough, to know the name is to know the background.

Modern Orthodox Israelis understand the origins of the state and the nature of Zionism, and they accept the fundamental precept of Rabbi Kook's teaching that God can use impious people in holy ways. Modern Orthodox hope and expect that Israeli society will become more religious over time, and they look forward to the remerger of the Jewish people and the erasure of divisions between Ashkenazic and Sephardic. *Haredim* do not see things this way at all. They believe that they are the true Jews, that they have a special relationship with God, and they live in Israel for religious reasons, not political ones. They coexist with the state, but are not really part of it. They look forward to the coming of the messiah and the redemption from heaven, at which time the secularists will be either transformed or pushed aside, and they will then rule as regent of the messiah. They therefore look upon Israeli secularists as lost souls, as virtual non-Jews. As a result of these attitudes, there is a deep divide in Israeli society between secular and religious viewpoints, and divisions within the camps.

Both as a social datum and as a molder of the public policy agenda, the secular-religious divide is more acute and more consequential for the future of state and society than the Ashkenazi-Sephardi divide. This is shown by the fact that, while the Sephardi groups tend to be less secular than the Ashkenazi ones, there are secularists of Sephardi origins. And they have more in common with and tend to vote in patterns similar to secular Ashkenazim rather than religious Sepharadim.

The secular-religious divide is a problem not just in the political sense but also in the wider social and cultural sense. Many would argue that unbridled secularism undermines social mores and cohesion over time, giving rise to a sense of purposelessness that generates alienation, the erosion of the family, crime, and various forms of escapism such as drug addiction. These are maladies common to all secular Western societies nowadays—including America—and it is no coincidence. On the other hand, forms of religion, such as that of the *haredim*, that try to freeze time or turn it backwards, become irrelevant to the needs of society and obscurantist in their own practices and understanding. That is why—in my view—both the maintenance of the Jewish character of the state and also the development of modern Orthodoxy in Israel is so important to Israel's future. Many believe, too, that Israel needs an even broader move toward religious pluralism to bridge the secular-religious divide. These are important issues because, as Deuteronomy says, "Men do not live by bread alone."[32]

But the secular-religious divide, deep as it is, should not be exaggerated. Again, most secularists are not anti-Jewish; they just oppose the lock the Orthodox rabbinate has on the state. Most desire that the state have a Jewish character, just as Thomas Jefferson believed that a religious sensibility should permeate American society. At the same time, modern Orthodox in Israel function as a buffer, and sometimes a bridge, between secularists and *haredim*. Things could be worse.

Relations with the Diaspora

We have already mentioned the relationship between the diaspora and Israel several times. From the diaspora has come capital and political support since the end of the nineteenth century. Much tourism to Israel, which is a mainstay of the economy, is undertaken by American, Canadian, British, French, and Australian Jews, as well as by non-Jews. Crucially, the diaspora is the source of new immigrant population, whether from the places noted above or, more likely, from the former Soviet Union, Latin America, and South Africa. We have noted the impact of official Orthodoxy in Israel on the sensibilities of Jews elsewhere.

But the diaspora is not just a place to Israelis, it is a concept that causes problems as well as confers benefits. Zionism is a negation of exile. Zionism presupposes that no refuge outside of Israel is ultimately safe or good for Jews. Zionism assumes that Jews in exile will perpetuate characteristics not of the Zionist new Jew but the old Jew of *galut*, and those unnatural characteristics should disappear. This is the myth. What happens when the reality turns out to be, or at least to seem, different?

The Zionist founders, like Ben-Gurion, were unbridled idealists who fully expected the majority of Jews worldwide to come to Israel in one or two generations. That didn't happen. Most people are not idealists; they don't live according to principles, and they don't generate transpersonal dreams that they then follow. In general, too, people don't move from a higher living standard to a lower living standard. More Israelis have left Israel for North America than North American Jews have left for Israel and, to committed Zionists, this really hurts.

Moreover, while some Jews in diaspora do exhibit characteristics of the old Jew—shyness and timidity, obsequiousness before power, bookishness, physical frailty[33]—most don't and, ironically, one of the reasons is the reflected light from Israeli strength and independence. Israel's birth, survival, and achievements have transformed Jewish self-images in diaspora, even though it hasn't brought these Jews literally to live in Israel. This is something Ben-Gurion and his colleagues apparently never expected. There is again Jewish creativity and growth in diaspora—in religion, literature, art, everything. This wasn't supposed to happen either.

Israel has been a refuge for Jews who needed it more than a spiritually liberating affirmation for Jews who wanted it. Israel's history so far has confirmed the Herzlian sense of its purpose more than the Ben-Gurion sense. The continued existence of the diaspora has eroded the Zionist prophecy, at least for the time being. That is why, incidentally, when Russian and Ethiopian Jews come in great numbers to Israel that native-born Israelis feel a rush of patriotism. This is what the state is for, especially to greet those who themselves are not just coming in desperation but with their Jewish hopes and dreams in train.

Israel and Zionism, truly, have a love-hate relationship with the diaspora. Israelis need and appreciate the diaspora for what it does for Israel, a state that does not hold even the majority of the world's Jews. But lots of Israelis resent it at the same time. Some particularly resent the American Jewish community, and it's worth a word or two to explain why.

America is to Israel both the rose and the thorn. It is a rose in the sense that the American government helps arm and protect Israel, and delivers vast amounts of largess out of an amalgam of idealism, enlightened self-interest, and political expediency. Additionally, American leadership of the democratic world, of which Israel is the only thoroughly Middle Eastern member (Turkey stands astride Europe and has a shakier democratic experience), has the effect of including Israel in the nest of civilized states and societies in what often seems (and no doubt is) a bitter and brutal world. And in America there lives the world's largest, wealthiest, and most politically powerful diaspora Jewish community, a community whose moral, financial, and political support for Israel succors its well-being.

But America, and even American Jewry, is a thorn to Israel, too. This is an irritating remark to those American Jews for whom Israel is more of an icon than a real place, but it's true just the same. Many Israelis, generally those left of center, believe with some justification that American aid has enabled Israeli governments to avoid the political and economic choices required to dig itself out from under the strategic paralysis of the post–1967 period. The paralysis over security policy was broken by the political will and electoral success of the Labor party in 1992, but the aid money still enables Israel to avoid—or at least consider less urgent—the economic reforms its own elite wish to make in order to escape the mendicant status that renders it vulnerable to American diplomatic pressure and, on that account, constrains its relations with other countries as well.

Moreover, the allure of America as a secure and relatively stable society sticks a finger in the eye of the Zionist conception of Israel as the best, or only, safe haven for Jews. Idealistic Zionist philosophy aside, the most powerful practical argument for a Jewish state always used to be: We need a place to be so that we can protect ourselves from those who would kill us all the day long whenever they could. This Zionist argument of last resort has always been very powerful, and rightly so, the modern world being the way it is. Lately, however, a problem has arisen, and that problem is America.

When the Jews of Russia began to leave the czar's domains in the 1880s, most went to America, not only because it was the land of economic promise but because it was considered safe—safe from external enemies because America was strong and safe from internal enemies because America was democratic. It was much safer, surely, than what was then a forlorn province of the Ottoman Empire. In the early 1990s, when Jews were again pouring out of the Russian empire, the overwhelming majority wanted to go to America. Why? Same reasons. It must be admitted, after all, that with unconventional weaponry and ballistic missiles abounding, the one place in the world today where millions of Jews could most likely be killed in a near instant is . . . Israel.

The truth is that some Israelis think America is safer than Israel—for Jews as well as others. It probably was safer than Israel during the January 1991 Iraqi Scud attacks. It's ironic, and maybe a bit sad, but some Israelis privately think of America as *their* place of refuge in a pinch should things go horribly wrong in Israel. Not everybody is brave, not even Israelis. Considering how many Israelis already live "temporarily" in the United States— many times the number of Americans who have made *aliyah* to Israel since 1948—this should come as no surprise. All this is despite the fact that in normal times Israel is at least as safe as America, if not safer, depending on where one happens to live.

Israel is nevertheless proud of its independence and self-reliance. This

---

Loaded with Options

My wife once called around to learn about renting and buying cars. One fellow, the owner of an establishment that sold cars that were formerly the property of rental car agencies, made a telling comment upon hearing that we were not temporary residents *(toshavim ara'im)*, a category preliminary to *aliyah,* but U.S. nationals in the country for the year on a B-1 visa. "Oh, good for you," he said. "You have options." It wasn't that he didn't want to encourage *aliyah;* it's just that in an unguarded moment he expressed a wistfulness about America that many Israelis feel.

---

is ideologically and historically the essence of the state: that it frees the Jews from dependency on others. But Israel has been in many ways dependent on the United States: in the beginning for food and diplomatic support, later for weapons and economic aid. Even here, Israel's history confirms Herzl's quest for a great power patron to advance the Zionist cause. American Jews have tried—with some success but not as much as is commonly thought[34]—to help Israel with money and by trying to bend U.S. policy to Israel's favor. American Jews, for years, took credit for success in helping Israel. They felt they were the big brothers, so to speak, and small Israel the little brother. When the community leaders and large donors came to Israel, they often acted the part—like the wealthy American couple in Salah Shabbati's forest.

Frankly, this sort of thing really ticked off Israelis. "Who is building this land from the ground up with their bare hands?" they would ask themselves and each other. "Who is living every day surrounded by a hundred million Arabs and who is willing to fight and die for this land? Who has made the ultimate personal commitment to the Jewish future?" Many Israelis formed an image of American Jews as haughty, ignorant, cowardly, soft, and bombastic.

Behind this, no doubt, was a degree of envy over the wealth, security, and political clout of American Jews who, after all, were in exile. There was much inward resentment toward the fair-weather American Jewish tourists who had money, lived in a safe country, and got to drink Johnny Walker whenever they felt like it. Americans had big trees growing all over the place without anyone having to plant them, and more water than they knew what to do with. They didn't have to save, steal, or borrow small fortunes to buy a car and an apartment. They didn't have to go to war or sit through shellings near border settlements. They could come to Israel for a couple weeks, feel noble, drop some cash, take some pictures . . . and then leave. It also privately bothered many Israelis that, Israeli military prowess notwith-standing, Uncle Sam could stick the entire state of Israel up his left nostril if he really wanted to. All this made for a tender and ambivalent relationship.

In recent years, the relationship has, if anything, worsened. American Jewish lay leaders took it upon themselves over the years to develop their own views of what was good for Israel. They sometimes lobbied in ways that diverged from those of the Israeli government. During the period of Likud and national unity governments in Israel, from May 1977 to June 1992, many American Jews adopted attitudes toward security issues that accorded with Likud positions. When Labor came back into power in 1992, some diaspora Jewish organizations actually opposed the policies of the Is-raeli administration. And this was after the Gulf War in January–February 1991, when many American Jews, including those inclined to Likud views, canceled trips to Israel by the thousands while Israelis sat with Iraqi Scuds raining down on their heads. If anybody thinks that Israelis missed the es-sential meaning of this behavior, they should think again.

This was the backdrop when in August 1992 Prime Minister Rabin dressed down the American-Israel Public Affairs Committee (AIPAC) for "straying from the reservation" all too often. The prime minister, and all muscular secular Zionists of the Israeli Left, wanted to know where self-appointed fat-cat American Jewish leaders got the right to lobby against the policies of the democratically elected Israeli government. This is what one of Israel's most prominent journalists, Aqiva Eldar, had to say in March 1994 when some American Jews made representation to Congress and the administra-tion about the status of Jerusalem. Eldar called the collection of eighty-two congressional signatures

> a cheeky action on the part of Jewish functionaries . . . that bear no responsi-bility for the consequences of their deeds and misdeeds. . . . Never before has a group of Jews so insolently exploited its political clout to thwart a diplo-matic compromise reached by Israeli and U.S. government leaders. . . . Ac-cording to them, Jerusalem is not just the capital of Israel but "the capital of the Jewish people." In a few days, as they do on Passover every year, they will proclaim "Next Year in Jerusalem" and proceed to check how the construc-tion of their villas in Beverly Hills and on Long Island is coming along.[35]

If that wasn't enough, Yossi Beilin, then deputy foreign minister and the *enfant terrible* of Israeli politics, proposed soon thereafter the reconstruc-tion of the World Zionist Organization and the Jewish Agency in a way that would give the Israeli government more control over the organizations at the expense of diaspora Jewish organizations. He also told American Jews to "keep their money" at home, using it for Jewish education. He pointed out that when people are secularists in Israel, they assimilate into a Jewish culture, but when Jews are secularists in America, they soon stop being Jews altogether. He repeated at length the assimilation statistics of American Jews—numbers that have to punch a hole in anyone's hubris about the health of the American Jewish community. (See Chapter 7 for specifics.) The implication? For secular Jews who really care about Jewish continuity, the only safe place, culturally speaking, is Israel. Religious Jews already know that, Beilin allowed. In other words, there are no good arguments left for not making *aliyah*, and giving us money won't change that. He implied that the money was a guilt offering, and that Israel didn't really need it. Beilin pointed out that private American Jewish aid, about $400 million per year, was less than 1 percent of a $62.5 billion economy (at that time).

Though without the direct call for American *aliyah*, this was nevertheless a take-no-prisoners Zionist speech, and it stunned the American Jewish leadership. Prime Minister Rabin disavowed Beilin's speech, but most Israelis, whatever he or she thought of the tactical wisdom of making such remarks, agreed with them. And many were happy to the point of sheer delight that, finally, someone had had the courage to get up and tell these people where to get off. It came translated to Israelis this way: "Think your money gives you the right to make decisions that affect us, and without even telling us first? Then keep your money."

Beilin's remarks also had a subtext addressed to Israelis. American pop culture—music, fashion, movies, and so on—is very popular in Israel. This puts Israel in the same category—for a change—as most of the rest of the planet. American cultural influence is huge, and no picture of Israeli society today would be complete without a description of it.

Places such as Tel Aviv, Herzliya, Raanana, and Kfar Saba can feel like a sort of weird transliterated America. Shop signs are often an amalgam of transliterated American words written in the Hebrew alphabet and some are just written in Roman script, which is a status symbol related to the "outside Israel" (*hutz la'aretz*) syndrome.[36] From the window of the 572 or 502 Egged bus that goes back and forth between Tel Aviv and Ramat Aviv on the one hand and Ra'anana and Kfar Saba on the other, a passenger can see, all in Hebrew letters, "The Big Boss" restaurant, the "Country Club," two "Burger Ranch" fast-food spots, and about a hundred other such signs.

Even Israeli breakfast cereals are modeled on American brands: Captain Loopy for Fruit Loops and Mixed Flakes (again in transliteration) for Special K, and so on. There is also more Chicago Bulls and Michael Jordan regalia in Israel than in Chicago—or so it seems anyway. The Simpsons, too, are everywhere. Kids prefer T-shirts with English writing. The eve of Rosh Hashanah (New Years) is a gift-buying frenzy season, indistinguish-

---

Roll Over Who?

Many Israelis don't only imitate the American present; they also imitate its past. LSD parties became fashionable in the summer of 1992; Jimi Hendrix videos are coveted collectors items; the radio plays the Beatles, Frank Sinatra, and Madonna. I was standing in a little store one afternoon ("little" meaning almost every store in the country outside of Tel Aviv that isn't the town Mashbir), and the Beatles' version of Chuck Berry's "Roll Over Beethoven" came over the radio. I like the song and I know all the words, and I absentmindedly started singing along in a low tone. A couple of Israeli teenagers noticed, and started looking at me like I was some kind of cultural super hero. The fact that I actually knew all these words, and presumably understood what they meant in all their wonderful, semi-secret significance—this was just too cool. They smiled at me. I felt stupid.

---

able in many ways from the nine-shopping-days-to-Christmas insanity that strikes America every year. Even the American cult of violence is exportable; I saw a paratrooper on guard duty in front of the Defense Ministry headquarters in Tel Aviv wearing a pack inscribed with the phrase "Psycho Killer." Made in the U.S.A.

There is also a habit of using English neologisms instead of Hebrew roots. There is, for example, a perfectly good Hebrew word for brakes—*ma'atzorim*. But most Israeli mechanics say "breaks," with the "r" sound dutifully transformed from the American dog-barking noise to an upscale Frenchlike trill. There's a perfectly good word for text—*tamlil*. People say "text." Need film for a camera? *Seret* makes a good word, just as *film* in English refers to both a movie and to what goes into your camera, but Israelis say "film." Is there a Hebrew word for sex? Sure: *min*. What do people say much of time? "Sex." Somehow sex sounds sexier to Israelis in English; Hollywood culture strikes again.

In short, as far as Israel and Zionism are concerned, America has made imitating and envying *goyim*[37] fashionable again. This creates uncomfortable incongruities for Israelis who take Zionism seriously. They worry that American influence is too great and on balance unhealthy, that the allure of American popular culture is colonizing the Israeli mentality with an imitative materialism smelling of envy. Some Israeli intellectuals, as with many European ones, still consider America utterly without real culture. It is, they think, crass materialism run rampant, a sordid kaleidoscope of the cheap, unhealthy, homogenizing, ugly, and soulless. It really bugs such people that

their own kids can't seem to get enough jeans and Western boots, hamburg-
ers and ice cream, Madonna and Michael Jackson, Mickey Rourke and Clint
Eastwood. Clearly, the cultural aspects of a relationship with America is a
major theme in Israeli intellectual life; even the theater illustrates the point.
In late 1994, the Camari Theater in Tel Aviv staged Motti Lerner's *Pollard*,
Lionel Goldstein's *Halperin and Johnson*, and Arthur Miller's *Broken
Glass*—all three about the Israel-American Jewish relationship.

As we recall from Chapter 1, the model of American democracy is one in
which ethnicity and religious particularism hold no noble or secure place.
The social basis of American democracy, and Americans' assumptions about
what an ideal democratic society is, differs markedly from other democracies. The ideal remains that of the melting pot, a phrase invented by a British
Jew, Israel Zangwill, around the turn of the century. Multiculturalism aside,
the ideal persists and, for the most part, the reality does, too. The hyphen-
ated Americanism that emerged from the 1960s and the reality of racial
differences obscure the connection between the ideal and the real, but the
impulse to make a new society out of shards of old ones is still strong and
will probably triumph in the end.

Israel's democracy is more like the European sort than the American,
even though the nature of Jewish peoplehood is more complex than those of
Europe. Clearly, Israeli democracy is Judeocentric. Now, if every other democracy were ethnocentrically based like Israel's—Japan's, Germany's, and
so on across the planet—there would be little sense of dissonance in Israel.
But the internationalism and humanism represented by American ideals appeal deeply to many Israelis, especially to secular Israelis who long to be
citizens of the modern world. America beckons because it promises for the
world the relatively decent harmony internationally that it has been able to
build in its civil society. But in this vision of a new international society,
what becomes of little Israel?

Muscular secular Zionism, therefore, says to Israelis: don't fall for the
allure of the diaspora world; it's like the foolishness of those newly freed
slaves long ago who yearned for "the fleshpots of Egypt."[38] What Beilin
and other modern secular and religious Zionists are saying to both American
Jews and Israeli Jews is that Israel is the center of the Jewish world now, and
the future of the Jewish people and Jewish civilization will turn on what
happens in Israel, not what happens in New York or Washington. The physical center of gravity of Jewish history has shifted back to its origin, and
those who affirm the diaspora had better understand this and get used to it.

The majority of American Jews, even those who clearly identify as Jews
and pay attention to Jewish-related news here and abroad, do not really understand this. The teenagers join organizations that are pro-Israel because

that has become a major facet of Jewish identity in America, and they celebrate Israeli Independence Day, and dance around singing Hebrew songs many of them don't understand, and proclaim that the people of Israel are one, and so on and so forth. As far as they (and their parents, for the most part) understand, there's no problem, no issue, no debate. But it's not so. The Zionist ambition has always been made up of two parts of roughly equal importance: to forge a new relationship between the Jewish people and the gentile world; and to forge a new Jewish people in the process. In this, nothing has really changed; the battle continues on both fronts, and after only a half century it's still too soon to come to a conclusion about the impact of Zionism on Jewish history in the diaspora and in Israel. Indeed, Zionism continues to hurl its mythos at reality and, sometimes anyway, it's reality that strikes out.

5

Political

Institutions

and Issues

By now something about the basic cultural, economic, and social undergirding of the Israeli political system should be clear. As noted earlier, a political system usually evolves out of a complex of more basic social behaviors in such a way that forms of government concord in their structure and function with the accustomed rhythms, expectations, and attitudes of social life. The keys to such concordance are mainly the definition of legitimate authority and the hierarchy of social statuses. If political structure reflects culture in these areas, and if it functions in accord with cultural expectations, then people tend to see the political system, whatever its flaws, as representative and legitimate in the broadest sense.

Political systems do not always evolve out of organic social and economic realities, however. Sometimes a political structure is imported or imposed from afar, as often happens when colonies become independent countries and adopt a variation of the metropol's political structure. Sometimes this sort of thing works out fairly well, at least compared to likely alternatives; India's adaptation of British parliamentary procedure is a case in point. Other times it doesn't work out so well, as when multiparty systems tend to worsen tribal or ethnic tensions in ethnically heterogeneous countries. Multiparty systems inherited from Britain and France have been widely abandoned in sub-Saharan Africa partly because of this problem.[1]

In Israel's case, the political system is a hybrid of the organic and the extrinsic. The Jewish communalism characteristic of basic Israeli social institutions is a function both of life in diaspora communities over the centuries and the conditions of building and maintaining the Yishuv in Mandate times. It is organic to the Jewish and Israeli experience. Israel's formal political structure—its parliamentary system, its electoral system, the structure and function of the judiciary—are adapted mainly from the British model. This model has served well since 1948 because the political structure has reflected cultural predicates for the most part, and it has acted in a way that has conformed to social expectations and values. It has therefore been accepted as legitimate, and therefore, too, it has been stable. Indeed, of all the several dozen countries that have achieved national independence since the end of World War II, no political system has been simultaneously as stable, legitimate, and democratic as Israel's.

But there have been problems and peculiarities. One problem is that no Israeli political party has ever been able to achieve an absolute majority, so all governments have been coalitions. This isn't a problem at all in the sense that it has allowed greater inclusiveness in government, and it has probably made the system more popular overall by giving a greater percentage of people the sense that they matter in government, and are represented by it. It *is* a problem in terms of democratic practice because small parties—especially the religious parties—have been able to market their strategic political support for financial and other favors that are way out of proportion to their numbers, and this has caused a good deal of resentment over the years.

One peculiarity is that all of Israel is one electoral district, a legacy of the organization of the Yishuv in Mandate times. There are no legislative subdivisions aside from municipal government, and municipal government in Israel is not very significant for the most part. Localities, therefore, have no "pull" on the national level because no one specifically represents them. On the other hand, for the same reason, government largesse is not politicized according to region. When Mendel Rivers of South Carolina was chairman of the House Armed Services Committee, where he served for many years, it was just uncanny how so much federal government money flowed to facilities somehow placed in South Carolina. As the Marxists used to say, this was no coincidence. American politicians believe fervently that charity (and reelection prospects) begins at home. Because there is no political districting, this sort of thing, at least, doesn't happen in Israel. Instead there has developed a national political class, a matter to which we will return below.

Some fairly significant changes have been introduced in the Israeli political system in recent years, such as the direct election of the prime minister, which occurred for the first time in May 1996. Change is easier to come by in Israel than in the United States, perhaps because much of the political system is not organic to the society and the culture, and, because it is also relatively new, Israelis do not have the same warm and fuzzy feelings about these arrangements that educated Americans have for the Constitution and the Bill of Rights. They have not yet attained the hoary, time-venerated status of a sacralized civil order. Israelis are therefore less hesitant about changing things and experimenting a bit.

It is also important to remember that, in any political culture, the formal structures of government mingle with the informal relationships and attitudes that define political interactions. Formal structures are important, but they cannot explain everything about any polity. Informal relationships are important, but they lack full explanatory power, too. Only when seen together, the formal with the informal, is the picture complete.

As noted, Israel's formal political structure is extrinsic, so one might expect dissonance or contradictions between formal structures and informal patterns. One might expect bureaucrats, for example, to work around formal patterns to get things done, as happens in many countries—most of the Arab countries are good examples—where formal structures do not accord well with custom. But informal workarounds are not that pervasive in Israel, especially not anymore. Bureaucrats and administrators usually go "by the book," sometimes too much so, and most people expect them to. What has happened over the years is that culture has permeated government processes and routines. Israel has taken the formal British model and penetrated it with custom, thereby making it both Jewish and mostly workable.

How did this happen? Remember the history presented earlier. Israeli political parties arose from social-political movements that *predated* the state, and that worked to define the state and the society, as well. In the early United States, on the other hand, the organization of the state—the formal system of government—simply suggested itself from experience and the traditional model of the British system, and individual parties and the party structure evolved *afterward* in accordance with it. Clearly, the reason we have a two-party system in the United States, for example, is not because it is directly written into the Constitution—it isn't, of course— but because it takes a majority of the electoral college to elect a president, and absolute majorities cannot be easily attained in a multiparty environment.

In other words, America was not brought into being as an independent country by a narrowly defined political movement, but by a fairly broad social revolt against an authority that had come to be seen as illegitimate. Zionism, contrarily, *was* a self-conscious political movement designed among other things to build a new Jewish society. It poured its ideological energies into everything it touched; as we have seen, from the start it produced a highly politicized society permeating everything from labor unions to youth groups, from theater companies to literary societies. Hence, shaping an extrinsic model of parliamentary government to fit Israel's circumstances turned out to be fairly easy for the dominant Labor Zionism political center once it achieved a state.

What is left to do in this chapter is to describe the workings of the formal and informal political system. The formal part of the trip will take us on a brief journey through the eleven Basic Laws, the parliamentary and electoral systems, the judiciary, and municipal government. The informal part includes brief tours of the political class, political parties and related interest groups, and the press and intellectual elite. We conclude with an observation about extraparliamentary activities.

The Basic Laws

As noted earlier, history and precedent matter. The Zionist movement always had its factions, and the only way to live together for the sake of the collective ambition of establishing a Jewish state was to live tolerantly. That meant, de facto, living democratically.

In 1947, when it seemed that the state would soon come into being, this benign habit was advanced into the precursor institutions of the state. The executive of the Jewish Agency and the Yishuv's National Council (Vaad Leumi) formed a Joint Emergency Committee to prepare the transfer of power from the British. This committee produced a draft constitution and a legal code, and it tried to line up government and military personnel for the new state. It also had a plan for government structure, naming and numbering government ministries and delimiting their authority. In March 1948, the Joint Emergency Committee transformed itself into a temporary National Council of State. On May 14, 1948, the National Council became a provisional government and divided itself into three parts: a state council that acted as a parliament; a cabinet elected from the state council; and a president also elected by the state council. Not surprisingly, Ben-Gurion became prime minister and defense minister. Also not surprisingly, Haim Weizmann was elected president.

This provisional government functioned until early 1949, wasting no time building the full gamut of administrative structures and policy directives anticipated by the Joint Emergency Committee. The provisional government, just in advance of the first national election, voted to transfer all its authority to a Constituent Assembly—that is, those who were about to be elected, which of course included nearly all the members of the provisional government. This Constituent Assembly convened on February 14, 1949, and declared itself the first Knesset, the first parliament. From a purely technical democratic-legal perspective, this is precisely how one should go about transforming a movement into a legally legitimate democratic government.

One of the first things the Knesset set out to do was to formally establish a written constitution. Pursuant to that, it quickly passed a Transition Law that, in essence, confirmed legally what had already become fact in the transition process from mandate to state. It said Israel was a republic with strong cabinet government and a weak, really only symbolic, presidency. Government procedures were based on common practices, which were in turn an amalgam of Yishuv experience and British administrative procedures under the Mandate. The Transition Law became known as the "small constitution."

Contrary to expectation, however, an actual "large" constitution was never written. The crucial reason, as noted earlier, was that no way could be found to integrate Jewish religious law into a document expressing its relationship to the state. The secularists would not agree that *halakha* should hold any privileged position in Israeli law overall, which would have ceded substantive authority to rabbis over a vast legal arena, and religious Zionists would not agree to a constitution that did not so privilege *halakha* at least in principle. Indeed, even the proclamation of the State, in May 1948, reflected this stalemate. Socialist Zionists wanted no mention of God in the proclamation; religious groups insisted on the reverse. So a compromise was worked out: the Proclamation refers to "the rock of Israel," which can be a reference to God or not, depending on how one chooses to read it. The result of the continuing inability to agree on how to deal with the relationship between the Jewish state and Judaism was the aforementioned compromise, agreed to more or less formally in June 1950, that maintained the status quo—a status quo with no written constitution.[2]

Instead, the Knesset agreed that clusters of necessary legislation be passed, each cluster called a Basic Law. In time, it was hoped that these clusters could be somehow grouped together, a preamble written based, presumably, on the May 1948 Proclamation of the State, and the combination called a constitution. Between 1958 and 1984, the Knesset passed or revised significantly eight Basic Laws: Knesset (1958), Lands (1960), Presidency (1964), Government (1968), State Economy (1975), Military (1976), Jerusalem (1980), and Judiciary (1984). In 1992, it substantially amended the Government basic law. Three others have come into being in the 1990s, Human Dignity and Liberty, Comptroller, and Freedom of Occupation.

Obviously, legislation dealing with almost all these subjects preexisted the passage of a Basic Law about them. But the Basic Law refined the law, consolidated it, and worked out contradictions or ambiguities in previous legislation. The Basic Law then took on the status of a near constitutional principle against which all subsequent legislative initiative on the subject would be based. To pass a normal law, a majority of those present and voting is sufficient. But to annul or change a law that falls under the rubric of a Basic Law, an absolute majority is required.

That's the formal side of the constitutional issue. There's an informal side too, as always, and in this case it is a function of a broad social consensus on four issues. First, Israel is a Jewish state. Second, the preservation of national security is the preeminent function of government. Third, therefore, the army has to remain outside politics. And fourth, Israel must function as a society defined by communitarian principles if not literal socialist ideology. These are obviously important areas of agreement, with enormous implications for law itself concerning such matters as the Law of Return, the limits of civil liberties and the swath of intelligence-related activities, and the basic dimensions of economic and social policy.

Only taken together—the Basic Laws plus the four fundamentals of social consensus—does one see Israel's actual political constitution. Otherwise, as we have already said, it doesn't formally exist.

Parliamentary Institutions, Cabinet Government, and the Presidency

The Knesset is formally the supreme authority of the state of Israel. It can initiate and pass laws, raise taxes, declare war, and so on and so forth, as can any democratically constituted parliament. It must also pass the budget each year, or there is no spending authority for the government.

The Knesset consists of 120 members who are elected for four-year terms by general and direct suffrage. The voting age is eighteen. The Knesset is unicameral—Israel has nothing equivalent to the U.S. Senate or the British House of Lords, which before 1910–11 really did matter in British politics.[3] Voting is by secret ballot; there is no absentee voting except for members of the Israeli diplomatic corps serving overseas.

But Israel has a parliamentary system, so people do not vote directly for people—with one important exception, explained just below—but for parties. Israel has always been awash in parties, and forming one is quite simple. In 1981, for example, thirty-one parties sought Knesset seats and ten succeeded. In 1984, twenty-six parties tried and fifteen succeeded. In the 1992 election, even taxi drivers banded together to form a party to run for Knesset. (They didn't win the minimal vote to get in.) In the 1999 election, thirty-three parties ran—a new record—and fifteen got in—another new record. All any group has to do is present a list with a few thousand signatures (in 1984 it was 2,500; in 1992 it was 1,500, and in 1996 and 1999 it was the same) and plunk down the equivalent of a few thousand dollars for processing fees. If the new list fails to get 1.5 percent of the vote, it forfeits its money; if it wins, it gets the money back. Lists already represented in Knesset do not have to go through these procedures.

With only a few exceptions, any Israeli citizen above the age of twenty-one can run for the Knesset.[4] In practice, party leaders choose their lists based on a variety of factors, including party and personal loyalties and connections, reputation, seniority, popularity, ethnic background, and profession. One rarely sees a *Mr. Smith Goes to Washington* kind of story in Israel, although it does happen. For example, one member of the current Knesset is a Russian Jew who got his start in Israel sweeping streets. Still, Knesset members form a political class for the most part.

Parties form a list of up to 120 candidates and voters choose a list. Every party adopts an alphabetical symbol, and that is what voters pick in the election. If a certain party wins, say, 20 percent of the vote, they're entitled to 20 percent of 120 Knesset seats, or twenty-four seats. That means that the first twenty-four names on its list get seats in the Knesset, and all those listed further down lose out. Until 1996, the top name on the list that does best became prime minister. Israelis refer to this position as *rosh hamemshalah* (head of government).

Actually, it isn't quite this simple. Some votes are cast for parties that fail to make the cutoff. (For a long time, the cutoff was 1 percent. Then, in 1992, the cutoff became 1.5 percent.) All votes cast for parties failing to meet the minimum are set aside when Knesset seats are calculated. The votes cast for parties that do make the cutoff are totaled up and divided by 120, which gives a quotient for each seat. Then the number of votes each party received is divided by the quotient to figure the number of seats it gets. This procedure leaves the Knesset short of 120 depending on the percentage of votes cast for parties that did not make the cutoff. The remaining seats are filled by a complicated calculation that tends to benefit the larger parties.

Before 1996, a government was formed when, after the seats are apportioned, the president asked the leader of the list with the largest percentage to try to form a government. If any one party were to get sixty-one seats, this would be a cinch, of course. But this has never happened. So the head of the largest party grouping[5]—either Labor or Likud—would go to the other parties of his or her (we mustn't forget Golda Meir!) choosing and try to get them to join in forming a government. What exactly does that mean?

If a smaller party agrees to join the lead party in a coalition, it means that it will vote with the lead party in the Knesset. The aim is to gather a group that will give the government at least sixty-one votes every time. Of course, getting a smaller party to agree to this isn't free or always easy. The smaller party will extract something in return for pledging its votes. It will get funds for its own party institutions such as schools, or certain cabinet posts that give the smaller party power over those ministries, or pledges that the larger party will support certain pieces of legislation that are of special interest to the smaller party and its constituency.

Since there are so many parties in Israel, it has frequently led the prime minister-designate to negotiate coalition agreements with more than one smaller party. This gets pretty complicated, especially if the two, or three, smaller parties do not see eye-to-eye on important issues. For example, in the government that Yitzhak Rabin assembled after the June 1992 election, Labor's coalition partners included Meretz, a secular Left grouping, and Shas, a Sepharadic religious party. Setting policy on a range of issues, and dividing coveted cabinet posts, turned out to be a rather contentious matter, and the contentiousness didn't end once the government was formed, either. These negotiations generally result ultimately in a coalition agreement, usually a written statement that amounts to the government's platform.

The formation of the government after the 1999 election was even more complex than usual. Ehud Barak stated his desire for a very large coalition, including both Likud and Shas if possible. He wanted a large coalition because a large coalition is more stable, all things considered—a point proven by the fragility of both the Rabin and Netanyahu governments before him. But while a large coalition may be more stable once formed, it is harder to form one. In this case, the secular and pro-peace Meretz party did not want to sit with the more hawkish, pro-settler National Religious party, and vice versa. And the stridently anti-clerical Shinui Party did not want to sit with the ultra-Orthodox United Torah Judaism (Agudah Israel) party. And the Russians organized in the Israel Ba'Aliyah party did not want Shas in the government, because the Russian Jews felt they had been treated badly when Shas controlled the Interior Ministry in the former government. When there is so much disagreement over basic issues, it is hard to write a coalition platform that everyone can agree to and at the same time make sense.

In this particular case, since Barak won so big and because, in general, the right-wing parties did so poorly, Barak had so many choices of parties to bring into his government that he was in a position to charge a sort of admission price for entry. Hence, to cite just one example, Barak wanted Shas in the government, and Shas wanted to be in the government in order to keep the funds flowing to its schools and social programs. So what was Barak's price? His price was Shas' support for changing the situation with regard to the number and nature of exemptions from military service on account of religious studies. A compromise was worked out that made it easier for Meretz to join the government.

The point is that, in Israel, the program of a government is a function of the coalition arrangement, not, as in the United States, a function of the ideology of a single major national party.

Of course, a prime minister can, if he wishes, change the coalition arrangement anytime he likes, or anytime he needs to do so. If one smaller party leaves the government or threatens to leave, the prime minister can open negotiations with another smaller party to bring it into the government. When smaller parties fail to vote as promised, or threaten to withhold promised support, the prime minister can counter that ploy by negotiating with other parties to replace them and by threatening to break aspects of the coalition agreement that benefit the recalcitrant party.[6] Sometimes the prime minister will be serious, sometimes he will be bluffing in such counterthreats. The recalcitrant smaller party in the coalition has to assess its strengths and its political alternatives, and take a guess. Sometimes they guess wrong. It was the National Religious party that finally brought down the Netanyahu government in December 1998, but once the government fell, the NRP regretted what it did. In the 1999 election, the NRP lost seats, the new prime minister is less to its ideological liking, and its clout on both counts diminished. But this is the sort of dynamic—coalition building and maintenance after elections—that makes parliamentary democracies so interesting but sometimes also so messy and unstable.[7]

Sometimes Israeli governments survive without formal coalition agreements. When Shas left Rabin's Labor-led coalition in 1994, Rabin was forced to rely on the tacit support of the six Arab members of Knesset. For political reasons, Rabin did not want to formally ask these Arab members, who were divided into two parties, to join the government. And the Arabs had their own reasons for supporting the Rabin government, for the alternative was thought worse from their point of view. So Rabin survived every challenge from the opposition—votes of confidence, as they are called in parliamentary government—even though he formally lacked sixty-one votes by coalition agreement.

While only sixty-one votes are needed, Israeli prime ministers do not like to rely on such a narrow majority if they can help it—and they certainly don't like to rely on a tacit majority. But, as noted, with every party added to the coalition, some price must be paid, so there is a trade-off between the benefits of a larger majority and the benefits of a more easily managed coalition.

In Israeli history, some governments have been a lot more placid and stable than others. Between 1949 and 1977, Labor always formed the government and the head of Labor was always the prime minister; the main coalition partner was the National Religious Party.[8] There was plenty of political intrigue, and more than enough speculation to fill the political gossip columns. Arguments raged over personalities, ideological issues, and factional disputes. But the arrangement was still basically stable because Labor didn't trespass in the domains set aside for the religious parties, and the religious parties did not make demands on Labor when it came to foreign or economic policy, or national security issues.

Since 1981, however, things have gotten more complicated. More parties won representation in the Knesset as the religious bloc split and the political Right enlarged and split as well. The religious parties have become more broadly politicized, too. More coalition combinations are possible, more jockeying goes on, and more wheeling and dealing takes place both before and just after elections—and often all through the year, for that matter. In general, maintaining coalition stability has become more difficult in Israel's last twenty years than it was in its first thirty.

Still, technically speaking, no Israeli government has ever fallen because it lost its majority and could not reconstitute one. In theory, an Israeli government can lose a no-confidence vote and, in parliamentary systems, this obligates the prime minister to return his mandate to the head of state (in Israel the president, in Great Britain the queen). The president of Israel, were he ever to be confronted by such a situation, could decide to ask the prime minister, still the head of the largest Knesset party, to form another government. Had the Rabin-Peres government fallen between 1992 and 1996, this is almost certainly what would have happened. The president could instead ask the leader of the next largest party to try to form a government, or he could call for new elections.

While no government has ever fallen because of a no-confidence vote, not every government has served out its full term. Indeed, since the days of David Ben-Gurion, rather few of them have. On several occasions, a kind of weakness and gridlock has overtaken the government and the Knesset voted a special law to end its term early and move to new elections before schedule. This happened in 1951, 1961, 1977, 1981, 1984, and 1998. In some cases, as in 1998, this is tantamount to a government falling, because the same votes that force premature elections would also be votes that would cast a vote of no confidence.

Also, sometimes the head of government dies in office (as with Levi Eshkol in 1969 and Yitzhak Rabin in 1995) or resigns (as with Menahem Begin in 1983), but this doesn't bring down the government. The leading party simply replaces the prime minister with another from its own ranks, and the president gives a pro forma mandate (technically two periods of twenty-one days each) for the new prime minister to form his government. This can and has, however, required shifting cabinet positions around and thus unsettling, if not destroying, coalition agreements.

Israelis tend to think about government a little differently from Americans. Israelis elect a government for four years, and then after the four years are up, they cast their votes based on its performance. In between, the general inclination is to leave the government alone to do the best it can. There is a general feeling that the country cannot afford massive levels of political uncertainty and sudden shifts in leadership for diplomatic and security reasons. Israel, therefore, isn't like Italy; both are parliamentary systems, true, but Israeli governments do not fall like Italian ones tend to fall. The reason for this is not formal but informal—it's not anything to do with a Basic Law, but with a dimension of the Israeli consensus on security issues.

Otherwise, it is important to note that, as with any democracy, the legislative branch doesn't function wholly in conformity with its formal structure. In Israel, two phenomena define this difference: the cabinet system and the committee system.

The cabinet is the crucial intermediary institution between the prime minister and the Knesset. About 95 percent of all legislation is designed and originated in the cabinet; nearly all government decisions are made by the cabinet; and nearly every Israeli government has an "inner cabinet," a group of five or six individuals who are the prime minister's closest colleagues and who make the key policy decisions on diplomatic and security issues. In addition, the prime minister's office has a director-general and a spokesman who are often informal members of the cabinet, and who generally have a great deal of political clout. These positions are roughly comparable in the American system to the White House chief-of-staff and the White House spokesperson.

It is also important to note that Israel does not have anything comparable to the American National Security Council system. In the United States, the president's national security apparatus is sprawling, and there is a national security adviser with powers sometimes comparable to those of the secretary of state. In Israel, crucial decisions on national security issues are made by just a handful of people grouped around the prime minister. This makes for fast decision making in crisis, but also holds the danger of impetuous decision making as well. Prime Minister Netanyahu tried to create a more systematic operation in the national security arena, but he did not get very far. It is still unclear if Prime Minister Barak shares Netanyahu's ambition in that sphere.

Also, the Knesset does not make laws as a whole body, but works by a committee system, just as occurs in the U.S. Congress. While the Knesset is open to the public, and its proceedings are even broadcast on television in recent years, committee proceedings are not open to the public and that's where the parliamentary rubber meets the policy road, so to speak. Committee assignments and leadership generally follow the political makeup of the Knesset as a whole, but this means something special in a parliamentary system.

In the U.S. Congress, there is a majority and a minority, and the committee chairmanships switch according to the relevant numbers. When Republicans are the majority in the Senate, for example, all the committee chairmen are Republicans. Inside committees, the committee head can always count on a majority. There will be one other major position to hear—that of the minority. In Israel, it's not so simple.

Key committees will be headed by the largest party, but somewhat less significant ones may be headed by a member from a smaller coalition partner. Inside any committee there will be several views, not just two. Moreover, in a committee discussing, say, the importation of meat, a coalition religious party may be supported by a religious party not in the coalition. The committee system, therefore, holds open the possibility of rogue combinations. But few bills will get past the whole Knesset unless they conform to the overall majority, and unless they past muster with the cabinet minister whose jurisdiction covers the area of proposed legislation. Still, sometimes an opposition party will side with the government on the basis of a deal worked out in committee. But it doesn't work the other way; a coalition member will not often vote against the government because of something that happened in committee because the entire government may be imperiled by it.

In America, therefore, the percentage of Democrats and Republicans who vote against the mainstream of their party is much higher than the percentage of Knesset members who violate party discipline. This is mainly because U.S. congressmen are often responsive to their local constituencies and because whatever they do cannot cause the fall of the government. In Israel there are no local constituencies and a collapse of party discipline, if broad enough, surely will cause the fall of the government.

Because of the closed nature of the committee system, Israeli citizens are sometimes surprised at legislation suddenly brought before the Knesset and passed before the man in the street has even a clue as to what is going on. This may seem less than ideally democratic, but in the United States a great deal of what actually affects citizens are administrative judgments made by bureaucrats whom no one has ever elected. This kind of thing also happens in Israel, but it is rarer simply because Knesset members jealously guard their prerogatives down to the smallest detail. In other words, in the U.S. Congress, laws tend to be less detailed and implementation is left to bureaucrats who actually write the rules for laws to be implemented. In Israel, the laws themselves tend to be more detailed.

As a result, the Israeli legislative process can be very protracted—slower even than in the U.S. Congress. All laws have to be "read" three times in the Knesset as a whole once they are reported out of committee. There, anyone can propose an amendment before it goes back to committee. This makes the legislative process slower still.

It is also fairly wild some of the time. When the Knesset does meet as a full body, decorum is often modest, to say the least. Whole clumps of deputies heckle and shout at the speaker, even when he is the prime minister, and seem often to go to considerable lengths to irritate and outrage each other. In 1992, a Moledet deputy, Rabbi Avi Ba-Gad, began to sing from the Knesset dais at one point, and at another donned a prayer shawl *(talit)* in the evening. This latter stunt managed to outrage both secular and religious deputies, albeit for different reasons. Avraham Burg, once a Labor member of Knesset and now Knesset speaker, once brought a condom-dispensing machine into the Knesset to illustrate a point about sex education, and the hall exploded in derision and counterderision. In 1994, then Foreign Minister Shimon Peres made a mildly disparaging remark about King David, not essentially different from what many great Biblical commentators have also said about him over the years, but he outraged several deputies from the religious parties.

These episodes can get very loud, as all Israelis know. As former Israeli President Haim Herzog once observed, "When kids yell in school, the teachers try to make them behave by telling them: 'This is not the Knesset!' "[9]

In recent times, there have been three significant changes in the Israeli political structure. First, starting in 1969, election campaigns have been financed by the government, although raising private funds was not disallowed. In general, the list system tends to depersonalize politics and emphasize programmatic and ideological elements instead. Campaigning tends to be less extravagant and less protracted. It is, indeed, limited by law to just three weeks before a scheduled election. Far less money is spent than in typical American campaigns.

But this is changing, too. For the first time in 1992, the Labor Party decided to move to a primary system to select its election list. This meant that party members would vote for their favorite politicians, and the party leaders agreed to respect the results. In the case of Labor, primaries tend to free the system from insider control, from Histadrut officials and old party leaders. Celebrities, such as mayors of larger cities, television personalities, retired army officers, even entertainers who haven't paid their party dues over the years can now more easily slip into Knesset. More important, in 1992 it meant that Yitzhak Rabin and not Shimon Peres would head the Labor list; Rabin won the primary from his long-time rival.

While Rabin won the primary and Labor won the election with him at its head, it did not mean that Rabin was suddenly more influential in the party than Peres. Peres retained much power, and his competition with Rabin went on after the election in the contest for the head of Labor's Central Committee, and also in the Histadrut elections. Over all, the primary system makes the process more open and more democratic, but it probably makes it harder for any single figure to control internally his own political constituency, and later even his own cabinet.

The change in the primary system has also made Israeli politics more personal and more expensive. For the first time in 1992, individual candidates used radio and television advertising to run for the list. The financial requirements for campaigning grew sharply and rapidly, and in March 1995 a scandal broke out revolving around Labor candidates illegally using Histadrut funds to run their campaigns. The temptation to solicit campaign funds from abroad—especially from Jews in the United States—also grew sharply.

This, in turn, has led to major Israeli parties and politicians hiring American pollsters and campaign consultants, which has Americanized Israeli elections to a considerable extent. In the 1992 election, Benyamin Netanyahu hired a Republican consultant named Arthur Finkelstein, and it clearly helped him a lot. He was also aided by a very wealthy Australian Jew named Yosef Goodnik, and a number of very wealthy American Jews. By all accounts, this enabled Netanyahu to beat Shimon Peres, since he won by less than 30,000 votes. Taking the lesson, Labor was not to be outdone the next time around. So Ehud Barak had at his disposal more funds from solicitation trips abroad, and the services of President Clinton's chief pollster, Stanley Greenberg, and the advice of James Carville.

None of this is illegal, but, arguably, it's not healthy either. The 1999 campaign in Israel was speckled with slick television advertisements, but there were no real debates, and the candidates did not bother to discuss issues in any depth or at any length. Compared to Israel's early elections, the tone of the 1999 campaign was as though it was taking place in a completely different country.

The third change was implemented in the May 1996 election, in which the Likud's Benyamin Netanyahu narrowly defeated Shimon Peres. The prime minister was for the first time elected by direct vote. The system now works like this—at least until it is changed back, or changed to some third method. To run for prime minister, a candidate must have at least ten current Knesset sponsors or show 50,000 petition signatories in support. This means that while smaller factions can still run lists for Knesset, there will not be more than three or four candidates for prime minister. (In 1996 there were only two; in 1999 there were five but three dropped out just before the election.) To be elected, a candidate must have 51 percent of the vote. If the first ballot does not provide a winner, a runoff is held.

This new system leaves open the possibility that the prime minister may one day be of a different party and a different view than the major party in Knesset. Nevertheless, according to the law, the president must ask the prime minister to form a cabinet even if his party does not hold a plurality of Knesset seats. Should the prime minister-elect fail to form a government after two 21–day periods, a new election must be held. Unlike the case in the previous system, the president may not turn to the leader of the largest Knesset faction, someone liable to be the second place finisher for prime minister.

This change puts the Israeli system somewhere between the American and the British, more like the French system, with a strong, directly elected chief executive and a parliament that can be headed by a different party. How this will work out in Israel in the future is unknown. Many academic analysts, and the new law's authors, hoped that the change would reduce the influence of the smaller parties and make for larger and more stable coalitions. The idea was that if the smaller parties could not play both ends against the middle by negotiating with the leaders of the two major blocs—for remember, only the elected prime minister can form a government—their leverage woud be reduced.

But others projected that instead of reducing the power of the small parties, as intended, the result would be the reverse: if a prime minister-elect cannot form a government without their participation, he might need to give them as much or more than ever. Many also fear paralysis if elected prime ministers fail on a regular basis to form a government after the elections.

The 1996 election results were a shock to those who thought that smaller parties would be rendered less important. Just the opposite took place. The two large blocs, Labor and Likud, between them lost 18 of 120 seats to smaller parties. It seems that voters reasoned that, having taken care of major security issues in their vote for prime minister, they could more freely and with less risk indulge their particularist affinities by voting for smaller parties. And they did. Three religious parties increased their power dramatically from 16 to 23 seats. New parties (Natan Sharansky's "Russian" party, called Israel Ba'Aliyah, and the Third Way party) got 11 seats between them (7 and 4, respectively) out of nowhere. The Arab parties also grew from 5 to 9 seats.

The 1999 elections led to an even more fractured result. Between them, Labor and Likud got only 45 of the 120 Knesset seats, by far the lowest ever. There were 15 parties in Knesset, not just 11. By now, almost everyone in Israel is convinced that the new law has failed to work as intended, and there has been a lot of discussion about going back to the old system. But that may not happen because party leaders—first Netanyahu and now Barak—did much better as individuals than did their parties. And if the major parties' leaders do not support changing the law back, it probably will not happen.

On the other hand, there is some reason to suspect that coalitions will be larger and less vulnerable to failure. The smaller parties, almost all of them, would have joined either a Peres or a Netanyahu government, meaning a coalition beyond seventy compared to Rabin's sixty-one. Barak's coalition, too, is fairly large and could have been—and may still be—even larger.

The other change in the system from the 1992 law is so far theoretical, but just barely so. In the past, a Knesset and a prime minister had to go out of business together. This is no longer necessarily the case. If there is a vote of no confidence that the government loses, or if a law to dissolve the government passes, as in December 1998, then the system works as it always did. But there are a few circumstances under which the Knesset can remain but a new election for prime minister has to be held. One is if a prime minister is voted out of office by a special supermajority. In another, he can be removed by a plain majority by the Knesset if he has been convicted of a crime of "moral turpitude" brought up by the Attorney General. In the Bar-On scandal during the Netanyahu government, where the prime minister appointed an unqualified Attorney General as a payoff to a coalition party, Shas, for its vote on the Hebron accord, the specter of a crime of moral turpitude seemed to rise up. In the end, things did not get so far; there was not enough evidence to convict Netanyahu of the deed, even though most Israelis then and now have been persuaded of his guilt.

Finally, by way of formal political institutions, there is the president, who is elected by the Knesset for a five-year term, and who may serve two additional consecutive terms. The president *(nasi)* of the state during Israel's formative years was always an elder statesman and most people got used to thinking of his duties as strictly honorific. This is not exactly true, however.

Technically, for example—before the 1992 change in the election law—the president did not have to ask the head of the largest party after an election to form a government. He could have asked the head of any party he thought could succeed in forming a government. If an election had been very close, the second-place finisher could have had a better chance of forming a government because of the array of smaller parties and how they did in the elections. For example, suppose Labor got forty-one seats and Likud thirty-nine in an election, but that smaller parties closer to Labor's views won only eight, while smaller parties closer to Likud's views won sixteen. A president might logically have decided to ask the head of Likud to try to form a government even though Likud came in second.

This is not just a theoretical case. The 1984 election was very close, and President Haim Herzog could logically have asked either Shimon Peres of Labor or Yitzhak Shamir of Likud to form a government. He asked Peres, who ended up having to settle for a government of national unity (where both major parties form a government together, along with some other smaller parties as well). Obviously, the president isn't necessarily politically disinterested just because he is an elder statesman. Herzog had been associated with Labor all his life, and he chose the Labor leader.

Because of this experience, the presidential election in 1993 became interesting and controversial. No one had ever really "run" for president before like Ezer Weizmann did then. It had usually been fairly obvious who the most prestigious elder statesman was at any given time, and the Labor establishment always named him. Israel's first president was Haim Weizmann, a man without whom the state might not have been born.[10] The next president was Yitzhak Ben-Tzvi, then Zalman Shazar, two men from the era of the Second Aliyah—both obvious choices. Then came two presidents who were less obviously elder statesmen: Efraim Katzir and Yitzhak Navon.[11] All faced token opposition only. Then came Herzog in 1983, who defeated Menahem Elon, a High Court justice, by a Knesset vote of 61–57. Herzog was a controversial president, and not just because he had chosen Peres in 1984 to form a government.

In the 1993 election, the Knesset ended up choosing Ezer Weizmann, the grandnephew of Haim Weizmann, former head of the Israeli Air Force and a former Likud defense minister turned political dove. But his election was not a foregone conclusion, largely because Ezer, as he is universally known in Israel, had demonstrated a strong tendency to say whatever came into his head, and this was not a trait liable to well serve a president of Israel, especially abroad. In any event, with his election the post of president appears to have been permanently politicized. He won again in the 1998 election, so he clearly did not justify fears that he would speak inappropriately—at least not to a great excess.

Besides picking a party head to form a government, the president has the power to pardon criminals, reduce jail sentences, and grant reprieves. This includes acting on behalf of political criminals or spies that the intelligence services want to trade for others. Once nominated by the appropriate agencies, the president appoints the heads of religious courts (Jewish, Christian, and Muslim), the governor of the Bank of Israel, the state comptroller, and the head of the *Magen David Adom* (the Red Shield of David, comparable to the Red Cross). The president also delivers something like a State of the Union address each year on the eve of Rosh Hashanah, which, because it is not obviously political, is an important unifying national event. The president also represents Israel abroad and his remarks in that context are often carefully chosen and politically significant. His function is thus not entirely symbolic.

Ezer Weizmann became especially active politically after Benyamin

Netanyahu became prime minister on June 18, 1996. It was largely public pressure mounted by Weizmann that persuaded Netanyahu to meet with Palestinian Authority head Yasir Arafat in September 1996. After that, too, the president kept an unusually active profile to force the Netanyahu government to negotiate in good faith with the Palestinians. Weizmann's stature as president has grown over time, and he may be a very important figure in the Barak era. We shall see.

The Judiciary, the Legal Adviser, and the State Comptroller

The Israeli court system is divided into civil and religious courts, as explained earlier. Religious courts, whether Jewish, Muslim, or Christian, handle family and related life-cycle issues. The civil courts handle criminal activity, business and tax law, and all the rest of what normally falls under the jurisdiction of American courts. This is managed under the Israeli Ministry of Justice.

The court system works in a hierarchy. At the lowest level, there are municipal and magistrate courts that handle misdemeanors and other minor matters. Such courts can impose fines and sentence people to light jail terms. There are also district courts, five of them, in Jerusalem, Tel Aviv, Nazareth, Haifa, and Beersheba. These courts handle appeals from lower courts, and they also deal with any offense that does not fall under the jurisdiction of municipal and magistrate courts. In both lower and district court proceedings, one judge usually presides. As is the case in France and most continental European systems, there are no jury trials in Israel.

In what are called capital, or major, offenses, where large sums of money or long jail terms are possible, three judges usually preside, one of them being a member of the Supreme Court.

There are also several special courts. There is a traffic magistrate to deal with offenses against a special law, the Road Transport Ordinance. There is a Labor Law Court that deals with disputes about union issues, pension funds, and the operation of the National Insurance Law. Special commissions of inquiry can be established by the government, too, such as the 1974 Agranat Commission that investigated the mismanagement of the 1973 war, and the 1984 Kahan Commission that investigated the Sabra-Shatilla massacres and led to the resignation of the then Israeli Defense Minister, Ariel Sharon. In special commissions of inquiry, the head of the Supreme Court names a chairman, who must be either a Supreme Court justice or a district court judge, and the other members of the commission.

Of the special courts, the most important are the military courts for those who disobey military regulations. But the military courts have a wider sway than this suggests, as detailed below.

Aside from the minister of justice, every Israeli government also appoints a special legal adviser called the Attorney General (or Procurator General). The legal advisor proffers legal advice to the government and also serves as a state procurator general, which is someone who can prosecute anyone on behalf of the state if he sees a need to do so. The Attorney General also has jurisdiction over questions of parliamentary immunity, in case a Knesset member is accused of a crime (this *has* happened). He can indict judges who behave improperly. He can also transfer cases to and from military and civilian courts as he deems necessary. And he is involved whenever state secrets are germane to legal proceedings.

The government can dismiss the Attorney General, but the office's high authority has rendered this rare.[12] The government cannot tell the Attorney General what to do or what not to do, and the legal adviser can indict a government minister if he sees fit. In 1976, the legal adviser, Aharon Barak, decided to prosecute Leah Rabin, the prime minister's wife, for having an illegal dollar account in the United States. It cost Rabin the premiership at the time and paved the way for Menahem Begin's accession to office.

Of special interest in Israel, as in the United States, is the Supreme, or High, Court of Justice—comparable to the U.S. Supreme Court in some, but not other, ways. Unlike the case in the United States, the High Court in Israel traditionally has not been able to invalidate legislation. But Aharon Barak's tenure as chief justice introduced, as of November 1995, a more aggressive form of judicial review in Israel.[13] Before very long, too, the Orthodox parties responded to the Barak court's judicial activism with unprecedented verbal attacks against the court. In another sign of the court's increasing power, on March 27, 1996, a Supreme Court justice ordered Rabbi Yitzhak Greenberg released from administrative detention (he had been picked up on March 10 for allegedly fomenting violence). It was the first time ever that the court overturned an order of administrative detention.

It remains to be seen if these changes will outlive the Barak-led court; there is considerable opposition to them from several quarters, not just the Orthodox parties.[14] But even if they do not, the court will maintain, as before, its ability to invalidate actions taken by bureaucracies if it deems them contrary to law. It can also invalidate a Knesset law if a technical error of some sort was made. (This has never happened, however.) And it can interpret the meaning of laws, which can lead to consequential judgments that affect political issues.

In the United States, the president nominates and the Senate approves Supreme Court justices, who serve until resignation or death. It doesn't work that way in Israel. Instead, a nine-member commission suggests to the president candidates for appointment to the High Court, which consists of ten justices. The commission is chaired by the minister of justice and consists of two other High Court justices, the president, two Knesset members-at-large chosen by secret ballot, one other cabinet minister, and two delegates from the Israeli Bar Association.

Until the 1984 Basic Law on the Judiciary, justices ended their tenure either by death, resignation, mandatory retirement at age seventy, or expulsion for disciplinary reasons by the president and at least five other justices. After 1984, seven of nine commission members—not other justices—can decide to remove a justice if the motion is offered either by the president or by any other High Court justice.

Unlike the American system, too, not all of Israel's justices hear every case brought before the court. Instead, the chief justice decides on a subgroup of (usually) three justices to hear any particular case. An activist chief justice, therefore, can be a very influential shaper of court decisions simply by reserving certain judges (including himself) for service on particularly significant cases.

All in all, it confuses some observers that in most democracies, including Israel and the United States, the highest judicial body is more or less immune from democratic control. But as part of the separation of powers, the founders of both countries understood that at least one branch of government had to be beyond the potential reach of a mob.

Before the mid-1970s, the Israeli High Court kept a fairly low profile. As noted, that is no longer true. The court's ability to strike down administrative edicts has been the main wedge with which it has widened its powers in Israeli politics. It is relatively simple and inexpensive for Israelis to turn to the High Court in a dispute over administrative rulings. Most important, the court's power of judicial review has always encompassed actions taken by the military administration in the territories occupied by Israel after June 1967. West Bank Arabs have turned to the court to stop administrative detention, land expropriations, expulsions, and other actions.[15] The court established a record of hearing such complaints and, especially during the period of Likud rule, often sided against the government and for the Arab complainant. The court has also ruled in favor of Israeli Arabs and Israeli bedouin specifically in cases involving expropriated land.

Those who opposed the Likud policies thought of the High Court as a kind of savior, but this in turn led many Israelis to fear a politicization of the legal system. Likud and other politicians, in any event, began to take more seriously the political impact of the court's administrative prerogatives, and the process of selecting justices has become more politicized, as with the office of president.

As noted, until November 1995 the court lacked the right to overturn law (judicial review), but it did interpret law definitively with regard to its implementation. This has included interpretations of various anti-discrimination laws, including laws against racism and laws against activity designed to jeopardize the Jewish character of the state. On the basis of these laws, the court banned the Arab nationalist group al-Ard in 1964, and it banned Kach, a far-right Jewish group led by Meir Kahane, from running for the Knesset in 1988. Both of these actions were generally popular in Israel.

The High Court used the same venue to grant itself the right to rule on whether a 1994 coalition agreement between Labor and Shas was legal because the agreement contained within it language about circumventing the purview of the court.

The High Court also has security-related functions. In 1948, the Knesset passed a Prevention of Terrorism Ordinance, which specified that terrorists were to be tried by military courts. The military courts fall under the general authority of the High Court, however; if they make mistakes or abuse their authority, the High Court can reverse judgments. On balance, however, the High Court has trod lightly in this area. Additionally, in 1948 the Provisional State Council passed a Law and Administration Ordinance, part of which (Article 9) gave the state the right to declare a state of national emergency whenever it deemed necessary. It did this the same day, intending the emergency to last only as long as the war. But the emergency has never been suspended; the Knesset extends it every year. It applied to all Israeli Arabs until December 1966. This same law is what has allowed military courts and administrations to function legally in the territories after 1967 and up until today. The High Court has the authority to interpret the 1948 law in such a way as to redefine the conditions for declaring an emergency, but it has not yet done so.

The High Court's status is such that certain national difficulties calling for non-politicized scrutiny that is beyond reproach involve it from time to time. The best-known example, perhaps, followed the massacre of Palestinians by Maronite Christians in Lebanon at the Sabra and Shatilla refugee camps in September 1982. The area in which the camps were located was at the time under general Israeli military control, and Israel's Maronite allies of the moment against the PLO took the opportunity to do their bloody deeds. Israelis were horrified by the massacre and demanded to know the extent to which the Israeli government was responsible. A three-man commission, the Kahan Commission mentioned just above, that included a current and former High Court justice, concluded that the government had been not guilty but partly responsible for what happened. As a result, not only did Defense Minister Ariel Sharon lose his post, but several military officers were censured as well.

In short, the High Court is one of the best-respected state institutions in Israel. Its status is high, its competence is widely respected, and its political interventions are more or less judicious. The creeping politicization of its role, however, threatens to undermine its status over time. A resolution of the status of the occupied territories, in particular, would go far in allowing the court to regain its lower profile.

Finally, the state comptroller, known more formally as the state comptroller and ombudsman. Israel's state comptroller, responsible only to the Knesset, is appointed for a five-year term by the president on the recommendation of the Knesset rules committee. Even more than the attorney general, the prime minister and the cabinet cannot touch this person, who can say whatever he or she likes. The comptroller cannot hold any government post because that would raise an obvious conflict of interest.

The job of the comptroller has changed over the years, but basically it has to do with auditing the entire public sector, which is enormous. The comptroller is supposed to audit all government ministries, the Bank of Israel, all local government agencies, local religious councils, university administrations, the television and radio networks, all state corporations, and the social security administration. Every year, the comptroller must issue a public report on government malfeasance.

In 1971, the comptroller was also made responsible for the Commission of Public Complaints, as if there wasn't enough to do already. What is the Commission of Public Complaints? Basically it's a suggestion box, like the kind you see on the wall in various places in the United States, only on a national scale. There's an address in Jerusalem that Israelis can write to if some bureaucrat irritates them. The commission averaged about 5,000 written complaints a year before the mid-1990s, when the numbers rose somewhat. In the September 1996–October 1997 period, there were 6,921 complaints.

Some of these complaints are serious, and the comptroller general's office settles them more or less as a judge would. In 1998, some 36 percent of the complaints were found valid and were acted upon. Indeed, the recently retired Miriam Ben-Porat urged the public to make more use of her office as a "High Court bypass road" in order to reduce the burden on the overworked justices. This gives some idea of how major some of the issues can be.

The very idea of a state comptroller trying to audit an entire government may strike some as amusing; after all, government and government-related agencies rarely tell the truth about what they do with taxpayer money. And local religious councils and university administrations? One could sooner melt the Antarctic with a Bic lighter than expect a straight or reliable financial report out of either one. On the other hand, when has the American

GAO (General Accounting Office) ever publicly audited itself or any agency of the U.S. government? When is the last time an American citizen was able to get a written report on how efficiently any agency of the U.S. government operated, or the government as a whole for that matter? In fact, Uncle Sam never allows a public audit of himself; at least in Israel they try.

Some try harder than others, too. During Prime Minister Rabin's 1992–95 tenure, the state comptroller was the estimable Miriam Ben-Porat, noted above. Ben-Porat is a woman with eyes of flint and a will of cold steel. Even with a modest staff and resources, Ben-Porat investigated a variety of government activities, finding most of them outrageously wasteful and some verging on illegal in their use of funds. She issued periodic reports, with readable summaries, that made newspaper headlines on a regular basis. She spoke like a Gatling gun and never seemed to blink on camera. Or smile. One had the feeling that given somewhat greater resources and a couple years' time, she could clean up any government mess, no matter how rotten or seemingly hopeless, just through the sheer power of intimidation.

The Parties and Their Discontents

We have often made mention in passing of Israeli political parties, but we have yet to describe them in any detail. Many texts on Israel spend multiple pages describing the intricate and complex political history of Israel's main parties over the years. Many books have elaborate and ornate charts that try to follow these developments, which are important for students who move on from an introduction to a more advanced grasp of Israeli history and political culture.

For our purposes, however, it is important to know that Israel's three main political streams—Labor Zionism, Religious Zionism, and Revisionist Zionism—have split and merged and split and merged again over the years based on ideology and personality differences. It is worth learning, too, what these three streams represent today in terms of the attitudes they exhibit. It is also important to learn to recognize the parties on the contemporary scene, and to know their basic positions on foreign policy-diplomatic and national security issues on the one hand, and on the secular-religious divide on the other. Relatedly—as illustrated in the charts on the following pages—it is important to see that, while there is some overlap between the two sets of positions, that overlap is incomplete, and the incompleteness is itself politically significant.

Of the three streams, Labor Zionism, to repeat, was the central ideological and political force behind the entire Zionist movement from 1904 through at least 1977. As a Left grouping, however, it was never immune from some

Chart 1

Spectrum of Major Israeli Political Parties on Foreign Policy/Diplomacy and Security Issues

<u>Dovish</u>   <u>Hawkish</u>

Israel Communist Party

Progressive List for Peace

    Meretz

        Shinui

          Labor

           Shas

            Israel b'Aliyah

             Agudah Israel

              Likud

               Nat'l Religious Party

                Moledet

                 Kach

Chart 2

Spectrum of Major Israeli Political Parties on Secular/Religious Divide

<u>Secular</u>

Israel Communist Party

Progressive List for Peace

Shinui

Meretz

Labor

Israel b'Aliyah

Likud

Moledet

Nat'l Religious Party

Shas

Agudah Israel

Kach

<u>Religious</u>

factionalism and, indeed, for purposes of running for the Knesset, Labor blocs or alignments were assembled beforehand from various factions. For a long time, for example, Labor Zionism consisted of Mapai (*Mifleget Poalei Eretz Israel*, or Land of Israel Workers Party), plus Mapam (*Mifleget Poalim Ham'uehedet*, or United Workers Party) plus Ahdut Ha'avodah.[16] In 1968, all labor factions except Mapam came together to form the Labor Party, and running with Mapam in elections starting in 1969, this political conglomeration was called the *Ma'arakh Ha-avodah*, or the Labor Alignment.

On several occasions early in the state's history and in the late 1980s, Mapam ran separately from the rest of Labor. In the early years, Ahdut Ha-avodah ran separately as well. In 1965, Ben-Gurion himself bolted from Labor and established his own party, called Rafi, which stood for election separately but eventually found its way back into Labor. Similarly, in 1977, Yigal Yadin led a brief movement called the Democratic Movement for Change, which did fairly well in the election—a sign of how tired the Labor establishment had become by then. The Democratic Movement for Change, however, was far closer to Labor on policy issues than to the parties of the Right; still, its challenge weakened Labor in that election and may have allowed the Likud to come to power.

In recent years, a more or less cohesive party to the left of Labor—but not communist—has formed from Mapam, Ratz (Citizen's Rights), and Shinui (Change), the latter two being small parties that existed in the 1970s and early 1980s. This party came to be known as Meretz, which means "energy" in Hebrew but which also is an acronym for the parties from which it was formed. It did well in its first showing in the 1992 election, and better since, winning nine seats in 1996 and ten seats in 1999. Meretz's appeal tends to be to the young, the secular, and those who are more dovish than the center of the Labor Party on peace process issues. It is not uniformly socialist on economic matters, and in this sense is not to the Left of the traditional Israeli Labor Party view. Its key personalities have included Yossi Sarid, Ran Cohen, Amnon Rubinstein, and Shulamit Aloni.

Labor itself remains the largest and broadest left-center party. It tends to be less doctrinaire about socialism. This means that, more than Meretz, as far as economic policy goes, Labor is willing to privatize state corporations and allow a greater function for the market when it comes to generating wealth. But it is not conventionally capitalist in the sense that it retains a strong dedication to communalism as social policy when it comes to deciding how to use and distribute wealth once it is produced. Americans tend not to think in terms of this distinction between economic policy and social policy, but lots of Israelis do.

When it comes to foreign and security policy, on the key issue Meretz favors the creation of a Palestinian state, subject to certain restrictions on its sovereignty agreed by treaty with Israel. This has led Israeli hawks to refer to Meretz and its supporters as being *tzimhoni* (vegetarian), which translates roughly into the English term spineless.

Labor favors something less than a fully independent state, preferring formal or less-than-formal confederation between Palestinian areas and Jordan. This may seem a small distinction, but in Israeli thinking it is not so small. Labor is also keen to preserve its relationship at the highest level with the United States, partly because the relationship is the key to Israel's qualitative advantages in military technology over its enemies. Meretz tends to be the home of muscular Zionism, and it is here that the anti-American biases related earlier tend to find the most hospitable home. Many Meretz members look instead to the social democracies of Western Europe for their ideal model.

Also very important, insofar as Israel has interest groups outside or parallel to the party structure, these interest groups are represented mainly within Labor. Two are most significant: unions (the Histadrut), and the agriculture lobby, which flows from the *kibbutzim* and *moshavim*. During Likud tenure, the Histadrut stopped being a Labor Party arm of the state and started behaving more like a classical interest group, ready to strike and otherwise hurt and embarrass the government. The Labor Party Central Committee has traditionally had very close ties to the Histadrut, although they are not technically the same thing. Sometimes Histadrut affiliates, like the medical or teachers unions, will strike even against a Labor government. And in 1994, as noted, Haim Ramon bolted from Labor, formed his own party, Ram, and won control of the Histadrut itself. This put Ramon in a strong position to bargain with Labor in advance of the 1996 election, and had it not been for Rabin's assassination, he probably would have bargained more vigorously than he did.

The agricultural lobby and its affiliates, such as Hevrat Ovdim, also do a lot better for themselves when Labor is in power. To take just one example, Labor ministers of agriculture are far more sympathetic to heavily subsidized prices for water than Likud agriculture ministers tend to be.

Farthest to the Left have been the Communists. Israel had a Communist party that predated the founding of the state. By 1924, there was an anti-Zionist Palestine Communist Party made up mainly of Jews, but also a few Arabs. It was very small for the simple reason that is wasn't very logical for Jews to come to Palestine and at the same time deny the legitimacy of Zionism. It was dedicated to class struggle, which took precedence over national issues, which was logical in a way because, theoretically at least, one cannot be an internationalist (Communist) and a nationalist (Zionist) at the same time. In 1943, the party split into three, and in 1948, two of the three splinters—one Jewish, one Arab—came together to form Maki, an acronym for Israel Communist Party *(Mifleget HaKommunistit HaIsraelit)*. It averaged around 4 percent of the vote in early Knesset elections, mainly Arab votes. In 1965, Maki split into two: the Israel Communist Party, mainly Jewish; and Rakkah *(R'shimat HaKommunisti Hahadasha,* or New Communist List), mainly Arab. Thus during much of the Cold War, Israel, a pro-Western country, had not one but two Communist parties while in the Arab states, most of which were pro-Soviet, Communist parties were almost always and everywhere illegal.

There were other "Arab" lists associated with Mapai, and this split the Arab vote about in half in most elections. Then in 1983, a group called the Progressive Movement–Nazareth—which elected a communist mayor in Nazareth in 1975—split from Rakkah and in 1984 merged with a small group of Jewish doves led by Mattityahu Peled and Uri Avnery to form the Progressive List for Peace (PLP). Maki more or less disappeared. So in 1992 Rakkah and the PLP held up the far Left, again taking most of the Arab vote. In 1999 yet another division appeared, with avowedly Muslim Arabs moving into the picture. The United Arab List won five seats, Hadash won three, and the National Democratic Alliance won two. The former represented the more religious Islamic part of the Arab community, while the latter two are essentially mixings and reformulations of the PLP and Rakkah.

The Communists were always outside Labor to its Left, and never participated in governing coalitions. The Arab vote, largely associated with the Communists, however, has become more and more important as the Arab population rises and becomes more politicized. The politicization really dates from the 1967 War, when the isolation of the Israeli Arabs ended. Just as Jews could go into the West Bank, so could Israeli Arabs. There they reconnected, so to speak, with their Arab brethren and acquired a wider political personality. Additionally, the politicization of Israeli Arabs has been a function of near universal elementary education among Arabs, and also a relatively sophisticated secondary school system, which undermined the traditional social structure of elder patriarchs.

The trend reached a new point of political departure in 1976, when Israeli Arabs called a general strike in Nazareth to protest land expropriations—which resulted in riots and six deaths, an event now commemorated each year as Land Day. Since then, in close elections such as those of 1984 and 1992, the Arabs rather than the religious parties have become Israel's new swing vote. This has had a lot of people scratching their heads.

The most dramatic expression of Israeli Arab political clout thus far occurred in May 1995, when the five Israeli Arab Knesset members threatened to help bring down the Rabin government if it did not freeze a land expropriation order concerning about 134 acres in East Jerusalem. Although the government weathered censure by the United Nations Security Council, the European Union, and the two Arab countries with which it was at peace—Egypt and Jordan—the Israeli government persisted until the Arab gambit stopped the expropriation in its tracks.

Like Labor Zionism, Revisionist Zionism was not a single party but a voting bloc for most elections, consisting of Herut, the Independent Liberals, and what remained of the General Zionists. During the 1960s, as Labor tended to consolidate into a single party, Revisionist Zionism did the same. In 1965 Herut and the Liberals combined to form Gahal (*Gush Herut Liberali*, or Liberal Freedom Bloc). Finally, in 1973, Likud was formed when La'am, a former Labor grouping, joined the Right, although factions still abounded within the Revisionist camp as within the Labor camp. The Revisionist movement was always non-socialist and more bourgeois on account of its social and economic origins. Labor Zionists came earlier, Revisionists later. The former came willingly, venerated agriculture, and looked to the task of creating the new Jew; the latter came as economic refugees, settled in cities, and saw ideology in far less idealistic terms, wanting personal security, political normalcy, and also, if it ever became possible, revenge against the *goyim*.

These very considerable differences remained fixed after 1948. But given the success of Labor Zionism in creating and defending the state, the Revisionist parties never got very far in elections before 1977. They were always the opposition, and the government pretty much ignored them all. By May 1977, however, the ossification of the Labor Party and the success of the Likud at exploiting Sepharadi resentment of Labor's Ashkenazi establishment led to the most dramatic electoral revolution in Israel's modern history: the election of Menahem Begin as prime minister. Begin had been the opposition leader since 1948, and his permanent status as a loser was so deeply entrenched that his victory in May 1977 left the Labor establishment stunned and speechless. The shock was comparable to what one would imagine would happen had a Massachusetts liberal fallen into a coma in 1962 and woken up twenty years later to find Ronald Reagan president of the United States.

Begin won election again in 1981, but fell ill and resigned into seclusion in 1983 during the war in Lebanon. He was succeeded by Yitzhak Shamir, his foreign minister. Shamir contested the 1984 election for Likud and wound up in a strange rotation agreement with Shimon Peres, where for the first eighteen months Peres was prime minister and Shamir foreign minister, and for a second eighteen-month period the two switched positions. This was a unique national unity government arrangement. The sides kept their bargain, and in the first eighteen months the two sides united to break the back of a terrible inflation raging in the country (recall Chapter 4) and to withdraw most Israeli troops from Lebanon. But on foreign policy and security issues the government was mainly paralyzed by the coalition arrangement. Shamir then won the 1988 election over Peres and led a Likud-led coalition with Labor until 1990, after which Likud ruled without Labor until the June 1992 election.

Shamir's tenure as prime minister was racked by internal Likud infighting. An older man lacking the long reputation as opposition leader enjoyed by Begin, Shamir's rivals began sniping at him almost from the start. These included all of the following: David Levy, Ariel Sharon, Benyamin Begin (Menahem's son), Moshe Arens, and Benyamin Netanyahu. After 1992, Netanyahu became Likud leader, but the sniping has yet to stop.

This infighting hurt the Likud, but it was not the only factor responsible for its losing the 1992 election. Clearly, the Likud rose to power in 1977 on the backs of Sepharadim disenchanted and angry at Ashkenazic domination of the establishment and its party: Labor. This remained a core constituency throughout the 1980s, and is still today to some extent. But the mobilization of the Sepharadim behind one particular party was a sign of their growing integration and political savvy. That growth has continued, and as it has Sepharadim no longer vote as a block to the same extent. As the 1992 election clearly showed, Sepharadic voters voted more on the issues than on ethnicity, and far larger percentages voted for Labor than was the case in the 1984, 1981, or 1977 elections.

What actually won the 1992 election for Labor, however, was not the Sepharadic vote but the Russian immigrant vote. Most observers had expected the Russians to vote for the incumbent Likud, and for three good reasons. First, Likud could use the power of incumbency to engender gratitude and pointedly directed patriotism toward itself. Second, new immigrants tend to be highly patriotic and nationalistic, even jingoistically so, and Likud rhetoric accorded far better with such vocabulary than Labor's. Third, the last thing people escaping from a socialist bureaucratic nightmare are liable to do is join a socialist party with a red flag still as its party banner.[17]

But most observers were wrong. Russian immigrants voted heavily for Labor mainly because the Likud grossly mismanaged and underfunded their absorption, preferring instead to throw money into settlement activity in the territories. To the immigrants, Likud *was* the bureaucracy. And the peace process brought hope that they would not have to live the rest of their lives in a virtual war zone. One could even say that Mikhail Gorbachev's benighted illusions about reforming communism, George Bush's insistence that Soviet Jewry émigrés go to Israel rather than the United States, and the ineptitude and nationalist blinders of Yitzhak Shamir's government all came together to elect Rabin prime minister in 1992.

Since 1992, the Likud has fallen on ever harder times. While Benyamin Netanyahu led a Likud-based government for three years, those years were characterized by great in-fighting in the party such that, by the time of the 1999 election, the Likud was shattered. Former Likud foreign minister David Levy had split and joined with Labor in the One Israel group. Former Likud defense minister Itzhak Mordecai and former finance minister Dan Meridor left for the Mercaz, or Center party, along with former Likud Tel Aviv mayor Roni Milo. In the 1999 election Likud won only nineteen seats; Netanyahu quit as the party's leader, and its future is very uncertain.

Within a few years after 1977, the secular right part of the political spectrum spawned other parties. The first notable one was *Tehiya* (Resurrection), formed in 1979. Led by Geula Cohen, Tehiya drew support from Likud hawks opposed to the March 1979 peace treaty with Egypt, from some Gush Emunim (see below) followers, and some Land of Israel followers who, unlike Gush Emunim, preached a secular form of extreme nationalism. Soon thereafter, a retired general and chief of staff from 1978 to 1983, Rafael Eytan, formed *Tzomet* (Crossroads). The major difference here was that Tzomet was resolutely secular. In 1984, however, Tehiya and Tzomet presented a common list and won five seats. The parties formerly merged in 1985, then split again soon thereafter. In the 1992 election, Tehiya was wiped out, winning no seats, but Tzomet continued to do fairly well, winning six. But in 1994, Tzomet split largely over personality issues, and two members of its Yi'ud faction were coopted into the Rabin government to shore up the sagging coalition. In the 1999 election, Tzomet failed to get into Knesset at all.

In addition, another former general, Rehavam Ze'evi, formed *Moledet* (Homeland) in 1988. Moledet is the most hawkish of all legal parties on the secular Right: it advocates expelling all Arabs from the occupied territories and annexing the land to Israel. Ze'evi even voted against the peace treaty with Jordan in 1994 and related legal normalization legislation because he argued that Jordan should be for the Palestinians, and that King Hussein of the Hashemites has no business ruling in Amman. In the 1999 election, the far right combined under the leadership of Benny Begin, Menahem Begin's son. It did not do very well, winning only four seats; after which Begin left politics, he said, for good.

Two groups even farther to the right, Kach and Kahane Hai, the latter being an offshoot of the former following the death of Meir Kahane in 1990, are both illegal as of 1994. Kahane did sit in the Knesset for a session (1984–88) before Kach was declared ineligible to stand for the Knesset in 1988 on the grounds that it was declared a racist organization by the High Court.

This brings us lastly to the religious parties. Kach and Kahane Hai are religious parties in a sense; Kahane was a rabbi and the rationale behind the group's view is self-defined as religious. But despite defining themselves as the only "true" Zionists, both groups are so far from the views of most Israeli religious parties as to fall into a separate category.

We have already distinguished the two shoots of Israel's religious parties: the Zionist Mizrahi movement that became the National Religious Party (HaMafdal, by acronym for *Hamiflaga Hadatit Haleumit*) and the non-Zionist Agudah Israel. Religious Zionism has had its fissures, too.

First, Mizrahi split in 1922 into two wings, the more left-wing parts calling themselves *Hapoel Hamizrahi* (Workers Mizrahi). In 1925 even Agudah Israel split, an industrial workers group forming Poalei Agudah Israel, which was less vociferously anti-Zionist.[18] In 1935 Agudah split again, with Neturei Karta (mainly the Israeli wing of the Satmar *hasidim*) moving into a radical anti-Zionist position. In 1956, the two Mizrahi branches came back together to form the National Religious Party. In 1948, all the religious parties ran as one list and won just over 12 percent of the vote. The two Agudah parties have frequently run as the United Torah Front. Before 1967, no matter how they organized themselves to run for Knesset, they got around 12 percent of the vote and Mafdal generally found itself in coalition with Labor. While in coalition, it more or less left diplomacy and security issues to Labor, while it was more interested in religious questions and resources for religious institutions.

The 1967 War changed things quite dramatically. Tzvi Yehuda Kook, following in the footsteps of his father, interpreted the 1967 War in jolting metahistorical terms: he saw it as a sign that the messiah would soon arrive. Various forms of religio-nationalist messianism slowly began to emerge and grow. This movement coalesced in part into *Gush Emunim* (the Bloc of the Faithful) around 1973. Originally, Gush Emunim arose within the NRP, but as an explicit settler movement with a more explicit and more theologically exotic point of view, gradually distanced itself from the NRP and came to associate instead more with Tehiya and, in more extreme form, with Kach.[19]

Another defection from the NRP in 1981 was Tami (an acronym for *T'nuah Lamasoret b'Israel*, or Movement for Tradition in Israel), a group of NRP members mainly of Moroccan origin led by Aharon Abu-Hatzeira. Tami did reasonably well at first, but did not last long as a party.

Then, in 1983, Rabbi Moshe Druckman founded a Zionist-Religious bloc out of the NRP called Matzad. Matzad then decided to join with Poale Agudat Israel (still a non-Zionist party but being pulled toward Zionism) in 1984, calling the combination *Morasha* (Heritage). Then in 1984, David Glass led a faction out of the NRP and into Labor in an attempt to form a religious faction within Labor. This did not get far, but it did hurt the NRP. The only two religious figures of note in the Labor party in recent years have been Rabbi Menahem Hacohen, the rabbi of the *moshav* movement, and Avraham Burg, son of former Mafdal head Yosef Burg, who became head of the Jewish Agency in 1995 and then Knesset speaker in 1999.

In 1984, Agudah split again along ethnic lines similar to Tami's split away from the NRP. In advance of the 1984 election, Sepharadim in Jerusalem felt as thought they had been locked out of Agudah Israel's list, and that the Ashkenazim had adopted a condescending attitude toward them—which they had. So under the direction of the former Chief Sepharadi Rabbi, Ovadia Yosef, they bolted and formed Shas, which stands for *Sepharadim Shomrei Torah*, or Sepharadi Torah Guardians. The name has additional resonance, however, because Shas is a common abbreviation—and has been for several centuries—for *shisha sidrei Mishnah*, the six books of the Mishnah, the inner core of the Talmud. In 1984, it won four seats. In 1988, it won six, and in 1992, it won six again and this time and entered a coalition with Labor. But this deal did not last very long, partly because Shas's public is more right-wing than its leadership, but at the same time less anti-Zionist or non-Zionist. In 1996 it won ten seats, and in 1999 it won seventeen, just two short of Likud. Shas has become the third largest bloc in the Israeli political system.

A final word may be said about the political orientations of Shas and Morasha and the syntheses they represented. Shas came out of Agudah Israel, which is non-Zionist, and Agudah Israel has not typically had strong views on nationalist and security-related matters. This is why even after 1967, when the NRP moved ever farther toward the nationalist Right, Agudah Israel remained a suitable candidate for explicit or implicit coalition with Labor. Shas follows that line; Rabbi Yosef has pronounced that *Klal Israel* is more important than *Eretz Israel*, that the people of Israel are more important that the land of Israel, meaning that security for the people is more important than the need to hold now and always all the territories bequeathed to the Jewish people by God. Shas thus follows Agudah's traditional political line in this respect.

But Agudah Israel itself has moved away from political neutrality on such issues, and this may cause further splits in the future. The Morasha synthesis indicated that some *haredim* are moving toward a more explicitly nationalist stance. Some call this new combination by the adjective *hurdal*, for *haredit datit leumit*, or ultra-Orthodox religious nationalist. *Hardal* also means "mustard," so it's a spicy little acronym at that.

One can see this phenomenon in two ways. First, the worldwide Lubavitch movement has adopted a nationalist position, spending millions of dollars advertising in American and Israeli papers against territorial concessions to the Arabs. Under the direction of its leaders, including the late Menahem Schneerson, the Lubavicher Rebbe, tens of thousands of *haredi* citizens of the state returned to Israel to vote in the 1992 election against Yitzhak Rabin and the Labor party. Also, some *haredim* have come to pray at the grave of Baruch Goldstein near Hebron, the man who killed twenty-nine Arab worshipers in February 1994. Until a few years ago, this kind of politicization of the *haredi* community would have been almost unthinkable.

Agudah Israel may split over this, for other groups within it oppose this position. The non-*hasidic* elements, remnants of the *misnagdim* led by Rabbi Eliezer Schach under the banner of *Degel HaTorah* (Flag of the Torah) within Agudah Israel, appear to oppose it, too. Nonetheless, the Agudah groups ran together in 1996 as Yahdut HaTorah, and won four seats. They won five in 1999.

The Media and the Intellectual Elite

The media are sometimes called the Fourth Estate, meaning the fourth branch of government outside of the executive, the legislative, and the judiciary. The media matter in Israel even more than they do in the United States in some ways. In the United States, newspapers and newspaper syndicates may sympathize with the Democrats or the Republicans, but they are not literally owned by a political party and their editorials are not determined by a party line. The Israeli press, however, began as a government press at least in part. Every major movement had its own paper during Mandate times. There were also independent papers, including the English-language *Palestine Post* (now *Jerusalem Post*) and several papers in European languages.

Since 1948, Israelis have continued to be avid newspaper and journal readers, just as they avidly listen to radio news. The number of daily newspapers sold per capita in Israel is the highest in the world. Nowadays, about a dozen papers publish daily. Four are in Hebrew, two in Arabic, one in English, several are in Russian, and there are three small-circulation papers in other European languages. There are also many regional weeklies.

The best paper by far is *Ha'aretz* (The Land), founded in 1919. Its coverage is most complete, its literary quality by far the highest, and its reputation for accuracy the best. It usually follows a left-of-center editorial line, which enrages the Right. Until recently there were two party papers. One was *Al-Hamishmar* (On Guard), the organ of Mapam, which stopped publishing in March 1995 for lack of funds. The other was *Davar* (Word, or Message), the organ of the Labor party, which finally folded in April 1996 for financial reasons. *Davar* was not at every newsstand like other papers, but was delivered to every Labor party and Histadrut member. It was Israel's second-best paper in literary and intellectual quality, and was modestly influential. *Ha-Tzofeh* (The Vista) is the National Religious party paper that caters to the religious community; hardly anyone else reads it. There are two tabloid mass circulation dailies, *Ma'ariv* (Evening) and *Yediot Aharonot* (Latest News . . . it looses a lot in translation), and these sell more than all other papers combined. The two compete vigorously for advertising and circulation. They tend to support conservative domestic policies and moderately hawkish, nationalist security and foreign policies, but like all the papers, their opinion columns and editorials reflect fairly diverse viewpoints.

The English language paper is the *Jerusalem Post*. It used to be slightly to the Left or centrist until the mid-1980s, when its ownership and editorial control shifted to those with right-wing points of view. This has caused some confusion because many Arab leaders read the *Jerusalem Post* because they don't read Hebrew, and many diaspora Jews subscribe to a weekly overseas edition, again because they can't understand Hebrew. This leads them to sometimes think that the opinions expressed in this paper represent centrist, mainstream views. Generally they do not.

Finally, an Arabic daily, *al-Ittihad*, is the organ of the Communist party. (Two Arabic papers also publish in Israeli-controlled east Jerusalem, *Al-Quds* and *an-Nahar*, the former tending to be pro-PLO and the latter pro-Jordanian.)

No Jewish-owned papers are published on Saturday, and all of the papers tend to publish their big "Sunday" edition on Friday. That's when the magazine sections and literary supplements are included. Circulation of the Friday papers is usually about double the circulation of dailies. If a paper has a major attention-grabbing article to run, if often saves it for the Friday edition.

Military censorship applies to newspapers in Israel. News stories have to pass the censor before publication in order to ensure that sensitive information isn't passed on to terrorists or other enemies. Foreign correspondents working in Israel—and there are many—must also submit copy for censorship; when they don't—as has happened on occasion—they may be asked to leave the country.

Some foreign news organizations resent this infringement on free speech, but those who feel this way often do not understand the damage they can cause. For example, when Scud missiles first hit Israel from Iraq on January 17, 1991, some foreign journalists dispatched reports by satellite that described where the missiles hit down. Iraqi gunners did not otherwise have this information and had no way to get it. Learning where their first salvos struck, they were able to adjust their fire and their next salvos hit downtown

Tel Aviv. It simply did not occur to the foreign reporters that such information could be used this way.

Most foreign correspondents like Israel—certainly far more than they like being posted in the Arab world. Israel is an open society, its night life is fun, and its amenities are substantial. For this reason, among others, Israel tends to get perhaps too much news coverage. Stories tend to come from where the correspondents and their camera crews are. Also, because few big-time foreign correspondents speak Hebrew or Arabic, they often rely on Israeli or Arab stringers to do legwork for them. This accounts for the occasional bias and error that creep into reportage from Israel. Some correspondents, too, are just biased against Israel—BBC reporters, it seems, every last one.

As for electronic media, the airwaves carry all sorts of sounds in Israel. The radio in Hebrew includes several *Kol Israel* (Voice of Israel) channels, the government station, and *Galei Tzahal* ([Radio] Waves of the Army), the military's own station. *Galei Tzahal* plays such good music that even "hip" teens in Amman have been listening to it for years, something I heard with my own ears in 1981. The BBC broadcasting in English from Cyprus is also audible, as are several Arabic stations broadcasting from Lebanon, Jordan, Syria, and Egypt. There have also been "pirate" radio stations, of left- and right-wing political views, broadcasting from ships in the Mediterranean.

As for television, in 1993 cable came to Israel, and made a significant change in everyday habits. There was no television at all in Hebrew until 1968, and then there was just one station, the government station, broadcasting programming for only a few hours a day. People were proud that there was Hebrew television, but the programming was not very popular. Nowadays, the Hebrew programming has become very sophisticated, especially programming for children, which includes *Rehov Sumsum*, Israel's version of *Sesame Street*. This explains why, in 1965, only 4 percent of Israel households had television sets, whereas by 1980, 90 percent did, and today virtually everyone does.

Much television programming is purchased abroad (from the United States, Australia, and Great Britain primarily) and subtitled in Hebrew—and sometimes also in Arabic. This includes animation dubbed in Hebrew. It is quite a shock for an American to hear for the first time the Ninja Turtles or Bugs Bunny holding forth in Hebrew. Many Israelis are a little worried about the long-term effects of cable TV on the country. On the one hand, it will make learning English easier for students, but on the other, Israeli children will be exposed to images and values that are not Israeli, Jewish, or even necessarily healthy—a problem with television fare in other places, too.

Friday night television includes special Arabic programming. There is a very popular variety show, subtitled in Hebrew, that features traditional Arab music. Some Israeli Arab soap operas appear, too, and an occasional black-and-white Egyptian-made or Lebanese-made movie classic from the 1950s is screened. The news, at different times of the day, is broadcast in Arabic, English, Russian, and French, as well as Hebrew.

The news shows are watched most avidly, and political interview shows, especially the nightly new show *Mabat* (Perspective or View), which is popular and influential.[20] Their main moderators, especially *Mabat*'s Haim Yavin, are national celebrities and the other journalists who participate, most of whom write for the newspapers too, are all household names. Another popular variety show is *Zeh Hu Zeh* (That's That), which is roughly analogous to *Saturday Night Live.*

In recent years, there has been agitation to open a second commercial Hebrew channel, *Arutz Shtayim* (Channel Two), but it took a long time to get going, and cable seems to have short-circuited it. Practically everyone has cable. This was not something the government did lightly, but several Israelis had managed to steal international cable signals—including those of U.S. Armed Forces TV in Europe—and then started selling lines in major cities, digging up soil and putting up poles all over the place. This was both technically illegal and lucrative, so, naturally, the government decided to intervene.

Municipal Government

As noted, municipal government in Israel is traditionally not very important or exciting. Most towns have mayors and local councils, and sometimes the elections are quite competitive. The mayors of Jerusalem, Tel Aviv, and Haifa have some national exposure and, given the right personality and a long tenure, a mayor from a major city can be a significant personage. Teddy Kollek of Jerusalem and Shlomo "Cheech" Lahat of Tel Aviv are good examples.

But the range of power and initiative that can be taken on the local political level is limited. Mayor Kollek used to complain that he didn't even have the authority or the budget to install streetlights in Jerusalem. He exaggerated, but not much.

The main limitation is money. Localities—and there are 256 municipal governments in Israel—cannot levy taxes without the permission of the Interior Ministry, and the Interior Ministry controls the level. Municipal government is therefore always dependent on subsidies from the national government to run local services, and even with those subsidies they are usually in debt. Nearly half of the municipal budget always comes from the national government, and often more than half. But remember, Israel is a single political district, so there is no obvious way that localities can lobby through the system for more money.

Moreover, most services are provided at the national level anyway, Israel being so small. Utilities, including water, do not depend on local government to administer them. All major roads are built and maintained by the state, not the municipality. The electrical grid is a national responsibility and so, of course, is police. No Israeli city has its own local cops the way American towns do. No city or town has an elected school board with its own budget, either; the educational system is national. Health inspections of restaurants are done by the Ministry of Health, and so on and so forth down the line. Beyond that, the state, or the political parties, or the Histadrut offer youth clubs, recreational facilities, and adult education. The private sector, too, increasingly offers services such as exercise clubs, tennis clubs, and swim clubs.

So there really isn't all that much left for municipalities to do besides keeping the library and town center (if there is one) in working order, planting flowers in public areas, cleaning up the streets, dealing with the garbage, and arranging public holiday entertainment (like the fireworks for Independence Day). One thing local government can do is raise and spend additional money for schools, which is why schools in some towns have better facilities than in others. The other thing local government can do, and which is important to many people, is reflect local feeling when it comes to the extent of public observance of the Sabbath, like whether public transportation will be available and whether shops will or will not be virtually forced to close on the Sabbath and holidays.

Local government has had some other important functions through the years, however. In the days when Israel was absorbing large numbers of immigrants from the Arab world and sending many to development towns, local government provided a way for these communities to feel as though they were represented at some level. It also enabled them to develop an understanding and experience with democracy, and to generate leadership for their communities. This was particularly the case after local mayors were elected directly by the people, an innovation from 1978; before then, people voted for city councils by list, and the councils then picked the mayor depending on how the vote turned out.

The same goes for the Arabs of Israel. Municipal government has enabled them to maintain and build their own organizations, preserve their political identity, and make organized representation to the national government. This they have learned to do with increasing sophistication and success.

Also, political coalition building on the municipal level has often been more flexible than on the national level. Revisionist parties, religious parties, and socialist parties sometimes cooperated in ways that would have been hard to imagine on the national level. In such a fashion, the passions of ideological politics are somewhat muted on the local and neighborhood levels.

Basically, however, local government bores Israelis. When local elections are held off-season from national elections, less than 50 percent of the voters usually bother to vote. (When held concurrently with national elections, the figure for municipal polling goes up to around 60 percent, extremely high numbers compared to U.S. voting averages. Voting in Arab municipalities regularly exceeds 90 percent of eligible voters.)

Municipal government is also a virtual dead end politically. In the United States, a political career typically starts locally, and the aspiring politician runs for office in ever widening constituencies: from local council to state representative to the House of Representatives to the Senate. But there is almost no crossover from municipal government, no matter how exalted, to the national level in Israel. Even popular mayors of large cities have trouble breaking into national lists at a high level. One of the reasons for this concerns Israel's political class, our next topic of discussion.

The Political Class and Challenges to the Mainstream

The ideal in American democracy is that there be no professional politicians and that there not be a political class. Our ideal is still very Jeffersonian: the gentleman farmer doing a stint of public service or Davy Crockett going to Washington to patch up the crack in the Liberty Bell. That's why the issue of mandatory term limits for congress members has been discussed so passionately of late. Americans look at Washington, follow the money trail, and become generally nauseated.

Israelis have a different history and a different idea about politicians in general. The last thing that the Zionist founders wanted to be was amateurs, part-timers. As far as they were concerned, there was nothing ignoble about a career devoted to one's people, to the cause, and in time to the state. After over 1,700 years of exile, the very idea of the free exercise of Jewish politics in the land of Israel was exhilarating. The notion that the work ahead was long and arduous, and required the very best from the best and brightest, was taken for granted. The idea of a professional politician really began, then, as the idea of a full-time dedicated public servant, activist, fighter, and thinker. Only after the state was created and things became relatively normal in Israel did this image turn into that of the professional politician. And even then, the image of the politician that came through was that of the country's heroes, such as Ben-Gurion and Moshe Sharett. They were full-time, nay, double-time professional activists and politicians. What was wrong with being like them? Indeed, the idea of the professional public servant-politician inheres in the very notion of *mamlakhtiyut* (statism).

Therefore, from the days of the Yishuv to our own time, Israel's elite has been made up preeminently of politicians and soldiers. The heights of the former are to graduate into statesmen, and of the latter to get to the top of the military and its related intelligence organs. The scientific, intellectual, and business elite are prestigious, to be sure, but not as much so, and a society attracts talent to various areas of work in proportion to the image of reward and status associated with them.

There are other reasons why elite interest in politics lacks the stigma in Israel that it has lately acquired in the United States. First, while political clout does help make one wealthy in Israel as elsewhere, the financial incentive is relatively modest. The ethos of Israeli politicians drives them toward status and fame, not wealth, and those motives don't seem as vulgar as wanting to be rich. None of the best-known politicians in Israel's history have been rich; the early Labor types were mostly ascetics in their personal tastes (outside of Moshe Dayan's appetite for collecting antiquities) and, with a few exceptions, the Likud types have shown no great appetite for personal wealth, either. There have been political scandals having to do with money over the years. There was a Knesset member named Shmuel Flatto-Sharon who engaged in both domestic and international illegalities. There have been various figures from the religious parties—especially Shas in recent years—taking money by dubious means, generally not for personal use but to benefit religious institutions. Avraham Shapira, an Agudah Israel member and former chairman of the Knesset Finance Committee, has been implicated in illegalities too numerous even to mention, and so has Aryeh Deri, the former head of the Shas party. Small-scale bribery and kickbacks are about as ubiquitous as they are anywhere else. But these incidents have generally not involved national leadership, and high-level scandal focused around money has been relatively rare compared to places like Italy—and the United States, for that matter.

Second, political leadership in Israel has always been associated ultimately with the striving for national survival. There has been a general consensus that government was very important because the decisions it made were, ultimately—as Israel's history has shown—ones concerning life and death. Decisions made by U.S. politicians—having to do with the Vietnam War, for example—were as important from time to time, but overall, most Americans do not take politics quite *that* seriously. This makes it somewhat easier for Americans to take a dim view of politicians.

Third, Israelis tend not to share the typical American attitude toward ideal government decision processes as expressions of collective common sense.

Americans often feel that any honest, reasonably intelligent person can figure out the right thing to do when it comes to public policy. We distrust
eggheads and experts, and that's one reason that most Americans would
trade away experience to get freshness in a politician five days out of six.
Israelis tend to appreciate the importance of experience, to think of politics
as an acquired skill, and—partly thanks to army training, no doubt—to believe that expertise is in fact useful in solving problems that can be very
complicated. Israeli attitudes are, in short, more European on this score. If a
typical American populist tried to explain the rationale behind term limits to
a typical Israeli, the American would think the Israeli thick and the Israeli
would think the American deranged.

Fourth, Israelis, especially secular Israelis, are nowhere near as puritanical as Americans, and do not project puritanical attitudes toward politicians.
When one thinks of what has happened to American politicians such as Wilbur
Mills, Gary Hart, Bob Packwood, Chuck Robb, Ted Kennedy, and others
because of their pecadillos with women and drink, one recognizes a pattern
here. Israelis, like Frenchmen, simply cannot understand Americans on this
score. Israelis expect their politicians to be rapscallions and many would be
disappointed if they weren't, for they would ask: How can they deal with
other rapscallions and not get fleeced unless they're rapscallions themselves?
It is fairly common knowledge, for example, that Tzomet leader Rafael
("Raful") Eytan built a house for his mistress right next to his wife's house
at Moshav Adumin. Few Israelis appear to care much about it one way or
another.

Even more interesting, in 1992 Benyamin Netanyahu tried to embarrass
his Likud rival David Levy by claiming that Levy's men had spied on him
while trying to get evidence of his marital infidelity. In fact, though everyone knows Netanyahu has been unfaithful to his wife Sarah, this incident
turned out to have been unproved, and was thought to have been instead an
effort by Netanyahu to hurt Levy. Understand what this says about Israeli
politics: it's worse to reveal someone's adultery on account of a political
motive than it is to commit adultery. Frenchmen understand this readily;
most Americans have a tougher time.

So much for attitudes. The fact is that there is an Israeli political class,
maybe a thousand people at any given time, from the conjunctions of a few
hundred families who overwhelmingly dominate elite politics. They tend to
be Ashkenazic—although this is changing—and to live in Jerusalem and Tel
Aviv. After all, the single electoral district is the sine qua non for the development of the Israeli political class. They generally have college degrees but
not advanced ones, for they've been working in the political trenches from
an early age. They pretty much all know each other and tend to socialize

with and marry each other, too. They have been doing this now for several generations. To a lesser extent, elite military families are engaged in the same patterns, and with a certain interweaving with the political elite. To some extent, even differences of ideology are muted by these social connections and the common sort of life that politicians lead, although it doesn't mute them entirely.

As a result, to understand Israeli politics—who trusts whom, who respects whom, who owes whom—it often helps to know the family histories and marital connections of the players. For example, Abba Eban and Haim Herzog, two Israelis with illustrious prior histories in the military and in politics, are married to sisters (Suzy and Aura neé Ambache) whose father was a prominent individual in Jewish Mandate-era society. Ezer Weizmann was married to his wife, Reuma, by Herzog's father, who was chief Ashkenazic rabbi during the Mandate. And similarly, Meretz Knesset deputy Naomi Chazan, an academic at Hebrew University, was able to make the switch into politics partly because of family ties: her father was Avraham Harmon, a former Israeli ambassador to the United States, and her mother was a member of the Knesset. (This is not to say, of course, that she does not have talents of her own.) One could easily multiply examples, although if one did so one would see that these family ties tend to be more significant in Labor than in Likud or other parties.

Aside from lateral entrances afforded by family connections, the political class is a circumscribed group—though not so much today as it used to be. There is still virtually no way into a party list through business, academia, the media, the foreign service, or municipal government. At the ground level, one works for the party. The Histadrut is another way in to the Labor political elite for, as before, the union is still to some degree a wing of the party. If one represents a particular community—Moroccan, Yemeni, Russian—and is hauling several tens of thousands of votes behind him, that can be a way in as well. Foreign Minister David Levy is of Moroccan Jewish descent and comes from the town of Beit She'an, where many other Moroccans live. Levy brought these votes to Likud, in return for which Likud made a place for him. In general, the Likud, as opposition party, was more amenable to such arrangements in the 1960s and 1970s than was Labor, and it paid off in the Likud's May 1977 electoral victory. Now, Levy's Gesher (bridge) faction is with Labor, and that helped Labor attract more Sepharadic votes in the 1999 election.

Most easily of all, a retired military man can slide sideways into politics at the upper level, and virtually no other kind of professional can do so. Israeli political history is full of generals entering politics: Rabin, Ezer Weizmann, Moshe Dayan, Yigal Allon, Ariel Sharon, Rafael Eytan, Avigdor

Qahalani, and Ehud Barak. Such is the status of the IDF that it carries instant political utility. Oddly, one of the reasons it works so well is not just because Israelis think of military men as competent, take-charge, no-nonsense leaders, but also because they are seen as less politically partisan just because of their having been mute on politics while in the army. Israelis aren't so much disgusted with politicians as they are with partisan backbiting. The generals turned politicians learn the routine soon enough, however, and the voters watch as their white knights turn gray.

Little by little, Israelis have begun to tire of their political class. A great many Israelis, when asked what Israel's biggest problem is, respond "a lack of leadership with vision." There is a certain creeping alienation from politics on the part of large numbers of Israelis, but this is natural in a way as Israel moves from its early revolutionary, heroic period to a more normal one. The problems have become less stark yet at the same time harder to solve. And every Israeli leader pales next to the image of Ben-Gurion.

Yet Israelis are not so disgusted with their political class that they are ripe for revolution, or a level of apathy that would in the foreseeable future bring voting patterns down anywhere as low as those in the United States. For politicians, then, these guys don't do such a terrible job. Still, there has been an increase in recent years in extraparliamentary activity on both left and right fringes of the political system.

The secular Right has stayed pretty much within the legal and political framework of the state, but the nationalist religious Right has tended to wander beyond conventional politics and sometimes well beyond the law—as the November 4, 1995, assassination of Prime Minister Rabin clearly illustrated. There is almost no way to express the magnitude of this particular example of extra-parliamentary activity. Rabin's life paralleled that of the state itself, and his killer was no loner, no weirdo, but a graduate of a noteworthy yeshiva, a former member of an elite military unit, and student at a reputable law school. Israel fell from its heroic stage with the assassination, and it will never be able to go back to it. Indeed, the lingering trauma of the assassination partly explains why Israel's 50th anniversary celebrations in 1998 were relatively subdued. The country was still in a state of mourning for its own innocence.

The assassination was not without notable prologue. During the 1980s, the Gush Emunim generated some small radical splinter groups that aimed at terrorizing Arabs in revenge for Arab terror against Jews, and one underground group plotted to blow up the Dome of the Rock mosque in Jerusalem so that space could be made for building the Third Temple. Some West Bank settlers in the 1990s have come to believe that the democratically elected government of Israel is illegitimate because it is contemplating withdrawing from territories the settlers believe to be theirs by divine right. A few have even threatened to secede from Israel and create the state of Judea. A few others, mainly from the illegal Kach and Kahane Hai groups, attack Arabs not just out of revenge but because they think that Arabs fall into the Biblical category of Amalakites, whom Jews are enjoined to fight in every generation.[21] They also want to create more violence to draw in the army and encourage the notion of "transfer"—the expulsion of the Arab population from the territories.

Haredim also engage in extraparliamentary activity from time to time. It often concerns archeology. Archeology?

The *haredim* believe in the coming physical resurrection of the dead in or after the time of the messiah.[22] Therefore, they oppose cremation and any disturbance of bones in burial areas, for this seems to them to make resurrection much trickier. Archeological digs appear to them to often intrude on areas where there might be ancient gravesites, and the *haredim* have been known to block and try to disrupt excavations. Sometimes the police intervene and a melee ensues, yielding photographs in the newspaper the next day of hundreds of men in black hats and coats pitching rocks at police as they run from their truncheons and water cannons. Back in their own neighborhoods, they occasionally continue their demonstrations by overturning trash receptacles and tearing down street signs. But since the *haredim* set themselves apart from the Zionist character of the state, their demonstrations are seen more as a nuisance and an embarrassment than as a challenge to the legitimacy of the political mainstream.

On the Left, extraparliamentary movements have included *Shalom Akhshav* (Peace Now) and a feminist protest movement called Women in Black, known for dressing in black and standing at different prominent spots in Jerusalem and Tel Aviv, usually on Friday afternoons. The Meretz party is the link between these groups and the Israeli political mainstream. These groups have not broken the law, but they have encouraged IDF recruits and reserves not to serve in the territories, which is technically against the law. Another organization generally of the Left is *B'tezlem* (In the Image),[23] which monitors human rights, particularly in the territories. It sometimes sponsors marches and demonstrations.

On the whole, there is no doubt that extraparliamentary activity has grown in the last twenty years. It has grown primarily on account of the divisive debate over the future of the territories taken in the 1967 War. Before 1977 or thereabouts, there were also extra-parliamentary activities, many of them based on protests by Sepharadi groups against unfair treatment by the government. There was once a group called the Black Panthers, mainly Sepharadi teenagers who went around scrawling graffiti in the Musrara quarter of Jerusa-

lem and in poorer neighbors in Tel Aviv, raging against "gefilte fish" culture.[24] These kinds of extraparliamentary activities have ebbed and practically disappeared, partly because first the Likud and now Shas has captured
those sentiments and brought them into the mainstream, into the Knesset.

In other words, political expressions that the system could not assimilate
rapidly in the mainstream and within the structure of normal politics gave
rise to demonstrations and organizations outside of it. This is normal in all
democratic cultures, and unless it breaks laws, is not prohibited. It does
signal, however, that the system is not responding as well as it might through
normal channels. It's a wake-up call. The health of a democratic political
system is measured not by the absence of extraparliamentary activism—that
could just as easily signal apathy and resignation—but by the system's capacity to integrate protest and bring discussion and solutions within normal
channels. The United States has done this well over time with extraparliamentary movements concerning abolition of slavery, women's suffrage,
unionization, civil rights, and anti-war movements against the Mexican and
Vietnam wars. Israel has a much shorter track record, and its population has
had less time to fully internalize democratic attitudes, but so far its record is
not abnormal or particularly bad.

Given the suddenness with which Israeli society has been composed
and the range and severity of its problems, one might wonder why there
hasn't been even more extraparliamentary activity. The answer, clearly, is
the sense of security siege; Israelis reasoned that they couldn't afford such
undisciplined and diversionary activity from the main threats at hand. Many
Israelis therefore wonder whether the coming of peace and a more normal
situation will result in sharper challenges to Israeli democracy, or whether
a solution to Israel's main political problems with the Arab states and the
Palestinians will remove most of the issues around which extraparliamentary
protest would congeal.

We will return to this key question in the final chapter. But now it's time
to look at Israeli foreign policy.

6

Foreign Policy:
Sources and Substance

Foreign policy generally refers to how the governments of states act in relation to other states. It can also refer to what governments do in relation to
international organizations, multinational corporations, political and military organizations that are not state actors, and sometimes even prominent
individuals. In Israel's case, Jerusalem has diplomatic and other kinds of
relations with many governments, with the United Nations, with several large
corporations that do business in and with Israel, with both the Palestine Liberation Organization and the American Zionist Federation, and publicly and
privately with individuals such as the late British businessman Robert Max-
well, Saudi financier Adnan Khashoggi, and even the pope. In this sense,
Israel is like any other country.

But it seems there is always the Israeli exception. Israel's foreign policy
is not like that of other countries in that it has a special kind of policy—or
better, an added dimension to its policy—toward countries with large Jewish diasporas, and even has a policy directly formulated for dealing with
those diasporas. At base, it seeks to draw those Jewish diasporas toward
Israel, to make its members citizens of the state. There is no other country in
the world—not even other projection states—with a foreign policy whose
major motive, among others, is to draw away specially defined population
groups from other countries and make them citizens of its own state.[1]

There is another important way that Israeli foreign policy differs from
that of the United States, but it is a characteristic it shares to one degree or
another with states like Jordan, Kuwait, and Taiwan. Interests tend to expand with power and, as President Truman's erstwhile secretary of state
Dean Acheson once said, influence is the shadow of power. The foreign

policy of a great power, or even a medium power whose security is not at obvious risk from stronger avaricious neighbors, separates out quite nicely from what is often called national security or defense policy. In other words, since the United States does not worry very much about threats to its territorial integrity and its literal existential security on a daily basis, it has the luxury of involving itself in any number of other international activities, good works, and adventures as it sees fit. This was even true to a considerable extent during the Cold War; it has been ever more true since 1991.

So the Department of Defense takes care of essential security routinely, and it and the State Department and all the other many bureaucratic constituencies involved in the making of U.S. foreign policy have plenty of time, energy, and money left over to worry about places like Somalia, Rwanda, Haiti, Cuba, El Salvador, Burma, Kosovo, and heaven knows where else—all places that cannot pose a major threat to U.S. national security. They also have time to worry about human rights, global environmental issues, the global trade regime, and the law of the sea. In other words, the U.S. government engages in most issues and in most places because it chooses to, not because it has to. Its foreign policy priorities and influence derive from its power, not its predicament.

Small countries that find themselves in a hostile environment do not enjoy the kind of distance that great powers can put between foreign and national security policy. In terms of priorities, the two roll into each other and become more or less indistinct.

Over the years Israel has had various foreign policies not connected to central ideological issues *(aliyah)* and central security concerns (survival), but they have not been of great importance. In the years before 1967 in particular, when Israel's long-term survival was not assured in the minds of most of its people, all aspects of foreign relations were bent to national security concerns. Even promoting *aliyah*, as we have seen, had a major security dimension to it. Israel's foreign economic dealings were related to development and the acquisition of technologies that were often defense related, or came to be in later years. Israeli embassies throughout the world were frankly engaged in many sorts of information collection, if not actual espionage, directly relevant to security concerns: learning about Arab military capabilities, pending arms sales to Arab states, and sundry political personalities, intentions, and intrigues. Its relations with the United States, France, Britain, West Germany, and other major industrial powers were overwhelmingly devoted to securing diplomatic support against the Arabs, military and economic aid, and direct military cooperation and even alliance to the extent feasible.

After 1967, and especially since 1991, Israel's security, while still the major policy concern, has not been as overwhelmingly pervasive as it was in earlier years. So, for example, when Israel negotiates economic agreements with the European Union, the general sense is that such agreements ultimately have more to do with the *standard* of living in Israel than with whether there will *be* living in Israel. The health of the Israeli economy is obviously still related to security concerns seen broadly, but increasingly such concerns have an independent rationale and psychology, as is the case in most normal countries.

The same is true for Israel's foreign relations farther afield. The peace process in recent years has enabled Israel to expand its diplomatic relations to include such major states as India and China. Such relations have important economic and symbolic dimensions that are of greater importance than their direct security relevance. But there is security relevance, too. For example, Israel's modest but not insignificant military relationships with China and India are related to its need to market defense-related goods in order to sustain Israel's own military industries, and that is a national security consideration.

Even when Israel does things like send medical triage teams to Rwanda or Kosovo in the midst of famine and disease bred by war, which it did in 1994 and 1999, respectively, it does so not just out of humanitarian concern—real though that is—but because Israel wants to be seen the world over as a civilized, engaged, responsible member of the international community that in no way remains a pariah state. It also wants to enhance its image in sub-Saharan Africa and the Balkans in order to blunt continuing Arab and Muslim efforts to isolate Israel or limit its presence worldwide. It's a minor scene within an act of a larger play: the Arab-Israeli diplomatic cold war, whose larger stakes are still rooted, albeit to a lesser extent than ever before, in core security concerns. Israel's small size and its general security predicament still order its interests, dictate foreign policy priorities, and define the nature of its limited regional and international influence.

Finally, Israel's foreign policy differs from many others in one final way: history and memory. Foreign policy is never just about interests: security, money, or power for its own sake. It is also about ideals, and as such it is a projection of the values and attitudes of domestic political culture. American foreign policy cares about democracy and human rights because the American people know at some level that their own civilization is based on these values.[2] These are subjects people tend to get emotional about, and it's no surprise that the United States enjoys its warmest relationships with countries whose people share most intimately the same values and the same kinds of experiences that shepherded them historically.

Israelis get emotional about some things in foreign policy, too, but they generally do it alone. Israel is the only Jewish state, and being a Jewish state

is what Israel is mainly about—certainly more so than it is about being democratic or "Middle Eastern." As noted earlier, Jews have long memories, and not
all the memories are pleasant. To say it plainly, memories of past anti-Semitism
of varying hues and intensities still color Israeli foreign policy today.

That's why when national leaders come to Israel from places like Latvia
or Hungary—or even Spain, owing to events that took place in the fifteenth
century!—they come not only as leaders of their respective states but as the
representatives of certain histories. They are ambassadors of memory; and
they know it. It has been the custom that, just as all state visitors to the
United States are taken to Arlington National Cemetery, state visitors to Israel are taken to Yad Vashem, Israel's national memorial to the victims of
the Holocaust. This isn't easy for some European leaders, the guilt of some
of whose predecessors is etched indelibly in history. In general, coming to
terms with history, at least on the symbolic level, is required before anything
like a normal relationship can develop between such a state and Israel.

For many European countries too, coming to terms with Israel is part of a
process of coming to terms with their own histories. Most of these countries
developed for centuries with Jews as the most salient minority within, and
now most have no significant Jewish population. How countries like Poland,
Ukraine, Hungary, Romania—as well as Germany, of course—read their own
travails with nationalism, fascism, and communism depends to some degree
on historical memories of how they related to Jews. Just as Israel cannot think
of such countries as just other countries—like it thinks of, say, Ghana, Australia, or Thailand—so these countries cannot think of Israel as "just another
country" either.

Just one example of these emotional and historical complications ought
to make the matter clear. In early 1995 news reports appeared that some
Israeli weapons had showed up in Serbia, and that some had made their way
to Bosnian Serbs as well. It's not clear how extensive the supply was nor
whether it got to Serbia by means of private arms dealers or whether the
Israeli government knew and approved of such transfers. And, of course,
even if the latter were the case, it does not mean that Israel supported the
Bosnian Serbs or approved of their tactics. Nevertheless, to get the full flavor of this affair, one has to know some facts that predate the establishment
of the state of Israel.

During World War II, a Bosnian Muslim S.S. unit existed and cooperated
with the Nazi occupation of Yugoslavia. The Mufti of Jerusalem, Haj Amin
al-Husseini, took a personal interest in the Bosnian S.S. and photographs of
his visits to them survive today. Most Israelis have seen them. (Muslim
support for the Bosnians, including weapons deliveries from Iran, made an
impression on many Israelis, too.) Additionally, Nazi Germany established

a puppet Croatian state led by an anti-Serbian fanatic named Ante Pavelić. The Croatian government was notoriously anti-Semitic as well as viciously anti-Serb, eagerly rounding up and deporting its Jewish population to concentration camps. Nowadays, many Croatians look upon the wartime puppet state with some nostalgia, though not mainly because it was anti-Semitic. After 1991, the newly independent Croatian government reinstituted the currency of that time and undertook some efforts to rehabilitate the memory of President Pavelić, which for reasons that should be obvious did not fare so well during the Tito regime. Meanwhile, the new president, Franjo Tudjman, wrote a book in which he made remarks about the Holocaust having been exaggerated.

During the war, on the other hand, the Serb population made up the bulk of the anti-Nazi partisan guerrilla army, and there are many documented cases of Serb peasants hiding and helping Jews being hunted by the Nazis and their Bosnian and Croat allies. Some of the survivors became Israeli citizens after the war. Given this history, what would one expect the attitude of the state of Israel to be with regard to the Balkan conflict, a conflict that otherwise directly impinges on Israeli interests not one whit? Given this history, too, some right-wing Israelis reasoned that Israel should support Serbian behavior in Kosovo in early 1999. But this view was widely rejected, and was thought to be an embarrassment, because another way of looking at Jewish history was counterposed against it. What if some power had intervened effectively in the 1930s and 1940s to stop the murder and pillage of minorities? Had that happened, many Israelis reasoned, perhaps the Holocaust would not have turned out the way it did.

Within this example are some of the themes that must be kept in mind in order to understand the deepest source of Israeli foreign policy. What is left is to describe the institutional structure through which the foreign policy of Israel is made, and then to review very briefly its history and current status in various areas of the world.

Institutions: Prime Ministry, Foreign Ministry, Defense Ministry, Intelligence Services

The foreign and security policy of Israel is made by the prime minister and the prime minister's inner cabinet. Historically, foreign and security policy has been as important, if not more important, than domestic policy. Therefore, Israeli politics and Israeli elections have often turned on the extent to which Israelis evaluated the toughness, experience, skill, and verve of the candidates to make the crucial decisions of war and peace, and to conduct Israel's relations with the country's most important allies.

In general, through the years the population has wanted hawks, just as the American electorate's assessment of presidential candidates during the Cold War generally turned on the same qualities. Ben-Gurion was certainly a hawk, and the competition he engaged in with Moshe Sharett in the 1950s turned on this issue. Indeed, for a brief period in 1953–55, Sharett became prime minister and pursued a somewhat softer line in security policy. When Ben-Gurion recovered the prime minister's office in early 1955, one of the first things he did was to launch a major raid on Gaza, which contributed a great deal to the sequence of events that led to the Suez War of 1956. But Ben-Gurion did it because that was what toughness demanded, and that was what produced popular leadership in the country.

Relatedly, Ben-Gurion's successor, Levi Eshkol, was sharply criticized for being indecisive in the crisis that led to the 1967 War, and his place in history has suffered on account of that. Similarly, Golda Meir is not held in high esteem by many Israelis for her actions on the eve of the October 1973 War, in which she allowed Israel to be attacked first so that there would be no doubt in the American mind as to who started the war. This decision proved costly in Israeli lives and many Israelis still think that she should not have given such weight to diplomatic considerations.

Yitzhak Rabin was elected in 1974 largely because he was the hero of the 1967 War and people trusted him. He was also the first *sabra* to become prime minister. Rabin was elected again in 1992 on a similar basis. In the 1992 election, the Likud opposition tried to discredit Rabin by recalling rumors that he had experienced a breakdown just before the 1967 War. True or not, the point is that this shows what the opposition thought was important in Israeli electoral politics. Shimon Peres's losing record as Labor's standard-bearer turns on his image of being untrustworthy and, for some, lacking nerve. Indeed, one reason, reportedly, that Menahem Begin ordered the June 1981 bombing of the Iraqi Osirak nuclear reactor before diplomatic efforts had run their course was his fear that if Peres won the upcoming election, he wouldn't have the nerve to order the raid. Clearly, the personality and temperament of the prime minister, or of whomever would be prime minister, matter a great deal in Israeli politics and history.

The other members of the inner cabinet on foreign policy and security issues usually include the foreign minister and the defense minister. The inner circle (but not the inner cabinet itself) also includes the director-general of the prime minister's office much of the time, people like Avraham Tamir, who worked for Peres; Yossi Ben-Aharon, who worked for Shamir; and Shimon Sheves, who worked for Rabin. If a decision involves a military operation, then often times the chief-of-staff of the military and the heads of Israel's foreign intelligence service, the Mossad, and its defense intelligence agency, Aman, also participate as a policy decision reaches the planning and implementation stage.

Israel's ambassador to the United States is also sometimes a close associate of the inner decision process on foreign and security policy. Over the years, a special relationship has developed between the prime minister and the ambassador to Washington for the simple reason that, even before 1967 when France was supplying most of Israel's sophisticated military equipment, Washington was still the country that stood able to help or hurt Israel the most when it embarked on a major diplomatic or military initiative. While technically the ambassador answers to the foreign minister, in practice he answers directly to the prime minister. This is the relationship Itamar Rabinovich had with Prime Minister Rabin, just as it is the relationship Rabin had as ambassador with Prime Minister Meir in the early 1970s—and as, for example, Ambassador Moshe Arens had with Prime Minister Shamir during a period of Likud leadership of the government.

The prime minister's diplomatic preponderance has also been in evidence since 1992 when, in the Arab-Israeli peace process, Prime Minister Rabin took direct responsibility for negotiations between Israel and the Palestinians, as well as between Israel and the Arab states. Foreign Minister Shimon Peres was responsible for negotiating follow-up details and for overseeing the multilateral track that developed out of the October 1991 Madrid Summit. (Not that Peres was happy with this arrangement.) Peres was, of course, deeply engaged in the Oslo track diplomacy that eventually produced the September 1993 Israeli-Palestinian accord.

The prime minister also chooses his own ambassadors elsewhere. As in the United States, most Israeli ambassadors are professional diplomats from the foreign service, but some are outsiders appointed by the head of government. Political appointment of ambassadors in the United States is more common than it is in Israel, but it still happens. After the Israeli-Jordanian peace treaty was signed on October 26, 1994, the two sides agreed to exchange ambassadors by December. Jordan quickly named Marwan Muasher, but Israel kept stalling. The reason was a heated dispute between Rabin and Peres over who should go to Amman. Rabin, the Palmah veteran, wanted someone he could personally trust, and for him that someone was Efraim Halevi, the deputy head of the Mossad who had been instrumental in bringing the intense secret diplomacy with Jordan to a successful conclusion. Peres wanted a foreign service professional who would be responsive to him, and argued that sending a Mossad official to Amman would be the worst possible signal to the Arab world in general. Peres also argued that the Israeli ambassador to Jordan would be a public emissary, and need not be a key policy player because Rabin and Peres's relationship with King Hussein was so close that any serious and important business would be conducted directly, over the phone or in person. Peres made the better arguments on this point, but Rabin still would not accept a foreign service official as the ambassador to Jordan. After an embarrassing hiatus, they compromised on Shimon Shamir, an academic and former Israeli ambassador to Egypt.

Obviously, the Knesset is very interested in diplomacy and defense policy, but on balance it has little input. It can debate and criticize, but other than its control of the budget for the army, it doesn't have much direct clout. And unlike the case in the United States, where the Democratic party has often urged the reduction of the defense budget, arguing that the threat has been exaggerated, Israeli politicians virtually never do such things. There is simply no significant constituency in Israeli politics for playing fast and loose with the country's security, or for downgrading the status of the army either, for that matter.

Finally, the Histadrut has undertaken projects abroad, often in connection with Israeli Third World aid projects. The Jewish Agency, too, clearly plays a role insofar as foreign policy is directed toward the Jewish diaspora. These are, however, second-echelon functions and second-echelon actors compared to the key security and foreign policy functions of the state.

The Paramountcy of Security: War and Peace

As noted, security and survival have been practically synonymous in Israeli history. Mess up security and lose a war, and the state's survival would be in jeopardy. Having said that, it would be misleading to suggest that Israel's leaders spent every moment of every waking day between the end of the War for Independence and the last several years perseverating over existential threats to the country's very life. They didn't.

This is as good a time as any to review in somewhat more detail the ebb and flow of Israel's security history since 1949. The fact that we've been able to talk about Israel, and in some detail, without having to relate the story of Israel's post–independence wars belies the common image that fighting wars for survival is all Israel ever does, or is all that it's about. Nonetheless, it is very important material.[3]

Israel's successes in 1948–49 were quite stunning, but when looked at analytically, as in Chapter 3, not all that surprising. But the divisions and other problems the Arabs faced in 1948 could not be counted on to last forever. And the Arab insistence on not accepting Israel's right to exist clearly constituted a major long-term problem. Israel's military doctrine, too, has been described: reliance on a small professional army determined on deterrence of attack, and armed with a tactical bias toward maneuver and preemption. Between 1949 and 1956, the Arab states never mounted a conventional military threat to Israel, but they did encourage Palestinians to violate the frontiers and engage in terror. It was difficult to police Israel's long border and not every terrorist raid could be stopped. Though not without controversy and argument, Israel decided under Ben-Gurion to adopt a strong retaliatory policy, punishing any incursion into Israel with a counterstrike many times more powerful. The Gaza raid of February 1955, mentioned earlier, was a prime example of this strategy. So were raids against the towns of Qibya (October 1953) and as-Samu (November 1966) on the West Bank of the Jordan. The aim of these retaliations was to raise the price to, in these cases, the Jordanian government of either encouraging or of just looking the other way when Palestinians undertook such operations. The Israeli thinking was that if it raised the price to the neighboring governments high enough, they would clamp down on the raiding in the interest of self-preservation.

The problem with this approach was twofold. First, it embarrassed and weakened the governments with which Israel ideally wanted to make peace, especially Jordan, making it harder for them to do so. Second, it got Israel in frequent trouble with the United Nations Mixed Armistice Commission officials, who were obligated according to the terms of the 1949 armistices to monitor those armistices against violations from either side. As a result, it also got Israel into trouble with the members of the Security Council, including the United States. For this and other reasons, U.S.-Israeli relations during the two Eisenhower administrations (1953–61) were often quite cool.

The former problem was especially acute with Jordan. Immediately after the 1949 armistices were signed, Israel and Jordan under King Abdallah engaged in intense secret negotiations aimed at bringing about a peace treaty.[4] The negotiations did not stay secret enough, however, and largely as a result of their being leaked, King Abdallah was assassinated in Jerusalem in July 1951 by gunman hired by the al-Husseinis. King Abdallah was a realist who recognized that Israel was an established fact, and an Arab leader whose ambitions were aimed mainly at Syria and Hejaz (wherein is Mecca and Medina), from which the Hashemite family had been expelled by the legions of Abdel Aziz ibn Saud in 1924. He saw both the British and after 1948 even the Israelis as potential allies in his quest. The Zionist-Hashemite relationship had long been pragmatically based and even cordial going back to 1919. While Abdallah's death had put an end to already diminished hopes that a treaty might be signed, it did not make particularly good sense to abuse Israel's most pragmatic and generally compliant neighbor, ruled after May 1953 by Abdallah's grandson Hussein.

As related earlier, Israel's foreign policy in its early years sought neutrality, but the importance of American aid and pressure over the Korean War

combined with Russian anti-Semitism and Stalin's erratic behavior gradually drove Israel toward the West. But given the coolness of the Eisenhower
administration toward Israel, and its refusal to supply Israel with weapons,
Ben-Gurion chose to nurture Israel's relations with France, West Germany,
and also Great Britain—the latter being an ironic twist of political fate for
both former enemies.

In 1952, the Egyptian monarchy was overthrown by a military coup calling itself the Free Officers. By 1954, Gamal Abd al-Nasir had emerged as
the Egyptian leader. Egypt, by far the largest Arab country with the largest
army, had always represented Israel's most serious military opponent. Under King Farouk and the fact of indirect British tutelage in Egypt, however,
there was little to fear from the Egyptians. Nasir was a different matter altogether—a strident Egyptian nationalist and populist who came to develop
an almost mystical power over the Egyptian people. Nasir was able to mobilize the Egyptian masses like the monarchy never could. He was also deeply
anti-British and had ambitions of uniting the entire Arab world—or as much
of it as possible—under his mantle. To do that, Nasir had fixed on the Palestine problem as the quintessential pan-Arab issue. To Israel, he looked like a
dangerous customer, plain and simple.

Under Nasir, Palestinian *fedayeen* raids increased in frequency and intensity into Israel from Gaza, which Egypt occupied in 1948 but never annexed to Egypt as the West Bank was annexed to Jordan. Between 1951 and
the Suez War in October 1956, more than 400 Israelis were killed and 900
injured in more than 3,000 incidences of armed infiltration, a large number
of these attributable to infiltration from Gaza. Ben-Gurion wanted to teach
Nasir a lesson and the U.N. Mixed Armistice Commission too, which seemed
to Israel to be providing a shield for attacks against Israeli civilians by claiming that there was no evidence that the Egyptian regime was complicit in the
attacks. The Gaza raid of February 1955 was the lesson, but it backfired
badly. The raid so shocked the Egyptian government, and so rattled the army,
that it accelerated Nasir's political inclinations and his impulsiveness. Nasir
made a deal with the Soviet Union through Czechoslovakia to acquire massive amounts of Russian weapons. At the same time, Nasir accelerated his
campaign to rid Egypt of all vestiges of British rule, particularly British
control over the Suez Canal.

The Egyptian-Czech arms deal stunned the United States, which at that
time under Secretary of State John Foster Dulles had been trying to assemble
an anti-Soviet alliance from among the Arabs. Some sort of an alliance,
directed by the British, had emerged in 1954–55 as the Baghdad Pact, which
included Pakistan, Iraq (then a Hashemite monarchy like Jordan), and Turkey. With the Egyptian-Czech arms deal, the Soviet Union had managed to

leapfrog the Baghdad Pact. Worse, with Soviet diplomatic backing, Nasir nationalized the Suez Canal in 1955 and drove the British out.

By driving out the hated British and bringing in the Soviet Union, Nasir had pulled off a diplomatic-strategic coup of enormous weight. He had also brought the Cold War directly into the Middle East, internationalizing a regional problem and making it much more dangerous for everyone. From the Israeli point of view, Nasir was now in a much better position to get sophisticated weapons and to bring about the military coordination of the Arabs against Israel. In the face of this, Israel all but begged the United States for a security alliance and for arms to offset the Soviet shipments to Egypt to come. Instead, the United States continued to push a secret plan for solving the Arab-Israeli conflict, known as Operation Alpha, that contained elements—like Israel's giving up substantial territory in the Negev—completely unacceptable to Israel. The British, under Evelyn Shuckburgh at the British Foreign Office, at first saw the growth of Egyptian power as a means to get Israel to buckle under to the demands of Operation Alpha. For a time, so did Shuckburgh's American counterparts. The United States also believed that Egypt's early dalliance with Moscow was not irrevocable, and tried to wean Nasir away from Moscow with offers of weapons and dams on the Nile.

The American reaction to Nasir's strategy sent a deep foreboding through the Israeli leadership. The Soviet Union had become a double enemy: an ally to those who would destroy Israel and a repressor of Jews inside its borders as bad as, or worse, than in the days of czars. Ben-Gurion concluded that war with Egypt—a second round—was inevitable and he wanted to fight it on terms most advantageous to Israel: that is, before Soviet arms shipments could be absorbed into the Egyptian order of battle. As it happened, Nasir's dalliance with the Soviets soon began to take on a air of being more permanent.[5] With the nationalization of the Suez Canal, the British under Prime Minister Anthony Eden began to see Nasir as an Arab Hitler— an exaggeration, to be sure, but Eden was a master of exaggeration and mental hyperbole. At the same time, the French colony of Algeria, in the heart of Arab North Africa, was rising in revolt and Paris saw Nasir's pan-Arabist agitation behind the trouble.

By early 1956, then, Israel, Britain, and France all had good reasons for wanting to get rid of Nasir. So they together tried to do just that. On October 29, 1956, Israel invaded Egypt. On the afternoon of the next day, Britain and France invoked the 1950 Tripartite Declaration—designed to protect the Suez Canal from the Soviets—as an excuse to intervene, ostensibly to stop the Israelis. The plan called on both sides to stop fighting and withdraw to positions ten miles from either side of the canal. This, of course, was the pretext the British wanted to reoccupy the canal themselves. According to the secret plan, Israel was to agree but Egypt would of course refuse. At this point, Britain and France were supposed to swoop down and occupy the canal, at the same time sending special forces to get Nasir. But the British, in particular, screwed up the operation royally. While the Israelis had taken Sharm al-Sheikh, at the far end of the Sinai Peninsula, by November 5, the British and French failed to occupy even a third of the canal before the U.N. called a cease-fire supported by both the United States—which had not been told of the plot—and the Soviet Union.

President Eisenhower and Secretary Dulles were furious with the British and the French, their key NATO allies. They believed that what had been done was illegal, wrong, and stupid, for it would push the Arabs into the arms of the Soviet Union.[6] Washington moved to undermine the British currency in forcing the British, French, and Israelis to get out of Egyptian territory. Not surprisingly, Nikita Khrushchev sought to take credit for the solution.

In any event, Israel withdrew by mid-1957, but with a promise from the United States and the international powers that the Red Sea and the Straits of Tiran, heretofore blockaded by Egypt, were international waterways. A U.N. buffer force was also introduced into the Sinai to prevent a recurrence of war. These arrangements opened up the port of Eilat and helped develop the Negev. Back in Israel, the quashing of the Egyptian army was hailed as a great victory, and its architect, Moshe Dayan, a great hero. In retrospect, however, the Suez Campaign, as it became known, does not look so glorious.

First, Israel's collusion with the hated European colonialists played into highly charged and highly erroneous Arab interpretations of Israel as a conspiratorial extension of European imperialism, an axiom of Arab nationalism for decades. It also magnified in Arab eyes their wildly distorted image of Israel as a ruthless aggressor with almost limitless expansionist intentions.[7] Second, the international guarantees acquired by Israel in 1957 and the U.N. buffer force both proved worthless when they were put to the test in 1967, and Israel had to go to war again to preserve its one diplomatic achievement from the 1956 effort. Third, despite the Egyptian defeat on the field of battle, Nasir actually emerged stronger, and the Egyptian-Soviet alliance of convenience emerged stronger, too. Israel's main design in the war—to break Nasir and end the eventual threat of a broad Soviet-Arab combination against Israel—flatly failed. The spinoffs from Suez almost led to the collapse of the Jordanian monarchy to pro-Nasir pan-Arabists, to the collapse of a similarly non-threatening order in Lebanon, and by 1958 it *did* lead to the overthrow of the Iraqi monarchy and the establishment of an anti-Western, and eventually pro-Soviet, military government (eventually inherited by Saddam Hussein). By 1956, too, France did lose Algeria, which also moved, seemingly anyway, toward the Soviet orbit.[8] Finally, the Suez War was a war of choice for Israel despite the reality of the threat to Israel's survival that Nasir's armed diplomacy portended. In 1982, many Israelis described the war in Lebanon as the first war Israel fought by choice rather than necessity *(milhemet ain brayra)*. But this was not strictly true.

None of these developments benefited Israel in the longer run. That it all flowed originally from a flawed American policy during the Eisenhower administration, whose standoffish attitude toward Israel brought about the very troubles it was designed to avoid, just goes to show that the mistakes of the mighty often come down upon the heads of the weak.

The Suez War did bring some benefit to Israel, however. Israel was now taken more seriously as a regional actor by the United States, Britain, France, and others—including others in the developing world—and it may well have bought Israel ten years of relative quiet, during which it worked hard to consolidate its newly forming society. It also ended the porosity of Israel's southern border for a long while.

After Suez the Israeli alliance with France deepened, and France became Israel's most important ally. Israelis learned French as a second language—answering a question posed in Chapter 1, remember?—and Israel acquired its first truly modern air force from France. More important perhaps, if secret at the time, Ben-Gurion had concluded that the general trend of the Arab-Soviet alignment called for Israel's attainment of a nuclear deterrent. The only way to deter a concerted Arab attack against Israel, organized and led by Nasir, was to threaten nuclear retaliation. Ben-Gurion's trusted aid, Shimon Peres, was put in charge of the effort and, with much French help, he succeeded in founding Israel's nuclear program at Dimona, in the northern Negev. No one knows for sure when Israel developed its first deliverable atomic bomb, but it was probably an accomplished fact by 1969—not in time for the June 1967 War. Israel's deterrent doctrine also developed in tandem: not to be the first to use nuclear weapons in the Middle East, not to affirm possession of a nuclear capability, but to leave no doubt that if ever pushed to the wall of its own survival, the aggressors had best be prepared to swallow a most bitter nuclear pill.

Again, from 1956 to 1967 the Arabs did not mount a serious conventional military threat against Israel. This was despite the continuance of Nasir's tenure in Egypt and considerable military aid to Egypt (and now to Syria) from the Soviet Union. The Arab failure to credibly threaten Israel was not from a general lack of desire, but on account of a lack of capability. This lack of capability, about which the Israeli leadership was generally aware, turned on three elements: Arab collective military inferiority; disunity and rivalry among the Arab states; and the diplomatic and military-technical dependency of the Arabs on both the Soviet Union and the major Western states, none of whom generally found their interests served by another Arab-Israeli war.

Nevertheless, in 1964, a new crisis in Arab-Israeli relations broke out over the construction of Israel's National Water Carrier. Arab summits met under Nasir to discuss ways to foil Israel's plans. Several schemes were hatched, including the diversion of waters in Lebanon and Syria that flowed naturally into Israel. Israel viewed such schemes seriously, for if implemented, they threatened the potential for the state's economic development and hence its long-term security. The Arabs viewed these schemes as rightful, for they were in a state of war with Israel. They believed that Israel's growing power would become a greater threat to them if, through the National Water Carrier, Israel was able to irrigate the Negev and expand its presence and population throughout what the Arabs still invariably called Palestine.

To most Israelis, it seemed ludicrous that the Arab world, with more than twenty countries and 200 million people, could seriously be worried about one Jewish state with, at the time, fewer than 4 million people. The Arabs, who believed that Israel was an extension of Western imperialism that hatched conspiracies against the Arabs on a near daily basis, could not comprehend how Israel could depict itself as such a benign, peace-loving entity. Hadn't Israel displaced the Palestinians, won two wars (1948 and 1956), and refused to define its final borders? Most Israelis could not appreciate how the Arabs thought about the conflict, simply not believing that the outlandish things they said were genuinely felt. And the Arabs could not appreciate how Israel saw things, could not understand that Israel took Arab political rhetoric at face value—something that Arabs among themselves rarely if ever do.

In the period before the 1967 War, the Arab-Israeli conflict was certainly real, but cultural differences clearly added a significant level of mutual misperception to the actual divergences of interest, which made everything worse. Both sides sincerely saw themselves as in the right, as the aggrieved party, and both sides believed that the other side couldn't possibly be serious about feeling that way. The other side, therefore, had to be lying, to be planning deceit, to be untrustworthy, to be cynical and capable of any enormity. When mutual expectations in a conflict take on these characteristics, it becomes very hard to solve the actual conflict, which may or may not be as acute as the emotions and mutual misperceptions make it seem.

The 1964 Arab summits, and Nasir's leadership of them, also led to another very portentous development. In 1964, under Egyptian aegis, the Palestine Liberation Organization was founded. Before 1964, the Palestine national movement was eclipsed by defeat and by the thunder of pan-Arabic rhetoric and hope at its heyday, in which individual Arab nationalism was subsumed beneath the desire to unite all the Arab world as the precondition to its renewed greatness and power. By 1964, Nasir's star was already fading. He had failed to unite the Arab world behind him, and now faced both republican opposition (as in Iraq after 1958) and monarchical opposition from Saudi Arabia and Jordan. The United Arab Republic, a union of Egypt and Syria formed in 1958, had fallen apart by 1961. Nasir's Egypt was at war in Yemen, fighting on behalf of one group and against another backed by Saudi Arabia. Egypt's economy had failed to perform; the nationalization of foreign interests and the bureaucratization of the Egyptian government and economy had lead to progressive ruin, and with it dependency on the Soviet Union. This dependency, rather than burnishing Nasir's reputation for independence and boldness, now sullied the image of Egyptian sovereignty. The creation of the PLO was a means of rebuilding Egypt's image behind the quintessential pan-Arab issue, and a means of fighting the Arab cold war Egypt was waging against Iraq, Saudi Arabia, and Syria. The origins of the June 1967 War simply cannot be understood unless the state of inter-Arab politics and the Egyptian position within them are understood first.

The Syrian regime grasped what the formation of the PLO was meant to do. So in opposition to Egypt, Syria found its own Palestinian proxies in the person of Yasir Arafat's al-Fatah,[9] an organization formed in Kuwait some years earlier. Syria armed and financed al-Fatah, which attempted its first raid against the Israeli National Water Carrier on January 1, 1965. It failed.[10] By 1965 then, Syria and Egypt, each with its own Palestinian proxy organization, were escalating their attacks on Israel, even though the real dynamic that drove events was less a determined effort to destroy Israel than a determined effort to wage the Arab cold war. Most Israelis were not overly concerned with the Arab cold war; all they knew was that their borders were again becoming increasingly perilous, and the occasional terrorist attack was succeeding in killing soldiers and unlucky civilians.

Troubles escalated sharply after February 1966, when a coup in Damascus brought to power a very radical Syrian regime under Nureddin al-Atassi that aimed to simultaneously challenge Nasir's leadership of the Arabs and Israel's ability to live in comfort. The Syrians challenged and ridiculed Nasir, and stepped up their anti-Israel acts, sponsoring terrorist raids and beginning diversion projects of the Banias, one of the three sources of the Jordan River. For about a year, between the spring of 1966 and the spring of 1967, tensions between Israel and Syria rose sharply. The Israeli air force attacked and destroyed Syrian water-diversion projects, a few minor land skirmishes were fought, and Syrian gunners intensified their shelling of Israeli civilian settlements from the heights of Golan.

Nasir did not want war with Israel; between 1964 and 1967 he made it clear on several occasions that the Arabs were not yet ready; that if they went to war they would lose. In May 1967, Egypt's best troops were still fighting in Yemen. But the Syrian challenges, and the increase in Syrian-Israeli fighting, forced Nasir to escalate his rhetoric to stay in the game with the Syrian regime. The Soviet Union, ally and military supplier to both Syria and Egypt, also played a mischievous role, exaggerating the dangers of an Israeli-Syrian clash to Egypt.

In any event, the Egyptian response to Syrian behavior led to a kind of war fever among the Arabs, and Syria and Egypt found themselves in a bidding war throughout 1966 and into 1967 to see who could be most bold, most bellicose, and most bracing in standing up to Israel. In mid-May, Nasir upped the ante. He proclaimed a national state of emergency, mobilized the entire Egyptian army, and moved troops across the Sinai toward the Israeli border. Then on May 16, Nasir requested the partial removal of the United Nations Emergency Force (UNEF) troops that had been placed there in 1957. To Nasir's surprise, the U.N. Secretary General, U Thant, confronted him with a choice: total withdrawal or none, and Nasir had no choice but to ask for total withdrawal. Thant complied even though, according to the terms of the 1957 arrangements, he lacked the authority to do so. Egyptian and Israeli armies suddenly stood face-to-face, with no buffer in between.

Naturally, Israeli Prime Minister Levi Eshkol watched these developments with great concern. On the one hand, he knew that Israel was strong and that the Arabs were mainly feuding among themselves. He doubted that Egypt really wanted to go to war. Instead, the Israeli government concluded that the most likely aim of Egyptian diplomacy was to force diplomatic concessions of some kind from Israel. It soon became clear what Nasir wanted. As the armies stood blinking at one another, Nasir declared the Straits of Tiran closed to Israeli-bound shipping, which locked in Israel's southern port area and the town of Eilat. Technically, this was an act of war. Diplomatically, it was clear that Nasir was trying to reverse the one gain Israel had made from the 1956 Suez War. The decision facing Israel was how to prevent Egypt from getting away with this scheme.

Israel turned first to the United States and the international community at large, which had solemnly guaranteed the international status of these waterways in 1957, and in consideration for which Israel withdrew its forces from the Sinai. Israel asked that the United States fulfill its promise and honor its commitments. It asked the same of France, Britain, and the other guarantors. Israel wanted some sort of international flotilla to sail from Aden to Eilat to demonstrate the 1957 pledge, and force Egypt to back down in the process.

The key, clearly, was in Washington, but President Lyndon Johnson was reluctant to act. Why? Because of the Vietnam War. American forces, including the U.S. Navy, were committed in Southeast Asia. America's European allies were not eager to buck Egypt either, worried that doing so would stir up a confrontation between the United States and the Soviet Union at a time when the American deterrent along the inter-German border was believed uncertain. Most shocking for Israel, its best ally, France, suddenly reversed its position under Charles DeGaulle and threw its support to the Arabs.

As a result of what happened in May 1967, Israel lost all confidence in the value of United Nations—and, for that matter, international—guarantees. It has not regained any confidence in them since, except U.S. guarantees to a limited extent.

When Israel saw that it stood alone, a national unity government was formed with Moshe Dayan, the hero of the Suez Campaign, as minister of defense. Israel made urgent and discreet inquiries as to what the U.S. attitude would be if Israel launched a war to break the Egyptian strategy. The American government was not of a single mind. A war in the Middle East between American and Soviet clients at the same time America was fighting in Vietnam might provide the Soviets with a chance to hurt an American asset—Israel—at a moment when U.S. forces were stretched too thin to reliably help. On the other hand, if Israel whipped Soviet-supplied allies and the United States did not move to stop them, then a signal of some power would be sent to Moscow. When there is a difference of opinion on such questions in the American government, the view of the man who sits in the Oval Office turns out to be the opinion that matters. President Johnson told the Israelis to go ahead if they had to, but not to count on the United States to come to their rescue if they got into trouble. In the meantime, Johnson promised to make sure the Soviet Union did not interfere; to this end, when the war began on June 5, the United States put its nuclear weapons in an upgraded alert status called Defense Condition 3 (Defcon 3) to indicate "hands off" to the Soviets. Moscow took the hint.

Meanwhile, the war fever had now spread to Palestinians living mainly in the West Bank, including many refugees from the 1948 War who now believed that the hour of their revenge against Israel and their "return" to Palestine was at hand. They rioted against the Hashemite king, who soon concluded that he had better join the forming Arab war coalition or risk losing his throne to a popular insurrection aided and abetted by Egyptian, Syrian, and Iraqi agents and sympathizers inside Jordan. This King Hussein did on May 30, 1967.

By early June 1967, therefore, Israel faced several very serious questions. Could Israel beat all the Arabs simultaneously, and quickly enough so that it would not have to assure itself of a major military resupply? After all, Israel's air force was French, and it had no assurance of being able to keep its air force flying for weeks on end now that the French diplomatic attitude had changed. Second, should Israel wait to see if the Arabs would strike first? Israel had never faced a real Arab war coalition before and the results of a war started by the Arabs on their terms and timetable could not be known for certain ahead of time. Even if Israel won such a war, what would the cost be? Moreover, Israel was now fully mobilized, and each day of mobilization destroyed the sense of normalcy in the country, not to speak of the economy. Israel could not afford the waiting period *(hamtanah)* after the mobilization for very long, or that alone would destroy the country.

The key questions for the Israeli leadership, then, were these: Assuming that the Arabs would not actually go to war, were the uncertainties of launching a war worth it to defeat Nasir's diplomatic strategy of reversing the gains of 1956–57? Especially if Israel's mobilization could not be maintained, would the Arabs have talked and postured themselves into making war anyway, even though it was not their intention from the start? What might the difference be in the outcome, and in the costs to Israel, if the Arabs were to strike first?

The Israeli political leadership thought through these questions as its military leadership frantically generated options to be reviewed. Israel would not allow itself to be defeated by Nasir's diplomacy, for the demands and pressures, they believed, would only get worse. Israel couldn't know that the Arabs wouldn't attack anyway, and both the costs of waiting and the costs of not going first were believed too great to bear. Moreover, in the street Israelis looked upon the situation in far less optimistic tones; they thought this might be the end of the state, and such a psychology could not be allowed to persist for long.

Besides, the Israeli military had devised a plan it believed would work. Israel also hoped it could at least keep Jordan out of the war, making it a two-front instead of a parlous three-front affair (as in 1948), and it communicated to Jordan via a third party that if Jordan did not shoot first, Israel would not either. In effect, Israel tried to recreate the relationship that worked in 1948.

Israel launched the war on June 5; the first wave was an air strike in which Israel destroyed virtually all of the combat-capable Arab air forces on the ground. The Arabs were confused, and began fighting without air cover or even a real plan of attack. The Jordanians had given command of armored forces in the West Bank to an Egyptian general, and when Jordan fired artillery shells into Israel, the war expanded to all three fronts anyway. In five more days of fighting, the Syrian, Jordanian, and Egyptian armies were all defeated and lay in ruin. The Jordanians again fought hard in Jerusalem, but this time they lost it along with the entire West Bank. A flow of about 250,000 refugees began into the east bank, some now refugees twice over who had moved to the West Bank from Israel in 1948–49. Syria lost the Golan Heights despite having the great advantage of that high ground. Egypt again lost the Sinai, its army not retreating in an orderly fashion but essentially leaving its equipment in the field and running away every man for himself. Token forces that had come from Iraq—as well as the Palestine Liberation Army in Gaza—were either routed or ran away.[11]

The Arab defeat was thorough, total, and utterly humiliating. Nasir offered to resign, but he was denied by the Egyptian people who acclaimed him even in abject defeat. Nasir and King Hussein agreed to make up stories about how the American and British air forces had helped Israel on the first day of the war in order to reduce the sting of the humiliation. Arab intellectuals believed that the rottenness and corruption of the Arab regimes had reached a new nadir.

In Israel, the reaction, naturally, was jubilation. The taking of the Old City of Jerusalem was by far the most poignant moment. This was, for secular as well as religious Israelis, the ultimate achievement; if Jerusalem was the heart of Israel, Israel now had a whole heart instead of only part of one. The entire country cried with joy, songs were written, spontaneous pilgrimages and festivals broke out. Religious Zionists of the Rabbi Kook school of thought, not surprisingly, interpreted the victory as the finger of God in history, as a sign that the final redemption and the rebuilding of the temple were at hand. Given that the average Israeli really didn't understand the actual balance of military power, and even less the divisions and capacities for ineptitude among the Arabs, the victory was widely hailed as a miracle even by those who were not swayed by Rabbi Kook's interpretation of Zionism. In fact, the war turned some people into believers, and the NRP experienced a temporary political boom.

More pragmatically, Israel's leadership hoped that the war would finally convince the Arabs that Israel was a fact, that it was here to stay, and that the Arab states had better make peace with it. Israel offered to return virtually all of the territories taken in the war for peace and normal relations, but the Arabs were not in a conciliatory mood. Their humiliation and sense of dishonor instead drove them to a postwar summit in Khartoum, Sudan, where they declared the "three no's": no peace, no recognition, no negotiations with Israel. With American help and Israeli assent, the U.N. Security Council in November 1967 developed Resolution 242, which called upon the Arabs to make peace, in return for which Israel would return territories taken in the June War.[12] The Arabs refused. Most Israeli believed that eventually the Arab states would sober up, and that the territories could be traded for peace. The Labor government of the day decided just to wait; meanwhile, it annexed East Jerusalem to the newer part of the city and began putting pressure on the Arabs by establishing first a paramilitary and then a civilian presence in the occupied territories in those areas seen as vital for security purposes: the Jordan Valley, around Jerusalem, and atop the Golan Heights in particular.

At the same time, Israel began an effort to improve the closeness of its relationship with the United States because it needed, more than ever perhaps, a reliable supplier of high-technology military equipment. The Soviet Union replaced Egyptian and Syrian losses, and through the defeat of their clients seemed to improve its position after the fact. And Israel could not hope ever again to get sophisticated equipment from France, which saw the oil crisis ahead as Europe moved from coal-fired to oil-fired industry throughout the 1960s, and determined to be on the right side of its own economic interests.

It is hard to exaggerate the impact of the June 1967 War on the Middle East and on Israeli history and society ever since. Three elements matter most.

First, pan-Arab rhetoric notwithstanding, the war for the first time joined the Palestinian issue with the actual concrete interests of at least some of the Arab states, for three of them had significant slices of their national territory now occupied by Israel. And whatever they might say, getting back that territory and restoring their national honor was liable to rank as a higher priority than helping the Palestinians. Without question, the first seeds of moderation toward Israel in Egypt began with the June 1967 War. It took more than a decade for those seeds to grow into something more definite, but time moves more slowly in the affairs of state than in the affairs of individuals. In a sense, the Israeli government in 1967 was correct to think that the impact of the war would contribute to a greater sense of realism on the part of the Arabs. It's just that the government was thinking in terms of a dozen months, not a dozen years, which is in fact how long it took before Israel and Egypt made peace in March 1979.

Second, the June 1967 War reignited Palestinian nationalism. Before 1967, as noted earlier, the Palestinian national movement was in eclipse, kept down by pan-Arabist ideology and, ironically, the parochial machinations of the major Arab states. The line of thinking had gone: we Palestinians will trust the Arab states to liberate Palestine for us, after which Palestine will form a province in a united Arab state. Now, with the Arab states defeated and disgraced, the thinking changed: we Palestinians will liberate Palestine ourselves, according to the guerrilla war model of Ho Chi Minh in Vietnam and Che Guevara in Latin America. Before 1967, the Palestinian leadership had

Map 3
Ceasfire Lines After
1967 Six-Day War

been that which more or less had presided over the disaster of 1948. With the discrediting of their Arab patrons, this leadership was discredited, too. If before the war the Arab states and their leaders were the vanguards of the Arab revolution that would liberate Palestine, now the Palestinian revolution was the vanguard whose success in Palestine would catalyze revolution in the Arab world and overthrow all the corrupt, sycophantic, and ineffective elites. In short, the direction of causation was reversed, and by 1969 Yasir Arafat's al-Fatah and other, smaller, newer, more radical, and generally more pro-Soviet and pro-Marxist groups had taken over what remained of the organizational corpse of the Palestine Liberation Organization.

The new Fatah-led PLO set up shop on the east bank of the Jordan River, and King Hussein and his army found it hard to stop them. With a new group of disgruntled refugees and a population on the east bank that was now majority Palestinian, the Hashemites continued to claim concern, aid, and sympathy for the Palestinians, part of which has always been genuine. But part has been for purposes of self-preservation. Remember: King Abdallah called what he annexed of Arab Palestine in 1950 the West Bank, not Palestine. The Hashemites have always looked upon Palestinian nationalism as a problem, as a rival to its own territorial claims and political legitimacy, and in this they have found much common interest with Israel, for whom Palestinian nationalism represents an existential political—though not a military—threat. When Nasir created the PLO in 1964, Hussein was furious, for Jordan had seized the claim to speak for the Palestinians—and do so in such a way that Jordan's interests would not be jeopardized. The eruption of Palestinian nationalism after 1967 was a threat to Jordan as well as Israel, and the Hashemites struggled to limit the damage it could do to them.

Fatah's aim in 1968–69 was to generate a war within the occupied territories against Israel on the model of the Viet Cong. It didn't work. The Palestinian Arab population of the West Bank remained sympathetic to Jordan, just as King Abdallah's Palestinian allies during Mandate times had come largely from the hill country of the West Bank rather than from the cities and more cosmopolitan areas of Palestine. When the effort failed, the PLO, with its new recruits from the refugee camps and new money extracted from Saudi Arabia and elsewhere, created a state-within-a-state in Jordan that increasingly assaulted the government's prerogatives in its own country.

After Nasir agreed in August 1970 to a U.S.-designed formula to end the War of Attrition[13] and begin a political solution to the Arab-Israeli conflict—infuriating and shocking the Palestinians—the more radical PLO groups catalyzed a civil war in September 1970. They hoped to seize control of Jordan and use it as a staging ground for liberating Palestine, displacing Arafat in the process. Like Nasir in 1966–67, Arafat wasn't eager for war and his reticence proved justified. The PLO lost the civil war and by the next September the remnants of its state-within-a-state was annihilated by the Jordanian army. The PLO fled to the Palestinian refugee camps in Lebanon, where they helped catalyze yet another Arab civil war five years later.

The point here is this: the reemergence of Palestinian nationalism in radical, militant form was a surprising development that imperiled Israel and Arab state interests in different ways, and the spate of Palestinian terrorism that erupted after 1970 proved the point, for it took in Israeli and Arab targets almost equally.[14] A truly independent and radical Palestinian movement threatened the Arab status quo in all those places where significant numbers of Palestinian refugees lived: Jordan, Lebanon, Kuwait, Gaza, even Syria. It meant that Arab states, even Egypt, could no longer manipulate the Palestinian issue while at the same time paying no real attention to Palestinian grievances. But still they tried. In October 1974, Jordan's right to speak for the Palestinians was given to the PLO by an Arab League hoping to moderate and gain leverage over the Palestinian movement in the context of an international diplomacy led by the United States.

For Israel, something even more serious was let loose and it has yet to be fully recontained. Before 1967, there was never a serious question of an independent Palestinian state coming into existence—the one scheduled to be born through UNSCOP in 1947 but destroyed in the 1948 War between Israeli power and Hashemite ambition. It was a matter of returning territory to Jordan for peace, or not; or of returning some territory for some peace. Now, gradually but ineluctably after June 1967, the demand for a Palestinian state reentered the diplomatic equation of the area. Jordan struggled against it but could not stop the tide. Israel gradually woke up to the fact that its greatest victory on the battlefield had destroyed its central diplomatic achievement of the 1948–49 era: the subjugation and eclipse of Palestinian nationalism.

It is very strange, but it happens so often in politics—and life in general—that it just has to be said: What often seems to be one's greatest triumph turns out to unleash forces that become one's greatest peril. On the personal level, Goethe put it this way: beware of what you wish for in youth, for you may get it in middle age.

Third of the three major consequences of the June 1967 War had to do not with the Arabs but with Israeli society. The war gave rise to a kind of nationalist triumphalism in Israel. The psychology of the country before 1967 defined Israel as always on the defensive, as if its existence were in literal jeopardy, as if the state's future might be short. The extent of the June victory was such that much doubt was wiped away in a trice. Some religious Israelis, as noted earlier, believed they were living in a transcendent Jewish passion play, with cosmic forces being worked out before their eyes. Secularists too, however, became more self-assured, more proud, less eager to propitiate Arabs and Europeans alike. And as time went on, Israelis grew used to the new security borders, and little by little settlements became entrenched in certain areas under occupation.

Speaking of Europeans, Israeli scorn for the French betrayal reached great heights. After 1967 the status of French as Israel's second language disappeared almost overnight, replaced by English.

Then came the October 1973 War.[15] After September 1970, Israel had kept waiting for the Arabs to offer a reasonable political settlement, and the United States supported Israel for very sensible reasons—one having to do with the conflict itself and one having to do with the Cold War.

UNSCR 242, read as designed, said that Israel was not obligated to withdraw from the occupied territories until the Arabs agreed to discuss genuine peace. Nothing in the resolution says or implies that withdrawal is a precondition for negotiations, nor that Israel is obliged to withdraw from all the territories. The resolution says Israel has to withdraw "from territories"—not even from "the" territories—this to be decided in direct negotiations between the parties. The American view, therefore, was that if the Arabs refused to sit, Israel was not obligated to move. American diplomacy was aimed at establishing direct negotiations, and at doing those things—including mediation between the parties—that might lead to direct negotiations. After all, Arab actions had brought about the 1967 War in the first place; the fact that the Arabs had lost the war was a different matter altogether.

As for the Cold War, the United States reasoned that the Soviet position in the Middle East was a function of the Arab need for weapons and support vis-à-vis Israel. But if the Arabs chose a political solution rather than a military one, it stood to reason that Soviet arms and diplomacy would come to matter less to them than an improved relationship with the United States, which, as Israel's main ally and supporter, was alone in a position to get Israel to satisfy minimal Arab aims. For this to work, the Arabs had to know that they could never defeat Israel in a war and, to make sure of that, after September 1970 the level of U.S. military aid to Israel in both quality and quantity rose sharply. In the summer of 1972, this approach paid a huge dividend: Anwar al-Sadat, Nasir's successor,[16] expelled the Soviet military mission from Egypt and made overtures to the United States precisely along lines predicted by President Nixon and his National Security Adviser, Henry A. Kissinger, a year and a half before.

Unfortunately, Washington didn't hear Sadat's overtures: Nixon and Kissinger were too busy with SALT I, détente with the Soviet Union, the negotiations to end the Vietnam War, and the opening of U.S.-Chinese diplomacy. The Israelis, meanwhile, now had a substantial new military arsenal and seemingly unlimited U.S. support to stoke their triumphalism. The view of the Golda Meir government was that if Arab weakness produced good results—like getting rid of Soviet forces from Egypt—then greater relative weakness would produce even better results.

While the Americans were inattentive and the Israelis complacent, Sadat grew desperate. He decided to make common cause with Syria and Saudi Arabia to blast the diplomatic stalemate into renewed activity. He decided to stage a military demonstration for diplomatic purposes. The Soviets, desperate to regain their position in Egypt, were willing to supply the weapons despite the risk that a new Middle East war might kill détente. The Syrians were willing to join in rather than be left out should the ploy work. The Jordanians were not invited. Because of changes in the oil market dating from the early 1970s, the Saudis for the first time had achieved an ability to simultaneously sit out the revenue loss involved in an oil embargo and still have enough money left over to finance a war. The plans were hatched in April 1973: the Egyptians and Syrians would attack, the Saudis would declare an embargo, and the Soviets would call for a quick cease-fire, consolidating Arab gains before Israel could strike a counterpunch.

This plan was implemented on Yom Kippur 1973. Things went better than planned at first for the Arabs, then not so well at all. The aim of the war was not to destroy Israel; none of the Arab planners were sufficiently distanced from reality to imagine they could do that. The aim was to score some initial victories and then dig in. But even though Israel knew the Arabs were going to attack at least twenty-four hours before they did, initial Arab successes were stunning. The Egyptians crossed Israel's extensive fortification by the Suez Canal—the Bar-Lev line—and killed many Israeli soldiers. The Syrians stormed passed the cease-fire lines and even penetrated the Green Line southeast of Lake Tiberias, crossing into pre-1967 Israel. The Saudis declared an embargo, neutralizing most West European support for Israel and dividing many Americans, too.

But the Arabs allowed their enthusiasm over their military achievements to sweep away their plans and feed their ambitions. They told the Russians to wait before demanding a cease-fire, and they pressed on farther. The Israelis mobilized and first turned their attention to the north, to the Syrians, for that was the attack with the greatest potential to endanger civilians. One of the most amazing feats of personal heroism took place during the early hours of this effort when an Israeli soldier, Avigdor Qahalani, almost single-handedly stopped a Syrian armored attack at a place that has come to be known as *Emek Ha-bakha*, the Valley of Tears.[17] The Syrians soon became interested in a cease-fire, lest all their gains be wiped out, but the Egyptians were making progress still and refused: the Arab partnership had already fractured.

Meanwhile, the Soviet Union began a massive resupply effort to the Arabs as the duration of the fighting exceeded expectations. After a delay of several days, the United States began a resupply to Israel.[18] The intensity of the armored warfare was like nothing seen since World War II, and the rate of modern ordnance usage was even greater.

After routing the Syrians and chasing them down the road toward Damascus, the Israelis turned their attention to the south, where they had been engaged in a costly holding action for more than a week. The Israelis repainted some two dozen Soviet tanks captured from the Syrians with Egyptian markings and shipped them south. In a brilliant move designed by General Ariel Sharon, Israeli armor punched a small hole through Egyptian lines and infiltrated these tanks through it. They then crossed the Suez Canal into Africa, pretending that they were returning from the front for refueling. Once across, they turned on the Egyptians and decimated them, anchoring themselves in a new bridgehead on the other side of the canal. Israeli forces poured through the hole and turned south. Before long, most of the Egyptian army was encircled in Sinai awaiting its doom.

At this point the Egyptians finally decided that a cease-fire would be a good idea. The Israelis, having lost many soldiers and now quite angry, preferred to utterly destroy the Egyptian army instead. The Soviet Union insisted on a cease-fire, and threatened to introduce its own troops unilaterally to bring it about. The United States, in response, called another Defcon 3 alert, this time publicly, and fears of a direct U.S.-Soviet clash—with all the morbid possibilities inherent in an escalation to nuclear war—erupted. The United States threatened to end the resupply to Israel if Israel did not accept a cease-fire, and Israel reluctantly did so. Secretary of State Kissinger (he had been thus elevated in April 1973) now seized upon the ambiguous outcome of the war—the Arabs had surprised and hurt Israel, but Israel had prevailed—to do more or less what Sadat had hoped: begin intense diplomacy to bring about the return of Arab lands taken in 1967 and, if possible, do something for the Palestinians. By September 1975, Israeli-Egyptian diplomacy was in full gear, and by November 1977, Sadat's dramatic visit to Jerusalem produced the psychological breakthrough that led in turn to the Camp David Accords of September 1978 and the Egyptian-Israeli peace treaty of March 1979.

The October 1973 War, like the June 1967 War, had major consequences. Just as the former was a rude awakening for the Arabs, the latter was a slap to the Israelis and the Americans, a wake-up call from their triumphalism and complacency. The regaining of the Arab sense of honor enabled them to compromise and move toward peace. The oil embargo that accompanied the war destroyed much of Israel's support in Europe, where governments quickly knuckled under to pressure from Arab oil producers. This behavior by the Europeans created serious strains in NATO, but at the same time the Soviet willingness to pull a fast one on the United States in the Middle East, in direct contravention to pledges made by Soviet leader Leonid Brezhnev at a June 1973 U.S.-Soviet summit, undermined the Nixon-Kissinger détente policy and the overblown expectations they had allowed to rise around it. U.S. policy was further undermined at that time by the collapse of presidential authority with the Watergate scandal. The October 1973 War and its aftermath were sad, soul-searching times in both Israel and the United States. The war also led to increasing dependency on the United States by Israel for arms and aid as well as diplomatic support.

The October 1973 War also accelerated the further entry of the Palestinian issue into regional diplomacy. The Saudis, in particular, carried the Palestinian case rhetorically even as the Egyptians, Syrians, and certainly the Jordanians tried to get Yasir Arafat to moderate PLO views and enter into a political dialogue with Israel. In retrospect, while it took until 1988 at the earliest for the PLO to finally do this, the process of its moderation may be said to have begun with the 1974 Rabat Summit and the consequent pressure on it from the Arab states. Also contributing to this process was the Lebanese civil war, which started in 1975 and which involved the PLO, the Israeli invasion of Lebanon in 1982, and the experience of the *intifada*—the Palestinian uprising that began in December 1987. But the October 1973 War was the source because it represented the real beginning of the Arab-Israeli diplomatic process, a process that reasserted the control of the Arab states over major regional diplomatic outcomes.

Israeli-Egyptian diplomacy made more progress than any other after 1973. There was one "disengagement" agreement between Israel and Syria in 1974, which reduced the amount of territory Israel held on Golan by a small amount, but the Syrians were not willing to move into consideration of normal relations with Israel and the political process stalled. To avoid its becoming isolated, Syria along with its Soviet patron and its associates in terror tried whenever it could to play diplomatic spoiler. This Damascus did well after the Israeli invasion of Lebanon, when Syrian diplomacy managed to wreck an Israeli-Lebanese accord negotiated by U.S. Secretary of State George Shultz in May 1983. By March of the next year, the deal was a dead letter thanks to Syrian intrigues.

Jordan, meanwhile, did not participate in the October 1973 War, but definitely wanted a role in the postwar diplomacy. In preparation for such an engagement, a series of secret summit meetings between King Hussein and Israeli leaders were held over the years.[19] But the other Arabs promoted the PLO at Jordan's expense, and Jordan's delicate domestic circumstances and general weakness precluded a bold move in opposition to the Arab consensus. Hussein therefore tried to bind Arafat into some kind of joint arrangement that would trade a restored Jordanian position for the brokerage Arafat needed and the king could provide with Israel and the United States. But Arafat either wasn't ready for political dialogue with Israel or the PLO was too fractured for him to "sell" the idea—or both—and tentative Jordanian-PLO arrangements constructed during the 1984–86 period deteriorated in acrimony and also some violence.

Israel and Jordan had come close to a secret deal in the 1971–72 period, but the king would not accept less than a full Israeli withdrawal from the territory taken in June 1967, and Israel would not offer quite that much. In light of what has happened since with Palestinian nationalism, both sides would have been much better off had some sort of deal been reached then. At the same time, Israel and Jordan built slowly but steadily on a de facto arrangement of non-belligerence. Between 1971 and the Israeli-Jordanian peace treaty of October 1994, not a single shot was fired in anger along that border by an Israeli or a Jordanian soldier—except at Palestinian infiltrators.

The next major event in the diplomatic process after the October 1973 War was an event in Israeli domestic politics: the May 1977 Likud electoral victory. The Likud view of the diplomatic process in general, and of UNSCR 242 in particular, was quite different from Labor's. The Revisionists believed that all of Israel—the West Bank, and Jordan too—was part of the original homeland promised to the Jews in 1917.[20] They never accepted the partition resolution of 1947. They never accepted the applicability of UNSCR 242 to the West Bank, and it was over this issue that Menahem Begin took the Likud out of the national unity government formed in 1967 on the eve of war. Likud ideologues believed that all of the land west of the Jordan River should be Israel; the Arabs would be Arab residents of this Greater Israel or, as it was called in Hebrew, *Eretz Israel ha-sh'leyma* (the complete land of Israel). The Palestinians, if they liked, should have their state where Jordan was—and the Hashemites, as far as Begin and his colleagues were concerned—should be sent packing back to Mecca where they came from in 1920–21.

On the other hand, the Likud was intensely interested in a deal with Egypt, for Egypt was the most dangerous state Israel faced. But it wanted no deal with either Palestinians or Jordanians that would lead to Israel's relinquishing control of the West Bank, which it invariably called by its ideologically tinged Hebrew names, Judea and Samaria. As for Syria, the Golan Heights, while technically part of Eretz Israel as far as religious Zionists were concerned, wasn't part of the Mandate. So it was harder to claim from a legal viewpoint. From a security standpoint, however, Likud like Labor found it hard to contemplate coming down from Golan unless and until there were some fundamental changes in the way the Syrian regime appeared to see the world. So the order of diplomatic business from the Likud point of view was Egypt now, Syria later, West Bank never. It should also be recalled that the shift in the orientation of Israel's religious parties, especially the NRP, strengthened this point of view in the country at large, and particularly within the Likud-led coalition.

To turn that set of priorities into reality, however, required cooperation from the Arabs and the Americans. In this context, Sadat's dramatic gesture in November 1977 was like a wind from heaven for Menahem Begin. The new Carter administration had precisely the opposite priorities, tending to think more like Europeans when it came to the PLO and the illusion of reaching an all-at-once, comprehensive settlement of the Arab-Israeli conflict. Indeed, Sadat went to Jerusalem mainly to short-circuit U.S. policy, which he saw as mortgaging the interests of those who wanted to make peace to rejectionists like Syria and the PLO backed by the USSR who clearly didn't. (Hint: Sadat was right.) Sadat's opening made it possible for Begin to engage in serious diplomacy for two years precisely on the level and area he desired, and to push aside everything else.

In the meantime, too, Likud settlement policy introduced after May 1977 differed fundamentally from that of Labor. Labor settlements were chosen for their relevance to security and future diplomacy, not to foreclose future diplomacy. Labor settlements were put along the old border far from Arab population centers. Likud settlements were the reverse; religious zealots were encouraged to move in right near Arab towns and cities. Their purpose was to create new demographic realities in the West Bank that would preclude that land ever being returned to Arab sovereignty of any kind. The Likud actively subsidized settlement activity, taking money from the budget for infrastructure and immigrant absorption programs to do so.

The Israeli settlement effort was kept out of the core of Israeli-Egyptian negotiations lest raising it cause Israel to dig in its heels and balk at peace diplomacy writ large. At Camp David, in September 1978, Begin thought he had finally achieved his main aim: peace with Egypt in return for all the Sinai (and even the evacuation of a few settlements, such as Yamit), but no significant concessions with regard to the West Bank or the Golan Heights— unlike Sinai, both parts of historic Eretz Israel. American efforts to extend the diplomatic process to engage Israel on these other issues got nowhere, and the Carter administration's foreign policy was soon consumed in any event by the Iranian revolution of 1979 and a second oil crisis, as well as by SALT II and the Soviet invasion of Afghanistan on December 25, 1979.

The advent of the Reagan administration in January 1981 seemed to promise Israel an easier time. Reagan was a deep friend of Israel, and so was his first secretary of state, Alexander M. Haig, Jr. Reagan was in any event more focused on domestic policy, and he wasn't inclined to pick a fight with a government that seemed as resolutely anti-Soviet as his own. Reagan despised the PLO for its terrorist record, and was disgusted by the obeisance paid to it by most of America's West European allies. Things might have remained placid had it not been for Israeli hubris, most of it in the person of Ariel Sharon, the architect of Israel's brilliant crushing of the Egyptian war plan in 1973.

In June 1982, just two months after the last Israeli troops had left the Sinai according to the terms of the Israeli-Egyptian peace treaty, Israel invaded Lebanon. The aim, the government said, was to attack the PLO, which had set up a state-within-a-state there that it used to attack Israel's northern border. The violence coming from Lebanon had been a real problem before July 1981—people had been killed and wounded in increasing numbers, including rooms full of schoolchildren—but between July 1981 and the Israeli invasion the border had been very quiet. Israel's aim in June 1982 was in fact grander than attacking the PLO and stopping terrorism. It was threefold: to settle finally the Lebanese civil war in a way that would establish the Maronite Christians as victors; to weaken the PLO so badly that Israel could annex the West Bank with minimal political and internal security repercussions; and to "settle" the Palestinian problem by undermining King Hussein in Jordan and creating a Palestinian state on the east bank.

The invasion achieved none of these aims. It did drive the PLO from Lebanon—with a good deal of help from Syria later in the year—which is how PLO headquarters ended up in Tunis and how PLO members were dispersed to places like Yemen and Iraq. What it also did—aside from getting more than 650 Israeli soldiers killed—was destroy good relations between Israel and the United States for a good long while, help engender Palestinian political moderation of the sort Begin and Sharon wanted least, as well as lead to Israel's protracted occupation of southern Lebanon, which let the Shiite genie out of its bottle.[21] There, combined with Iranian and Syrian support, Shiite political power in the form of Hizballah—the party of God—has created as much of a problem for Israel in the decade since 1985 as that represented there by the PLO in the decade before 1985.

It was thanks to the Lebanese debacle that Labor made a partial comeback in the 1984 election. Shimon Peres's tenure as prime minister was marked by strenuous efforts to advance the peace process, particularly with Jordan. But the rotation agreement of the national unity government made real progress effectively impossible. Discussion had settled on the West Bank and the Palestinian issue, and Likud views precluded any negotiated agreement with any Arab party, and guaranteed as well considerable acrimony in relations with the United States over the problem.

It took the end of the Cold War, the Gulf War of 1990–91, and the mutual exhaustion occasioned by the *intifada* to bring about the next major change in the diplomatic-strategic constellation in the area. We save this discussion for Chapter 7, but meanwhile let's take a brief tour through the state of Israel's foreign relations today, recognizing from the outset that in this venue we cannot do full justice to the complexity of these topics.

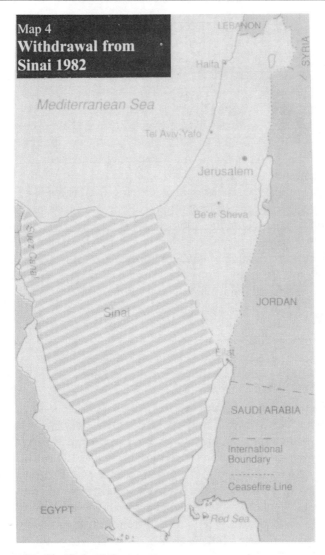

Map 4
Withdrawal from Sinai 1982

Relations with the United States

Israel's relations with the United States have been an important facet of Israeli history from the start. From what we have already discussed, several points may be gleaned and are worth reviewing in brief.

Americans have always been interested in Jews and in Israel (or Palestine before 1948) for reasons of history and theology. An American naval officer, James Lynch, was the first to explore and map the Jordan River in modern times (1847). American missionaries and missionary schools established themselves in the Middle East, including Jerusalem, along with the British, French, and Russians in the nineteenth century, and a certain amount of trade followed in turn. At the collapse of the Ottoman Empire, Great Britain, through Foreign Minister Balfour, at first suggested that America's status should entitle it to take the Mandate for Palestine, but President Wilson demurred and the British anyway soon changed their view. Nevertheless, through the Versailles Peace Conference in 1919 and the famous King-Crane Commission of 1919–20, the United States did involve itself to some extent in the formation of the Mandate system and followed developments in Palestine quite closely.

During and after World War II, with the full emergence of the United States as a superpower in competition with the Soviet Union, America became further enmeshed in the Middle East. President Truman supported Zionism and tried to pressure the British government on its behalf in the 1945–47 period. Against the advice of many of his own aides, including his secretaries of state and defense, Truman pushed for partition, quickly recognized the state in 1948, and immediately provided important economic and diplomatic support—but not weapons. Cold War concerns led to a far less affable relationship during the two Eisenhower administrations as the two countries quarreled over a host of issues, but President Eisenhower himself was a deep friend of Israel, and had push come to shove, and Israel's existence was in direct jeopardy, Eisenhower would certainly have acted in Israel's defense.

While many disagreements over particular issues continued, in general U.S.-Israeli relations grew friendlier before the June 1967 War during the Kennedy and Johnson administrations. With an uncomfortable lull in 1969–70, the relationship grew closer still after the Jordanian civil war, and even closer after the October 1973 War during the Nixon period. This was ironic because, as the White House tapes show, Richard Nixon was no special friend of Jews. Yet he admired Israel's spunk, and his administration's judgments, like those of most others, flowed from strategic calculation and not sentiment. Nevertheless, all through this period Israel and the United States were not formally allies. No treaty ever passed the Senate, as required by the Constitution, and until a Memorandum of Strategic Cooperation was signed during the Reagan administration as an executive agreement, no formal document bound the United States to Israel.

U.S.-Israeli relations were cooler during the short interregnum of President Ford, as the two sides disagreed on peace process tactics after the second Israeli-Egyptian disengagement agreement of September 1975. Then, with the arrival of the Likud government in 1977, U.S.-Israeli relations in the Carter and Reagan periods entered an era of sharp ups and downs. The relationship was up whenever strategic interests coincided—as with the press for an Israeli-Egyptian peace—and down when they did not—as over the invasion of Lebanon and the frustrations of dealing with the West Bank and the Palestinian issue. Interspersed with the major issues were other ups—for example, the sharing of intelligence and military-technical innovations that saved the U.S. military billions of research and development dollars—and also other downs—such as the Jonathan Pollard affair, where Israel recruited an American Jew to steal unredacted documents about Arab military capabilities and other matters for Israel, and the question of possible Israeli-South African cooperation on nuclear research and technology.

Israel's relations with the United States today are by most measures special and extraordinary despite the continued existence of differences over some issues. The United States is by far Israel's most important ally, providing crucial economic and military aid and diplomatic support. The first free trade agreement negotiated by the United States was with Israel, a country 6,000 miles away. Since then, Israeli exports to the United States have gone up as a percentage of the total, and by 1996 amounted to nearly half.

The Israeli currency is also tied to the dollar and this has many and sometimes major impacts. For example, when the dollar suddenly weakens, as it did in the spring of 1995, it either makes Israeli products more expensive or, if products are sold for the same dollar amount, reduces profits. This in turn leads Israeli manufacturers to lobby for depreciating the sheqel against the dollar, but that fuels inflation, which in 1994 was back to 14.4 percent. Relatedly, a strong dollar tends to raise housing prices in Israel, which are generally denominated in dollars.[22]

Also, with most U.S. aid recipients, the money is part loan and part grant. U.S. aid to Israel—roughly $3.5 billion annually in recent years—is all grant and has been since 1986. With every other U.S. aid relationship, very little money is ever transferred to the recipient; instead, a credit is forwarded and services rendered largely by American companies are provided. But Israel's aid money is provided by the U.S. Treasury directly near the beginning of the fiscal year, and Israel uses the money more or less as it sees fit, and earns interest on it as the year passes. Israel has also long been the largest single recipient of American aid; since 1979 it has amounted to roughly $3.5 billion per year, this for a country then with barely more than 5 million people. Almost forgotten nowadays, too, is how important U.S. economic aid to Israel was in the early years. While no military assistance was provided, between 1949 and 1965 over $740 million was provided in grants, loans, and technical assistance.

In addition to formal and public government-to-government relationships, there are also private and less formal ties. The intelligence cooperation between the United States and Israel has been close for many years. Not all information is shared, and Israel has frequently been frustrated with American reluctance to share data, but the relationship is nevertheless quite extensive, rivaling that which the United States has with its closest NATO allies, such as Great Britain.

Informal U.S.-Israeli ties are dominated by Israel's relations with American Jewry, and American Jewry's many organizations, which include the American-Israel Public Affairs Committee (AIPAC), the Anti-Defamation League of B'nai Brith, the American Jewish Congress, the American Jewish Committee, the American Zionist Federation, and importantly, an umbrella group called the Presidents Conference of American Jewish Organizations. But the informal ties go beyond that. Many American Christians and Christian organizations are very interested in Israel for historical and theological reasons. American tourism to Israel is extensive, and forms a valuable part of the Israeli economy. American direct private investment in Israel is also significant—from Jews and non-Jews—and will become more important if and when Israel further reduces the bureaucratic impediments to such investment.

These facts suggest a remarkably close relationship, and that would be correct. But the relationship has not always been smooth. U.S.-Israeli relations are a lot like a family affair, necessarily close owing to historical factors and coincidences of interest, but sometimes very tempestuous and even bitter. As Sören Kirkegaard once pointed out, the most bitter battles are not fought between strangers, but within families. Neither country has forgotten the Jonathan Pollard spy affair, in which an American Jew was recruited to spy for Israel, nor hints that the United States, too, has spied on Israel. The United States has been unhappy with what it thinks are selected violations of Israeli pledges not to re-export U.S. military technology, particularly to countries such as China. The United States wishes on one level that Israel would sign the Nuclear Non-Proliferation Treaty, for this would make extending and strengthening the treaty in the Middle East far easier, but on the other hand it knows that Israel is unlikely to do so as long as states like Iraq and the Islamic Republic of Iran can potentially threaten Israel with unconventional weapons.

On the other hand, Israel once tried to engage North Korea in a form of diplomacy that would involve stopping or limiting North Korea's sale of missiles to Syria and Iran, but the United States, which then preferred a policy of enforced isolation against North Korea, pressured Israel to abandon well-advanced efforts. The United States also has conducted a public diplomacy that defers generally to Chinese efforts to isolate and delegitimate Taiwan; Israel has reluctantly followed the American lead in this regard as well. In the summer of 1995, Cuba expressed a desire to open diplomatic relations with Israel, and Israel was willing until the United States insisted that it not do so.

More generally, however, as long as Israel and the United States have sitting governments with more or less compatible views on the Middle East peace process, basically good relations are not hard to maintain. The continuance of the peace process is believed to serve U.S. interests in general, although the urgency of the matter was relieved by the collapse of the USSR and the general retreat of Russian power from the region. Beyond that, Democratic administrations tend to have more of a domestic stake in good relations with Israel because most American Jews still vote Democratic and participate actively relative to their numbers in fund-raising and other political advocacy roles. The politically weaker a Democratic administration is—and this applied to the Clinton administration after the November 1994 midterm election—the less eager it is to get into a spat with Israel. When the administration recovered its political bearings, winning the 1996 presidential election, it was less reluctant to get into a spat with Israel, and get into several spats it did.

Israel, for its part, desires a greater independence from the United States, but it knows that, for the foreseeable future, its American connection will remain important. Yet the advent of a government in Washington that does not really care much about domestic pressures from American Jews—that is to say, a Republican administration—in combination with an Israeli government that has incompatible views about the peace process—that is to say, a Likud-led government—could lead to a quick deterioration in general comity between Israel and the United States. The same is the case between a second-term Democratic president and a Likud prime minister, and on the eve of the U.S. presidential election of 1996 many observers anticipated difficult times in a Clinton-Netanyahu era. Those anticipations proved correct.

Indeed, the future holds many questions for the U.S.-Israeli relationship, most of them more broad and consequential than tactical disagreements between leaders over peace process issues. We take up these questions in the final chapter as well.

Relations with Europe and Russia

Israelis have very mixed feelings about the country's relationships with European countries and Russia. On the one hand, European history and power provided the backdrop for the creation of the Jewish problem that in turn engined Zionism itself. Many Israelis see Europe as a graveyard for Jews, a place of sadness and exile. Nevertheless, France, West Germany, Great Britain, the Netherlands, Belgium, Norway, and other European states were de facto allies with Israel during the Cold War, and before 1967, owing in part to the mutual socialist ideologies of the ruling parties of Israel and many West European countries, relations were good with most.

Gradually, however, West European sympathy for Israel eroded. Many Europeans ascribe the reasons to Israel's becoming an occupier after 1967, and an anti-socialist state under the Likud after 1977. Europeans have been critical of Israel's human rights record in the territories. This, say most European officials, is why the European Community tended to support the Palestinian cause beginning in 1973—so much so that it diverged appreciably from U.S. policy and caused strains in U.S.-European relations. Israelis and others have a different general explanation for the change in European attitudes: fear of the Arab oil weapon, political weakness, and moral obloquy. Had it not been for American protests, most Israelis believe that the West Europeans would have been even more obsequious in their fawning before the Arabs.

There is still very little love lost between Israeli government officials and most foreign ministry officials among the NATO-European countries. This is particularly true among the Likud. Some Labor party members and officials sympathetic to the Labor line still admire European taste and refinement, still remember the good relations of the 1950s and 1960s, and still retain their personal friendships from that time. A good example in this regard is Shimon Peres. Nevertheless, at poignant moments it doesn't take much for the basic antipathy to show through. For example, the European Community, whose pretense to a unified foreign policy is belied almost daily by divisions on practically every issue, insisted upon and received a place at the Madrid Summit of October 1991. The speech delivered by the EC minister struck most Israelis as preachy and extraordinarily hypocritical given the significant role of European imperialism in creating the Arab-Israeli conflict in the first place. The Syrian speech, not surprisingly, and the Palestinian one too, had much harsher things to say about Israel. But the Israelis saved their sharpest private disdain for the West Europeans.

Israel does not have the luxury, however, to express its dislike for European politicians in public, or to lose its patience and act undiplomatically. The reason is money. Europe has been and remains an important trading partner for Israel. But the European Community, now European Union, has organized itself increasingly as an economic unit, and dealing with it requires negotiating extensive arrangements that must be periodically renewed. From the late 1950s onward, Israel has tried to maintain a favored position in these negotiations, for Europe was the prime market for exports of Israeli citrus, diamonds, flowers, specialized electronics, and other goods. Over time, this has become more and more difficult. The expansion of the EC in

January 1986 to include Portugal and Spain cut deeply into Israel's advantages in exporting citrus, for Portugal and Spain, once inside the European Community, gained special trading privileges. The EC further reduced Israel's traditional advantages by negotiating associate arrangements with several North African countries.

In recent years the EU has increasingly turned into a trading bloc, cartelizing more and more of its trading relations as its own economic performance has become less robust. As former Warsaw Pact countries, such as the Czech Republic, have found out, the EU countries are happy to make use of cheaper Central European labor and even to locate some production facilities outside EU borders, but they adopt protectionist barriers against foreign goods in order to protect their own producers (and political constituencies), and EU investments abroad are designed mainly to repatriate profits rather then to generate fixed capital investment abroad. In the Israeli case, the EU has thus far denied Israeli companies the right to bid on public tenders, and has tried to use economic incentives to press Israel on political points, less for their own sake, Israelis suspect, and more to curry favor with their Arab trading partners, with whom most of them run trade deficits.

Beyond that, the reach of European military-strategic and diplomatic power is fairly modest, but French, British, German, Italian, and also Swedish arms manufacturers have a longer reach. All have usually been eager to sell weapons and military technology—including dual-use technologies that might be used for unconventional weapons programs—to the Arab states and to Iran. Israel has, quite naturally, been unhappy with this enthusiasm and so, for the most part, has the United States. On November 28, 1994, the EU decided that, as a gesture to Syria to reward its supposed diplomatic moderation, it was lifting a freeze on weapons sales. At the same time, Syria was known to be working on a chemical warfare capability and importing intermediate-range ballistic missiles from North Korea. Israel protested the lifting of the freeze, but in vain.

Finally, with regard to Western Europe, Israel has had some especially good relations with a few states and some especially bad relations with a few others. When virtually all West European governments stood in thrall to the power of Arab oil in 1973 and thereafter, the Dutch government bucked the tide out of sheer devotion to principle. As a result, Holland was singled out in 1973–74 for specially harsh treatment from the Arabs. Israelis appreciated this gesture and still have a special place in their hearts for the Dutch. Dutch teenagers, too, have established a large summer presence on Israeli *kibbutzim* in programs that let them be part-time volunteers and part-time tourists; a number of Dutch citizens have stayed in Israel, some marrying Israelis. The two countries are also bound together by their still-lingering strong hatred of Germans, and by the epochal story of Anne Frank, a Dutch Jewess. Israel also has good and improving relations with Spain since the end of the dictatorship of Francisco Franco in 1975.

As far as poor relations go, mention has already been made of France after 1967. As far as Israel could see, the French government led every push within the EC to move Europe away from a pro-Israeli position toward a pro-Arab and pro-Palestinian one. France (and Italy) even made deals with the PLO in the 1970s to spare themselves terrorist events at the price of exporting them to their neighbors.

Also a sore point has been Israel's relations with Austria. Israelis could never understand why the Allies treated Austria as an occupied nation instead of an ally of Nazi Germany. Austrian anti-Semitism was legendary, and Austria's avid participation in the S.S. was well documented. And then came Kurt Waldheim, first as United Nations secretary general—something that surely did not help endear the United Nations to Israel—and then as the elected president of Austria. The Austrian people elected Waldheim after his Nazi past had become well known, suggesting that as a nation they really didn't much care. This made it difficult, to say the least, for Israel to maintain normal diplomatic relations with Austria.

And finally there is the Vatican. Israel's relationship with the Vatican is encrusted with about as much historical baggage as it is possible to heap on a relationship. A careful reconstruction of the history of Jewish-Papal ties shows a mixed relationship, sometimes extraordinarily cordial as in the early Middle Ages and sometimes extraordinarily poor. In post-Balfour Declaration times, this relationship turned on four factors: the Vatican's claim to have a say in the administration and future of Jerusalem; the Vatican's role during the Holocaust; the Vatican's generally pro-Arab advocacy in the Arab-Israeli dispute from its inception; and the official Vatican attitude toward the Jews insofar as it affected the status and security of Jews worldwide, for all Jews, says Israel, are its business.

Until the 1960s, relations remained poor on all points. Since then things have gradually improved. Pope Paul VI issued a Papal Encyclical in 1962 absolving Jews living today from the "deicide" of Jesus. (After all that had happened over the centuries, many Jews felt this proclamation so long overdue as to be almost surreal.) More recently, the Church has admitted behaving wrongly during the Holocaust. Because of changes in the Arab world too, the Vatican has moderated its anti-Israeli attitude, which was largely a function of the fact that the Church has institutional and evangelical interests in Catholic communities in the Middle East. Thus, despite continuing to disagree about Jerusalem, Israel and the Vatican succeeded finally in establishing diplomatic relations in 1994.

As far as the Eastern and Central European countries are concerned— former Soviet satellites every one—there are similarities and differences with Western Europe. The old history and the memories are the same; the recent history is quite different. With Romania partially excepted, Hungary, Poland, Czechoslovakia, Bulgaria, Albania, Latvia, Lithuania, and Estonia had no independent policies in the Cold War with regard to the Middle East— indeed, the three Baltic States were not even formally sovereign. Upon their reemergence as independent states after 1989, all were eager to establish relations with Israel. There were many reasons.

One of these reasons was the expiation of historical demons, as mentioned earlier. Another was to ingratiate themselves with the United States, for Israel was looked upon, sometimes quite exaggeratedly so, as a channel to Washington. Another was to demonstrate true independence from Russia by doing exactly what they had been prevented from doing heretofore. Another was as reaction to the often bad experience these countries' officials had with the Arabs during the Cold War. Still another was to connect to the Israeli military mystique in the belief that Israeli liaisons could improve their security status. And finally there were the presumed benefits of trade with Israel, whose advanced technology in many fields, including medical, was attractive to the Central and East European countries, all of whom "enjoyed" living standards inferior to Israel's.

For the most part, Israel reciprocated these gestures. It too had several reasons. First, there were still small numbers of Jews in many of these countries; Israel sought their coming to Israel or their protection where they chose to remain. Second, new relations reduced Israel's diplomatic isolation and pariah status. Third, trade could be mutually beneficial; Eastern and Central Europe offered some natural resources cheaper than could be gotten elsewhere, and since Israel was still locked out of Western Europe to some extent, the expanding market for Israeli exports was viewed positively. This included, potentially at least, military exports. And fourth, relatedly, many of these countries—the Czech Republic and Poland in particular—had developed arms-supply relationships with Syria, Libya, and Iraq; Israel hoped to restrain those relationships in the future.

As to Russia itself, Israel's main concern overwhelmingly was hope for continued Jewish emigration to Israel. This was a factor largely out of Israel's control, of course; it depended on domestic developments and Russia's international circumstances. But that just put a premium on getting Jews out as fast as possible. This raised a paradox. The better things went in Russia as far as political and economic reform, the better for the world in general, but then Jews would have less incentive to come to Israel. A Russia verging on civil war and economic collapse, on the other hand, was dangerous for the world—what with about 27,000 nuclear weapons lying around—but good for Israel, for Jews would leave faster and in greater numbers. Despite the logic of the situation, Israel did not advocate or promote destabilization in Russia, not least because it would put Israel afoul of all its major international allies.

After 1993 the situation in Russia, and in other places with substantial Jewish populations—Kazakhstan, Ukraine—stabilized to some extent. Reform has not been reversed, but neither has it moved forward fast. As of this writing, anything could still happen. For some of the same reasons, and for some different ones, Israel, America, and the rest of the world are still watching and waiting. As Russia struggled after its international economic default of August 1998, Jewish immigration from Russia to Israel began to rise again.

Beyond the central issue of *aliyah* and Russia's future, Israel's interests are served by de facto Russian subservience to U.S. policy in the Middle East peace process, and the general reduction of Russian influence in the Middle East. The reduction of Russian influence leaves Arab states such as Syria, Iraq, and Libya high and dry when it comes to heavy-weight external helpers, and this makes their policies either more compliant or less dangerous to Israel. In particular, Israel hopes that Russia will not feel compelled to sell weapons and nuclear technology to countries like Iran in order to raise hard currency. Israeli leaders know that Russian motives are no longer mainly political, and they are not really directed against Israel for ideological reasons or reasons of Cold War competition. This makes the Israeli-Russian dialogue far less apoplectic than it used to be. But money is a powerful motive, so it doesn't make the issues much less easier to solve to mutual satisfaction.

Otherwise, Israeli-Russian trade is increasing, largely through recent immigrants with connections back home. Israeli trade with other former Soviet republics has increased, too, for the same reasons. Israel, for example, made considerable effort to penetrate markets in Central Asia, principally through large Israeli companies like Yossi Maimon's conglomerate Merhav. The reasons are partly economic: Israel has much to offer countries like Kazakhstan and Uzbekistan with regard to modern agriculture, and those countries have vast energy and other natural resources to pay for them in trade. But there was a diplomatic angle, too. The five Central Asian republics are Muslim countries, but not Arab. All but one—Tajikistan—are part of the Turkic cultural world.[23] Maintaining normal relations with such states blunts Arab and Iranian attempts to isolate Israel, and an Israeli presence makes intelligence work easier pertaining to Israel's fears that nuclear weapons materials and technologies will "leak" from the former Soviet republics into unfriendly hands.

Origins of the Kazakh Mango

As guests of the government of Kazakhstan in October 1992, some colleagues and I were treated to several banquets. These banquets featured almost the same food each time: vegetables, cold horse meat, oddly colored potatoes, and limitless amounts of vodka and a semisweet brandy that only Russians, not Kazakhs, appeared ever to drink. Once, however, at an especially fine meal with a member of the government cabinet, we were treated to small glasses of mango juice. During the meal, I excused myself to take my ablutions and, as I passed the kitchen door, I saw Hebrew writing. A quick and quiet investigation revealed several cases of mango nectar, all imported from Israel.

The Israeli government has developed an especially cordial relationship with Kazakhstan's President Nursultan Nazerbaev. Thanks in part to the activities of Merhav, Israel has done Kazakhstan's elite several small favors. Nazerbaev's books, including his extremely turgid doctoral dissertation, have been translated and published in English in Israel through Merhav, although neither "Israel" nor "Merhav" appear in or on the books. Israel has also supplied what by current barely post-Soviet-era Kazakh standards have to be considered luxury goods for the Kazakh elite.

With increased trade between Israel and the Commonwealth of Independent States (CIS) has also come increased crime and smuggling related thereto. In the 1970s, this problem was associated largely with Georgian Jewish immigrants, but since then it has spread to other groups. Drugs, prostitution, extortion rings, loan sharking, and the violence that goes with them are more prevalent in Israel as a result of all this. Israelis see vividly what kinds of citizens, what kinds of attitudes, what extraordinary levels of cynicism and selfishness, got engendered in people—even Jews—under Soviet communism. The entire interchange between Israel and Russia over the last decade, then, has been very much a mixed bag.

Relations with the Third World

Finally, a word about Israel's foreign relations with the rest of the world, most of it the so-called Third World. For most of its early history, Israel's relations with the emerging Third World were a function of two primary considerations: the demonstration of Israel's formal non-aligned credentials, and Israel's desire to have the broadest possible diplomatic representation so as to blunt Arab efforts to isolate Israel. These efforts in the days after independence met with considerable success, especially in sub-Saharan Africa. Several new African states that became independent in the late 1950s and early 1960s looked to Israel as a model of self-sufficiency and social coherence. Some, like Ghana, the former British Gold Coast, also saw in Zionism a model for ethnic revival and cohesion along local African tribal lines. Israel established convivial relations with many sub-Saharan African states, especially in West Africa, but also with Kenya, and advanced this relationship by bringing many scores of African students to study at universities in Israel.

Israel's opening to the Third World was a source of great pride to the Labor Zionist leadership of the period. It proved to the world Israel's progressive spirit, its non-racist attitudes, and the nature of its aid programs exalted its technological competency and skill. However, these optimistic relationships did not last; most fell prey to post-1973 efforts by oil-rich Arab states—especially Saudi Arabia—to effectively bribe these African states to break relations with Israel.

Israel also tried to cultivate relations with Latin American states, but this was never a major priority. Most important to Israel were those countries with substantial Jewish populations, mainly Argentina and Brazil, but including Venezuela and also Cuba. As time passed, some Latin American countries became markets for Israeli weapons, but again, in the general scheme of things, Latin America has never been a major interest of Israeli policy.

Until the early 1990s, Israel's relations with much of the Third World were at a standstill. The 1975 U.N. General Assembly resolutions equating Zionism with racism exacerbated the situation. The consequences of this diplomatic problem were mainly symbolic, but nevertheless worrisome. The breakthrough in the peace process following the Gulf War in 1991 broke the barriers to normal relationships, however, and Israel rapidly reestablished its Third World presence thereafter. Relations with the Third World are not the highest priority in Israel's foreign relations, but still serve a significant symbolic function. Now that South Africa has attained majority government, Israel's relations in sub-Saharan Africa may attain useful if modest practical dimensions, too.

This may take time, however, for the new South African government resents Israel's closeness to the white governments of the past. That closeness was partly a function of Israel's being ostracized by black African states at Arab urging after 1973, but also partly a function of Israel's concern for South African Jews. Indeed, one of the largest *aliyah* communities in Israel in recent years as a percentage of the total diaspora population is the South African Jewish population. It is true, too, that some Likud politicians in the late 1970s and 1980s saw a more positive affinity between Israel and South

---

Breaking Up Is Hard to Do

An Israeli diplomat once told me an amusing story. He had been posted to the Ivory Coast in the mid-1970s when Arab pressures had finally forced the Ivorian government to break diplomatic relations with Israel. Israel's relations with the Ivory Coast had dated from Ivorian independence from France in 1960, and that closeness had been aided at that time by excellent Israeli-French relations. A high-ranking Ivorian diplomat very friendly to Israel had come to tell the Israelis at the embassy the bad news, that diplomatic relations would be broken tomorrow. The Israelis said they understood the problem, and hoped one day things could be put normal again.

The next day the announcement was made and the Israeli delegation prepared to leave the country. When the Ivorian official heard about this, he rushed to the Israeli embassy and shouted: "What are you doing?! Where are you going?!"

"Well," said the Israeli ambassador somewhat quizzically, "You have broken relations with us, and so we are going home. What did you expect?"

"But no, you misunderstand," said the Ivorian. "We told the Arabs we would break relations. We never told them we would make you leave. Just lower your flag, that is all. We are still friends, yes? What's a flag anyway? Flag-shmag."

Africa based on their both being polities of Western cultural origin in non-Western environments. Some Israeli politicians even said as much, and not always in a delicate way—an unfortunate and tactless mistake for which Israel is still paying diplomatically in Africa.

As for the United Nations, the common Israeli attitude is still quite negative. Israeli attitudes derive from the disappointing and frustrating experiences of post-1949 Mixed Armistice Commission episodes. Once the U.N. General Assembly came under the influence of the Soviet-led Third World voting bloc of the 1970s, the Israeli attitude toward the United Nations suffered yet another blow. Israel ceased to take the United Nations seriously, and also ceased to take seriously the work of its functional agencies, such as the World Health Organization, the International Labor Organization, and UNESCO. Israel was either expelled or nearly expelled from all three in the 1970s.

In practical terms, this probably hurt the United Nations more than it hurt Israel. Appropriately, there's a common phrase Israelis use in reference to the United Nations: *Oom-Shmoom. Oom* is an acronym for United Nations in Hebrew—*HaOomot Hame'uhadot. Oom-Shmoom* is therefore roughly equivalent to Yiddish-like formulations of casual disdain such as fancy-shmancy, cute-schmoot, or flag-schmag.

The U.N. Security Council, on the other hand, has retained a certain symbolic cache. Here Israel has expected the United States to protect its interests, and when, for various reasons, the United States did not do so, Israel suffered what seemed to it to be a significant diplomatic defeat.

With the advent of the peace process in its post-1993 configuration—with the Arab world divided by PLO action—the U.N. General Assembly has lost most of whatever negative potential it once held with regard to Israel. As for U.N. Security Council deliberations, they were, after all, mainly a function of Cold War diplomacy and the Cold War is over.

Finally in this regard, it is worth pointing out that Israel has ample experience of the difference between peace keeping and peace making. Where the United Nations has been involved in the Arab-Israeli conflict successfully, it has been when all parties engaged were determined to keep a peace made on serious and mutual terms. In such cases, as with Egypt and Israel in the Sinai after 1979, multilateral peace-keeping efforts have been effective, but this arrangement is outside U.N. jurisdiction. The U.N. Emergency Forces on the Golan Heights works because Syria and Israel wish it to work. But where U.N. troops were inserted, as in southern Lebanon, where there was no peace to keep and where local conditions augured more for war than for peace, the operation came mainly to grief. Most Israelis thus view the United Nations, and its peace-keeping operations, as something less than fully serious or effective, and observations of the U.N. force in the Balkans in the 1993–95 period only strengthened this view.

Overall, much of Israeli diplomacy—that segment not devoted to the principle concerns of security, immigration, and diplomatic help at the highest level—have been devoted to fending off attempts to isolate Israel. Much like Taiwan, which has had similar problems particularly since 1972, Israel has gradually succeeded in expanding its worldwide status and presence. Much of this success of late has had to do with the peace process, an important subject within our final chapter.

Israel in the Middle East

Nowadays, Israel also has relations with other Middle Eastern countries, even Arab countries. While the next chapter retells how such things came about, we would be remiss here not to sketch out the basics of the regional picture in Israel's own area.

Israel reached a peace agreement with Egypt in March 1979, and with Jordan in October 1994. It has been openly negotiating normal relations with the PLO since September 1993. It has consular relations with Morocco, Tunisia, Oman, and Qatar. And it has secret relations of varying degrees of depth and utility with other Arab states as well.

This latter phenomenon is nothing new. Something has been said already about the longstanding Zionist-Hashemite relationship. An interesting subrosa relationship used to exist, as well, between Israel and Morocco. For example, there was the Ben Barka affair of 1965, when the Mossad helped its counterparts in Rabat to assassinate opponents of the king. Shortly thereafter, Israel began training Moroccan special forces units and the royal guard. Certain Moroccan interior ministers actually helped Mossad agents in the country for use against their own and the regime's enemies. In the 1973 war, Morocco dispatched some hot-blooded political troublemakers to fight Israel from the Golan Heights. The Morrocan secret service duly informed Israel of their whereabouts, whereupon most of the group was *really* dispatched.

But this is all "ancient history," as they say. Today, Israel has become part of regional diplomacy in a fuller and more open—and very complicated—way. Israel and Jordan have a close strategic relationship, even if they do not see eye to eye on many political matters. Israel essentially "covers" Jordanian air space with its own air force, a quiet dimension to the Israeli-Jordanian peace arrangement. Israel has also spoken of its investment in theater ballistic missile defense as potentially covering the Palestinians as well as Jordan, to protect them against possible future attacks from Iran or Iraq.[24] And through Israel, with America's blessing and encouragement, Jordan has become a junior partner to the Israeli-Turkish alliance, the most important single regional strategic development since the end of the Cold War.

Israel and Turkey, a Muslim but non-Arab country, have rapidly improved their relations in recent years. It involves commercial, diplomatic, economic, and military aspects. Both countries are, after all, worried about Syria and Iraq, both are close U.S. allies, and both have less than smooth relationships with the countries of Western Europe. This relationship has already paid big dividends to Turkey. In October 1998, Turkey threatened to invade Syria if it did not expel Abdullah Ocalan, head of the insurrectionist Marxist Kurdistan Workers' party (PKK according to its Kurdish initials), from Syria. The Turks had threatened many times before and the Syrians had simply ignored their demands. This time, with Turkish troops to the north and Israel on the south, Syrian president Hafiz al-Asad complied in record time. Ocalan was eventually seized by Turkish commandos in Kenya and returned to Turkey to stand trial for subversion and murder.

Israel has also been trying to open lines of communications to Iran, but this has not been easy. One of Israel's motives is the safety and eventual immigration of more than 25,000 Iranian Jews. But in Iran's current power struggle, where things look very murky politically even to most Iranians, this is a tough game to play.

The point is that Israel has regional allies, Arab and non-Arab, and regional adversaries, Arab and non-Arab. It has complicated relations with countries like Egypt, with which it is at peace, but which, for example, looks unkindly upon the closeness of Israeli-Turkish ties. For once, something completely normal about Israel!

7

Peace

and

Normalcy?

The Zionist movement has lived its entire modern existence under a sense of siege. First the Jewish problem in Europe enveloped its concerns and gave the movement the impetus for its very birth. Then the Yishuv struggled against economic underdevelopment and hardship, an increasingly unfriendly Arab population, and an increasingly uncooperative British Mandatory authority. Then after the state came into existence, just three years after the Holocaust, Zionism found its principal achievement—the state of Israel—in a state of war with all its neighbors. Soon enough, Israel's enemies found a super-power patron in the Soviet Union, a country that even without Josef Stalin was one of the most anti-Semitic places on earth.

As we have seen, the sense of siege, based largely on realities and not just perceptions, has played a major role in shaping Israeli society and its institutions. Difficulty, and the social determination it has more often than not inspired in Israelis, is part and parcel of the national character.

Today, by contrast, Israel is strong and prosperous. Not that it would be simple or easy, but few military experts doubt that the Israeli Defense Force (IDF) could defeat all of its immediate neighbors simultaneously in a conventional war. (A war involving conventional attack, massive internal upheaval among Arabs in and near Israel, and unconventional external attack all at the same time—tanks, knives, and missiles—would be another matter, and a worrisome one.) Israel's $100 billion economy is larger than those of Egypt, Syria, Jordan, Lebanon, and the Palestinians put together. On April 1,

1997, a remarkable thing happened, remarkable even though few people knew of it at the time: the International Monetary Fund officially began classifying Israel as a "developed" rather than a "developing" country.

And that isn't all. Israel has the world's greatest power, the United States, as its closest ally, and Turkey, the largest regional military power, as its next best friend. The Soviet Union no longer even exists. Most important, Israel is formally at peace with two of its immediate neighbors—Egypt and Jordan—and is either negotiating toward that end with all the rest, or is about to do so.

The obvious question, then, is this: Can Israel cope with peace and normalcy as well as it has coped with war and emergency? No one really knows.

Of course, there is no guarantee that the peace process will produce real peace. Between May 1996 and May 1999, many observers wondered if Israel really wanted peace with the Palestinians. The government of Benyamin Netanyahu lacked the warmth or optimism that the Rabin and Peres governments seemed to have for the process, if not always for the Palestine Liberation Organization (PLO) as a partner. The Netanyahu government seemed to go out of its way to act in a manner that demeaned and humiliated the Palestinians. What got lost in this change of mood was that the PLO did not often keep its contractual agreements—to speak about peace in Arabic to its own people, to curb terror, to collect illegal weapons, and more besides. Would the PLO have kept its word if the tone of the Israeli government had been different? We'll never know, but it is not a foregone conclusion one way or the other. Now with the ascent of the Barak government, one far more similar in tone to Rabin's than to Netanyahu's government, we may finally find out if Yasir Arafat is a real partner for peace, or a false one bent on tactical advantage for some "ultimate" victory over Israel.

But the uncertainties about the prospects for peace go even deeper than that. Treaties alone cannot prevent war, either in the Middle East or anywhere else. Governments in the Arab world that make peace can be overturned and treaties can be unilaterally nullified. Countries that do not border Israel—such as Iraq, Iran, Libya, Algeria, even Pakistan—may come to pose serious military threats from afar with ballistic missiles and unconventional warheads.

Even closer at hand, there is no guarantee that Israel, regardless of its governments' intentions, will be able to achieve peace treaties with Syria, Lebanon, and the Palestinians. For historical and strategic reasons, making peace with Egypt and Jordan was much easier than it will be with the Syrians and Palestinians. Israel and Egypt did not have any essential territorial dispute: the Sinai was not part of the Palestine Mandate and does not carry the status of being part of historic Eretz Israel. Israel has always enjoyed relations of mutual respect and, more often than not, pragmatic cooperation with the Hashemites—even in time of war—and the two have shared a mutual adversary in Palestinian nationalism. The treaty with Jordan, moreover, did not require Israel to evacuate significant territories. Also, Jordan today does not consist of any land west of the Jordan River, so again there is no religio-historical problem between the two.

This is not the case with Syria. The Golan Heights, while as strategically important as Sinai, never was part of the Palestine Mandate.[1] But it is definitely part of historic Eretz Israel and was inhabited by Jews over many centuries. Israeli and Syrian strategic competition over Lebanon also impinges on the possibility of coming to a peace agreement. Ideally, Israel would like to see a fully independent Lebanon without foreign forces on Lebanese territory; but Syria sees Lebanon as part of Greater Syria and is loath to see its considerable influence there diminished.

As for the Palestinians, here the claims of the two national movements overlap very considerably, and in some cases—as with Jerusalem—almost completely. While recognizing the need for compromise, both sides in their heart of hearts believe that all the territory west of the Jordan River rightfully belongs to them. Because of this, and because of additional conflict over Jerusalem, refugee issues, and how to deal with the endemic violence against civilians that characterizes the problem, it is by no means assured that Israelis and Palestinians will come to a full and stable peace any time in the next several decades. Still, they might. Most likely, relations between Israelis and Palestinians will be characterized by neither real peace nor all-out war, but by simmering conflict within new political and security parameters that limit both the levels of violence and the ability of either side to get its way entirely on any major issue in dispute.

If the conflict can be tamed and regularized, even if not ended, it will still represent progress. And if the conflict enters what we may call a higher quality level of belligerence, most observers believe that the Israeli economy, and possibly the Palestinian and Jordanian economies as well, will grow rapidly.

In any event, Israeli power and prosperity, together with the present and prospective future achievements of the peace process, suggest a possibility for at least relative normalcy for the first time in more than a century of the Zionist movement. The purpose of this final chapter is to sketch the future direction of some of the major themes involved in a possible departure from emergency, war, and siege to a condition of normalcy, peace, and relative calm.

The Peace Process Since Camp David: A Brief Sketch

Before we can get very far in assessing how much progress we may expect of the peace process in the future, we have to take a step back and review progress to date.

As explained in Chapter 6, the first major breakthrough toward peace came in the Israeli-Egyptian relationship. The June 1967 War, by joining the concrete interests of the Arab states to the conflict, engendered moderation on the Arab side, and the shock of the October 1973 War engendered realism on the Israeli side. Nurtured along by intense and generally quite skillful U.S. diplomacy, this moderation and realism came together in September 1975 at the signing of the second Israeli-Egyptian disengagement agreement, which in reality was more than a military affair. In November 1977, not because of but despite new U.S. diplomacy, Egyptian President Anwar al-Sadat broke down the psychological wall by visiting Israel. By September 1978, the Camp David Accords were signed, which included an Egyptian-Israeli track and a prospective Israeli-Palestinian track that the Palestinian leadership refused at the time to take advantage of. By March of 1979, Israel and Egypt concluded a treaty of peace, which was signed on the White House lawn in the company of President Jimmy Carter. According to the provisions of the treaty, Israel was to withdraw step by step from the Sinai. This was finally achieved in April 1982 as agreed. A small remaining dispute over the Taba border problem, near Eilat, was eventually settled by arbitration mainly in Egypt's favor.

The peace process made no major progress after 1979 until 1991, owing mainly to the unwillingness of Israel's Likud-led governments to withdraw from remaining territories occupied in 1967, and equally to the unwillingness of the Arab parties—especially Syria and the PLO—to recognize Israel's right to exist, to negotiate directly with Israel, or even to speak about their desire for genuine peace.[2] A partial exception was Israel's relationship with Jordan, which was quietly if selectively cooperative for the most part, amounting to an informal relationship of nonbelligerency.

Three things drove the stalemate into renewed activity. First was the *intifada*, the Palestinian uprising against the Israeli occupation that began in December 1987. The *intifada* was for the Palestinians a lot like the October 1973 War for the Egyptians: while it gained nothing concrete, its symbolic successes and the sacrifices it entailed restored the Arab sense of honor. Palestinians could now look Israeli soldiers in the eye. They could inflict pain. They could be unmanageable, for whatever Israel did to defeat the *intifada*, it never fully succeeded. They could provoke disagreement and dissent within Israel as a result. They turned the occupation from something that benefited the Israeli economy overall to something that drained it. They could manipulate international media against Israel. And they could do all this with civil disobedience and stones, not knives and guns.

The *intifada* was a major turning point in the Israeli-Palestinian dimension of the Arab-Israeli conflict because of the change in perceptions it engendered on both sides. On the Israeli side, the *intifada* signified that the future had finally arrived. Ever since June 1967, Israel was waiting for the future, when the Arab states would sober up and agree to make peace to get their land back. But the future never seemed to arrive, and Israelis got used to having the territories under their control. Returning to the 1967 borders, especially for those who had no adult memory of them, seemed absurd. The Arab population was passive for the most part, and most Israelis—the 97 who percent lived inside the Green Line—went about their business as though the territories did not exist, except when they had reserve duty there. The *intifada* changed all that forever; Israelis knew that there would be no going back to the easy management of a passive population. After four and half years of spilled blood and mutual exhaustion, the desire to finally settle this matter, one way or another, led to the election of Yitzhak Rabin in June 1992 and gave him a mandate for change.

As for the Palestinians, the *intifada* was not just a revolt against the Israeli occupation, but also to some extent a social revolution within Palestinian society against the generation of elders who had failed to confront the occupation and whose passivity had brought dishonor and shame. The role of youth (the *shabab*), of women, of refugees, of intellectuals, changed from one of subservience and low social status to one of ad hoc leadership in revolutionary times. As a result, too, a new generation of local West Bank and Gazan leaders arose independently of the PLO, whose leaders lived abroad. The *intifada* was not started from the PLO headquarters in Tunis, and it surprised Arafat as much as it surprised Shamir. For years thereafter, the PLO tried to find ways to muscle in on, take credit for, and direct the *intifada*. Ultimately, and with Israel's help, it more or less succeeded in doing this; but the changes in Palestinian society have not been undone. On account of their own organization, Palestinians now expect more, demand more, and can extract more from a leadership and a government than can other Arab populations. Indeed, it is no exaggeration to say that Arafat decided to make his deal with Israel because he feared that, if he didn't, the Palestinians in the territories would negotiate without him. And in time they probably would have done so.

The second factor after the *intifada*, both in timing and in relative importance, was the Kuwait crisis and Gulf War of 1990–91. The war, whatever else it did, marginalized the Arab rejectionists and helped the moderates. It brought Egypt, Syria, and Saudi Arabia—the same combination of key Arab states that made war in 1973—into a pro-U.S. alignment. Now, with the Iraqis defeated and their allies (Yemen, Libya, Sudan, and the PLO) marginalized, these three states could make peace if they chose to do so. The PLO was greatly weakened by the war, for Arafat chose the wrong side. The PLO's huge subsidies from Kuwait and Saudi Arabia were cut off as a result, and the PLO was impoverished. The PLO was unable to control events inside the territories and was battered in the war. By the summer of 1993, Arafat concluded that making major concessions and establishing a relationship with the United States and Israel were the only things that could save the PLO from oblivion. He was probably right.

The third factor was the end of the Cold War and the collapse of the Soviet Union at the end of 1991. Even before then, by 1990 for certain, it had become clear—at least in Damascus—that the Soviet Union was not going to be the kind of ally for the radical rejectionist Arabs that it had been since the late 1950s. Moscow was no longer interested in or willing to buck American policy for the Arabs' sake; rather, it put improving relations with the West far ahead of fighting the Cold War in the Third World. The Soviet Union reestablished diplomatic relations with Israel in January 1991 and made significant rhetorical changes in its traditionally anti-Israel policy line.

The reduction and finally the disappearance of Soviet support—military and diplomatic—for the Arabs was a major psychological blow, comparable to Iraq's defeat in war. The key impact was to persuade Syria that it needed to create a new working relationship with the United States, which is one reason why it joined the allied coalition against Iraq.

President Bush and his secretary of state, James Baker, saw and understood the general impact of these changes. While the Arab-Israeli conflict did not represent nearly as significant a danger for the United States after the Cold War, Bush and Baker decided to seize the opportunity to complete some unfinished business, long a part of the U.S. diplomatic agenda: solving the Arab-Israeli conflict. These efforts produced the Madrid Summit of October 1991.

The Madrid Summit was a major watershed in the history of the Arab-Israeli conflict. For the first time, all of Israel's remaining adversaries after Egypt sat in direct public negotiations with Israel. Pictures of Israelis in the same room with Syrians, Palestinians, Saudis, and others were beamed around the Arab and Muslim world. The iron wall of Arab rejectionism, nihilism, and psychological denial of Israel's very existence came down with a great crash.

Madrid generated Arab-Israeli negotiations on three tracks. The first was a series of bilateral negotiations between Israel and Jordan, Israel and Syria, and Israel and Lebanon. The aim of these negotiations was a final treaty of peace. These negotiations were not formally linked to one another, but in practice everyone knew that Lebanon would not go forward without Syria, and the Arabs feigned coordination, lest lack of progress on one track reduce the leverage remaining to the other Arab parties on other tracks. In practice, such coordination proved to be no more than lip service.

The second track was Israeli-Palestinian negotiation, the aim of which was not a peace treaty but an interim accord on Palestinian autonomy or self-government within the territories. After autonomy had been created and put into practice, it was expected that the parties would then begin negotiations about final status issues, leading, if successful, to a final peace treaty. Israel negotiated with a Palestinian delegation that was a part of the Jordanian delegation. This was necessary because Israel under the Shamir government refused to negotiate with the PLO, and the Palestinians needed some Arab umbrella outside of the territories themselves to attend the Madrid Summit.

In fact, the Palestinian delegation was picked largely by the State Department with Israel's participation.[3] In practice, however, even though the delegation was not composed of PLO members, it could not operate apart from the PLO's influence. So while the Palestinian delegation was formally part of the Jordanian delegation, Israel knew that this delegation was in coordination with, if not actually taking orders from, the PLO in Tunis. The Palestinian delegation, then, derived part of its legitimacy from its connection to the PLO and part from its ties to the Palestinian "street" in the *intifada*. These latter ties were not particularly strong, but strong enough so that the Washington delegation either would not or could not concede enough to Israel to reach a general declaration of principles that could lead to a negotiated accord over Palestinian autonomy. Thanks to the *intifada* and its "insider" origins, the delegation had a standing independent of the PLO, but not independent enough to escape a virtual PLO veto over its biggest decisions. As a result of all this, while the bilateral tracks progressed to one extent or another, the Israeli-Palestinian track got nowhere fast.

The third track created by Madrid was the multilateral track, a collection of five working groups (on refugees, water, environment, economic cooperation, and arms control) under the auspices of the great powers, whose aim was twofold. First, broad international participation in the working groups was supposed to lend a wider legitimacy to the peace process, and begin a process of normalization between Israel and all Arab and Muslim states. Second, it was designed to evoke international financial support for agreements reached between Israel and its neighbors as a means to create incentives for peace and to bolster agreements reached on other, more basic political levels.

The Shamir government was reluctant about Madrid. It did not really want negotiations if they were likely to lead to a showdown over the territories with the Palestinians, and therefore trouble with the United States. Labor governments had always accepted the principle of relinquishing territories taken in 1967 if they could be traded for real peace. On both legal and security grounds, Labor governments were not willing to return to the exact pre-June 5, 1967, lines, but they were willing to make major territorial concessions. The Likud position from 1967 onward was that Samaria (Shomron) and Judea (Yehuda) were not occupied territories but liberated territories. It rejected any return of any of these territories to Arab sovereignty. It suggested autonomy for what it called "the Arabs of Eretz Israel," refusing to acknowledge a specifically Palestinian people or the legitimacy of a specific Palestinian nationalism.

The model for this autonomy, which had been invented by the founder of Revisionist Zionism himself, Vladimir Jabotinsky, was the Jewish Pale of Settlement in the czarist empire, a place where Jews exercised limited autonomy under the sovereign purview of the empire. Shamir thus went to Madrid talking about "autonomy for the people," not for "the land."

The United States, for its part, did all it could to get the Israelis to Madrid. Every demand the Shamir government made—no PLO, no Palestinians from Jerusalem, no discussion of final status questions with the Palestinians, no preconditions—the United States granted, for it knew that without Israeli participation there would be no peace process at all. Shamir thus decided to go to Madrid because he received an invitation from Washington that he could not refuse. Even after accepting, however, Shamir had hoped that Syria would reject the American invitation; when Syria also accepted, Israel had no choice but to go. Whereas Menahem Begin would have responded to this circumstance by energetically lecturing the world at large on Jewish history and Israel's rights, Shamir treated the occasion more like a visit to the dentist. His main aim was to delay a real reckoning over the problem of the West Bank, for that would lead inevitably to a crisis in relations with the United States, which has always supported the Labor view of territorial compromise for peace that accords with its interpretation of UNSCR 242.

Most likely, the peace process would have gone nowhere with a Likud government in Israel, and the *intifada* in one form or another would have continued. First Rabin's primary victory over Peres and then the Labor victory in the June 1992 Israeli election are what changed the overall context. Rabin had won a mandate to deal with the Palestinian issue, and after more than a year of trying to work a deal with the Palestinian delegation to Washington, he realized that this delegation was not strong enough or independent enough from either the Palestinian "street" or the PLO to deliver an agreement. He also realized that Islamic opposition among the Palestinians to any negotiation and any agreement with Israel was growing, and so was its capacity for terror and violence.

When Rabin decided to move, he did so by reaching down and elevating a low-level dialogue that had been started in Oslo by Israeli academics and

Palestinian intellectuals and officials, and generally overseen by Foreign Minister Peres and his closest aides, Deputy Foreign Minister Yossi Beilin and the director-general of the Foreign Ministry, Uri Savir.[4] The so-called Oslo track was not very important in the beginning, but it made unexpected progress and was clearly endowed by the Palestinians with an increasing importance as an alternative to the Washington negotiations. Israel began to get signals from Arafat that he was prepared to grant Israel terms much more advantageous than anything Israel had heard from the Palestinian delegation that emerged from Madrid, but only on the condition that Israel publicly recognize the PLO as the legitimate interlocutor for the Palestinian side. Secret negotiations continued throughout the summer of 1993, and on August 20, Israel and the PLO signed the outline of a Declaration of Principles in Oslo, Norway.

These negotiations had been kept secret. The Knesset did not know. Israel's main negotiator in Washington, Elyakim Rubinstein, did not know. The Israeli chief-of-staff, Ehud Barak, did not know. No American diplomat knew either.[5] When the agreement was made known a few days later, the world was shocked.[6] Some were shocked and pleased, some were shocked and displeased, most were just shocked. The Declaration of Principles was formally signed on the White House lawn in the presence of President Clinton on September 13, 1993. On that occasion, Prime Minister Rabin reluctantly shook hands with Chairman Arafat, and the real promise of the Madrid Summit began to emerge.

Jordan followed quickly in the PLO's footsteps, signing its own Declaration of Principles with Israel the very next day.[7] It took until May 4, 1994, for the Israeli-PLO Declaration of Principles to be fleshed out, and its first stage, called Gaza-Jericho, to be implemented—somewhat longer than expected. In July, Arafat and his aides arrived and took up residence in Gaza. For the rest of 1994 and roughly the first half of 1995, PLO-Israeli relations were poor. Violence against Israelis from Islamic groups opposed to Arafat and the PLO, mainly Hamas and Islamic Jihad, rose sharply, undermining support for the accord and those who negotiated it in Israel. In the meantime, owing to frequent and increasingly long-lasting closures of the Israeli border to Palestinian laborers and its simultaneous opening for the export of Palestinian produce, the standard of living went down in Gaza and Jericho, undermining support for the deal and those who negotiated it on the Palestinian side.

Arafat's failure—or unwillingness—to get control of his opposition, and to do the necessary things to acquire promised international aid, threatened the entire process. But Arafat was trying to avoid a showdown with his opposition and trying to avoid looking like a pawn of the Israeli occupation, which would undermine what nationalist credentials Arafat had and doom his prospects. Israel did not want to undermine Arafat, for that would serve no purpose, but it couldn't afford to let Arafat ignore his obligations on the security side of the agreement. Arafat's balancing act with his own constituency, and Rabin's balancing act with his, composed the inner dynamic of the Palestinian-Israeli track during the period after May 4.

The immediate aim of Israeli-PLO diplomacy after May 4, 1994, was to hold Palestinian elections. Israel promised in the May 4 accord that it would withdraw the IDF from populated centers in the West Bank so that free elections could take place. But given what had happened to the security situation in Gaza, Rabin was reluctant to move ahead toward elections until Arafat achieved better control. This was a particularly serious matter, owing to the number of Jewish settlements and settlers in the West Bank. There were only a few thousand settlers in Gaza, and for the most part the settlements were concentrated in a single area called Gush Katif, where they could be easily defended. The security problem in Gaza concerned mainly attacks originating there but targeted on Israel proper. In the West Bank there were about 140,000 settlers—half of them children—spread over a large area and interspersed with areas of large Arab population. Most of the settlers lived in the greater Jerusalem area and in other settlements adjacent to the old border, but many lived elsewhere. The security problem involved in withdrawing the army, therefore, was qualitatively different from the case in Gaza.

Arafat, meanwhile, demanded that elections be held as soon as possible so that his authority could expand in the West Bank beyond the Jericho enclave. In effect, Arafat was saying to Rabin, "Give me more authority, and I'll be able to give you more security," and Rabin was saying to Arafat, "Give me more security, and I'll be able to give you more authority." Finally, on September 24, 1995, the two sides finished hammering out a compromise, which quickly became known as Oslo II, that would allow elections to be held.

Oslo II was a complex agreement, administratively and otherwise. It was also very detailed, partly because Israel insisted that it would not allow the agreement to be as vague as Oslo I, and very controversial in Israel, passing the Knesset by a 61–59 vote. Oslo II also brought about the decision of Yigal Amir to stop the process by murdering Prime Minister Rabin.

Although Amir didn't succeed in stopping the process, he did complicate it and slow it down. Rabin's murder had the initial effect of driving the Israeli political spectrum back to the center, toward a cautious consensus on peace, after the September 1993 handshake on the White House lawn had split the country nearly in two. The emotional catharsis of the mourning period deepened the commitment of the pro-peace constituency, drew the undecided and the hesitant closer to Rabin's vision, and muted criticism from those opposed. This process was deepened by facts on the ground: the Israeli army completed the bulk of its withdrawal from the West Bank in December and January in an atmosphere almost totally bereft of violence. Things finally seemed to be working out, to be turning nearly normal; something like actual peace seemed, for the first time ever, to be possible. Not since the beginning of the *intifada* in December 1987 had there been such a sustained period without significant violence.

In essence, Oslo II involved the withdrawal of the IDF from all major Palestinian-populated urban areas in the territories (not including East Jerusalem and, for a different reason, Hebron) and a redeployment around other Arab towns and villages. By December 28, 1995, this withdrawal was basically completed: Israel had finally stopped being responsible for the daily lives of well over a million Palestinian Arabs.

In this relatively positive environment came the Palestinian election of January 20, 1996, which went more smoothly than most predicted. Relatedly, as anyone who read a newspaper in Israel knew, both pre-election maneuvering and the election results showed Hamas's strength to be diminished; Arafat had outflanked and politically neutered his opposition and was fast turning Hamas into a not particularly loyal, but what seemed to be a relatively docile, opposition. In short, Arafat's capacity to be a partner in Israel's general security environment seemed to be waxing, precisely as peace process architects planned and predicted.

The fact that there was no bloodletting or trauma over the withdrawal or the election meant, in effect, that this, literally the most consequential part of the peace process with the Palestinians, became defined for Israelis as more "normal" than not, as in effect part of the flow of expected events. And if this were not enough, the possibility of a breakthrough with Syria seemed suddenly possible, and with it the prospect that Israel might one day soon be at peace with all of its immediate neighbors.

In consequence, by mid-February 1996, after months of internal debate, even the majority of the opposition Likud bloc had come to terms with the reality of the peace process with the Palestinians. Their predictions of catastrophe after the signing of Oslo II in September had not come to pass, and Likud's begrudged moderation showed that it lacked a distinct alternative position to that of the Labor government. Israel's religious parties, too, both on account of their own soul searching and in light of political realities, were moving away from the militant, quasi-messianic nationalism of recent years into a posture to join a Labor-led coalition after the May 29 election—and they would have done so had Labor won. Taken together, all of this was cause for a glint of optimism in a society deeply inured to a skeptical, pessimistic attitude toward political life.

What Israel expected in return, now that Arafat's authority had expanded with Israeli withdrawal and the Palestinian election, was much greater personal and psychological security than had been the case during the early months after the September 1993 handshake. Things seemed to be going smoothly for a while, and then all of a sudden the entire peace process was thrown into jeopardy. A series of four spectacular suicide bombings between February 25 and March 4, 1996 killed fifty-nine Israelis in Jerusalem, Tel Aviv, and Ashqelon. Never in the entire history of the state had so many civilians been killed in so short a time. The country was stunned, its morale temporarily sapped, its anger rising.

The spate of grisly terror bombings was shocking even by ingrained local standards, and those standards are defined by a regrettably high threshold of pain. But the real reason for the unprecedented shaking of Israeli confidence was not just the frenzied frequency and lethality of the attacks, nor their symbolically central sites in Jerusalem and at Tel Aviv's Dizengoff Center, nor even the fact that, once again, little children were victims. The reason for the stunned shock was that it flew in the face of new and hopeful expectations. This is why the bombs hurt so badly; precisely in proportion to the hopefulness engendered in the months before was the hurtfulness of this terror offensive. To be wounded in hope is in many ways worse than to be wounded in hatred. Who could blame the average Israeli for careening back toward pessimism, fear, and anger—to the chilly comfort of familiar emotions?

The peace process was thus brought to the brink of political collapse. The positive developments listed above were not illusory but real: Israel as a political community had come closer together in support for peace, the Palestinian Authority (PA) was slowly gaining the upper hand, and Hamas was weaker and more divided than ever. Insofar as they bore political meaning, these attacks illustrated the desperate effort of some of its competing extremist factions to stop the peace process before it became irreversible. But the emotional flow in Israel was strongly in the opposite direction; people felt betrayed, abused, even ashamed of allowing themselves the luxury of imagining that they could bequeath a normal life to their children, a life forever without killings and hatred, air-raid shelters, and gas masks. The odd juxtaposition of the hopeful changes of recent months and the horror of recent days thus defined the moment.

Prime Minister Peres affirmed the peace process but demanded that Arafat and the PA act as a partner, as it had promised. He demanded that the Palestinian National Covenant be amended or junked to be rid of phrases about Israel, Zionism, and Jews that were incompatible with peace. Israel also showed that despite the withdrawal under Oslo II, the IDF could effectively seal and segment the entire West Bank, and do so without having to set foot in any street in any major Palestinian city.

Before the bombings, Shimon Peres seemed a sure bet for reelection. Within hours, literally, the bombs destroyed Peres's lead in the polls. Between mid-March and May 29, Peres and the Labor party worked and hoped to project an image of toughness, but also of wanting peace. (This was illustrated, partly, by the Israeli assault on southern Lebanon in April, which followed a Syrian and Iranian-abetted assault on northern Israel by Hizballah, the Lebanese Shiite party of God.) Peres, and all Israelis for that matter, focused hard on Yasir Arafat, for the post-bombing period was the first real test after the Palestinian elections and the expansion of the PA's power in the West Bank of Arafat's willingness and ability to be the partner in peace that he had agreed to be. The PA's record improved markedly, although it remained imperfect. The covenant issue was managed if not fully solved before the Israeli election, and Palestinian security forces scored some successes. But it still did not do everything it might have, as Arafat continued to prefer indirect and protracted means of squeezing and reducing his Islamic opposition to confrontational ones.

As a result, the Israeli electorate decided on May 29 that it was better for the country to be united around a hesitation than divided over a gamble. While Likud's Benyamin Netanyahu defeated Labor's Shimon Peres by only 29,490 votes, with 50.3 percent of the vote, Jewish Israelis voted for Netanyahu by a margin of about 55.5 to 44.5 percent—a spread of ten points, a true mandate. Israelis, it seems, were worried by Peres's utopianesque statements and his reluctance until after the bombings to press full enforcement of Oslo II on Arafat and the PA. Many also believed that Likud's diplomatic version of "tough love" with the Palestinians would bring peace.

The Knesset results confirmed the verdict of public opinion. The Meretz party sunk from twelve to nine seats, Labor from forty-four to thirty-five. The Third Way party's three seats could still be counted as basically pro-Labor, and increased seats for the Arab parties and for the Shas could not be assumed to be anti-peace process, but it is still clear that the body politic shied away from pursuing the peace process with the Palestinians at the same speed and in the same way as before.

In June 1996, when Prime Minister Netanyahu had just formed his cabinet and his government, it was generally agreed that if he stuck close to his campaign pledges—no more territorial concessions, no Palestinian sovereignty over anything ever, no symbolic compromises over Jerusalem, no withdrawal from Hebron as pledged in Oslo II, and a go-ahead to expand and build new Jewish settlements—then the Israeli-Palestinian track could blow up and the *intifada* return. But it was not clear if Netanyahu would do as he promised during the campaign or if he would be more moderate once in office. Some early evidence pointed one way, other evidence the other way. September 1996 brought matters to a head.

The Tunnel Door Episode

Benyamin Netanyahu's election as Israel's prime minister on May 29, 1996, was greeted by a great international gnashing of teeth. A dismayed horde of experts and pundits feared that, efforts at rhetorical placation notwithstanding, the Netanyahu government would follow its ideological instincts to the thorough befouling of the peace process. They predicted retrograde motion in every dimension of the Arab-Israeli conflict in consequence.

This was not immediately clear. Lost amid the bewailing was the critical fact that Netanyahu's election reflected an *already existing* crisis in the anemic record of Palestinian autonomy. On balance, as of the spring of 1996 autonomy had failed to deliver the goods: security and a sense of genuine Arab acceptance for Israelis; economic relief and restored honor for Palestinians. As a form of diplomatic art, autonomy was a good idea: the parties could not agree to more, yet a majority of both communities was sufficiently dissatisfied with the status quo to settle for less. But autonomy as practiced was not working, and the popularity of the peace process suffered accordingly.

As of June 18, when the new Israeli government was installed, the key question was whether or not Netanyahu and Arafat could fix autonomy. The answer promised to tell us whether the basic foundation of the peace process, as defined in Oslo in the summer of 1993, was sound or not. If it could withstand the new pressures of a new political combination between Israel and the Palestinians and emerge perhaps stronger for it, we would have known that its principles were mightier than the personalities that formed it, and sturdier than the tempests of Israeli and Palestinian domestic politics that buffeted it.

But such knowledge was slow in coming. As the first three months passed, fears over the Netanyahu government's projected course neither abated nor were vindicated. The reason was that the government proved more adept at "planning" its administration than at actually doing anything. All watched for signs revealing true intent, and signs there were; but they were ambiguous. Infrastructure Minister Ariel Sharon ordered roads and bridges built that suggested further Israeli territorial digestion, but Netanyahu hinted at relieving the closure of Palestinian areas. The prime minister said Israel would make a withdrawal of the Israeli army from Hebron but insisted on renegotiating the terms nearly from scratch. The settlement freeze was lifted, but no new settlements were authorized. The Israeli government postponed major decisions and avoided specifics whenever possible; even a brief spate of secret diplomacy regarding Syria and south Lebanon early in the Netanyahu period seems to have been designed mainly as a tactical delay, to keep the Americans deflected from the Palestinian track and to place any onus for the lack of progress on the Syrian track on Damascus.

But the government could not tread water forever; either decisions had to be made or they would eventuate by default. Clearly, the future depended more on what Netanyahu and his lieutenants did than on what they said, and in that respect the new team appeared to be learning as it went. Its principals did not expect to win election, and a combination of inexperience and early tenure-shock produced a clumsy coalition-building process, an abundance of intercabinet conflict over matters both foreign and domestic, and an unprecedented catfight between the prime minister's office and, in turn, the foreign ministry, the defense ministry, and the state security services.

At this early point, there was still a case for expecting a happy ending. Not every aspect of autonomy had gone wrong, after all; the trade already made—Israel's relinquishing of responsibility for the majority of the Palestinian population and the PA's assuming it—was one neither side wished to reverse. Both sides had much to lose, and they seemed to know it. Netanyahu also appreciated the peripheral benefits of the peace process: the economic boom it helped midwife and the growing normalization of Israel's position in the region and beyond. He worked hard to maintain both in early visits to Washington, Amman, and Cairo.

Moreover, while it had been a fetching campaign slogan to claim that the Labor government had "subcontracted Israeli security to Yasir Arafat," it was an exaggeration: after all, the IDF had segmented and subdued the West Bank in March 1996 within thirty-six hours after the grisly spate of terror attacks and kept it that way at will. Besides, the Palestinian police and intelligence forces were slowly becoming a serious if still imperfect partner with Israel, and if Netanyahu had done what he said he would do during the campaign—send the IDF everywhere throughout the West Bank and Gaza in search of terror suspects "over the heads" of Palestinian policemen—Israel would have quickly ended up with less security and more terror, not the other way around. So, while Netanyahu could barely bring himself to say "Oslo," he recognized that he could not deliver personal security to Israelis under current circumstances without the PA.

Most importantly, Netanyahu was not elected to stiff-arm the peace process but to reduce its costs and enhance its benefits. His ministers were right to argue that they were in a better position than Labor to demand compliance from the PA. Shimon Peres, they pointed out, was associated so closely

with the process that making such demands necessarily reflected prior failures, so he was reluctant to press them—until exploding buses and body
parts littered the streets of Jerusalem and Tel Aviv. The new government, it
was said, had no such problem, and no such reluctance.

And there were demands worth making. The Palestinian leadership could
have done much more to quell terrorism, could have turned over captured
terrorists to Israel as required by agreement, could have stopped praising
murderers and calling their acts "jihad," and could have avoided breaching
the agreed rules over Jerusalem. For its part, Israel was obligated to withdraw from most of Hebron, release the last security prisoners it promised to
release, create a safe passage between Gaza and the West Bank as agreed,
and ease the closure of the territories if the PA did its part on the security
side. There was no inherent reason why patient diplomacy could not have
achieved this amalgam of transactions had there been the intention to proceed. But there was no certainty that the will existed to do so, and that brings
us to the case for pessimism.

Such a case was composed of several parts. Palestinian expectations of
the peace process were excessive, and Yasir Arafat did not help by fanning
these expectations with repeated proclamations of the imminence of a sovereign Palestinian state "with its capital in holy Jerusalem." Meanwhile,
formal Likud positions—on not just some, but all, final status issues-in-wait-
ing—were so inflexible as to engender despair among Palestinians, elite and
commoner alike. The government program, promulgated with the introduction of the new government, called for the current territorial status quo to be
frozen, for existing Jewish settlements to be expanded and new ones established, for no Palestinian sovereignty over anything ever, for no compromise (not even symbolic) over Jerusalem, and for a freer hand for the IDF in
the territories. Nor was it clear during the summer of 1996 whether Netanyahu
would ever meet with Yasir Arafat—though he sent Foreign Minister David
Levy to do so despite catcalls and complaints from some of his own Likud
backbenchers. In short, while Israeli and Palestinian expectations of where
the peace process would ultimately lead diverged significantly ever since
the evening the Oslo accords were initialed, never before were those expectations so wide apart as they were during Netanyahu's first one hundred
days in office.

The PA's willingness to be a partner with Israel on security problems
depended in large part on its expectations. If the peace process was to lead
essentially nowhere, or nowhere beyond where it already was, then one had
to wonder how strong Arafat's incentive to be a full partner could be, especially when doing so posed a risk to his own still unstable position amid a
riven Palestinian community. Pessimists worried that Israel's possible un-

willingness to negotiate in good faith and at reasonable speed would jeopardize Arafat's position, help his Islamist opposition, and lead to violence. If the violence were major, it was thought, Israel would have little choice but to assume the full burden of security, an undertaking that, by reversing the two-year flow of authority to the Palestinians, would almost certainly spawn new terror recruits and terrorist acts. If, at the end of such a process, the large Palestinian towns, designated as Zone A in the Oslo II agreement, were all that was left to effective PA control, and if terrorism was known to flee, hide, and incubate there, Israel might find itself obliged to re-enter those "cities of refuge" even against its desires. And if it did, who knew how many of roughly 30,000 armed PA policemen would try to stop them? Arafat himself, amid a burgeoning new armed conflict that he could neither staunch nor manage, might well exile himself from the scene lest he be buried trying to control it. Hamas would inherit the vacuum, and the Oslo process would be dead.

Who was right, and why? To understand what happened next, we must go back to basics for just a moment.

In the Israeli-Palestinian case, a mutually intolerable status quo, the result of a dialectic of suffering occasioned by protracted Israeli military occupation and seemingly endless Palestinian *intifada*, led to a basic bond of partnership in 1993 that involved Israel and the Palestinians trading one instrumentality and one basic principle each. That trade, which had to begin in words and only afterward be able to move to firmer reality, was this: The Palestinians forswore the use of terror and violence as bargaining leverage and accepted explicitly the legitimacy of Israel's existence as a Jewish state; Israel foreswore the annexation or permanent military occupation of the bulk of the non-Israeli land west of the Jordan River, and accepted that the Arabs living there had not only basic human and residency rights, but at least some kind of *political* rights as well.

As noted, in the earlier phases of the implementation of the interim agreement—Oslo I—the limits of partnership were breached, in effect, by Yasir Arafat. Although his own domestic problems were serious, Arafat learned too slowly to appreciate the Labor government's domestic political circumstances. He was too sly and too slow in dealing with his extremist Islamist opposition, and he abetted what amounted to the offloading of the price of Palestinian political adjustment to autonomy onto Israel in the form of multiple terror and trauma. Yitzhak Rabin skirted the edge of the political chasm throughout most of 1994 and in the months of 1995 before he was murdered as well, but Shimon Peres, it may be said, learned "too fast," giving Arafat more of the benefit of the doubt than was wise. As a result, he got himself into irredeemable political trouble at home.

The combination of Arafat's slowness and Peres's speed led to the grow-ing impression in Israel that Arafat was insincere about the essential ele-ments of partnership, that he was indirectly using his oppositions' own violent acts to acquire political leverage, and that he was, in essence, double-talking and double-dealing. If he was to keep his promises against the temptations of playing to his domestic gallery, he would have to be *made* to keep them. More than anything else, this sentiment is what brought Benyamin Netanyahu to power.

With Netanyahu's arrival, the Israeli-Palestinian partnership suffered a sudden shift in valence. After the February-March 1996 terror bombings, in particular, Arafat finally moved against Hamas, a success illustrated by the fact that there were no suicide bombings between mid-March 1996 and the end of May when Netanyahu was elected, and he greatly advanced Israeli-Palestinian security and police cooperation. All of this came too late to save the Labor government, but it made Arafat a more reliable partner than he had been before. This was ironic because the more ideological elements in the Likud, as well as its coalition partners farther to the Right, had already concluded that Arafat was not and never would be a real partner. While Netanyahu held open the prospect of fixing autonomy, others that he brought into the government were interested less in fixing autonomy than, in their view, unmasking it for the dangerous charade that it was.

Thus, while Arafat had become the partner-in-waiting to Netanyahu that he had never been to Rabin, Netanyahu's most powerful domestic opposi-tion turned out to be that within his own cabinet. So with Arafat ready and needing to go faster to justify to the Palestinian "street" the steps that he had taken against his political opposition, he suddenly found himself with an Israeli interlocutor in Netanyahu wanting to go slower—and half of Netanyahu's cabinet wanting to go backward.

Netanyahu's mandate, and his intention as far as anyone could see, was to improve the peace process by asking for more from the Palestinians and giving them less—which made much political and diplomatic sense under the circumstances. But such was not the policy. Instead, the new govern-ment demanded more of Arafat even as it denied his achievements, and it gave nothing in return. It practiced a combination of "thumb-in-the-eye" and stall diplomacy that was deeply destructive to Israeli-Palestinian ties.

Several examples of the thumb-in-the-eye tactics may be cited. Israel lifted a crane over the wall of the old city in Jerusalem to demolish a Pales-tinian building that was being used as a day care center without a license; this occurred just days after Arafat agreed to shut down two technically illegal PA offices in east Jerusalem. Thus, a Palestinian concession followed by an Israeli indignity was taken by the Palestinians as an act of deliberate humiliation. Netanyahu's refusal to meet with Arafat, and then doing so belatedly and coldly, and without substantive results, was part of the pattern, as was keeping Arafat's helicopter in the air for forty minutes before allowing it to land in Ramallah. Israel also ostentatiously announced the expansion of Israeli settlements and a land-eating road-building program in the West Bank, under the auspices of Ariel Sharon, which was clearly aimed at segmenting it into enclaves.

At the same time, the Netanyahu government was achingly slow to decide anything relating to the negotiations with the Palestinians. The government dithered for months over what to do with respect to Hebron. It also procrastinated in establishing a common agenda with the PA for the further implementation of the rest of the Oslo II accord, and, after that agenda was finally established in early September, almost nothing of substance was discussed, let alone agreed upon, thereafter. Netanyahu also claimed movement on several occasions in easing the economic closure of the territories by issuing more Palestinian work permits. But in fact no such permits were issued before the outbreak of violence on September 24, and the Palestinian economy deteriorated even further.

So, in the first one hundred days of the new Israeli government, a new dialectic of political deterioration came into play in the Israeli-Palestinian partnership. While part of the problem flowed from Palestinian missteps, which confirmed the Likud's least charitable assumptions about Arafat's motives, the greater part of the problem flowed from Netanyahu's failure to put into effect his own stated plan.

The net result of Netanyahu's first one hundred days was the loss of most of the accumulated benefits of partnership built up since the summer of 1993; rather than understanding the other's domestic circumstances, each side increasingly tended to collapse its partner and its domestic extremist opposition together; to wit: they behave the same, so for practical purposes, they must *be* the same—Netanyahu and Sharon as far as the PA was concerned, Arafat and Hamas as far as the Likud was concerned.

Netanyahu's sudden downshifting of the peace process threw Arafat for a loop, but Arafat had made matters worse for himself by exaggerating the expected outcome of the peace process. He did this partly to justify his concessions, and partly to finally bury his opposition by romantically, but irresponsibly, outbidding it. Having stuck out his neck, Arafat and his lieutenants panicked when Netanyahu threw on the brakes. They threatened to return to violence and mocked the very idea of partnership by extolling mass murderers like "The Engineer," by naming public squares after them, and by otherwise displaying sentiments inconsistent with their promises.

It is against this background that the infamous tunnel door episode must be understood. On the evening of September 23, 1996, Israel opened a second doorway to a tunnel from the time of Herod that ran as a continuation of the Western Wall along the perimeter of the Temple Mount. Netanyahu himself made the decision, urged on by the mayor of Jerusalem, Ehud Olmert, and the minister of tourism, who expected greater revenue from the project. Opening the new door was in itself innocuous, and Arab claims about what it suggested—a conspiracy to structurally undermining the Dome of the Rock in order to rebuild Solomon's Temple—were absurd. But the way it was done, furtively and unilaterally, fit a pattern of deliberate humiliation.

The tunnel opening had been discussed for years with the Islamic *waqf* (religious endowment/administration), and Israel had proffered opening Solomon's Stables nearby as a possible site for Muslim worship in tandem with the tunnel opening—and something of an implicit understanding on this exchange seems to have been reached during Peres's tenure. But instead of pursuing the negotiations—assuming he knew about them in sufficient detail, which is not clear—Netanyahu proceeded unilaterally and without informing the *waqf* in advance. This was interpreted by the Arabs as an intentional subordination of Muslim rights in Jerusalem to Jewish ones.

Arafat ordered demonstrations, the demonstrations turned into riots, and during those riots some Palestinian policemen joined the mobs and fired at Israeli soldiers, killing fifteen. Seventy-four Palestinians died before things calmed down almost three days later.

Given the background of distrust that had built up, the Likud government initially saw the violent upheavals of September 24–26 as deliberate incitement to violence on the part of Arafat and the PA—a fundamental repudiation of partnership. It did not see, or would not admit, that its own behavior contributed to the violence. And the Palestinians saw Israel's opening of the tunnel door, amid its failure to bargain in good faith, as a repudiation of partnership as well. They did not see, or would not admit, that their own behavior also contributed to the violence.

Exaggerations and half-truths were hurled about as the dust settled and the fresh graves were filled. Many Israeli officials became surer than ever that Arafat intended violence when he called for demonstrations and that he had ordered his police to shoot at Israelis. They did not believe, or care to believe, that the reaction of many undertrained and inexperienced Palestinian policemen was a function of the chaotic logic of the moment, even though the pattern of interaction between the Palestinian police and the Israeli military was highly variable from place to place. They did not consider the possibility that Arafat might have called for demonstrations because he knew they were coming anyway, and thought it better to get in front and try to control them rather than let them run amok, possibly ending with the demonstrators aiming their wrath at him.

At the same time, Palestinian officials quickly came to believe that the tunnel caper was no error in Israeli judgment but another deliberate humiliation to undermine their authority. Nor did they believe that Israel's use of tanks and helicopter gunships against rioters was either a necessary or a proportional response to events. They called what happened a "massacre," and they believed it, even though the Israeli use of force was extraordinarily restrained under the circumstances. Had orders been given to IDF soldiers to fire indiscriminately, hundreds and perhaps even thousands of Palestinians would have been killed, not seventy-four.

Indulging in such delusions, however, helped both sides with their most problematical domestic constituency. The press focused on Arafat's gains, and they were real. The tunnel door "thumbing" offered Arafat an opportunity to reverse his sinking fortunes. Indeed, it furnished, in essence, a pretext—clear enough from the fact that Arafat had tried and failed a few weeks earlier to generate mass demonstrations by calling for a general strike and a massing at the Al-Aqsa mosque. Equally clear were Arafat's motives: to create a cost for Israeli foot-dragging and, as important, to deflect growing Palestinian displeasure with the PA onto Israel. What had not worked in early September was, however, ready to work by late September. With the temperature of the Palestinian "street" rapidly rising, the shock of the tunnel door opening in Jerusalem allowed Arafat to dwarf local displeasure with the PA's many sins—nepotism, corruption, police brutality, press intimidation and censorship, and general administrative incompetence—to join ranks with and rhetorically lead the entire Arab and Muslim world, and to show Netanyahu that even the mere *mukhtar* of Gaza, as Arafat's detractors sometimes call him, could exact a political price for demeaning him.

But the violence helped Netanyahu, too—not with the broader Israeli electorate, to be sure, or with world public opinion (whatever that is worth), but with the brawling Likud princes in his own cabinet who had given him the most trouble from the start. His uncompromising rhetorical and military response to the rioting shut them up, at least for a while. But the fact that, in the end, the violence helped both Arafat and Netanyahu politically is *precisely what was wrong with it.* Partnership is about a willingness to take political heat for the sake of joint aims, not a willingness to set partnership aflame for the sake of domestic political ease.

This being the case, the task at hand for the impromptu Washington Summit of October 1–3 was clear from the start: prevent the Israelis from assuming that the Palestinians were bent on using violence, hence repudiating their basic commitment, and prevent the Palestinians from assuming that Israel was bent on avoiding good faith negotiations, hence repudiating its basic commitment. Moreover, this reassurance had to be built simultaneously: if the Likud-led Israeli government were to think that the Palestinian forswearing of violence was conditional and disingenuous rather than principled, then it would not give away the option to repudiate Oslo; and if the PA were to think that Israel did not intend to negotiate in good faith, then it would be foolish to forswear the use of violence because it is virtually the only instrumentality the Palestinians have.

Fixing matters also meant restoring partnership in the sense of getting each side to be realistic about the domestic political limits of the other. This implied having patience and some degree of trust, not giving carte blanche for all misdeeds and trusting beyond prudence, the latter being simply out of the question for Israelis, who watched in horror as Palestinian policemen turned their guns on Israeli soldiers. Producing some degree of trust was difficult, but it seemed at the time to have been a major achievement of the summit—especially the three-hour Arafat-Netanyahu tête-à-tête on Wednesday night, October 2. King Hussein's pleadings, as well, seem to have done some good: they galvanized Netanyahu's fears that he might have jeopardized Israel's most important Arab relationship—that with Jordan.

Netanyahu's changed demeanor showed in his *Nightline* interview the next day, in which he made statements about Arafat and the PLO that he had never even come close to making before: recognizing the Palestinians as a people and the PLO and Arafat as their only negotiating address, and stating that the interests of Israeli and Palestinian children were intertwined. Afterward, too, Netanyahu retrieved his initial comments about Arafat's motives. As a result of that meeting, he said, there was now a basis for trust with Arafat, and he now believed that, just as he did not intend the tunnel door opening as incitement to violence, neither did Arafat give orders to shoot or likewise intend violence. Both had used bad judgment; the achievement of the summit was that Arafat and Netanyahu were able to admit that to one another. If indeed, as Netanyahu said, "the ice was broken" in Washington, that mutual admission was the icebreaker.

So despite much complaint at the time, the summit did not fail. It broke the downward spiral and provided a quality-time encounter between Arafat and Netanyahu that made a difference. It also created a "next step" in the negotiations over the status of Hebron.

Clearly, the biggest choices, at the summit and after, were left to Netanyahu. Again, some signs were positive for the continuation of the peace process, some not. Netanyahu ordered his aides to stop calling the summit an Israeli "victory" and stopped accusing Arafat of sins for which he had no evidence. He stopped his aides, too, from threatening publicly to have the Israeli army move into the major Palestinian cities to disarm 30,000 Palestinian police. But he did not try to get his followers to stop referring to the riots as "Shimon Peres's chickens come home to roost," as though the policies of his own government had had nothing whatever to do with the violence. And on the key question—whether he would stand up to the ministers in his own cabinet who did not share his stated goal of fixing the peace process—the jury was still out as of November 1996.

Indeed, the evidence continued to be ambiguous after the tunnel door incident. On the one hand, Netanyahu proposed that after the Hebron redeployment, Israel wanted to move to final status negotiations. Those negotiations, not scheduled to be completed before May 4, 1999, seemed to many observers to be most likely to freeze all further movement on the ground. Netanyahu's logic, or part of it anyway, was clear: If Israel gave up more and more territory in interim steps, what leverage would it retain when final status negotiations began? Moreover, Israel's hard-line approach to the Hebron renegotiations suggested no real change in approach. So, as was the case before the riots, Israel's signals remain mixed, between modest gestures and largely empty smiles, on the one hand, and rock hard, uncompromising, and profoundly unhurried negotiating behavior, on the other.

Arafat's behavior also returned to form. He claimed that the tunnel door should still be closed because it was the "al-Burak" area of the Haram al-Sharaf and therefore holy to Muslims. This was playing with fire. Also incendiary was his statement on October 9 that he could not prevent a new *intifada* from breaking out, which suggested he might not try, which in turn contradicted what he had earlier said to both Netanyahu and Ezer Weizmann.

So that is how the Netanyahu era began. When it ended about two years later, it did so after more of the same. Sometimes the trajectory of negotiations was upward, most of the time it was stalled or heading downward. Much of the time the United States took a standoffish position, believing that the parties had to work out their problems on their own; other times, especially as time passed with no progress, the United States became intensely involved for fear that if it did not, all that had been gained in the previous three years would be lost. But at no point in the Netanyahu tenure did the necessary development of mutual trust and respect between the sides reach the point that it had before the Rabin assassination and, as abstract as it may sound, trust and respect are what is important when adversaries try to become partners.

Part of the reason for this lack of trust was that the Palestinian side never clearly demonstrated its commitment to real peace, and that continued to undermine support for the process in Israel. Netanyahu also made many tactical mistakes. One was ordering an assassination attempt against a Hamas political operative living in Amman. The attempt failed, King Hussein was embarrassed, and to get Israel's captured operatives back, Netanyahu had to agree to release Sheikh Ahmed Yassin, the head of Hamas, from an Israeli jail.

Netanyahu's main tactical error, however, was to entice the United States into a far more intrusive and direct role in the diplomacy. Netanyahu thought that using the United States as a more direct mediator would end up bringing more pressure on the Palestinians, but Arafat saw his opportunity, stayed on his best behavior, and by the end of the Netanyahu period, was coming to Washington at will, while Netanyahu was treated as a virtual *persona non grata*. As important, Netanyahu was hamstrung by his own narrow coalition. He became a hostage to its anti-peace process wing even though he knew that the majority of the Israeli electorate felt differently.

How did Netanyahu feel, and what did he believe? Sometimes he acted like a believer in the peace process weighed down by an unruly coalition. Sometimes he acted like he opposed the whole arrangement but could not say so for fear of alienating the United States, Egypt, Jordan, and the majority of the Israeli electorate. Most of the time he acted like a amateur politician, weaving and leaning in whatever direction seemed to serve his needs at the moment. He is gone from power now, and the answer to this question is *still* not clear. And all this went on while the clock was ticking toward May 4, 1999, the expiration date of the five-year interim period—a pressure point Arafat used with some success in advancing the sense of inevitability about a Palestinian state.

What is clear is Netanyahu's legacy, which seems to have been part deliberate and part accidental. Despite his misgivings, Netanyahu did preside over two agreements with the PLO: the Hebron Accord of January 1997 and the Wye Plantation agreement of October 1998. The result of these two agreements was to deliver the Likud constituency to the idea of a political solution to the problem with the Palestinians, a solution that made the old Revisionist aim of controlling all the land west of the Jordan River impossible. As prime minister, Netanyahu ended, at least for the time being, the dream of Greater Israel. This was confirmed in a remarkable agreement in January 1997 among Labor and Likud Knesset factions as to final status talks with the Palestinians. From that time on, there has been a rough consensus in Israel as to what a final status arrangement can and cannot be. By the time Netanyahu fell in December 1998, this consensus covered most of the country. A plain majority of Israelis now believes that a Palestinian entity of some sort is a price of peace, and they are willing to pay it in territorial coin. That could not have happened without a man like Benyamin Netanyahu: namely, an anti-Oslo advocate promoting, however slowly, pro-Oslo diplomacy for lack of any alternative.

Netanyahu did something else for peace, and, unlike the foregoing, this was on purpose. Netanyahu managed to enforce a level of reciprocity in

Palestinian behavior that Rabin and Peres never achieved. The PA police and security forces have proven that they can handle Hamas and other disruptive forces if they want to. During Netanyahu's tenure, the level of terrorism directed against Israeli civilians dropped considerably. Once it was not clear if Palestinian terror took place because Arafat *could* not stop it or because he *would* not stop it. It is now clear that Palestinian terror can be stopped, and this is Netanyahu's accomplishment.

The odd thing is that, while Netanyahu achieved these things, and objectively advanced the peace process as a consequence, he was never able to truly embrace his own achievements. He deserved to sip champagne, but to him it tasted like vinegar. That is one reason—though not the only one—why the Israeli electorate threw him out of office in May 1999.

The election of Ehud Barak holds out promise for progress in the peace process, both with the Palestinians and with other Arabs. But Barak is no dove. His map of final status is not very different from Netanyahu's map, and he likes interim steps no more than Netanyahu did. Barak abstained in the cabinet vote on Oslo II, believing that it was not wise to give up territorial assets in interim agreements with the Palestinians because Israel would need them in final status negotiations. Moreover, his coalition includes parties that will not look kindly upon a set of negotiations in which strict reciprocity with the PA is not enforced.

Nonetheless, Barak's tone is liable to be much different from Netanyahu's. Relations with the United States and Jordan will improve, and the United States will be able to sit back a row or two from the diplomatic action, which benefits both U.S. and Israeli interests in the long run. Given the change in tone, we may now see what sort of partner Arafat really is. Thus far, Arafat and the PA have made no major concessions, just temporal ones that can be retracted at will. The Palestinians have not budged on their demands for land, and have recently enlarged them, demanding the borders of the partition resolution of 1947, not of early June 1967. They have not budged their positions on refugees, Jerusalem, or water either, even though ever since September 1993 Israel has been relinquishing territory, suffering terror attacks, and taking the long-term security risks of legitimating the existence of Palestinian political claims to parts of Eretz Israel.

This cannot go on much longer, and one may doubt that Barak will let it. If the Palestinians do not evince a capacity for serious negotiations, and serious compliance with undertakings already assumed, the peace process will go nowhere. The difference is that, with Barak in office instead of Netanyahu, the PA is far more likely to be blamed for the impasse than Israel, and not only in American eyes.

In any event, even if the Palestinians do show a willingness to deal in good faith, it is unlikely that final status negotiations will succeed to the satisfaction of both sides. Israeli and PA positions on every dimension of final status are too far apart to be easily bridged. As noted above, the best that can be expected is a higher quality level of belligerence, a deal about the modalities of future dispute, not a true peace born of their final resolution. But that is not an insignificant thing considering how deep and how long this conflict has been. Moreover, even if most Palestinians today are not reconciled to the legitimacy of a Jewish state in the Middle East, the process itself can be a vehicle to change those views. Sometimes hypocrisy is the advanced wave of a new truth. It is hard to think of any other way to proceed, which is, when all is said and done, the peace process' best friend: the lack of any plausible and available alternative.

The Broader Impact of the Peace Process

Whatever happens within the Israeli-Palestinian relationship, the Arab-Israeli conflict writ large seems to have changed permanently. While Israel's relationship with the Arab states—especially Jordan and Egypt—is sensitive to the Israeli-Palestinian relationship, there are definite limits to that sensitivity. So beyond the working of the Palestinian track of the peace process as such, and regardless of who is the Israeli prime minister, the detachment of the Palestinian problem from the interests of the Arab states seems to be irreversible. It resulted in the de facto end of the Arab boycott even during Rabin's tenure, and this has major economic implications for Israel.

The end of the boycott means that Israeli trade directly with the Arab states is likely to grow, but this is not of special economic importance because Israel's economy doesn't "fit" the Arab economies in most respects. Israel is too high-tech to find many markets in the Arab world, and the Arabs do not produce much that Israel wants or needs. The economies at the lower-technology levels are competitive, not complementary—although this could change in time.

But the end of the boycott signals greater stability, and that means that the largest international corporations that either avoided Israel altogether or did only modest buying and selling there will now think about integrating Israel more fully into their essential operations. Israel offers a highly talented and competitively priced labor force, the key to a country's success in the new knowledge-based economic environment. Israel's location—a hub linking Europe, Africa, and Asia—is ideal as well. Israel's international business connections are well developed and its infrastructure is modern. Also, Israel's science-based research and development capabilities are very impressive for such a small country, as are, say, those of Sweden.

Indeed, as the peace process proceeded in the 1993–96 period, foreign investment poured into Israel at an unprecedented pace. But as the peace process soured, the flow slowed notably, and the Israeli economy went into a slump—another reason Netanyahu lost the 1999 election. "There can be no dispute," said Jacob Frenkel, the governor of Israel's Central Bank, "This is not a political statement. It is a factual statement. Our ratings agencies, our investors, all look at the geopolitical situation, and they vote with their feet."[8]

But to make good use of its new opportunity, Israel needs more than peace. It is also going to have to reform its state-dominated economy to a greater degree. Between 1984 and 1994, for example, the cost of subsidies as a percentage of government expenditure dropped from 13.2 percent to 4.9 percent, but there is more to be done in this and other areas. There is a fragile consensus favoring greater privatization—as discussed in Chapter 4. It may be deepened and accelerated by the prospect of greater and more lucrative integration in the top ranks of the international economy. If so, the per capita Israeli income could even surpass that of the United States within a quarter-century. Israel could, in short, become the combined Hong Kong-Silicon Valley-California Tech of the Middle East.

Another positive economic sign is that, with the reduction of the military burden—assuming that remains the case—more money could be spent on capital investment. Already Israel has reduced reserve-duty requirements (from a maximum forty-five days per year to just twenty-nine) thanks to an increased population, and it has changed the age requirements as well. Men in combat units now have to serve until age 45; in non-combat units, 51. It used to be 55 for all categories. Woman have to serve until their mid-twenties, depending on the category of their work; it used to be the mid-thirties. All this frees up hundreds of thousands of work-hours that would otherwise have been spent in *miluim*.

Military expenditures as a percentage of government expenditures fell from 24.5 percent in 1981 to 11.0 percent in 1995, to around 10 percent or a bit lower in 1998. Israel also has too many eighteen- and nineteen-year-olds for its military needs. There is talk of reducing the period of basic conscription, and the army is granting more unsolicited exemptions from military service than ever before, particularly to women. In a few cases, Israeli women have protested their exclusion for, as explained earlier, military service is the key ticket to all sorts of state benefits. Clearly, if the demand for military manpower is reduced sharply—and it likely will be[9]—adjustments in this entire ticket-punching process will become necessary.

Aside from changing the role of the army to some degree, what changes within Israel would this kind of economic shift imply? For one thing, it would change the structure of employment. There would be more education-intensive employment, which would tend to be "indoor" urban work and have less emphasis on agriculture. This is positive in the sense that such changes would virtually solve Israel's water problem. More than 65 percent of Israel's water is used for irrigation, not drinking. Reducing the percentage of the economy devoted to agriculture will make the water problem far less severe.

This is not positive, say many Israelis, because the claim to the land depends essentially on living on the land and working it. Already Israel's urban population density is rising, and the new economic changes in the works will accelerate that trend. This is precisely the reverse of what the government did in the early years of the state by establishing development towns and building new agricultural settlements to disperse the population.

Again a positive consequence of such a new economic profile for Israel is that Israel could absorb many new immigrants without worrying about settling large numbers of people in the Negev—a very expensive and questionable proposition. A negative consequence that many Israelis worry about is urban sprawl and the virtual destruction of open spaces in those parts of Israel where people live. Israelis don't want the whole country north of Beersheba to look like a Hebrew version of Singapore. They still love the land. And they don't want the pollution that comes from urban sprawl either. But if you can't "keep 'em down on the farm after they've seen PCs," then how to prevent this from happening?[10]

So much for the Israeli-Palestinian diplomatic track and some of its most important implications. The other dimensions of the peace process are important to Israel too, notably those with Jordan and Syria.

Israeli-Palestinian problems did not stop the Jordanians from moving ahead to a formal peace treaty. Israel and Jordan negotiated intensely, largely in secret, and finally signed a peace treaty on October 26, 1994. Israel returned small parcels of land sequestered over the years for security reasons, and agreed to give Jordan a somewhat larger water allotment. The Israeli-Jordanian treaty in turn cleared the way for the normalization of Israel's relations with Morocco, Tunisia, Qatar, Oman, and other Arab states, and for the effective end of the Arab economic embargo against Israel. It was a major positive development from the Israeli strategic point of view because it meant that Jordan could not be used as a staging ground for a unified Arab attack from the east, a main concern of every Israeli military planner after 1949.

Jordan's move also underscored another very important fact. Once the PLO took responsibility for the burden of Palestinian history, it meant that the Arab states could pursue their own interests with regard to Israel without much concern for the Palestinians. Since the creation of the Arab League in 1945, Palestine was the quintessential pan-Arab issue. We have seen how it played in inter-Arab political maneuvering, especially in the 1964–67 period. With the Israeli-Palestinian Declaration of Principles, the Arab states have now largely severed their own policies from the plight of the Palestinians. Jordan signed a final treaty with Israel before the Palestinians had got past even the first stage of a Gaza-Jericho interim accord. Syria may or may not make peace with Israel, but either way it won't be because of what happens or does not happen to the Palestinians.

As to Syria, Israel's negotiations with Syria since Madrid have given rise to many expectations but few results. This is the area of the peace process in which the United States, mainly in the person of Secretary of State Warren Christopher, most intimately involved itself. The Rabin-Peres government expressed a willingness to withdraw from nearly all of the Golan Heights—nearly all, but not all. Syria, for its part, signaled a willingness to make peace but was not willing to define what it meant by peace. Israel wanted an asymmetrical military arrangement after withdrawal to accord with the differences in strategic depth on either side of the Heights. Syria insisted on a proportional withdrawal. Israel wanted direct secret talks at the summit plus some public gesture to assure the Israeli public of Syria's sincerity. Syria offered neither, preferring the mediation of the United States. In December 1994, the Syrian and Israeli military chiefs of staff met privately in Washington and reportedly had a serious conversation, but since then the Israeli-Syrian track has fallen into the deep freeze. With the ascent of the Likud after the May 29, 1996, election, and the withdrawal of Israel's offer to leave Golan, nothing much was likely to change in the peace process here—except a worsening of relations in and around southern Lebanon, which is exactly what happened.

If the Syrians ever develop the political will to move to a settlement, technical issues will not be a major problem. But no one knows if and when Syrian President Hafiz al-Asad will get the urge. He will have to pay a high price for peace: with regard to domestic politics, where the Syrian people have been fed an unremittingly hostile line toward Israel for more than forty years; with regard to Iran, whose friendship Syria will probably lose; and with regard to Lebanon, where peace may require a long-term diminution in Syrian influence. What would Asad get for this? A better relationship with the United States, but owing to Syria's stygian domestic system, not a cordial one. He would get back most of the Golan—1,190 square kilometers out of a Syrian total of 185,180 square kilometers—less than 1 percent of Syrian territory, and an area not of special interest to the minority Alawite ruling group. Getting it back, too, would deprive the Alawites of an issue around which to ingratiate themselves to the majority Sunni population. The chances of a genuine and full Israeli-Syrian breakthrough to peace, then, are at best uncertain.

Despite these circumstances, Ehud Barak seems determined to test the waters. He also seems determined to get Israeli troops out of southern Lebanon. The complexities of these issues transcend the scope of this text, but, suffice it to say, none of this will be easy.

Nevertheless, from the Israeli point of view, the detachment of the interests of the Arab states from the Palestinian problem is a very positive development even if the Syrian regime tarries in making peace. Just as the end of the Cold War has made the Arab-Israeli dispute much less dangerous for the world as a whole—since now neither an oil embargo nor a U.S.-Soviet confrontation can grow out of a regional war—the treaties Israel has signed with Egypt and Jordan have turned the Palestinian problem from a regional one to a local one. In a sense, the scale of the Palestinian issue is once more what it was before May 1948. It is much smaller, so even if the Palestinian-Israeli track does not result in a stable final peace, the peace process has succeeded in progressively shrinking the size of the Arab-Israeli conflict and its general danger to the world at large.

Hopes and Fears: Israel's Internal Peace Process Debate

A good deal of what Israelis think and worry about in their future pertains to the peace process and the future of relations with the Palestinians and other Arabs. Virtually all Israelis say they want peace and virtually all genuinely do want peace, but they know that they can't have a perfect peace given the level of hostility toward them among many Palestinians. For several decades now, the problem has really come down to this question: "Are we Israelis better off externalizing the problem, which means getting the bulk of hostile Palestinians outside our control, or are we better off keeping it internal, holding on to the land and dealing with the population as best we can?" There are risks and benefits to both approaches as most Israelis see it. On balance, Labor has favored externalizing the problem, Likud has favored internalizing it. That explains the main differences between the two camps on peace-process strategy since 1967, even if one does not raise religious and historical issues and questions. And now, as explained above, Likud in its post-Oslo incarnation is resigned more or less to the Labor point of view.

After the June 1967 War, Labor governments favored returning most of the West Bank to Jordanian control in return for peace with Jordan. This was called the Jordanian Option. But the rise of Palestinian nationalism, and the level of support it got in the Arab world, undermined Jordan's position over the years. Jordan has undertaken a series of tactical retreats, most notably in July 1988 when it renounced responsibility for the West Bank. Nevertheless, Jordan retains important interests and even a few ambitions in the West

Bank, particularly over Jerusalem. While the classically defined Jordanian Option is no longer realistic, Labor still favors a confederative relationship between whatever Palestinian entity might emerge from the peace process and Jordan.

Until 1996, therefore, Labor's platform opposed an independent Palestinian state. In 1996 the opposition was dropped, but nothing was put in its place. It does not object to a Palestinian anthem, a flag, a parliament, even a United Nations seat. But it does still object to a level of sovereignty that would allow a Palestinian entity to have any weapons it chooses, to allow any foreign army on its soil it chooses, and to have any external ally (such as Iran or Iraq) that it chooses. Obviously, from the Israeli point of view, limiting the prerogatives of a future Palestine by binding it with a country with which Israel already has a peace treaty—Jordan—is an attractive option. It also makes it easier for a future Labor government to persuade the Israeli people that relinquishing territory does not carry inordinate security risks.

The Likud still does not formally accept the principle of permanent territorial compromise in the West Bank; however, informally it does. In coming to this changed view, the Likud also came to change its view of a Jordanian-Palestinian federation.[11] Many of its thinkers used to argue that any such a federation would, in time, be dominated by the majority of Palestinians who could then nullify the Israeli-Jordanian treaty and use the entire area of what used to be Jordan before 1967 as a staging ground to wage war against Israel. This is not a fear that can be dismissed out of hand. But the Likud's view of Jordan has changed, and some of its principals, including Sharon, now see Jordan as a possible ally and substitute for the PA in some respects (e.g., security maintenance). But Jordan does not share the Likud's view of Jordan's role.

To the left of Labor is the Meretz party. Its view is that a neutral and demilitarized Palestinian state should come into being along side of Israel. It not only takes this view on moral grounds, but also on practical grounds: a federation with Jordan is politically impractical given Palestinian views of the Hashemites, and indeed it could backfire on Israel in the fullness of time. The political views of those to the left of Labor also believe that a Palestinian democracy is vital for Palestinians and Israelis. Most Labor analysts do not believe that Palestinian society is ready for democracy or yet capable of sustaining it, and most prefer instead that someone be in control even at the expense of democratic processes and civil liberties for the Palestinians.

There are also political views to the right of the Likud. The Tzomet and especially the small Moledet Party have favored "transfer," a euphemism for ridding the West Bank of its Arab population. Some would go about this slowly, by making life increasingly difficult for the Arab population; others would load the Arabs onto trucks and buses, drive them into Jordan, and just leave them there. This was a logical response to the conundrum of how Israel could keep the land it believes belongs to the Jewish people, but without the headache that comes from occupying nearly two million Arabs. But it is such a radical response that few Israelis ever supported the idea, and with the end of the occupation it has become largely moot. That, in turn, explains why the far right did so poorly in the 1999 election.

The idea of transfer, however unpopular today, won't go away completely, and it is liable to become more popular to the extent that every other means of dealing with the Palestinians and Palestinian extremist violence against Israelis fails. If, for example, militarized Islamic fundamentalism succeeds in capturing Palestinian politics, and Israelis conclude that no dialogue with such forces is possible, then transfer may become a popular idea notwithstanding its many negative aspects.

Another critical issue concerning the territories and the Arabs in them has to do with what kind of economic and day-to-day relationships Israel might have with the Palestinians in the future. The agreements signed so far between Israel and the PA call for the area they share to be a single economic space. This means that labor, capital, and goods should be able to flow freely among Israelis and Palestinians. On paper and in theory, this is what all economists would argue is the ideal relationship from a strictly economic point of view. But more is involved than economics.

First of all, Israel itself is a protected economy where services, goods, and capital do not flow freely. Second, where Israel's economy is $100 billion and the Palestinian economy is around $2.5 billion, it is hard to see how the Palestinians could avoid becoming, or remaining, hewers of wood and carriers of water for a more sophisticated economy. Such unequal relationships are not conducive to stable political relations based on mutual respect. And lastly, there is the security issue. The possibility of Palestinian violence against Israeli civilians will persist probably even if a contractual peace agreement is signed between Israelis and Palestinians.

The truth is that most Israelis do not want peace *with* the Palestinians, but peace *from* them. The frequent closure of the territories after May 4, 1994, has been popular in Israel, even though the security payoff of the closures has been modest in terms of preventing terrorist incidents. Palestinians with work permits to enter Israel almost never have been responsible for incidences of violence. But most Israelis still want separation, and that is what Prime Minister Rabin promised them after January 1995, even if it took building physical barriers to free movement. This is also the attitude of Prime Minister Barak, which helps to explain why he could get elected as a Labor candidate while Shimon Peres, an advocate of "integration," could not.

Some Israelis also want separation because they believe that use of Palestinian labor in menial work has distorted the Zionist project. Ora Namir, a former minister of labor affairs, made a particularly sharp point of reemphasizing the original Zionist project when it came to the nobility of work, and with so many new immigrants unemployed, it made little sense to hire Palestinians to do work that Jews could and should be doing.[12]

Likud supporters and ideologues have generally opposed separation. They generally have claimed that they oppose it because it would redraw the Green Line that Likud governments strove to erase in order to maintain perpetual Israeli control over the territories. But those businesses in Israel—especially housing contractors—that have had the most financial interest in maintaining the availability of cheap Arab labor tend to be Likud supporters. Ideology aside, it is hard to escape the conclusion that these interests are prepared to live with a greater level of security risk that comes from relatively open borders and free movement in order to maintain their profit margins. Nowadays, the Likud, here as with the problem of Jordanian-Palestinian relations in the future, has moved toward traditional Labor views supporting separation.

Because of the *intifada*, Israelis were eager to solve the question of the future of the West Bank and that is why, as noted earlier, they preferred Labor versus Likud to do it in 1992. But Israelis were not very eager to change the status quo with respect to the Golan Heights, and they still aren't. Because of Israeli power and Syrian prudence, the Golan might be the safest place in the eastern Mediterranean. Its geographical characteristics make it an important strategic high ground. Not only does Israeli control of the Heights make it impossible for Syria to shell Israeli settlements, as it did before June 1967, but it also puts Israeli forces within virtual sight and shelling range of Damascus. This offsets and neutralizes to a considerable degree the strategic significance of the Syrian position in Lebanon, and the more than 35,000 Syrian soldiers stationed in Lebanon's Bekaa Valley.

Nevertheless, many Israelis believe there are benefits to an Israeli peace with Syria that are worth giving up virtually all of the Golan Heights. The most important of these benefits is that the satisfaction of Syria's grievance regarding its national territory will greatly reduce the Syrian incentive to make war on Israel. Since Syria has missiles that can reach Israeli civilian population centers, and will probably be able to deliver unconventional ordnance in due course, Israel wishes to avoid a war in which thousands of Israelis might be killed even if Israel wins the war. Syria is the Arab country most able to cause severe civilian damage in a war, so naturally the Israeli army and foreign service are dedicated to limiting or eliminating that prospect, despite the lack of any public enthusiasm to make territorial concessions in order to do so.

Many Israeli analysts also believe that if Israel is at peace with all of its immediate neighbors, then the animus toward Israel from farther afield—

Iran, Iraq, Libya—will also be reduced and undercut. For Syria to make peace with Israel would mean to break its close ties with Iran, a shift that would serve both Israeli and U.S. interests in the region.

Finally, Israe! would like to withdraw from the security zone that it established in southern Lebanon in 1984, but it is unwilling to do so if that means that Hizballah will fill the vacuum and start attacking Israel's northern towns and villages as the PLO used to do before 1982. A deal with Syria has to cover Lebanon, and the political solution to Israel's problem in southern Lebanon is best attained through Syria. This is paradoxical, since Syrian efforts to eradicate Hizballah in the context of breaking its ties with Iran would strengthen the Syrian presence in Lebanon, at least temporarily. Israel's longer-term interest is not just in solving the Hizballah problem but in seeing Lebanon as free and clear of Syrian domination as possible. It is not yet clear how Israel will be able to manage this aspect of its problem with Syria.

The problems of the Palestinians in the West Bank and of the Syrian-Lebanese track are daunting and are unlikely to be finally solved any time soon. Quite aside from the religious and historical issues involved and the conventional security problems that inhere in dealing with the territories, there is the less conventional security issue of water. About 40 percent of Israel's drinking water comes from the main aquifer under the West Bank. According to most interpretations of international law, the ownership of the water is a function of traditional use, so most of the water is Israel's. Palestinians do not see things this way, however, and some sort of negotiated arrangement concerning water and water quality will be necessary for a final deal to be made. This will not be easy. Similarly with Syria, the ultimate source of the Jordan River is the snows of Mount Hermon in the Golan Heights. The path the water takes is mainly below ground, but the water does emerge here and there in the Golan and is theoretically subject to diversion. The Banias, remember, one of the three sources of the Jordan, was controlled by Syria before 1967. Clearly, then, working out a water deal in the context of a Syrian-Israeli peace negotiation could be daunting, too.

Without doubt the internal debate over these issues, and the shifting political alignments that go with them, will continue for some time. So will reference to American diplomacy which, in the Syrian-Lebanese dimension to this problem, remains a main actor. So it is to the future of U.S.-Israeli relations we now turn.

The Future of U.S.-Israeli Relations

Virtually every seasoned observer of U.S.-Israeli relations suspects that this relationship is bound for major changes in the near future. Several factors are commonly cited as reasons: the end of the Cold War, the possibility of Arab-Israeli peace, the maturation and stabilization of the Israeli economy, shifting relations between diaspora Jewry and Israel, and other reasons besides. Another, more intuitive source of this expectation is simply that no relationship so peculiarly intense can last very long.

Before May 29, 1996, U.S.-Israeli relations were unusually close, cooperative, warm, and relatively untroubled. But appearances can be deceiving. U.S.-Israeli relations have always been constructed from both "soft" factors of common values and "hard" ones of geopolitics. Additionally, as noted earlier, American Jewry has functioned as a connective tissue for the relationship within U.S. domestic politics. The nature of both soft and hard factors in the U.S.-Israeli relationship is changing, and the character of the connective tissue is changing, too. These changes dwell at different depths below the surface, but they are there. Let us look first into the shallows, and thereafter gaze more deeply.

Early on in 1993, the Clinton administration adopted a strongly pro-Israeli point of view, which was easy to maintain since American views of the Middle East peace process coincided with those of Israel's Labor government. The Rabin government's policies became the linchpin of American diplomacy in the region. Gone, more or less, were the acerbic disputes about settlements, aid levels, supposedly illegal arms-technology transfers, kickbacks and payoffs over aircraft engines and the like, espionage, and a whole host of lesser irritants that plagued the Bush-Shamir epoch and many of those before it.

But the Clinton administration's affection for Israel had more to do with American politics—prospects for the first re-elected Democratic administration since that of Lyndon Baines Johnson, most notably—than any deep sympathy for Zionism or Israel. Whatever the source of its affection, it certainly did not want to quarrel with Israel. But as other friendly U.S. administrations have found, circumstances as well as misunderstandings can ignite conflicts. As the peace process approached several moments of truth over negotiations with Syria, the potential for U.S.-Israeli argument rose with it. But it never rose very high.

Moreover, the Rabin government's private view of President Clinton and his administration was mixed from the very beginning. It appreciated the positive public demeanor, the willingness to consult, the continuation of high aid levels, and the continuity of basic policy. But it is no secret that Yitzhak Rabin wished for George Bush's victory in the 1992 election for fear that Clinton's lack of experience and inclinations toward gutting the U.S. defense budget would lead to the abandoning of an active American role abroad. Rabin's fears were not for nothing. American diplomacy in the Arab-Israeli domain during the Clinton administration was appreciated in Israel during Rabin's time more for its relative quiescence than for its creativity or skill. Israeli diplomacy, in turn, occasionally arched its back to produce that quiescence.

As a result of the surface harmony between the United States and Israel, the hypotenuse of the U.S.-Israeli triangle, so to speak—the American Jewish community—was relatively composed. With a solid if not vast majority at home with the Democratic party and a pro-peace Labor government in Israel, the wrenching choices of the Bush-Shamir period all but vanished. But look more closely and see another reality.

Divisions in the American Jewish community and between it and Israel are real and growing.[13] A vocal minority of American Jews, encouraged in their attitudes during the period of Likud ascendancy in Israel, thought they knew better than the Israeli Labor government elected in 1992 what was best for Israel, and most Israelis do not appreciate sermonesque hyperventilations from afar. Meanwhile, less politicized but more careerist leaders of organized American Jewry are scandalized when senior Israeli officials tell them to "keep their money" as well as their opinions. A certain subset of American Jewry thus likes Labor's positions on the key issues well enough, even if they have been made nervous by the Israel-PLO agreement, but they like not at all how Labor's newly muscular Zionists see and talk with the representatives of American Jewry.

History shows that transient circumstances and the occasional sharp personality can set the tone of U.S.-Israeli relations, for better or for worse. Yet even during bad times, it was clear that the relationship could weather its share of storms because it was solid at base. Before Bush and Shamir there was Begin and Reagan during the siege of Beirut, Begin and Carter at Camp David and after, Ford and Rabin in 1976, Eisenhower and Ben-Gurion, Dulles and Sharett. Through it all, over nearly half a century, the U.S.-Israeli relationship emerged strong, effective, seemingly unbreakable.

But what of this solid base today? Politics being unerringly a province of irony and surprise, could it be that, despite appearances, the U.S.-Israeli relationship is in more trouble today than ever before? Might the next storm—inevitable sooner or later—not just rock the ship as before but sink it? If so, changes in the very bases of the U.S.-Israeli relationship, both soft and hard, would be the reason.

Cynics notwithstanding, the soft aspects of the relationship have always been very important: the sharing of democracy and basic Western political institutions and civilizational norms; the mutually reinforcing ideological exceptionalism of Zionism and American nationalism; belief in the Judeo-Christian ethic; the objective multiculturalism of both societies; the leavening role of American Jewry; shared trauma and guilt over the Holocaust. What of these soft factors in the future?

Israel and the United States are still both democracies, true. But in a relatively de-ideologized world context, this may matter less to Americans and Israelis as a common bond that both will recognize as significant. Moreover, as we have seen, Israeli democracy is different from the American variety, not just because it is parliamentary as opposed to presidential in structure, but also for reasons of political cultures. Let us not forget: Israel's founders were socialists and proud of it, and Israeli society is still characterized by many aspects of a communitarian as opposed to an individualist ethos. The more Americans understand about Israeli democracy, the less sure they are of liking it.

Beyond that, the psychic cohesion afforded by the Holocaust is receding before the passage of time and memory, as it must. Efforts to use the Holocaust for various purposes, too, whether in building museums in Washington or in the rough and tumble of Israeli politics, have—rightly or wrongly—irritated more than a few who believe that the subject has been overplayed for less than fully sincere purposes.

As for social comity generally, the truth is that the Judeo-Christian ethic aside, America and Israel liked each other more when both were more secular during the 1960s and 1970s. Now that each society in its own way is having second thoughts about unbridled materialism and modernity, the real and specific differences between Christianity and Judaism may come to matter as much or more than their general similarities. Beyond that, as we have seen, many Israeli intellectuals resent the Americanization of Israeli popular culture, just as a smaller number of Americans (Gore Vidal and Patrick Buchanan being examples) resent what they believe to be the Judaicization of American arts, letters, and public life.

What about American Jewry's role now and in the future? In the main, American Jews are growing more distant from both Israel and Judaism. As to Judaism, rates of assimilation and intermarriage are going up about as fast as rates of Jewish education are going down. American Jews as a group are becoming Jewish Americans, the shift of noun and adjective indicating the shift of primary identification. Gradually, too, Jewish American educational and career patterns are becoming less distinctive within the American milieu, suggesting that Jewish American voting patterns and patterns of political identification will become less distinctive over time, too. That may mean that American Jews will become less pointedly powerful as their efforts and interests are diffused.

Diaspora Jewish identification with Israel is also changing. For years one of the main if unspoken motivations for American support for Israel was guilt. American Jews sympathized deeply with Israel but were themselves unwilling to sacrifice a higher standard of living to move to Israel and tough it out with the rest. So they gave money instead. Sharp emotional association with Israel came also to rest with sympathy for Israel's security dilemma and general plight. Nowadays, however, the Holocaust and the heroic epoch of Israel's founding are passing into history and the generations that experienced them first-hand are passing with them. Over time, too, the war in Lebanon and the *intifada* reduced the level of sympathy for Israel, as did the rough edges of the Netanyahu government, as it was obviously no longer seen as a perpetual underdog, and the peace process is reducing the plight. It would not be surprising if, in another few generations, Israel will mean as much to most American Jews (by then mostly Jewish Americans) as Italy does to most Italian Americans. In short, American Jewry's role as leavening agent between Israel and America may be wasting. After all, no yeast has an indefinite shelf life.

The full development of the hard part of the U.S.-Israeli relationship came after the soft one, but it was never an insignificant aspect of the partnership. Indeed, while general sympathy with Israel in the country at large, in the press, and within the halls of Congress has always been important, the evidence suggests that from Truman to Clinton, the executive branch in the end has always made its decisions based on the national interest, not sentiment.

Sometimes, particularly during the Eisenhower presidency, the executive branch viewed Israel as more of a geopolitical liability than an asset, but never to the point of considering abandonment of the essential American pledge to Israel's existence. Moreover, for the most part, geopolitical considerations have brought the two countries together more than they have driven them apart. From the 1950s onward, Israel and the United States shared the same global enemies in the Soviet Union and its local Arab proxies and allies. Israeli strength added to American strength. Israel's location suggested many forms of coordination; Israel's technical talents offered many occasions for joint effort; Israel's intelligence capabilities provided ways to multiply America's own.

But what of these hard factors today? With the Cold War over and an Arab-Israeli peace a real possibility for the first time, can the hard factors possibly seem as important or urgent as they once did? No, they can't. In a world generally less armed and less broadly ideological, even the distempers of the Middle East are likely to lose much of their headline-grabbing potential in the years ahead.

Some see Islamic fundamentalism as a replacement for the common bond of an enemy once supplied by the Soviets and their local Arab clients. No doubt, Islamic fundamentalism is a problem with many facets, but it is far-fetched to expect it to replace Soviet imperialism as a source of U.S.-Israeli alliance motivations. Islamic fundamentalism is neither united nor armed in superpower array, and its battles are for decades far more likely to be played out within Islamic societies than projected from them. And why would Israel, whose Zionist forebears chose to live among hundreds of millions of Muslims, go out of its way to enter what would inevitably appear to be an anti-Muslim crusade as the junior partner of the "great Satan" itself?

Moreover, the Gulf War demonstrated for many Israel's relative incapacity to act in a pinch in defense of the West's oil supply, not just because of operational limitations but also because of political ones. For years it was implied, if not explicitly argued, by Israel's supporters (if not also by some Israelis) that, in one fashion or another, Israeli strength could be bent in support of keeping oil flowing out of the Persian Gulf, a mission that has not disappeared with the Soviet Union. But now everyone knows that, in a pinch, this is something the United States must do directly, together with its European, Asian, and Arab allies. In such a constellation, Israeli assets are diluted and, on occasion, politically problematical.

As far as the region as a whole goes, the "expansion" of the Middle East with the liberation of the Balkans, the Caucasus, and Central Asia from communist rule has elevated Turkey over Israel as the pivot of American strategic calculations in the region. The demise of the Soviet Union and the reemergence of the Great Game in the heart of Eurasia has changed geopolitical calculations in important ways. They are slowly sinking into consciousness now, a decade after the events that produced the upheavals. Direct Russian aggression against the core Middle East is no longer a matter of pressing concern, nor is the spread of Moscow's power via its local clients. Now, the relative vacuum in Central Asia, the chaos in the Caucasus, and the competition within the Muslim world between secularist and religious visions of the future are what matters. Israel was well placed and well fitted to be America's partner in the earlier era; Turkey is better suited for the present one.

Also important, both Israeli and American notions of deterrence and their military doctrines are changing. For most of the past several decades, Israeli and U.S. military analysts thought on similar wavelengths and used compatible—often times identical—vocabulary. That appears to be changing. American thinking is inchoate, but there appears to be a strong impulse to de-emphasize nuclear weapons, to draw back the global U.S. overseas basing system that affords opportunity for rapid reaction to crises, and to avoid any commitment that might overly tax the frail fabric that today knits the U.S. military to American society at large.

But for Israel, nuclear deterrence is likely to remain of paramount significance long into the future, for both diplomatic and military reasons. Its reliance on high-technology advantages to support a preemptive crisis strategy will probably remain a fixture of Israeli thinking simply because demographic and geographical realities mandate it. And as long as Israel maintains the IDF as a simultaneously professional and citizens army, it will be on balance much less reluctant to use force for fear of popular displeasure.

There is thus a potential for a parting of the ways between Israeli and U.S. military thinking, and U.S. non-proliferation policy is a good example of an issue on which basic U.S. and Israeli views are irreconcilable, as the spring 1995 arguments over this issue showed. Washington might desire a nuclear free zone after the signing of peace treaties if one could be created; Jerusalem, almost certainly, would not.

Relatedly, the future of the U.S. alliance system is in some doubt. Throughout the Cold War, the American obligation to defend Europe brought U.S. power and weapons close to Israel, and it entailed planning for eastern Mediterranean contingencies should a global struggle with the Soviet Union ever break out. With the prospect for general war in Europe now quite remote—indeed, the vaunted central front in a divided Germany is now simply gone—the relationship of NATO and its strength to Israel is less clear than ever. In the past, lack of NATO consensus over how to handle out-of-area issues constituted a problem with regard to Middle Eastern contingencies, true, but out-of-area isn't the same or as severe as out-of-business.[14]

Nevertheless, despite all these potential problems, there are still important areas of overlap between the United States and Israel. Both countries share interests in the success of "dual containment" against Iraq and Iran. For that reason and others, both understand the importance of Turkey and both have good relations with Turkey.

Both share an interest in combating terrorism and preventing the flow of nuclear weapons and expertise from the former Soviet republics into the Middle East. Both have good reason to continue to refine the coordination of logistics, planning, intelligence, and military research and development, for each operates as a force and financial multiplier for the other.

For all these reasons, too, both have an interest in the general economic well-being of the other. This interest should in time bring mutually agreed change to the aid relationship and to expanding opportunities for U.S.-Israeli trade and investment.

If Israel and the United States are destined to drift apart, then there are important implications for Israel, for American Jewry, and, despite Israel's small size, perhaps for America itself. But is it really true? Are the hard and soft bases of the U.S.-Israeli partnership being undone by the plate tectonics of historical and cultural change? Or are these merely temporarily unsettled times whose long-range impact we naturally, but mistakenly, exaggerate? We'll just have to wait and see.

Israel and World Jewry into the Future

A similar uncertainty surrounds the future of Israel's relationship with world Jewry. At the beginning of the Zionist enterprise, the Jewish world center was still in Europe. Established Jewish populations with their own traditions in the Arab world, Iran, Turkey, and even the North American diaspora, were all more important demographically and culturally than the small Jewish population in Palestine. The rapid growth of the Yishuv after 1917, and the destruction of European Jewry between 1939 and 1945, radically altered the balance. By the time Israel reached its first birthday, in 1949, there were really four centers of world Jewry: North America, the Soviet Union, the Sepharadic world, and Israel. By the time Israel reached its tenth birthday, in 1959, the Sepharadic world had largely been absorbed into Israel.

By the time Israel reached its fortieth birthday, in 1989, the Jews of the Soviet Union were facing a major choice: leave for Israel or elsewhere, or face likely cultural disappearance in Russia. It may well be that those Jews who left the former Soviet republics between 1971 and 1993 are the overwhelming majority of those who will ever leave, at least leave as Jews. A Jewish revival in Russia is possible, but a major revival is unlikely. More likely is periodic instability leading to a further flight of Jews to Israel. Jewish communities in Latin America, Australia, South Africa, Iran, France, England, and elsewhere in Europe tend to be small and are growing smaller because of either assimilation or emigration. This leaves the U.S. and Canadian Jewish diasporas as by far the largest non-Israeli centers of world Jewry. For most purposes then, North American Jewry *is* or will sooner or later become *the* diaspora.

There are more Jews in North America than there are in Israel—about 6.5 million compared to around 5 million. But large numbers of North American Jews are highly assimilated, and do not associate with the Jewish community in any way. Intermarriage rates are around 50 percent, and the children from most mixed marriages are not raised as Jews. Even Jewish children today receive less Jewish education than ever, and an absolute majority—54 percent is the estimate—receive no formal Jewish education at all. With statistics like these, the number of Jews in Israel will probably exceed the number of Jews in North America within two generations—in about thirty-six years.

But demography is not the whole story, or even the main part of it. What matters more than numbers of Jews hither and yon are how these Jewish people live, what they do, how they think, and the issues they care about. In Israel, non-religious people assimilate into an Israeli culture defined largely by Jewish civilization as attenuated by the modern Israeli experience. It doesn't look, feel, sound, smell, or taste like centers of American Jewish population, such as Flatbush or Miami Beach, but it is definitely Jewish. And because Israeli culture is an amalgam of Jewish cultures from all over the world, it is arguably far more deeply and authentically Jewish than the run-of-the-mill example one is liable to find anywhere outside of Israel. But when a North American Jew assimilates into the general culture, that culture is an attenuated Christian one. There are Jews who cross their fingers for luck and say "knock on wood"—remember the question in Chapter 1?—without realizing that both folk superstitions reference the cross of the crucifixion and are of Christian origin. By such measures, even a secular Israeli Jew is more Jewish in many respects than many if not most non-Orthodox American and Canadian Jews.

In the last twenty years there has been a major cultural, literary, and intellectual revival of American Judaism. But this revival—which has included the expansion of the Jewish day school system, a publishing renaissance, and a trend toward Orthodoxy—has gone on simultaneously with the general trend toward assimilation. In a few decades, American Jewry will consist of three parts: *haredim,* who have large families but stay apart from society will grow as a percentage of American Jewry; modern Orthodox communities, which will probably grow but will also furnish increasing numbers of Jews making *aliyah* to Israel; and the rest, the great majority of whom will have ceased being American Jews and will have become Jewish Americans, as noted above, as a temporary way-station to total assimilation.[15]

I am not judging this phenomenon; this sort of thing has happened repeatedly in the past and there is little reason to think America will be any different in this regard in the Jewish historical experience. The point is only that soon there will be no argument about where the center of the Jewish world is: Israel. It is already so by most significant measures, but many American Jewish lay leaders either do not understand this or will not acknowledge it. This shift is bringing with it several neuralgic problems, some of them previewed earlier. Israel doesn't need American Jewish money as it once did. Israel doesn't need American Jewish political lobbying as it used to either. And given the export of Israeli political divisions into the American Jewish context after 1977, many Israelis incline to see it nowadays as more of a nuisance than a benefit.

In addition, the secular-religious dissonance in Israel is loud enough to hear all the way across the ocean, especially for Israelis attracted to America or American Jews attracted to Israel. The secular-religious divide gets tangled up in the Israeli-diaspora divide and produces some very interesting results.

As noted, most secular Israelis (and many modern Orthodox) want to be worldly, but they speak a world-minority language written in a world-minority alphabet that would be in danger of disappearing if their humanist

Separating Synagogue and State?

One evening in September 1992, the local Ra'anana school had back-to-school night for parents. Most of it was totally unexceptional; I heard nothing new, only I heard it in Hebrew instead of English.

There was one exception, however. In the fifth grade classroom a heated argument erupted about what to do with the extra hour to be added on to the school day after Succot. The mayor's office in Ra'anana recommended that part of this hour be used to teach the Siddur (the prayer book), not as a vehicle for prayer but as an exemplar of Jewish literature a thousand years in the making. How could anyone object?

Someone did. "Why waste our children's time on such stuff when it could be used to teach science or computers? I am secular; my kids will never use this lesson. Next thing we know, we'll be teaching Rashi script* and preparing children for *Bar Mitzvah*," the latter said in deprecatory tones. But another said: "I am happy about this change. It is scandalous that children come out of public schools in a Jewish country without knowing the front end of the Siddur from the back. I too am secular, but this is part of our heritage. It is not theology that we are talking about; it is heritage, and no less important than teaching archeology, which all the schools do." Others joined in and the debate went on for an hour.

I suddenly realized that the same arguments and tensions that fill American Jewish life from left-wing Reform to right-wing Conservative go on in Israel—only not in synagogue offices and meeting rooms, *but in public schools!*

---

*Rashi script is a special way of writing the Hebrew alphabet used by Rashi, a famous and revered twelfth-century scholar. He used it to make sure his commentaries on the Torah and Talmud were easily distinguishable from the actual texts being commented upon. Later scholars used the script in a similar way, and thus to study rabbinic commentaries at any depth, one must master Rashi script.

hopes for the world at large really came true. In an abstract way at least, most Israelis fear the gentile world but still crave Levis 501s, German bathroom fixtures, Marlboros, and upscale rock videos. On the other hand, American Jews live in the freest and one of the most secular societies in history, and most still want to remain Jewish—the name for a religious civilization in which individual liberty and secularism don't figure high on the chart. The passions of Israelis to move from particularism to universalism and of American Jews to move from universalism to particularism cannot but create difficulties. They get telescoped in Israel.

American Jews living in Israel offer a special perspective on these matters. Some North American-born Israelis like the Americanizing influence in today's Israel; it makes them feel more at home away from what used to be home. (I realize that this last sentence is convoluted, but so are the lives of most of the people to whom it applies.) It also makes them less inclined to hop on a ten-hour flight to experience again some of what they left. There is also that special category of the American Jewish tourist—the ones who wear the funny clothes, use all four words of Hebrew they know at every opportunity, and ask the waiter to explain the lunch menu down to the last microgram—who are amused by the Americanization of Israel.

But many American Jews, religious and not, come to Israel for the same reason that lots of Israelis leave and go to America: Israel is a pressure cooker. Many idealistic American Jews come to Israel looking for the challenge of living life on a heroic scale; America is too comfortable for that. So they get off the plane, head into Tel Aviv, and find, to their dismay, Burger King in transliterated Hebrew. This is also why, for the militant political messianists who come from the United States, living in the territories seems more "authentic" to them than living within the Green Line.

Conversely, most Israelis who come to stay in the United States do so for a variety of reasons, but the main one seems to be that they don't want to be heroes and they don't like living in a pressure cooker. American Jews shouldn't blame them unless they're willing to move to Israel and take their places. And for every Israeli who leaves for America, several others at least think about it.

None of this—this crazy-quilt amalgam of mutual attraction and repulsion among Israelis, Americans, and American Jews—is going to end. It's just going to get more interesting. And it's going to play a critical role in the future of Israel, Jewish civilization, and the Jewish people.

These kinds of changes will have a major impact on Israeli society and political culture. Israel will continue to develop its own special cultural personality that will be increasingly different from the diaspora model of centuries past. Israelis will thus have less in common with Jews remaining in the diaspora as time passes. This will pose problems for Israelis, who want to move into the Jewish future, but who also cherish the value of a unified Jewish people—Jews as a sort of meta-tribe.

But Israel's problems with the growing divide pale compared to the problems that North American Jewry will face. If Israel as a culturally distinct and normal society can no longer furnish the same powerful organizing principle around which a basically irreligious North American Jewish community congeals, and if a return to some variant of Orthodoxy is unlikely for the majority, and if massive *aliyah* is equally unlikely in the absence of some totally unexpected social catastrophe, then American Jewish lay leaders face a problem that has no solution. Over time, Israel will become not only the center of the Jewish world—a sun to the North American Jewish moon—but virtually the only light in the Jewish sky.

This is, of course, precisely what Zionism predicts must happen to Jews living as minorities in alien cultures; it is also, not incidentally, what the traditional American social attitude says *ought* to happen. As Woodrow Wilson told a group of immigrants: "You cannot become thorough Americans if you think of yourself in groups. America does not consist of groups. A man who thinks of himself as belonging to a particular national group in America has not yet become an American."[16] American Jews are often masters of denial on this score, but the truth is that Jewish and American identity vectors point in almost opposite directions. Plain logic and the statistics both say so, but when wishes and reality clash, so much the worse for reality most of the time.

Hence, as the process of Israeli growth and diaspora decline continues, a kind of dissonance between Israel and the diaspora is likely to increase. American Jewish leaders have only recently begun to feel the kindred sting of modern Zionism—being told to hold their money, tend to their own problems, and keep their political mouths shut.

It isn't Zionism that has caused this tendency toward the accelerating marginalization of the diaspora, although it would have if it could have. Zionist theory, remember, in its essence has always negated the diaspora and Zionists like Ben-Gurion wanted all Jews to come to Israel to live. What has caused this tendency is the Holocaust and the very strong anti-traditional biases of modernity—especially in America, but elsewhere, too—that have vitiated much of traditional Jewish culture outside Israel. For reasons only partly of its own making, Israel has thus become precisely what the Zionist founders wanted it to be: a new Jewish society that is the overwhelming center of gravity for the Jewish world, the vanguard of all future Jewish history, and where the creative energies of the Jewish people in science, religion, literature, and art come together to form a new reality.

The dilapidation of the diaspora is in many respects the price of this achievement. Perhaps it is inevitable, but looking back on the creativity of the diaspora—which has nourished Israel itself through the people who have come to live there—thoughtful observers cannot help but feel a bit sad about it all the same. History, however, does not respect—or even seem to notice—such feelings.

Peace and Israeli Society: The Challenge of Normalcy

As noted at the outset of this chapter, Israelis have never thought they lived normally, although, of course, they really have to some extent most of the

time. The self-sustaining and comforting conceit that "things are never boring" partly masked the reality that things were in fact really difficult and
often frightening. To wake up each morning realizing that about a hundred
million of one's close and more distant neighbors would slit one's throat if
they could is just not something normal people do, even if it happens to be
true. So people say "things are never boring" instead.

In reality, it was never the first thing on a hundred million Muslim Arabs'
minds to slit the throat of some Jewish Israeli on any given morning over the
past fifty years. It may have been the third or tenth thought, but not the first,
and life being what it always is everywhere, people rarely have the time or
the energy to act on any of their not-so-pressing thoughts.

Gradually, the awareness of the near normality of their lives has come
over Israelis, and the younger they are, the more normal normal appears.
With the Arab-Israeli peace process at least half succeeding in putting an
end to the kinds of conventional military problems Israel has lived with for
decades, normalcy is coming ever more clearly into view. But since peace
and normalcy themselves are not normal, present circumstances are therefore abnormal for a new reason! So normalcy, like everything else, will take
time to set roots in Israeli society.

But what if it really does? A few Arab intellectuals over the years, recognizing that Arab soldiers and weapons were unavailing against Israel, have
wondered whether a different approach would work: Levantanization.
Levantanization refers to the de-Europeanizing of Israeli society, making
Israel like the rest of the Levant, an antique but quite lovely word of French
origin for the eastern Mediterranean. According to this notion, a de-Europe-
anized Israel would cease to be Zionist, cease to be afflicted with a manic
work ethic, and cease to be so organizationally competent. In short, a
Levantinized Israel would cease to be an acute ideological, economic, and
military problem for the Arabs. In time, the Jews would be assimilated into
the Arab Muslim sea, or those not assimilated would be reduced to a minority in a new millet system. How long would this take? Maybe a century.
Maybe three. But Arabs are patient; it took three centuries to get rid of the
Crusaders, many reason, and the Israelis aren't liable to be a tougher nut to
crack than that.

This isn't likely to happen, at least not to such an extent. But a normal
Israel made up overwhelmingly of *sabras*, and without the memory or living reminder of a creative, syncretic diaspora, will be a different sort of
place. The tensions and demands of diaspora, over so many centuries, without a doubt brought forth exceptional energies from Jews. Normalize the
environment and probably one also normalizes motivation, achievement,
and expectations. There is, in short, a price to be paid for normalcy, and
Israelis don't quite know what it is. Neither does anyone else.

In a way, Israel faces a crisis of normalcy that represents what can only be described as historic victories. After all, Zionism was created to produce a Jewish state, and the state has striven to producer security and a normal life for the majority of world Jewry. Israel is on the verge of having done just that. It has won. So now what? This is how Eliot Cohen has stated the problem:

> For a century, neatly divided by Israel's birth in 1948, Zionists undertook and believed in two epic struggles: creating a defensible state for a stateless people and gathering in communities of Jews sundered by distance but united by faith and destiny. At 50—middle age for a human being, and in this case, a state, too—Israel sees these epic tasks largely accomplished and the epic dreams correspondingly faded.

And the result?

> The way in which Israel completed the tasks set by Zionism in the first half of the century has bred new and perplexing challenges for the future—challenges not amenable to the energetic ingenuity that has brought Israelis so much success thus far. Israel's democracy, political culture, open door to Jewish immigrants, paternalistic elites, historical verities, unifying army—none evoke the old certainties.[17]

What this means, in essence, is that the ways and means Israel used to complete the project of its first century are not necessarily appropriate for dealing with the project of its second century. And that project is the remanufacturing of Jewish nationhood, culture, and history now that normalization seems to have been more or less accomplished. That means not putting off, but facing the social tensions Israel has always experienced, but has always agreed to put off thanks to the external siege it felt itself under.

The results of the 1999 election give evidence of this process at work. Part of the shift away from the right and toward the left is temporal—a disgust with Netanyahu and a hope for Barak. Hard right, "Greater Israel" sorts of positions have clearly waned in Israel as voters see the utter impossibility of such programs ever becoming policy. But the 1999 election was also the first in which the size of the state was a secondary consideration to what kind of state Israel should be. The peace process was much less in the minds of voters than the religious-secular divide, and the related but not identical divide over whether Israel should be a normal state for Israelis, or a "special" state also for Jews everywhere.

The impact of these debates is reflected in the fracturing of the party system in Israel. The reason why the two main blocs, Labor and Likud, have lost so much support is that their reason for being has been overcome by events. Doctrinaire socialism no longer interests many Israelis, and neither does "statism" or the pioneer spirit. So much for Labor's raison d'être. Likud's hawkish views no longer fit reality, and its more free market attitude toward economic policy is widely accepted by all. So much for its distinctiveness. Hence the oddity that while for Israel's first forty years, political stability cohabited with sharp disagreement on policy, now a general policy consensus cohabits with a fracturing political party system—just the opposite of the traditional situation.

Most likely, the Israeli party system is in the throes of adaptation to a situation in which new realities and new issues are redefining the political agenda. But no one can guarantee that things will settle out, and new major political blocs will form again as new tensions are faced and debated.

What are these tensions? Some are obvious, and we have already talked of them. There is the problem of Sepharadim who think they are marginalized in Israel. The success of Shas, however, ironically proves the reverse. Their louder, more assertive rhetoric is a way to achieve symbolic equality. It will happen. What appears to be a worsening problem is, most likely, a sign of health. The same is true, most likely, in the case of Israeli Arabs. They are more assertive and effective politically, so they can articulate their grievances more pointedly. This is a sign of integration, not separation.

There is also a philosophical divide, between those who want Israel to be fully normal and those who still think of Israel as a modern representation of the "light unto the nations," the carrier of the Prophetic tradition, which is hardly a formula for normalcy. As suggested above, this latter position comes in both secular and religious versions. As Israeli political scientist Yaron Ezrahi has put it:

> Modern Israel has been beset by a bitter struggle between those who believe that the earth belongs to the living and those who believe that the living belong to the earth—that it is their duty to make sacrifices to ensure that the land under Israeli control will remain the land of the Jewish people.[18]

Religious nationalists take the latter position, but so do many secular Labor and Likud adherents. On the other hand, many "post-Zionist" Israelis care not one whit for the Jewish dimension of history or state, and many ultra-Orthodox see no lasting or transcendental meaning to the state. Such differences come out in seemingly minor debates. For example, Edgar Bronfman, a wealthy Canadian Jew who has done much for Israel and for Jewish causes worldwide, expressed in early 1999 the wish to ultimately be buried on Mount Herzl—Israel's most hallowed cemetery ground. Israelis who think of Israel as an expression of the Jewish people as a whole, and of Jewish history in which Judaism is the key factor, were prepared to entertain the idea. Those who see Israel as an Israeli state first and a Jewish state second attacked the suggestion as indecent and extraordinarily presumptuous.[19]

Similarly, during Israel's 50th anniversary celebrations, a multipart serial appeared on television that recounted the history of Zionism and the state. The series, called "Tkumah, the Founding," raised a storm of controversy. Some believed that telling the full truth about history, warts and all, was the sign of a mature polity that had come to terms with normality. Others decried the revisionist maligning of the state's heroes and its great purpose. This had nothing to do with the secular-religious divide, for advocates and critics of the series could be found in both camps.[20]

While this temperamental and philosophical divide is not exhausted or well drawn by the secular-religious cleavage in Israel, that divide is also real and is arguably growing both wider and less civil. This chasm is not just between religious nationalists (the Gush Emunim type and the new variety of *hardal*, remember) and secular leftists, and it is not just about the future of the territories and relations with the Arabs. It is about something much deeper.

Most secular Israelis see Orthodox religion as atavistic. Their very definition of Zionism excludes religion and puts a premium on modern Israeli nationalism as an alternate system of devotion, sacrifice, and meaning. Religious Israelis reject this conception altogether, seeing religion as the raison d'être of both the Jewish people and Israel.

More basically, religious Israelis stress the continuity of Jewish history; secular Israelis tend to stress the novelty and the pioneering nature of modern Israel. Religious Jews, like religious people everywhere, believe deeply that without reverence and respect for God, societies eventually destroy themselves in nihilism, purposelessness, and moral degradation. Most secular Israelis are liable to identify religion with intolerance, illogic, superstition, and lack of personal and intellectual freedom. They are simply aghast at the idea that God—if they believe in God—would have anything to do with such antics as can be found in organized religion of nearly every sort.

Moreover, religious Israelis see Judaism as the key to Israel's cultural uniqueness. They don't want Israel to be just like the other nations, including the other Western nations, and they do not credit a version of Jewish exceptionalism that can also be secular. They don't want the depredations of modernity as they see them: moral relativism, lack of respect for elders and teachers, high crime rates and drug use, social violence, and the deterioration of family life. They argue that turning Israel into just another province of the American pop-culture-dominated global village is just assimilation in another form: instead of Jews assimilating into secular diaspora society, Israel as a whole will assimilate into secular world society. The result, they argue, will be the same and equally unfortunate. If Jews are a chosen people, they should act like it; if Jews lose their memory of their own purpose on earth, they say, then they will lose everything.

Secular Israelis tend to emphasize the liberal values associated with a fuller integration into the world. Why should Jews always stick out and be different? Hasn't this caused us enough problems over the years? Enough of remembering the past, they say; think backwards and you'll act backwards. Look ahead, but not too far. As the great Israeli witticist and former Mapam leader Yaakov Hazan once put it, Israel was created so that Jews could act like *goyim* in their own country.

In other words, secularists tend to put a higher value on the freedom, mobility, material affluence, and cultural consanguinity with other peoples represented by global integration. They aren't interested in living life according to abstract principles that, for the average person, are burdensome and impractical. Some are even flatly embarrassed by the impulse of religious Jews to turn inward, to invoke versions of cosmic chosenness, to reject what seems to them to be the general direction of humankind.

These two notions of Israeli society, the secular and religious, are deeply antithetical. For them to coexist in the world is not surprising, but for them to exist within a Jewish state poses a special problem. The question must therefore be asked: can a house divided along such lines long remain standing?

So far, secular Israelis and modern Orthodox Israelis have learned to live and let live fairly well. They live together, serve in the army together, and so forth, as we have seen. But without the exigencies imposed by war and the emergency mentality, will this live-and-let-live attitude persist? Or will each group develop new forms of chauvinism and intolerance? This is not just a theoretical question: anyone even passingly familiar with Jewish history and the contents of the book of Ezekiel—to name just one of several that fit the case by way of example—knows that ancient Israelites tore their country and each other apart more than once over precisely such issues. This is probably the greatest uncertainty stalking the longer-term future of Israel.

I don't know how this will turn out. But I do know that high and rapidly growing levels of material prosperity often function as a lure, separating people from the values—such as family, fidelity, and the ability to distinguish right from wrong—that they are generally well advised to nourish. And if Israel's security situation does become more or less normal, Israel's economy could be in for a sustained economic boom that will produce heretofore undreamed of levels of material prosperity.

A richer and more urbanized Israel will look and feel very different from the Israel of the 1950s. It will be less communally organized, quicker paced, more crowded, less naturally beautiful, and arguably a less contemplative and interesting place to live. Taking the longer and broader view, wealth isn't free.

Or maybe Israel won't change in these ways. Maybe it will find a way to preserve what is best from its heroic revolutionary period—the period of protracted if intermittent national emergency from 1948 to 1994—and still wax wealthy and supermodern. Nobody really knows. Israel has been an exception in history and in modern times in so many ways, maybe it will be an exception here, too.

Reconciling Myth and Reality

One thing that can be predicted with confidence is that Israeli life will continue to be formed by that dialectical process between mythos and reality that we have come back to again and again throughout this book. This is why the philosophical argument between secularists and religious Jews over the nature of Israeli society is probably the key to Israel's future. Whichever set of values becomes most dominant as time passes will be the set of values after which Israel will fashion and, in a real sense possess, its own future. If it makes basically the right choices with regard to what matters most in life, things will be fine. If it doesn't, things won't be so fine.

In Jewish history up until now, a way has always been found, somehow, to adapt Jewish civilization to current challenges without destroying the core of Jewish values. Whether it was coming to terms with Babylonian science and letters, the Hellenic world and that of Rome, with Moorish civilization and the Aristotelian philosophy it carried, or the European Enlightenment, Jewish civilization managed—after great arguments often lasting centuries—to emerge stronger and still Jewish. Indeed, as a cultural system wrapped around a core community of human beings, it has outlasted all its conquerors, all its adversaries.

It has achieved this feat by careful, tender, painstaking adaptation, by mixing and merging points of view and ways of thinking. So far there is only the faintest sign of a creative merger between secular and religious visions of the future in Israel, but that doesn't mean it will not arise. The future is stretched out long before us; in Jewish historical terms, fifty years is as if a few seconds. But unless a merger of some kind evolves, dealing with the strains of peace, wealth, and normality might be more dangerous to Israel's future health than anything the Arabs ever cooked up.

This problem flows to some extent from the contradictory impulses that have always inhered in Zionism. One school wants Jews to have the right to live just like other peoples, speaking their own language, doing their own things, in safety and peace. Another says Jews are special, chosen, and that a Jewish state has an obligation to be a model of decency in the tradition of the Prophets. The first kind of Zionism doesn't demand as much as the second, but the second is more in tune with the Jewish historical self-image.

For the former, it makes sense to embrace new organizing principles of social and political life to replace divisive ethnic-based nationalisms. The second vision, that of Jewish particularism, would resist such amalgamation and collective assimilation.

This second vision remains a very strong force in the Israeli and Jewish soul. Orthodox Jews have their own reasons for preserving the Jewish people apart from others, and for why the state of Israel matters beyond its function as a night shelter. But the Jewish sense of being apart from others also exists among secularists divorced from the original reason for Jewish separateness, which is the Torah and the special relationship of the Jewish people to God. But *why* do non-religious Israelis (and most non-religious diaspora Jews) feel a need to preserve the Jewish people as a people? This is a hard question to answer; it brings us back to Yaakov Hazan.

Hazan was right, but in a way more profound than perhaps even he understood. The unvarnished truth is that the socialist Zionist founders of Israel were determined to escape two kinds of people: anti-Semites and rabbis. In Europe, many modernist Jews were all for being friendly and open with everyone else, even more or less on everyone else's terms if that's what it took, but the anti-Semites on the one hand and the rabbis on the other made that impossible. In their private honesty, more than a few original Zionists believed that the anti-Semites and the rabbis caused each other or, at the very least, reinforced the mania each had for the other. In Israel, it was hoped, normal Jews could escape both kinds of tormentors. Notwithstanding the rabbinate's hold over life-cycle phenomena in Israel, Israelis can, if they like, live a life free from both anti-Semites and rabbis. The army keeps the former at bay, and the personal choices that most Israeli Jews make keep the rabbis about as far away as most people want to keep them.

For centuries before this one, the Torah is what united Jews everywhere. In Israel today, the Torah is what divides Jews. This is inevitable considering when, how, and why Israel was founded, and considering the role of Jews historically in the evolution of modernity. But it may not be so healthy in the long run. Could it be that Jews remained whole as a nation *in exile* because of a common active religion, but will cease to be a single people *in their own land* because of the lack of a common active religion? Wouldn't that be the irony of ironies?

Questions such as this one are, in any event, what Israelis argue about with both subtlety and ferocity. The country's future depends on how this argument gets resolved. After all, there is no legitimate historical *Israeli* claim to the land of Israel predating 1948, only a legitimate *Jewish* one predating practically everything. In the end, this is what matters most in terms of both international politics and the very soul of the modern state of Israel.

Epilogue

When I put down my pen in late June, the Barak government in Israel was just a few weeks old. Now, as I write in early October, 1999, a few more things have become clear.

First, Barak knows how to run a government. While some of his cabinet appointees were criticized as being unimaginative and docile and Barak as a would-be king instead of prime minister, the government has been running professionally, and Barak's close hold of policy has not turned out to be such a bad idea.

Second, the Israeli-Palestinian track of the peace process has been revivified, just as I said it would, and so have U.S.-Israeli, Jordanian-Israeli, and Egyptian-Israeli relations. But this was not easy. After having persuaded the Americans to take a less direct role in the diplomacy, Prime Minister Barak proposed to Yasir Arafat that the October 1998 Wye agreement be revisited and renegotiated. The agreement's implementation had been suspended as the Netanyahu government tottered and then collapsed in the fall of 1998, and Arafat wanted Barak to continue implementation exactly as agreed—which meant more Israeli territorial withdrawals. Barak explained that he would implement the agreement as written if Arafat insisted, but he thought the tow of them could do a better job and fold the implementation of Wye as the final "interim" Israeli-Palestininan agreement into a formula to launch final status negotiations. Barak suggested that if Arafat were flexible now, he'd get more in the end and that if he wasn't flexible now, he'd get less.

Eventually, a sort of compromise was reached as the two sides negotiated under Egyptian auspices at Sharm al-Sheikh. Israel agreed to some further modest territorial withdrawal, already implemented but the PA agreed to fold the final Wye withdrawal into final status issues. The sides agreed to complete a framework for final status by February 2000 and to complete and agreement by September 2000. U.S. intercession was allowed to help the sides clear up some last minute disagreements about prisoner releases and other matter.

Whether the timetable can be kept is not clear. I am skeptical that a final status negotiation can fully succeed, as I have suggested above. But we shall see.

As to the Syrian and Lebanese arenas, Israeli negotiations with Syria have not gone as well or as quickly as many predicted back in June (although I made no such predictions—see what I said in "Israel the Exceptional" in the Fall 1999 issue of *The Washington Quarterly*, which I wrote in mid-June). But Syria did crack down on radical Palestinian groups long resident in Damascus, and the "body language" of Syrian officials has changed for the better. Some believe that Hafiz al-Asad's declining health will push him to make a deal before he passes from the scene. Others are not persuaded of this scenario. Here, too, we shall see.

Other than that, life in Israel goes on as usual, which is to say, unusually. Things are still not boring

Notes

Preface

1. I've used footnotes, like this one, whenever I want to alert students to the existence of important issues that cannot be handled in a primer, to point them toward more reading on those topics, and to provide basic definitions and information that might be confusing were I to put them directly in the text.

Chapter 1. Introduction

1. *Mythos* refers to the symbolic expression of the patterns of core beliefs in a culture. I use this word instead of myth because in common language, *myth* means to many students simply a nice story that isn't literally true. That misses the point altogether; cultures are constituted by beliefs that, while not literally true or objectively provable, express the values and attitudes that allow a purposeful collective life to exist.

2. Hebrew is a Semitic language. Its closest still-existing linguistic cousins are Arabic and Amharic (the language of Ethiopia), but these three languages are written in three different scripts, and spoken orally they are not mutually intelligible. Yiddish, the language of most Jews in Eastern Europe in recent centuries, is not a Semitic but a Germanic language, so Yiddish and Hebrew are not mutually intelligible either, despite the fact that Yiddish contains many Hebrew words. Finally, while many people—Jews and Arabs included—use the word *Semitic* to refer to kindred racial groups, there is no scientific justification for this usage. The term *Semitic*, while derived from the name Shem (one of the three sons of Noah), was coined in the nineteenth century by a German philologist to refer only to language groupings. That remains its proper, precise usage.

3. On this subject see Thomas Sowell, *Race and Culture* (New York: Free Press, 1994).

4. See Howard Wiarda, *Introduction to Comparative Politics: Concepts and Processes* (Beaumont, CA: Wadsworth Publishing Company, 1993), p. 22.

5. They have to be arbitrary or the same meanings would be attached to the same phonemes in different languages, and this is obviously not the case. A cute example from translating Hebrew into English is that young students learn that *me* is "who" and *who* is "he" and *he* is "she," and she is the teacher, so better pay attention.

6. Hebrew has no capital letters. Throughout the book, however, I have capitalized Hebrew words when their corresponding English terms would be capitalized.

7. See Wiarda, *Introduction to Comparative Politics*, p. 18.

8. See the glossary for the translations, and a way to answer the question.

9. Most Israelis pay their utility bills automatically through standing orders.

10. An excellent illustration, with photographs, of this point may be found in Joel Greenberg, "A Land of Tribes, Again," *New York Times*, May 9, 1999, p. 6 (Week in Review).

11. Important information on Israeli beer for those interested in such things is found in Chapter 3, note 7.

12. Answer: It's to prevent people from getting electrocuted when they wash the floor. As noted, the electrical current is powerful; if water gets inside the sockets they sort of . . . blow up.

13. This really happens sometimes.

14. This is a joke, but also one that really happened. Some years ago, Margaret Thatcher, when still British prime minister, paid a visit to Israel. The government ordered the roads she would travel on cleaned up so as not to make a bad impression. At a subsequent news conference, Mrs. Thatcher commented on how impressed she was with the countryside's cleanliness. Most of the Israelis in the room could barely stop themselves from laughing, and some did not quite succeed.

Chapter 2. In the Beginning

1. Yehuda Ben Meir, "Israeli Public Opinion," *Final Status Issues: Israel-Palestinian*, No. 6 (Tel Aviv: Jaffee Center for Strategic Studies, 1995), p. 7.

2. C.E. means "Common Era." B.C.E. means "Before the Common Era." These terms are used by Israelis and by Jews outside of Israel who are self-conscious of their identity. They are equivalent to A.D. and B.C. for most Americans, these terms being abbreviations for Christian phrases (Year of our Lord from the Latin *anno domini*, and Before Christ) that are theologically unacceptable to Jews. Obviously, whatever abbreviations are used, the year 1 refers, theoretically if not actually, to the birth of Jesus, which is problematic for Jews as a way to mark a calendar because Jews do not see in that event anything special. But culturally, Christian European power overwhelmed and virtually united the planet between the fifteenth and nineteenth centuries, and so won the right to establish the global calendar benchmark. Virtually the entire world these days accepts 1999 as the global standard for the present year, even if it is more for the sake of convenience than as obeisance to the superiority of European civilization. But Jews have their own calendar too, with different names for the months that date back several thousand years, and 1999 corresponds in the main to the year 5759, dated by tradition from the creation of the world. Muslims, including Israeli Arab Muslims, have their own calendar too, and count forward from the *hijra*, the migration of Mohammed from Mecca to Medina. The year 1996 corresponds to the Muslim year 1419 A.H. (After *Hijra*). The Jewish New Year in Israel is marked not on January 1 but on Rosh Hashanah, which in the Jewish lunar calendar usually falls some time in September. January 1 is called St. Sylvester's Day, after a pope (314–335 C.E. whose saint's day is December 31—and it isn't a holiday in Israel. Religious Jews (and Muslims) generally use their own calendar not just for religious purposes but also in day-to-day affairs. More secular people aren't so particular.

3. The term *Hebrew Bible* refers to what Christians usually call the Old Testament. Jews call their Bible simply the Bible, the New Testament being a term generally used to refer to Christian scripture *outside* the canon. As with the calendar, the names commonly used for things stand for larger universes of difference, and expressing those differences is generally a deliberate cultural statement. For Jews the calendar business is optional; the Bible business isn't. The Hebrew word used for the Hebrew Bible is *Tanakh*, which is an acronym made up from its three main parts: *Torah* (the Five Books of Moses), *Nevi'im* (Prophets), and *Ketuvim* (Writings).

4. See Avi Erlich, *Ancient Zionism* (New York: Free Press, 1995).

5. I use a lower case *m* when I use the word *messiah* to distinguish it from the upper-case Christian concept.

6. After the collapse of the Second Commonwealth and the exile, many rabbis developed far more mystical and theologically exotic ideas about the messiah, linked to more developed notions of an afterlife. In rabbinic Judaism, as opposed to the Judaism of the Bible and pre-exilic times, such subjects became important.

7. Some anti-Zionist polemicists, especially Arab Christians, speak of Jesus as having been a Palestinian. This is false; he was a Jew and the land he lived in was called Judea at the time.

8. The Talmud consists of the Mishnah, the core of the oral law, which is written in Hebrew, and a longer and later commentary called the Gemorrah, written in Aramaic. The Mishnah was codified by Rabbi Yehuda Ha-Nasi around the beginning of the third century; the Gemorrah was completed around the middle of the sixth century. There are two versions of the Talmud, the Bavli (Babylonian) and the Yerushalmi (Jerusalem), of which the former—written in Babylonia by the ancestors of the community exiled there centuries earlier—is generally the more studied and more authoritative. The Talmud is a long book containing law, homeletic stories and fables, some history, and even medical advice. This is not the place to describe the Talmud further except to say that its mastery has been the goal of Jewish religious scholarship for 1,500 years.

9. For more information, see Gershom Scholem, *Shabbtai Sevi: The Mystical Messiah, 1626–1676* (Princeton, NJ: Princeton University Press, 1973). Sevi is known more commonly as Shabbtai Tzvi, or Zvi. This is because the first letter of his last name is a Hebrew *tsadi*, which has a *ts* sound, and for which there is no English equivalent. There are different systems of transliteration; Scholem used a technical one, with a dot under the letter *s* to indicate the *tsadi*. Most transliterations are less technical. While we're talking about transliteration, below I use an English *h* to represent the eighth letter of the Hebrew alphabet, the *het*. The *het* is a light guttural for which English has no equivalent. The fifth Hebrew letter, the *hey*, is the *h* sound. But there is a stronger guttural, too—the twelfth letter, the *khaf*, which is somewhat akin to the *ch* in "Loch Lomond," properly pronounced. Sometimes the *khaf* is transliterated as *ch*, which leads some people to pronounce some transliterated Hebrew words as if they contained a *ch* sound, as in chicken. But Hebrew doesn't have such a sound, nor a soft *g*, either. Now, a little later I talk about a man named Haim Weizmann. The *H* in Haim is a *het*, the light guttural. It is widely transliterated as "Chaim," which makes no sense because its first letter is not a *khaf*. Worse, it leads some people to pronounce it like "chime," as in what bells do. To a Hebrew speaker, this makes the person sound like an idiot. I use Haim instead of Chaim to avoid that because we all have better things to do than to laugh at mispronounced foreign words.

10. It was not that so many Jews moved east in a short time, but that because of the second partition of Poland, the majority of the Jews of that land fell under the Russian realm.

11. Incidentally, *Holocaust* is not a good word to describe what happened to European Jewry in World War II. A holocaust is, according to the dictionary, a natural disaster: a hurricane, a tornado, an earthquake. What the Nazis did was anything but *natural*, something that just happens and about which human beings are essentially powerless. The murder of 6 million Jews was an act of human volition and, as such, could have been prevented by other humans with another volition. But it is hard to fight common usage, so I use the word. The Hebrew term *Shoah* suffers from a similar problem.

12. Bernard Lazare, *Job's Dungheap* (New York: Schocken Books, 1948), p. 67.

13. In time it came true: it was called *Mikveh Yisrael* (Hope of Israel), and was established in Jaffa in 1870.

14. Ascent to Israel. This word is rich with ancient historical and religious referents. On the pilgrim festivals (Passover, Shavuot, and Succot) in ancient times, people would ascend to Jerusalem to the temple for prayer and celebration. Still today, when someone is called to the Torah during prayer services, it is called an *aliyah*. The Zionist appropriation of the term includes both historical and religious allusions.

15. This was deliberate. Just as American Negroes in the 1960s decided to use the negatively connoted word *black* to express a defiant new pride, so Herzl decided to use the word *Jew*, as opposed to less charged terms "Hebrew" or "Israelite" then in use, to do the very same thing.

16. Another chance to correct a widespread misconception about the holy land. The idea of Israel being a holy land is a Christian, not a Jewish, one, but the Zionist mystique about the land has created the notion of Israel as a holy land in the modern Jewish mind. As far as Jewish law and tradition are concerned, God is holy, not real estate. Indeed, the only mention of the phrase *admat qodesh* (holy land) in the entire Torah refers to Mount Sinai, which is not part of Eretz Israel (the land of Israel), Exodus, 3:5. The land bears theological significance not because of any inherent mystical quality, as seems to inhere in the Christian notion of *terra sancta*, but because there are several commandments (*mitzvoth*) that can be performed only inside the land. Similarly, in the Prophets, Jerusalem is referred to as the "holy city," but only because the temple rites took place there and the "holy of holies" was located there. Note that religious Jews quote Isaiah 6:3 thrice daily in a key part of their prayers: "Holy, holy, holy is the Lord of Hosts, the whole world is filled with his glory." The point really could not be any clearer, and yet most modern Jews still accept the idea of Israel as the Holy Land as though it were a Jewish idea.

17. The best compendium of essential texts in English is Arthur Hertzberg, ed., *The Zionist Idea* (New York: Atheneum, 1969).

18. Again we run into a curiosity of terminology. The New Testament, and most English-speaking Christians, call this lake the Sea of Galilee. Arabs call it *Bahr Tabariya*, Lake Tiberias in Arabic. Israelis call it Yam Kineret, or just Kineret, after a diminutive form of the word *kinor*, or harp. Why? This is because seen from above, on the Golan Heights, the lake is shaped rather like a harp, and when camping on the shores, especially on the southeastern side near the rocks and reeds, at night the wind seems to make harp music as it blows across the water. Lake Tiberias takes its name from the town of Tiberias on the western shore, which is in turn named after a Roman governor-general. Lake Tiberias, Kineret, Bahr Tabariya, Sea of Galilee—it's all the same lake.

19. See Chapter 4 for a discussion of how a *kibbutz* and a *moshav* differ.

20. For the full story, see Ronald Sanders, *The High Walls of Jerusalem* (New York: Holt, Rinehart and Winston, 1983).

21. Many believe that the British promise to the Jews overlapped with and contradicted the promise to the Arabs. A close look at the pertinent documents suggests otherwise. See Elie Kedourie, *The Anglo-Arab Labyrinth* (New York: Cambridge University Press, 1976).

22. See my essay, "On the Origin, Meaning, Use and Abuse of a Phrase," *Middle Eastern Studies* 27, 4 (October 1991).

23. The brigade, as the first real military achievement of the Zionist movement in a country in which the military matters a great deal, has found a place of honor in Israeli history. Practically every town in Israel has a street named *G'dud Halvri* (The Jewish Brigade).

24. For details, see my *War, Water, and Negotiation in the Middle East: The Case of the Palestine-Syria Border, 1916–1923* (Tel Aviv: Tel Aviv University, 1994).

25. Described and explained in Chapter 3.

26. Jews did not return to Hebron until 1968, and the Jews that returned then were ultranationalist in character; they have bedeviled relations with local Palestinians and the peace process as well. But given the modern history of the town, and the fact that it is sacred to Jews because of the Cave of Mahpelah—where Abraham, Sarah, Isaac, Rebecca, Jacob, and Leah are supposedly buried—it is no easy thing for Jews to abandon the town once again. The Netanyahu government did manage to make a compromise over it in 1997, however.

27. *Etzel* stands for *Irgun Tzvai Leumi*, or National Military Organization. *Irgun* means "organization."

28. Many argue that the Revisionists engaged in terrorism, but this depends on the definition of terrorism. The best analyses of terrorism distinguish between violence against random civilians designed to generate maximum horror and shock on the one hand, and violence directed against uninformed military personnel on the other. If one accepts this distinction, then most of what the Irgun and the Stern Gang did, as well as acts like the blowing up of the U.S. Marine barracks near the Beirut airport in October 1983 by Muslim extremists, or the Irish Republican Army's attack on British soldiers in Belfast, was not terrorism, but more on the order of guerrilla or irregular warfare. That, of course, doesn't mean it's a nice thing to do.

29. In 1960 a popular movie called *Exodus*, starring Paul Newman, was made based on these events.

30. A minority position called for a single binational state.

Chapter 3. Society and Polity at Independence

1. Lehi and Etzel are acronyms from Hebrew of the Stern Gang and the Irgun, respectively (*Lohamei Herut Israel*, and *Irgun Tzvai Leumi*). See Benny Morris, *The Birth of the Palestinian Arab Refugee Problem, 1947–1949* (Cambridge: Cambridge University Press, 1987), pp. 113–31. In recent years it has come to light that the Arabs much exaggerated the scale of the Deir Yassin massacre in hopes of stirring up more international support for their position. What happened was the reverse: their exaggerations scared local populations and contributed to their abandoning their homes. The testimony of an eye-witness to the propaganda effort, Hazem Nussaibeh, is captured in a BBC television series, "Israel and the Arabs: A 50–Year Conflict." See also Eric Silver's summary in "Arab Witnesses Admit Exaggerating Deir Yassin Massacre," *Jerusalem Report*, April 2, 1998, p. 6.

2. For background, see the excellent book by Issa Khalaf, *Politics in Palestine: Arab Factionalism and Social Disintegration, 1939–1948* (Albany, NY: State University of New York Press, 1991).

3. For extensive detail and analysis, see Bruce Maddy-Weizman, *The Crystallization of the Arab State System* (Syracuse, NY: Syracuse University Press, 1993), especially Chapter 3.

4. For background on types of land ownership, which was important to this result, see Kenneth W. Stein, *The Land Question in Palestine, 1917–1939* (Chapel Hill: University of North Carolina Press, 1984).

5. A wadi is a stream bed that is dry most of the year, and wet during the rainy season (November–February).

6. As noted in Chapter 1, Israelis do not think in terms of degrees Fahrenheit and statute miles, but degrees Centigrade and kilometers.

7. We noted in Chapter 1 the relative lack of taverns and bars. The reason is part cultural (both Jewish law and common sense made public drunkenness inadvisable in exile) but part climactic: people in warm climates drink less hard liquor. There are

locally made Israeli brandies, and they're terrible; but Israel has two popular local beers, Goldstar, which is excellent, and Maccabee, which is fair, and beer goes down well in hot weather—point proven.

8. Rainfall figures appear regularly on the last page of the first section of *Ha'aretz* during the winter months.

9. See Daniel Hillel, *Rivers of Eden* (New York: Oxford University Press, 1994), p. 46.

10. Israel State Comptroller Report, 1991, p. 545.

11. This is when a south wind pushes temperatures very high and humidity down to nearly zero. This is dangerous weather; it makes some people ill. For technical meteorological reasons, the end of a *hamsin* can trigger intense, short showers.

12. When the British and the French finally agreed on the border between Palestine and Syria in 1923, the Banias was placed provisionally in Syrian territory because of a strategic road that connected Lebanon to the city of Kuneitra and the Yarmuk Valley. The deal was that the issue could be reopened, and the Banias returned to Palestine as had been originally intended, if a bypass road was built for the price of about £5,000. The Zionists never came up with the money and the British soon lost interest. See the discussion with accompanying documentation in my *War, Water and Negotiations*, p. 130.

13. Dead Sea is the English name, so called because nothing lives in it. The Hebrew name, both Biblical and modern, is *Yam Hamelah* (The Salt Sea). In Arabic, it is *Bahr Lot* (Lot's Sea) because, according to both the Torah and Qur'an, it is where Abraham's nephew Lot lived, near Sodom and Gomorrah, and where Lot's wife turned to a pillar of salt when she looked back on the city in disobedience to God's command. Traditionally, the origins of all that salt, and the mindbogglingly lunar look of the land south of the sea, comes from the fire and brimstone God rained down on the evil people of those two cities.

14. See my *Water, War and Negotiations*, Chapters 3–5.

15. Druze are a heterodox religious sect of Islam—so heterodox that most Muslims consider them outside the fold. Circassians are a Muslim people from the Caucasus who either came, were sent, or were exiled to the Middle East during Ottoman times.

16. The antagonism between Zionists and Orthodox traditionalists in the pre– and post–World War II American context is depicted brilliantly by Chaim (*his* spelling, not mine) Potok in his book *The Chosen*. There is also an excellent film of the same name.

17. See Yossi Katz, "The Religious Kibbutz Movement and its Credo, 1934–1948," *Middle Eastern Studies* 31, 2 (April 1995), pp. 253–280.

18. A *yeshiva* is an institution for advanced religious studies.

19. See Chapter 5 for details about Israeli communist parties.

20. David Ben-Gurion was born Dovid Gruen in Poland. Moshe Sharret was born Moishe Shertock in Poland. Levi Eshkol was born Levi Shkolnick in Russia, and was known to slip back into Yiddish in private conclave whenever issues of great importance were discussed. Golda Meir was born Golda Mahovitz in Russia, but went to Palestine in 1921 from Milwaukee. (By the way, Meir is a shortened form not of Mahovitz but of Meyerson, her husband's name.) Both Menachem Begin and Yitzhak Shamir came from Poland in the 1920s. Shimon Peres was born in Poland, too. Yitzhak Rabin was Israel's first prime minister born in Eretz Israel.

21. A *moshav* is an agricultural settlement where land owned by the state or the Jewish National Fund is leased to families—sixty families is the mean number—and where machinery and marketing are done in common. Health care and schooling are also communal responsibilities. But houses are private, budgets are private, and each family decides what to grow on its own.

22. Jabotinsky's remains were flown to Israel in 1964, about a year after Ben-Gurion's tenure as prime minister came to an end. As coincidence would have it, I saw the plane in Paris on my way to Israel for the first time.

23. Until December 1966, Israeli Arabs were subject to emergency military regulations. The trouble they caused, however, was minimal and much less than anticipated in 1949. See Chapters 4 and 5 for more about the Arabs in Israel.

24. This applies to groups, too. The state, and even the rabbinate, has sometimes been very pragmatic about such matters. In the case of Ethiopian Jews, there is much doubt about the authentic Jewishness of this community, but the rabbis swept this aside in the interests of harmony and the future—although they still give the Ethiopians some trouble when they want to marry. In the case of Jews from the former Soviet Union, too, the rabbis have not looked too hard at the documentation, fearing that if they did they might cause Jews to languish, and possibly perish, as a result. See Chapter 5 for details about the argument over who gets to decide "who is a Jew."

25. For detail see Rogers Brubaker, *Citizenship and Nationhood in France and Germany* (Cambridge, MA: Harvard University Press, 1992), pp. 168–171.

26. Tahal is an Hebrew acronym for *Tikhnun Hamayim L'Israel*, Israel Water Authority.

27. It means "Sources," but in a literary manner can also mean "Fountains."

28. Electricity is a slightly different matter. Producing electricity from water power involved a concession given to Pinhas Rutenberg by the Mandatory government in 1924. Rutenberg was one of the planners of Palestine's future water system, but he got the concession as a private business venture and planned to make money from it. The Palestine Electric Company also was responsible for building other power generating plants and for building the grid and related infrastructure. Only after 1948 did the Israeli government have much to do with this aspect of the economy.

29. See Yehuda Bauer, *From Diplomacy to Resistance* (Philadelphia: Jewish Publication Society, 1970). This is a translation of a Hebrew book published in 1963.

30. Today the Shin Bet is called the *Shabak*, an acronym for *Shirut Bitahon Klalit*, General Security Service.

Chapter 4. Society and Political Economy in Contemporary Israel

1. Remember: Sepharadic here combines all the non-European peoples. The term is really a misnomer: it really should refer to Spanish-Portuguese Jewry only, but it has come to include Jews from the Arab world, Iran, Turkey, India, and elsewhere.

2. Senator Jackson believed deeply that the best way to know how a country would act in its foreign relations was to look at how it treated its own people. No one has ever improved on this advice.

3. This was a very controversial issue for American Jewish organizations and a difficult one morally. American Jews supported Israel, but as a matter of principle many of the lay leaders had trouble with the idea that Israel was an inherently more suitable place for Soviet Jewish émigrés than America. They argued in terms of principle: the right of people to live where they wished, and the rightness of relatively open American policies of political refuge. But in truth, many were worried by the implication that if Israel was the "proper" place for Jews, their own status in the United States would somehow be affected—the Montagu syndrome revisited. If Ben-Gurion had been still alive, he would have said: "See, I told you so; you American Jews are not Zionists, you are only pro-Zionist." And he would have been correct. The moral issue was this: many Soviet Jews, given only a choice between going to Israel or staying put, would choose to stay put. As a result, their lives might be endangered, and a new anti-American government in Moscow might once again be able to use them as political pawns while still employing their skills in the service of the state. No one wanted this, but the Israeli

government—and the Bush administration—took the risk. Only the future will tell how wise it was.

4. Interestingly, most anti-Zionist arguments have claimed that Jews are not entitled to a state because Jews are not a people but a religious group. The Zionism-is-racism argument implied just the reverse—that Jews are not a religious group but a people who act in ethnically exclusionary ways. Logically, one cannot hold both of these views simultaneously, but many detractors of Israel did so anyway, sometimes even in the same speech to the General Assembly.

5. For evidence, if you ever get the chance, sample the standard fare of Jordanian, Palestinian, or Syrian street humor to find out what the average person thinks of an Egyptian or a Saudi.

6. The Green Line refers to the pre-June 1967 borders. It is so-called both because the land was always greener on the Israeli side thanks to systematic irrigation and because the actual line on most of the old maps was green.

7. See Youssef M. Ibrahim, "When Nations Draw Lines, the Druse Find a Way," *New York Times*, April 20, 1995, p. A4.

8. Palestinians do it, too. After the Beit Lid bomb in February 1995 killed twenty-one Israelis, Palestinian extremists boasted of having killed twenty-one "pigs" and wounded sixty "monkeys."

9. For example, see Anton Shammas, *Arabesques* (New York: Harper and Row, 1988).

10. Revelations that, in both the 1956 and 1967 Wars, Israeli officers had ordered the execution of Egyptian prisoners of war scandalized the country. See "Israel Reportedly Killed POWs in '67 War," *Washington Post*, August 17, 1995, p. A30.

11. See Clyde Haberman, "Can Israelis Be Polite? A Phone Call Could Tell," *New York Times*, June 26, 1995, p. A4.

12. See Andrew Album, "Israel: Privatisation Slows to a Crawl," *The Middle East*, March 1986, p. 17.

13. This decision in favor of a six-day work week was also strongly supported by religious Zionists. The commandment about keeping the Sabbath holy starts with the imperative "Six days thou shalt labor and do all thy work." Religious Jews take the first part of the commandment as seriously as they take the second part.

14. A Stakhonovite was a proletarian workaholic of Stalinist Russian fame.

15. Israel hosts an international Jewish Olympics every four years, called the *Maccabiya*, after the Macabbees.

16. Many Israelis eat finely cut vegetable salads with breakfast, which most Americans find weird. They also eat a kind of yogurt called *leben*, bread, cheese, fruit, and often chocolate—including a chocolate spread. Boxed cereal is not very popular largely because Israeli brands are horrible—they get soggy in a nanosecond and the taste of the cereal and the carton are indistinguishable—and imports are very expensive. Also, boxed cereal is a processed food and Israelis eat much less processed food than Americans. Raw foods are less expensive and in Israel, which is so small, people's kitchens are not that far from the farms where produce is grown. America's food-growing and distribution system is so far-flung that packaging is necessary for transport requirements and to prevent waste, although we probably overdo the packaging for other reasons.

17. During this period it was impossible to enforce currency laws. Despite indexing, private citizens always took dollars if they could get them, and a black market in currency exchange developed. Prices for investment items, especially real estate, began to be denominated in dollars and still are for the most part. Also, remember the *asimonim* mentioned in Chapter 1—the public telephone tokens? Chronic inflation is the reason for them: it was easier to change the price of the tokens than to retool every public telephone in Israel each time the phone rates changed.

18. Over the years, the inflation has wrecked havoc with the money. In 1948, 1000 *prutot* (*prutah*, singular) equaled 1 Israeli pound, commonly called a lira. By 1960, the prutah had become economically obsolete, so now 100 agarot equaled one lira, and all the coins and stamps had to be changed. Then, by December 1980, agarot had gone the way of prutot. In 1960, the cost of first class domestic postage was 18 agarot; by November 1980, it was 4.30 lira. So as of December 1980, 10 lira equaled one sheqel; the word *lira* reverting to agarah for amounts less than 1 sheqel. But by December 1986, even the sheqel had sunk so low that it had to be replaced by the new sheqel. So now 100 sheqels equaled 1 new sheqel, and old sheqels again were called *agarot*. This means that 1 prutah à la 1948 is worth one millionth of a new sheqel. We in the United States still have our cents and dollars after more than 230 years. When Americans complain that a dollar isn't the same as it used to be, they ought instead to be grateful that it even exists.

19. Reported on the television show *Mabat*, April 5, 1995.

20. The large literature on the *kibbutz* is as much a function of the interest of liberal and left-wing academics in this mini-utopia as it is of the intrinsic importance of the institution in Israeli society.

21. The word *necessarily* is important here; the union of church and state lasted more than 1,400 years in Christendom and helped define the Western legacy itself, but this union did not come about for theological reasons, but rather despite them.

22. Wondering how the prohibition against idolatry has a public dimension? Go to any American or European city, and along the streets, parks, and public squares there will be statuary of people, sometimes on horseback. There are a few such statues in Israel, but they're very rare. As with Muslims, Jewish art is non-iconographic, and the Biblical prohibition against making idols is the reason why.

23. There are two because the two communities have sufficiently different traditions and hierarchies to require separation. Neither chief rabbis is recognized by the *haredim*.

24. Such phenomena are not limited to Israel. In Virginia, until recently, stores were not allowed to sell pets or plants on Sunday. Why? It's a residual effect of antebellum blue laws prohibiting slave markets from operating on the Christian Sabbath. The principle embedded in latter-day blue laws was that nothing living should be sold on Sunday.

25. Not to get too technical, but even for Orthodox Israeli rabbis, Conservative and Reform Judaism, while treated more or less the same, aren't the same. The key is *halakha*, the religious law which is the very core of Jewish religion. Reform Judaism formally rejects the authority of *halakha*, which puts it beyond the pale as far as all Orthodox Jews are concerned. Conservative Judaism accepts the authority of *halakha*, but interprets some aspects differently from the Orthodox. The problem is that *within* Conservative Judaism there are also sharp differences about interpreting aspects of *halakha*, to the point where there is no longer unity of practice within the Conservative movement. Therefore, an Orthodox rabbi can, if he wishes, accept the authority of a Conservative rabbi whom he knows personally to be a *halakha*-observant Jew. But since the Conservative movement contains rabbis who are not *halakha*-observant Jews, as Orthodox understand it, the movement as a whole, since it does not expel such individuals, cannot be accepted. Since one of the main social purposes of *halakha* is to assure Jewish unity by assuring uniformity of practice, argue the Orthodox, any movement that allows that kind of diversity works against unity, and that is bad. Hence the Orthodox oppose the Reform and Conservative movements on somewhat different bases, and the opposition is neither baseless nor wholly political in inspiration.

26. In Jewish law, it is the mother who determines the identity of the child; Jewish mother, Jewish child, non-Jewish mother, non-Jewish child.

27. If the person is not circumcised, he must be. If he already is circumcised, just a drop of blood from a delicate pin prick is required in the ritual.

28. A major exception is that secular Israeli women dislike the divorce courts. A woman does not have the same level of legal rights in such a situation as a woman in the United States. An example is the problem of the *agunah*, a woman who has been abandoned by her husband and cannot locate him or his body either to get a divorce or to prove him deceased. Under rabbinic law, that woman cannot remarry. Outside of Israel, religious Jews choose to live under the edicts of the rabbinic courts and accept their status as *agunot*, but in Israel there is no choice, and that is the rub.

29. Some speak Hebrew only on the Sabbath. This may be the only case known of a substantial group of people who are bilingual in this manner.

30. This is not due to religious law but to a custom designed, ostensibly, to make the women unattractive to anyone but their husbands—so as not to court adultery.

31. See Charles S. Liebman and Elihu Katz, eds., *The Jewishness of Israelis: Responses to the Guttman Report* (Buffalo: State University of New York Press, 1997).

32. See Chapter 8, verse 3.

33. *This* is why most Israelis don't like Woody Allen and don't think he's funny.

34. U.S. support for Israel is best explained by strategic and political-historical factors, not by the power of American Jewish lobbying for Israel. See A.F.K. Organski, *The $36 Billion Bargain: Strategy and Politics in U.S. Assistance to Israel* (New York: Columbia University Press, 1990).

35. Aqiva Eldar, "Jewish Nerve," *Ha'aretz*, March 21, 1994, p. B1 [Author's translation].

36. Basically, the idea that anything made outside Israel is better than anything made inside it. This goes for everything from hot dogs to education. Often it's not true, but most Israelis still believe it. It's the ubiquitous "grass-is-greener-on-the-other-side-of-the-fence" idea, only in Hebrew.

37. A mildly (or not so mildly) deprecatory word meaning non-Jews. It literally means "the nations."

38. The reference here is to Exodus 16. Virtually all adult Israelis know it. Remember how we noted earlier that Jews, and Israelis, think and argue in terms of events that are sometimes thousands of years old? Here's a good example.

Chapter 5. Political Institutions and Issues

1. Other reasons, such as avarice, greed, and megalomania, have also been at work.

2. This bothered some but not others, who reasoned that England has done fairly well since 1688 as an evolving democracy without a written constitution; so if they can do it, why not Israel?

3. It is important to know basically what happened in England in 1215, 1688–89, 1830–32, 1867, and 1911 in order to understand how legal democracies develop and function, whether in England, the United States, Israel, or anywhere else. Original examples are generally important examples.

4. Candidates not eligible include senior army officers or senior civil servants, the president, the state comptroller, the two chief rabbis, judges, and any cleric of any religion who gets paid for holding a religious office. Also, the courts may revoke voting rights in some cases. Prisoners and diplomats abroad can vote.

5. I have to add the word *grouping* because for most of Israeli history neither Labor nor Likud was really a single party, as explained below.

6. It sometimes happens that individual members in the major parties will break party discipline, too. But not often. If they do it too much, or if they really influence the outcome of a close vote, they are nearly sure to lose their place on the party list come next election.

7. Note that in presidential systems like the American one, coalitions have to be formed *before* elections for the purpose of electing a president with a majority of the electoral college. This is what primaries and party conventions are all about. The matter of when and how ruling coalitions are formed is perhaps the most significant distinction between parliamentary and presidential forms of democracy.

8. During and after the June 1967 War (until the spring of 1970) there was a government of National Unity, where all Knesset factions were in the government. Agudah Israel was also part of the governing coalition between 1949 and 1951 only.

9. Personal communication.

10. It is true that the post was first offered to Albert Einstein, then living in Princeton. Einstein declined.

11. Navon was the only president elected so young that he thought of using the presidency as a stepping stone to "higher" office. He declined to run for reelection, but though popular as president, his political career never really took off.

12. It only happened once, in 1962.

13. See Peter Hirschberg, "The Lawgiver," *Jerusalem Report*, August 24, 1995, pp. 12–16.

14. See Daniel Schreiber, "The Supreme Coup," *Jerusalem Report*, March 21, 1996, p. 59.

15. For example, in August 1995, Shawqi Issa of the Palestinian Land and Water establishment appealed the decision to build twenty bypass roads in the West Bank as a consequence of the Israeli-Palestinian agreement on interim Palestinian autonomy. See *Palestine Report*, 18 August 1995, p. 5.

16. Ahdut Ha'avodah was a part of Mapam in the early days of the state; it split in 1954 over Mapam's pro-Soviet orientation. It split earlier, in the early 1940s, with Mapai as well.

17. That's why, by the way, one used to see red flags on some *kibbutzim* on May 1. It's May Day. This is not just a theoretical possibility: I witnessed such a thing myself on May 1, 1993.

18. Agudah Israel was formed in Poland in 1912.

19. Meir Kahane went even beyond Tzvi Yehuda Kook in developing an explicit theory of messianic history. To sum it up, he believed that after 1967, God had given the Jews forty years—like the forty years in the wilderness after the exodus from Egypt—to expel the Arabs and rebuild the temple. If they failed, the Jews would themselves be again exiled, as they had in 135 C.E.

20. Recall mention of *Mabat* in note 19 to Chapter 4.

21. See Exodus 17:8–16, and Deuteronomy 24:17–19. Needless to say, this view is far-fetched and is not accepted by more than a few rabbis.

22. By the by, mainstream rabbinic Judaism is divided on this topic. Since the time of Maimonides (eleventh century C.E.), all traditional rabbis and devout Jews have believed in the immortality of the soul, but not necessarily in the physical resurrection of the body.

23. Again, unless one knows the Torah it is not possible to understand the power of this name or its resonance in Israel and among Jews. "In the Image" refers to God's having created man in his image, which means to Jews not a literal physical image but a spiritual image. In other words, God is merciful, compassionate, and loving, so human beings should try to be the same. God is one, a unity, so human beings should recognize their common ancestor and common source and act accordingly. This principle is the essence of Judaism, so naming an Israeli human rights organization B'tzelem could not be more apt.

24. This referred to a kind of prepared fish, often eaten with a horseradish condiment, that only European Jews ate, hence the use of the symbol.

Chapter 6. Foreign Policy: Sources and Substance

1. As described in Chapter 4 with regard to Ethiopian and Soviet Jewish immigration. Israel is truly unique in this respect. Australia wants more people, true, and it is somewhat particular about who they are, but its reasons are social and economic, not religio-historical. It makes a difference. Germany welcomes other Germans, but doesn't actively seek their return. The same is true for the newly liberated Baltic States and places like Croatia, Armenia, and Ukraine. Israel, then, is in this regard unique.

2. That doesn't mean, of course, that U.S. foreign policy cares *only* about democracy and human rights, or that it is always possible or even wise to try to export such values to others.

3. I concentrate here on basic details, motivations, and the implications for Israeli society and politics. For more on the international diplomacy of the period, U.S. policy, or domestic developments in the Arab world, other sources should be consulted.

4. The negotiations proceeded quite far. By February 1950, an agreement of non-belligerency was initialed. By April, a draft treaty was completed. (For the texts, see the appendices in my *Israel and Jordan in the Shadow of War* [New York: St. Martin's Press, 1992].) Actually, Abdallah seemed in more of a hurry to complete the treaty than Israel, and was willing to make many concessions. Indeed, his general ambitions are what led him to make many territorial concessions to Israel in the 1949 armistice negotiations. Why was Israel reluctant? One reason was that the Zionist movement still believed that all of Palestine west of the Jordan River should be the Jewish state, and signing a peace treaty that would turn the 1949 armistice lines into an international border would mean an official, legal renunciation of Israel's right to the West Bank. Not even Moshe Sharett, a relative dove, was prepared to enter into such a pledge lightly. Had things gone differently on the Jordanian side, had Abdallah lived, it is a matter of conjecture as to what Israel would have done. The point? That Israel was not so weak and vulnerable that it was ready to sign a peace treaty at any price.

5. Whether Nasir intended this all along, or was dragged into it by circumstances, remains a matter of scholarly debate.

6. After he left office, President Eisenhower regretted having acted as he did, for almost simultaneous with the Suez fiasco was the Hungarian uprising, which the Soviets crushed as the West stood passively by. See Peter W. Rodman, "Eisenhower's Remorse," *Foreign Affairs*, September/October 1994, pp. 182–183.

7. Arab propaganda had convinced the man on the street that Israeli leaders have thought of Israel's ideal borders as being from the Nile to the Euphrates. This is what many Arabs still think of when they hear "Greater Israel." Yasir Arafat used to claim that the two blue stripes on the Israeli flag represented these two rivers, with Israel in between. Despite a poetical allusion in Genesis to such a definition of Israel's border, no modern Zionist has ever held or stated such a notion. But many Arabs believe differently nonetheless.

8. It is worth pointing out that some Israelis and many Americans exaggerated the pro-Soviet potential of Arab nationalism during this period. The Arab states were concerned most of all about securing their independence, and were equal-opportunity consumers of Cold War situations.

9. Yasir Arafat is a nom de guerre, Arafat being the name of the valley outside Mecca where Mohammed rested as he migrated from Mecca to Medina. His real name is Mohammed Abdel Rauf al-Quda al-Husseini, and he was born in Egypt of Palestinian parents. He is a distant relative of the Mufti.

10. The commander of the sabotage squad, Ahmed Musa, was killed not by an Israeli soldier but by a Jordanian one when Musa would not halt as he tried to recross the

border. This proved an apt metaphor for much of what would happen within the Israel-Jordan-PLO triangle in years to come.

11. Be aware that, while this is what happened, many committed partisans on both the Arab and Israeli sides still refuse to accept it. Many partisans of Israel still believe that from the start Nasir planned a war of annihilation. Many Arab partisans still believe that Israel planned aggression against Syria, and that Nasir's actions in Syria's defense in no way threatened Israel to the point that war was a proportional response. Israel, they say, just used the diplomatic crisis as a pretext to seize land. Israel's partisans call the June 1967 War a preemptive war of self-defense against a credible threat of doom; Arab partisans call it a war of premeditated Israeli aggression.

12. UNSCR 242 is the most important document pertaining to the Arab-Israeli peace process, and is worth reading in its entirety.

13. The War of Attrition consisted of roughly a hundred days of relatively low-level military activity on the post-1967 frontiers. It was begun by Nasir in March 1969 in hopes of making Israel's occupation more painful and less tenable. Israel escalated the conflict, however, in hopes of deterring Egypt, and other fronts erupted too, including among the PLO in Jordan. A major war seemed in the offing. It was at this point that U.S. diplomacy tried to avoid a new war and turn matters toward diplomacy. War was avoided—at least for a while—but the anticipated diplomacy fell victim to the Jordanian civil war and Nasir's sudden death.

14. The first victim of Palestinian terror after the Jordanian civil war was Jordan's Prime Minister Wasfi al-Tal. The most infamous, probably, was the murder of eleven members of Israel's Olympic team in Munich in 1972.

15. Like many things in this story, different people use different names for the same events and places, as we have already seen. The Egyptians call this the War of the Crossing, for they crossed the Suez Canal back into the Sinai. Americans and American Jews call it the Yom Kippur War because it began on Yom Kippur, and most of them think that this is what Israelis also call it. But that's wrong. Most Israelis refer to it, then and now, as *Milhemet Yom Ha-Deen*, the War of Judgment Day. Judgment Day is another name for Yom Kippur, but it connotes something special: that the war was also a judgment on Israel's diplomacy between June 1967 and October 1973. The October War is the most neutral name, so that's the one we use here.

16. Nasir died of a heart attack in September 1970, just after the Jordanian civil war.

17. The phrase derives from a universally known hymn sung every Friday evening called *L'kha Dodi*.

18. There is still much debate about why the United States delayed the resupply to Israel. (See Joseph J. Sisco, "America in the Middle East, *Orbis* 39:2 [Spring 1995].) It is clear, however, that one of the reasons President Nixon ordered it was a message from Prime Minister Meir saying that if Israel were to soon feel itself in mortal danger, it would have no choice but to use nuclear weapons to save itself.

19. These are detailed in my *Israel and Jordan in the Shadow of War.*

20. They were, and remain, quite wrong about this. For a short explanation, see Bernard Wasserstein's article in the *Jerusalem Post*, June 17, 1983. For a more detailed discussion, see my *War, Water, and Negotiation in the Middle East*, pp. 100–109, 137–143 in particular.

21. Shiites are heterodox Muslims. In Lebanon, they were a large but virtually powerless confessional sect until the Israeli invasion. Israeli soldiers were greeted with flowers and rice by Shiite villagers, grateful for Israel's liberating them from the thuggery of the PLO. But Israel overstayed its welcome and, thanks to Iranian interference, Shiite fundamentalists now represent a serious problem. Israel has maintained a security zone in southern Lebanon ever since its main withdrawal in 1984, and there it supports a mainly Christian Lebanese force called the Southern Lebanese Army (SLA).

Israel's position is that as soon as the Lebanese government takes control of the area and prevents attacks against Israel, Israel will withdraw to the international border. In fact, Lebanese foreign policy has been dictated by Syria since the late 1980s, and Syria—allied with Iran—finds Hizballah useful leverage in Syria's competition with Israel.

22. *Davar*, August 15, 1995, p. 2.

23. Tajiks speak Dari, which is similar to Persian.

24. See Barbara Opall-Rome, "Israel Promotes Regional Arrow," *Defense News*, May 10, 1999.

Chapter 7. Peace and Normalcy?

1. Some claim otherwise, but their history is faulty. See my *War, Water, and Negotiations*, pp. 143–144.

2. In 1988, Yasir Arafat, chairman of the PLO, did make the requisite statements demanded by the United States back in 1975 in the context of the second Israeli-Egyptian disengagement agreement. Arafat recognized the validity of UNSCR 242 and UNSCR 338 (passed after the October 1973 War to implement UNSCR 242), and renounced terrorism. This was enough for the United States to open a relationship with the PLO, called a dialogue, but it did not satisfy the Likud government in Israel. The United States eventually broke off the dialogue in 1990, when the PLO either would not or could not honor its commitment to abjure terrorism.

3. The problem of a Palestinian delegation long bedeviled the negotiating process. Israel insisted it would not negotiate with the PLO, which was dedicated to Israel's destruction. Over a period of several years, Israel moved from complete opposition to negotiating with non-PLO PLO appointees, to a position of deliberately not checking too closely the credentials of Palestinian delegates, to a position of negotiating with the PLO indirectly via the Washington delegation after Madrid, to a position of negotiating directly with the PLO in secret, and finally to a position of negotiating directly with the PLO in public. Israel's positions changed, but only because those of the PLO did, too.

4. The director-general of the Foreign Ministry is the highest-ranking civil servant in the ministry, as opposed to the political appointee, who is foreign minister. Israel's foreign service is a professional one, much like that in the United States and the European countries.

5. The relevant American diplomats knew something was going on in Oslo, but not what it signified nor any details.

6. Except the Egyptian leadership, which was kept informed of Israeli-PLO negotiations.

7. Actually, this agreement had been reached the previous October and then put in a form of political-diplomatic escrow until the Israeli-Palestinian track caught up. Jordan was always very reluctant to get too far out in front of the PLO, owing to the fact that more than half of Jordan's population on the east bank is Palestinian in origin.

8. Frenkel quoted in William J. Orme, Jr., "Israeli Business Flies Like a Dove," *New York Times*, October 18, 1998; and see Yaron Ezrahi, "In Israel, Peace Means Prosperity," *New York Times*, January 21, 1997.

9. Even if Israel continues to have problems with countries like Iran, which does not share a frontier with Israel, solving these kinds of problems does not rely on armored divisions and the thousands of men who soldier them. It relies on high technology solutions that are not as manpower intensive.

10. Another thing Israelis are going to have to get used to eventually is a thing called a train. There is a train from Jerusalem to Tel Aviv (that moves about as fast as a nine-year-old's go-cart), and another that goes up and down the coast between Haifa and Tel

Aviv. But Israel doesn't have a sophisticated commuter rail system, and it needs one badly. If Israelis keep buying cars and building highways at the present rate to alleviate traffic congestion—and if the rate increases as the economy grows—the entire country will slide into the Great Rift Valley from the sheer weight of the concrete.

11. In early 1995, Likud leader Benyamin Netanyahu began speaking about West Bank Palestinians friendly to Jordan as an alternative to the PLO. After the peace treaty with Jordan, the Likud developed its own version of a Jordan Option, which must rank as one of the greatest ironies of Israeli history. It wasn't clear, however, if Netanyahu was serious or merely grasping for ideas amid accusations that Likud had no alternative to the Labor government's policies.

12. In recent years, Israel has taken to importing foreign labor—Thais for agriculture and Romanians for construction, for example—because despite Namir's efforts, Israelis simply would not take the jobs. This has caused lots of problems. See Serge Schmemann, "Foreign Workers Replacing Arabs on Israeli Farms," *New York Times*, August 14, 1995; and Soug Struck, "Joblessness, Slaying Stirs Israel Anger at Foreign Workers," *Washington Post*, April 27, 1998.

13. See, for example, Sidney Blumenthal, "The Western Front," *The New Yorker*, June 5, 1995, pp. 36–42.

14. Out-of-area is a term of the art for how the alliance should act with respect to problems that were not sited on the national territory of any of the sixteen NATO members.

15. See Arthur Hertzberg, *America and Its Jews* (New York: Simon and Schuster, 1989).

16. President Wilson is quoted in Arthur M. Schlesinger, Jr., *The Disuniting of America* (New York: W.W. Norton, 1992), p. 35.

17. Eliot A. Cohen, "Israel After Heroism," *Foreign Affairs*, November–December 1998, p. 113.

18. Yaron Ezrahi, *Rubber Bullets: Power and Conscience in Modern Israel* (New York: Farrar, Straus, and Giroux, 1997), p. 71.

19. See Deborah Sontag, "Israelis Debate Burying Bronfman among Heroes," *New York Times*, February 3, 1999.

20. Joel Greenberg, "Israel's History, Viewed Candidly, Starts a Storm," *New York Times*, April 10, 1998.

Glossary

of Hebrew Terms

and Acronyms

admat qodesh   holy land, a phrase appearing but once in the Five Books of Moses, with reference not to Eretz Israel but to Mt. Sinai.

agarah (pl., **agarot**)   a monetary unit, 100 of which at various times have made up an Israeli pound, a sheqel, or a new sheqel.

agunah   a woman who has been abandoned by her husband and cannot locate him or his body either to get a divorce or prove him deceased.

Ahdut Ha-avodah   Workers' Unity Party; socialist political party presently within the Labor Party.

Al-Hamishmar   On Guard; the newspaper of the Mapam Party.

aliyah   ascent or going up, the act of immigrating to Israel; also, the ascent to the reading of the Torah in synagogue ritual.

Aman   Israeli Military Intelligence.

Asefat Hanivharim   Assembly of the Elected; Israel's proto-parliament during Mandate times.

Ashkenaz   old Hebrew word for Germany; refers to Jews of European background.

asimon (pl., asimonim)   public telephone token.

Ayrutz Shtayim   Channel 2; Hebrew television station.

Bank HaPoalim   Workers' Bank; the bank of the socialist Yishuv formed during Mandate times.

Bar Mitzvah   Son of the Commandments; the ceremony by which adolescents assume personal moral responsibility for keeping Jewish law.

Bezek   Flash; Israel's state-owned communications company.

B'nei Israel   Children of Israel; refers literally to Jacob's twelve sons and generally to the Jewish people.

bor bitahon   security hole.

botz   mud; Hebrew slang for Turkish coffee.

B'tezlem   In the Image; Israel's most prominent human rights organization.

cafe hafookh   upside-down coffee; *cafe latte.*

Davar   Word, or Thing; Labor Party newspaper.

Davidka   a noise-making mortar cannon that supposedly convinced the Arabs of Safad in 1948 that the Jews had some superweapon ready to use against them.

Degel HaTorah   Flag of the Torah; Agudah Israel Party faction led by Rabbi Eliezer Schach.

Edot Hamizrah   Oriental Jewish communities.

Ein Gedi   Well of the Kid; a large spring near the Dead Sea.

Emek Ha-bakha   the Valley of Tears; refers to a battle in the Golan Heights during the October 1973 War, but also a phrase from a well-known Friday evening hymn.

Eretz Israel   Land of Israel.

Eretz Israel ha-sh'leyma complete land of Israel; commonly known in English as Greater Israel, meaning Israel and most of the territories occupied in June 1967.

Etzel acronym for Irgun Tzvai L'umi, National Military Organization; Revisionist Zionist para-military organization in Mandate times.

Galei Tzahal Waves of the Army; the IDF radio station.

galut exile.

garinim sunflower seeds.

G'dud HaIvri Jewish Brigade; the Yishuv's military force in World War I.

Gemorrah second part of the Talmud.

goy (pl. goyim) nation; literally means "gentile," but is sometimes used in a deprecatory sense.

Gush Emunim Bloc of the Faithful; religio-nationalist settler group that emerged after 1967.

Gush Herut Liberali Liberal Freedom Bloc; Revisionist Zionist party.

Ha'aretz independent newspaper.

Ha'avara transfer of Jews and Jewish property out of Germany to Palestine in cooperation with the Jewish Agency before 1939.

HaBimah The Stage; Israel's national theater.

Haganah Defense Force; the military wing of the Zionist movement in Mandate times.

halakha Jewish religious law.

haluka charity collected for religious institutions.

halutz (pl. halutzim) pioneer.

HaMashbir HaMerkazi Central Supplier; economic institution of the Yishuv in Mandate times.

hamtana   waiting period after mobilization.

hanta-reesh   male bovine feces.

Hanukkah   Rededication; minor Jewish holiday celebrating overthrow of Hellenic domination and reestablishment of Jewish independence in 165 B.C.E.

HaOomot Hame'uhadot   United Nations.

Hapoel HaMizrahi   Workers' Mizrahi; labor wing of the Mizrahi movement.

HaPoel HaTza'ir   Young Worker; socialist Zionist political faction in Mandate times.

hardal   acronym for haredit datit leumit; ultra-Orthodox religious nationalists; also means "mustard."

haredim   those who fear God; non-Zionist or anti-Zionist ultra-Orthodox.

HaShahar   The Dawn; nineteenth-century Hebrew literary journal in Russia.

hasidim   followers; religious movement of some ultra-Orthodox.

haskalah   enlightenment.

Hatikva   The Hope; Israeli national anthem.

Ha-Tzofeh   The Vista; newspaper of the National Religious Party.

herum   emergency.

Herut   Freedom; Revisionist political party.

Hevrat Ovdim   Workers' Association; cooperative economic institution of the Yishuv founded in 1923.

Hiriya   a large garbage dump south of Tel Aviv.

Histadrut   the labor union federation.

hutz la'aretz   outside the land of Israel.

Irgun Tzvai L'umi   National Military Organization; also Etzel by acronym, or just Irgun for short.

jinjee   red-head.

Kach   Thus, or This Way; right-wing political movement.

Kahane Hai   Kahane Lives; right-wing political movement split off from Kach.

kibbutz (pl. **kibbutzim**)   socialist agricultural collective settlement, derived from the Hebrew word for group, *k'vutzah.*

kinor   harp.

kipah (pl. **kipot**)   skullcap.

Klal Israel   All Israel; the people of Israel.

Knesset   Israeli parliament; from the word for assembly, *kinnus.*

Kol Israel   Voice of Israel; state radio station.

konninut   mobilization.

Kupat Holim   Sick Fund; Histadrut-associated national health-care program.

La'am   For the People; Labor party faction that joined Likud.

leben   yoghurt.

Lehi   acronym for Lohamei Herut Israel, see below.

Lohamei Herut Israel or **Lehi**   Stern Gang, a Revisionist paramilitary group during Mandate times.

ma'abarot   temporary tent cities for immigrants owing to lack of housing.

Ma'arakh Ha-avodah   the Labor alignment.

Ma'ariv   Evening; mass-circulation newspaper.

Mabat   Perspective or View; popular television news show.

Maccabee   Hebrew name of family after which the Hasmonean dynasty was founded; also name of an Israeli brand of beer.

Maccabiya   Israel's Jewish Olympic games.

Mafdal   acronym for Hamiflaga Hadatit Haleumit; National Religious Party.

Magen David Adom   Red Shield of David; Israeli equivalent of the Red Cross.

Maki   acronym for Mifleget HaKommunistit HaIsraelit; Israel Communist Party.

mamlakhtiyut   statism.

Mapai   acronym for Mifleget Poalei Eretz Israel; Land of Israel Workers Party.

Mapam   acronym for Mifleget Poalim Ham'uehedet; United Workers Party.

mekhes   customs duty.

Mekorot   Sources of Fountains; Israel's semiprivate water engineering company.

Meretz   left-wing political party formed from Mapan, Ratz, and Shinui.

Merkaz Ruhani   Spiritual Center; the Mizrahi movement.

miklat   bomb shelter.

Mikveh Yisrael   Hope of Israel; agricultural school established in Jaffa in 1870.

milhemet ain brayra   a war without choice.

Milhemet Yom Ha-Deen   the War of the Day of Judgment; the October 1973 War.

miluim   military reserves.

Mishnah   the first part of the Talmud.

Misrad HaKlitah   Ministry of Absorption.

misnagdim   those whose oppose the *hasidim.*

mitzvot   commandments; the 613 laws of the Torah and other religious injunctions derived from them.

Mizrahi, Merkaz Ruhani   Spiritual Center.

Moledet   birthplace and homeland; also a right-wing political party.

moshav (pl. mos havim)   a cooperative agricultural settlement but with private ownership and private profits.

Mossad   Israel's foreign intelligence service.

nahal   a paramilitary settlement.

nasi   president.

nes   miracle; also slang for instant coffee.

Ofek   Horizon; a satellite launched by Israel in March 1995.

Ohel   Tent; Yishuv theater company founded in 1925.

olim   immigrants.

Oom-Shmoom   deprecatory phrase for United Nations.

Palmah   Haganah elite special forces unit.

protexia   protection; business or political connections.

prutah (pl. prutot)   a monetary unit, 1000 of which equaled an Israeli pound.

rabbi   Jewish clergyman; means "teacher."

Rakkah   acronym for R'shimat HaKommunisti Hahadasha, New Communist List.

Ratz   Citizen's Rights Party; now part of Meretz.

raysheet tzmihat g'ulatanu   the beginning of the dawn of our redemption; the State of Israel as conceived by religious Zionism.

Rehov Sumsum   Israel's version of *Sesame Street.*

rosh hamemshalah   head of government; prime minister.

Rosh Hashanah   New Year; major Jewish holiday in the autumn.

Sepharad   Hebrew word for Spain; refers to Jews of Iberian and Oriental background.

Shabak   acronym for Shirut Bitahon Klalit; General Security Service, Israel's internal security service.

shaliah (pl. shlihim)   emissary· representative of the Jewish Agency to the diaspora.

Shalom Akhshav   Peace Now; Israeli pro-peace group.

Shas   acronym for Sepharadim Shomre Torah; Sepharadic Torah Guardians; also an acronym for shisha sidrei Mishnah, the six books of the Mishnah.

sharav   a hot dry wind (*hamsin* in Arabic).

Shavit   Comet; Israeli ballistic missile.

shelemut ha-moledet   the entirety of the homeland; Revisionist Zionist concept or demand.

sheqel   weight; monetary unit.

shikun   housing and neighborhood; the Yishuv's housing construction company.

Shin Bet   short for Shirut Bitahon; security service; Israel's internal intelligence service. (See **Shabak**).

Shinui   Change; political party now part of Meretz.

Shoah   disaster; the Holocaust.

Shomron   Samaria; northern part of the West Bank.

siddur   Jewish prayer book.

Solel Boneh   Paving and Building; semiprivate construction company with origins in the Yishuv.

taharat neshek   purity of arms; concept concerning use of military force.

tal   dew; also a name.

talit   prayer shawl.

Talmud   Study; book of Jewish law and commentary made up of the Mishnah and the Gemorrah.

Tami   acronym for T'nuah Lamasoret b'Israel; Movement for Tradition in Israel, a Sepharadi political party.

Tanakh   the Hebrew Bible; an acronym made up from its three main parts: Torah (the Five Books of Moses), Nevi'im (Prophets), and Ketuvim (Writings).

Tehiya   Resurrection; now defunct right-wing political party.

tilim   projections, missiles; also, the range of extinct volcanoes on the Golan Heights.

T'nuva   Produce; cooperative economic institution dating from Mandate times.

Torah   Scroll of the Law; Five Books of Moses.

Tzahal   acronym for Tzvah Haganah L'Israel; see below.

Tzvah Haganah L'Israel   Israeli Defense Force.

tzimhoni   vegetarian; slang for a dovish politician.

Tzomet   Crossroad; right-wing political party.

Vaad Leumi   National Council; Zionist executive authority in Mandate times.

Yad Vashem   Hand and Name; Israel's memorial to the victims of the Holocaust.

Yam Hamelakh   The Salt Sea; the Dead Sea.

Yam Kineret   Lake Tiberias.

Yediot Aharonot   Latest News; mass-circulation newspaper.

Yehuda   Judea; southern part of the West Bank.

yerida   going down; emigration from Israel.

yeshiva   religious studies academy.

Yishuv   resettlement; the Zionist community in Palestine during pre-state times.

Zeh Hu Zeh   That's That; a popular television variety show; also the name of Israel's best-selling anti-lice medication.

Zohar   Splendor; the Jewish book of mysticism.

Suggested Readings

General Texts

Peretz, Don. *The Government and Politics of Israel.* Boulder, CO: Westview Press, 1983.

Reich, Bernard. *Israel: Land of Tradition and Conflict.* Boulder, CO: Westview Press, 1985.

Wolffson, Michael. *Israel: Polity, Society and Economy, 1882–1986.* Atlantic Highlands, NJ: Humanities Press International, 1987.

General Histories

Hohenberg, John. *Israel at 50: A Journalist's Perspective.* Syracuse: Syracuse University Press, 1998.

Idinopulos, Thomas A. *Weathered by Miracles: A History of Palestine from Bonaparte and Mohammed Ali to Ben-Gurion and the Mufti.* Chicago: Ivan R. Dee, 1998.

O'Brien, Conor Cruise. *The Siege: The Saga of Israel and Zionism.* New York: Simon and Schuster, 1986.

Perlmutter, Amos. *Israel: The Partitioned State.* New York: Scribner, 1985.

Sachar, Howard M. *A History of Israel from the Rise of Zionism to Our Time.* New York: Knopf, 1976.

———. *History of Israel, Vol. II: From the Aftermath of the Yom Kippur War.* New York: Oxford University Press, 1987.

Zionism and History of Zionism

Avineri, Shlomo. *The Making of Modern Zionism: The Intellectual Origins of the Jewish State.* New York: Basic Books, 1981.

Erlich, Avi. *Ancient Zionism: The Biblical Origins of the National Idea.* New York: Free Press, 1995.

Halpern, Ben. *The Idea of the Jewish State.* Cambridge, MA: Harvard University Press, 1970.

Hertzberg, Arthur, ed. *The Zionist Idea.* New York: Atheneum, 1969.

Laqueur, Walter. *A History of Zionism.* New York: Holt, Rinehart and Winston, 1972.

Vital, David. *The Origins of Zionism.* Oxford, UK: Oxford University Press, 1975.

325

————. *Zionism: The Formative Years.* Oxford, UK: Oxford University Press, 1982.
————. *Zionism: The Critical Phase.* Oxford, UK: Oxford University Press, 1987.
Wheatcroft, Geoffrey. *The Controversy of Zion.* Reading, MA: Addison-Wesley, 1996.

The Mandate Period and the Yishuv

Bauer, Yehuda. *From Diplomacy to Resistance.* Philadelphia: Jewish Publication Society, 1970.
Bell, J. Bowyer. *Terror Out of Zion: Lehi and the Palestine Underground, 1929–1949.* New York: St. Martin's Press, 1977.
Cohen, Mitchell. *Zion and State.* Oxford, UK: Basil Blackwell, 1987.
Hen-Tov, Jacob. *Communism and Zionism in Palestine.* Cambridge, MA: Schenkman, 1974.
Horowitz, Dan, and Lissak, Moshe. *The Origins of the Israeli Polity: Palestine Under the Mandate.* Chicago: University of Chicago Press, 1978.
Hurewitz, J. C. *The Struggle for Palestine.* New York: W.W. Norton, 1950.
Lucas, Noah. *The Modern History of Israel.* New York: Praeger, 1975.
Sanders, Ronald. *The High Walls of Jerusalem.* New York: Holt, Rinehart and Winston, 1983.
Shapiro, Yonathan. *The Israel Labor Party, 1919–1930.* Beverly Hills, CA: Sage, 1976.
Stein, Kenneth. *The Land Question in Palestine, 1917–1939.* Chapel Hill: University of North Carolina Press, 1984.
Stein, Leonard. *The Balfour Declaration.* New York: Simon and Schuster, 1961.
Sykes, Christopher. *Crossroads to Israel.* New York: World Publishing, 1966.
Wasserstein, Bernard. *The British in Palestine.* London: Royal Historical Society, 1978.

Selected Political Analyses

Aronoff, Myron J. *Power and Ritual in the Israeli Labor Party.* Armonk, NY: M.E. Sharpe, 1993.
Baker, Henry E. *The Legal System of Israel.* Jerusalem: Israel University Press, 1968.
Dowty, Alan. *The Jewish State: A Century Later.* Berkeley: University of California Press, 1998.
Ezrahi, Yaron. *Rubber Bullets: Power and Conscience in Modern Israel.* New York: Farrar, Straus and Giroux, 1997.
Fein, Leonard. *Politics in Israel.* Boston: Little, Brown, 1967.
Inbar, Efraim. *War and Peace in Israeli Politics.* Boulder, CO: Lynn Rienner, 1991.
Isaac, Jean Real. *Israel Divided: Ideological Politics in the Jewish State.* Baltimore: Johns Hopkins University Press, 1976.
————. *Party and Politics in Israel.* New York: Longman, 1981.
Kieval, Gershon. *Party Politics in Israel and the Occupied Territories.* Westport, CT: Greenwood, 1983.
Lazin, Frederick A., and Mahler, Gregory S., eds. *Israel in the Nineties: Development and Conflict.* Gainesville, FL: University of Florida Press, 1996.
Lehman-Wilzig, Sam. *Wildfire: Grassroots Revolts in Israel in the Post-Socialist Era.* Albany, NY: SUNY Press, 1992.
Mahler, Gregory S. *The Knesset: Parliament in the Israeli Political System.* Rutherford, NJ: Fairleigh Dickinson Press, 1981.
Medding, Peter Y. *Mapai in Israel.* Cambridge, MA: Cambridge University Press, 1972.
Nachmias, David, and Rosenbloom, David H. *Bureaucratic Culture, Citizens, and Administrators in Israel.* New York: St. Martin's Press, 1978.
Oz, Amos. *In the Land of Israel.* New York: Harcourt, Brace Jovanovich, 1983.

Peri, Yoram. *Between Battles and Ballots: Israeli Military in Politics.* London: Cambridge University Press, 1983.
Rackman, Emanuel. *Israel's Emerging Constitution, 1948–1951.* New York: Columbia University Press, 1955.
Roberts, Samuel J. *Party and Policy in Israel.* Boulder, CO: Westview Press, 1990.
Rubinstein, Amnon. *Israeli Constitutional Law.* Tel Aviv: Schocken, 1980.
Sager, Samuel. *The Parliamentary System of Israel.* Syracuse: Syracuse University Press, 1985.
Sharkansky, Ira. *What Makes Israel Tick?* Chicago: Nelson-Hall, 1985.
Shimshoni, Daniel. *Israeli Democracy: The Middle of the Journey.* New York: Free Press, 1982.
Sprinzak, Ehud. *The Ascendance of Israel's Radical Right.* Oxford, UK: Oxford University Press, 1991.
Wolfsfeld, Gadi. *The Politics of Provocation: Participation and Protest in Israel.* Albany, NY: SUNY Press, 1988.
Yaacobi, Gad. *The Government of Israel.* New York: Praeger, 1982.
Zidon, Asher. *Knesset: The Parliament of Israel.* New York: Herzl Press, 1967.
Zohar, David M. *Political Parties in Israel.* New York: Praeger, 1982.

Society and Economy

Abramov, S. Zalman. *Perpetual Dilemma: Jewish Religion in the Jewish State.* Rutherford, NJ: Fairleigh Dickinson Press, 1976.
Aharoni, Yair. *The Israeli Economy: Dreams and Realities.* New York: Routledge, 1991.
Aronoff, Myron. *Israeli Visions and Divisions.* New Brunswick, NJ: Transaction, 1989.
Badi, Joseph. *Religion in Israel Today.* New York: Bookman Associates, 1959.
Ben-Rafael, Eliezer. *The Emergence of Ethnicity.* Westport, CT: Greenwood, 1982.
Curtis, Michael, and Chertoff, Mordechai S., eds. *Israel: Social Structure and Change.* New Brunswick, NJ: Transaction, 1973.
Deshen, Shlomo, Liebman, Charles S., and Shokeid, Moshe, eds. *Israeli Judaism.* New Brunswick, NJ: Transaction, 1995.
Efrat, Elisha. *Urbanization in Israel.* New York: St. Martin's Press, 1984.
Eisenstadt, S. N. *Israeli Society.* New York: Basic Books, 1967.
El-Asmar, Fouzi. *To Be an Arab in Israel.* London: Francis Pinter, 1975.
Elon, Amos. *The Israelis: Founders and Sons.* New York: Holt, Rinehart and Winston, 1971.
Etzioni-Halevy, Eva. *Political Culture in Israel.* New York: Praeger, 1977.
Evron, Boas. *Jewish State or Israeli Nation.* Bloomington: University of Indiana Press, 1995.
Friedlander, Dov, and Goldscheider, Calvin. *The Population of Israel.* New York: Columbia University Press, 1979.
Goldscheider, Calvin. *Israel's Changing Society: Population, Ethnicity, and Development.* Boulder, CO: Westview, 1996.
Hareven, Alouph, ed. *Every Sixth Israeli: Relations between the Jewish Majority and the Arab Minority in Israel.* Jerusalem: Van Leer Foundation, 1983.
Harkabi, Yehoshafat. *The Bar Kochba Syndrome.* New York: Rosel Books, 1983.
Horowitz, David. *The Economics of Israel.* New York: Pergamon, 1967.
Jones, Clive. *Soviet Jewish Aliyah, 1989–1992: Impact and Implications for Israel and the Middle East.* London: Frank Cass, 1996.
Kanovsky, Eliyahu. *The Economy of the Israeli Kibbutz.* Cambridge, MA: Harvard University Press, 1966.
Kimmerling, Baruch. *Zionism and Economy.* Cambridge, MA: Schenkman, 1983.

————. *The Interrupted System.* New Brunswick, NJ: Transaction, 1985.

Kraines, Oscar. *The Impossible Dilemma: Who Is a Jew in the State of Israel?* New York: Bloch, 1976.

Landau, Jacob. *The Arabs in Israel: A Political Study.* London: Oxford University Press, 1969.

Leibman, Charles S., ed. *Conflict and Accommodation between Jews in Israel.* Jerusalem: Keter, 1990.

Leibman, Charles S., and Don-Yehiya, Eliezer. *Civil Religion in Israel.* Berkeley: University of California Press, 1983.

————. *Religion and Politics in Israel.* Bloomington: University of Indiana Press, 1984.

Luttwak, Edward, and Horowitz, Dan. *The Israeli Army.* New York: Harper and Row, 1975.

Mittelberg, David. *Strangers in Paradise: The Israeli Kibbutz Experience.* New Brunswick, NJ: Transaction, 1988.

Perlmutter, Amos. *Military and Politics in Israel.* London: Frank Cass, 1969.

Rouhana, Nadim N. *Palestinian Citizens in an Ethnic Jewish State.* New Haven: Yale University Press, 1997.

Schiff, Gary S. *Tradition and Politics: The Religious Parties of Israel.* Detroit: Wayne State University Press, 1977.

Smooha, Sammy. *Israel: Pluralism and Conflict.* London: Routledge and Kegan Paul, 1978.

Sprinzak, Ehud. *Brother against Brother: Violence and Extremism in Israeli Politics from Altalena to the Rabin Assassination.* New York: Free Press, 1999.

Wistrich, Robert, ed. *The Shaping of Israeli Identity—Myth, Memory, Trauma.* London: Frank Cass, 1995.

Foreign Policy

Amir, Shimon. *Israel's Development Cooperation with Africa, Asia, and Latin America.* New York: Praeger, 1974.

Ben-Tvi, Avraham. *The United States and Israel: The Limits of the Special Relationship.* New York: Columbia University Press, 1993.

Bialer, Uri. *Between East and West: Israel's Foreign Policy Orientation, 1948–1956.* Cambridge, UK: Cambridge University Press, 1990.

Brecher, Michael. *The Foreign Policy System of Israel.* New Haven: Yale University Press, 1973.

Cohen, Avner. *Israel and the Bomb.* New York: Columbia University Press, 1998.

Crosbie, Sylvia. *A Tacit Alliance: France and Israel.* Princeton, NJ: Princeton University Press, 1974.

Davis, Moshe, ed. *World Jewry and the State of Israel.* New York: Arno Press, 1977.

Draper, Theodore. *Israel and World Politics.* New York: Viking, 1968.

Inbar, Efraim, ed. *Regional Security Regimes: Israel and Its Neighbors.* Albany: SUNY Press, 1995.

Kimche, David. *The Last Option: After Nasser, Arafat and Saddam Hussein.* New York: Scribner's, 1991.

Kleiman, Aaron. *Israel's Global Reach: Arms Sales as Diplomacy.* Washington, DC: Pergamon-Brassey, 1985.

————. *Israel and the World After 40 Years.* Washington, DC: Pergamon-Brassey, 1990.

Laufer, Leopold. *Israel and the Developing Countries.* New York: Twentieth Century Fund, 1967.

Rabinovich, Itamar, and Reinharz, Judah, eds. *Israel in the Middle East.* Oxford, UK: Oxford University Press, 1984.

Reich, Bernard. *Securing the Covenant: United States-Israeli Relations after the Cold War.* Westport, CT: Praeger, 1995.

Reiser, Stewart. *The Israeli Arms Industry.* New York: Holmes and Meier, 1989.

Sela, Avraham, and Maoz, Moshe, eds. *The PLO and Israel: From Armed Struggle to Political Solution, 1964–1994.* New York: St. Martin's Press, 1997.

Stock, Ernest. *Israel on the Road to Sinai, 1949–1956.* Ithaca, NY: Cornell University Press, 1967.

Arab-Israeli Conflict

Bar-Zohar, Michael. *Facing a Cruel Mirror.* New York: Scribner's 1990.

Ciment, James. *Palestine/Israel: The Long Conflict.* New York: Facts on File, 1997.

Dowty, Alan. *Middle East Crises.* Berkeley: University of California Press, 1984.

Eisenberg, Laura Zittrain, and Caplan, Neil. *Negotiating Arab-Israeli Peace: Patterns, Problems, Possibilities.* Bloomington: Indiana University Press, 1997.

Fraser, T. G. *The Arab-Israeli Conflict.* New York: St. Martin's Press, 1995.

Garfinkle, Adam. *Israel and Jordan in the Shadow of War.* New York: St. Martin's Press, 1992.

Grossman, David. *The Yellow Wind.* New York: Farrar, Straus and Giroux, 1988.

Harkabi, Yehoshafat. *Arab Strategies and Israel's Response.* New York: Free Press, 1977.

Kemp, Geoffrey, and Pressman, Jeremy. *Point of No Return: The Deadly Struggle for Middle East Peace.* Washington, DC: Carnegie Endowment, 1997.

Mendes-Flohr, Paul R., ed. *A Land of Two Peoples: Martin Buber on Jews and Arabs.* New York: Oxford University Press, 1983.

Morris, Benny. *Israel's Border Wars, 1949–1956.* Oxford, UK: Oxford University Press, 1994.

———. *1948 and After.* Oxford, UK: Oxford University Press, 1990.

———. *The Birth of the Palestine Refugee Problem, 1947–1949.* Cambridge, UK: Cambridge University Press, 1987.

Ovendale, Ritchie. *The Origins of the Arab-Israeli Wars.* New York: Longman, 1984.

Reich, Bernard, ed. *Arab-Israeli Conflict and Conciliation: A Documentary History.* Westport, CT: Praeger, 1995.

Rubinstein, Alvin Z., ed. *The Arab-Israeli Conflict: Perspectives.* New York: HarperCollins, 1990.

Saunders, Harold H. *The Other Walls.* Washington, DC: American Enterprise Institute, 1985.

Shalev, Aryeh. *The Intifada: Causes and Effects.* Boulder, CO: Westview Press, 1992.

———. *Israel and Syria: Peace and Security on the Golan Heights.* Tel Aviv: Jaffee Center, 1994.

Sheffer, Gabriel, ed. *Dynamics of a Conflict.* Atlantic Heights, NJ: Humanities Press International, 1975.

Sicherman, Harvey. *Palestinian Autonomy.* Boulder, CO: Westview Press, 1992.

Tessler, Mark. *The History of the Israeli-Palestinian Conflict.* Bloomington: University of Indiana Press, 1994.

Wagner, Abraham. *Crisis Decision-Making: Israel's Experience in 1967 and 1973.* New York: Praeger, 1974.

Yaniv, Avner. *Dilemmas of Security.* New York: Oxford University Press, 1987.

Relations with the United States

Arens, Moshe. *Broken Covenant.* New York: Simon and Schuster, 1995.

Blitzer, Wolf. *Territory of Lies*. New York: Harper and Row, 1989.
————. *Between Washington and Jerusalem*. New York: Oxford University Press, 1985.
Melman, Yossi, and Raviv, Dan. *Friends in Deed*. New York: Hyperion, 1994.
Quandt, William. *Decade of Decisions*, 2nd ed. Berkeley: University of California Press, 1994.
Reich, Bernard. *Quest for Peace*. New Brunswick, NJ: Transaction, 1977.
————. *The United States and Israel: Influence in the Special Relationship*. New York: Praeger, 1984.
————. *Securing the Covenant: United States-Israel Relations after the Cold War*. Westport, CT: Greenwood, 1995.
Safran, Nadav. *Israel: The Embattled Ally*. Cambridge, MA: Harvard University Press, 1981.

Biography and Autobiography

Allon, Yigal. *The Making of Israel's Army*. New York: Universe Books, 1970.
Bar-Zohar, Michael. *Ben-Gurion: The Armed Prophet*. Englewood Cliffs, NJ: Prentice-Hall, 1968.
Begin, Menachem. *The Revolt*. New York: Nash, 1981.
Ben-Gurion, David. *Israel: A Personal History*. New York: Funk and Wagnall, 1971.
————. *My Talks with Arab Leaders*. Jerusalem: Keter, 1972.
Dayan, Moshe. *Story of My Life*. New York: Morrow, 1976.
————. *Breakthrough*. New York: Knopf, 1981.
Elon, Amos. *Herzl*. New York: Holt, Rinehart and Winston, 1975.
Eshed, Haggai, *Reuven Shiloah—The Man behind the Mossad*. London: Frank Cass, 1997.
Gervasi, Frank. *The Life and Times of Menahem Begin*. New York: Putnam, 1979.
Haber, Eitan. *Menachem Begin: The Legend and the Man*. New York: Delacorte, 1978.
Herzog, Chaim. *Living History*. New York: Pantheon, 1996.
Meir, Golda. *My Life*. New York: Putnam, 1975.
Pawel, Ernst. *The Labyrinth of Exile: A Life of Theodore Herzl*. New York: Farrar, Straus and Giroux, 1989.
Peres, Shimon. *David's Sling*. New York: Random House, 1971.
Prittie, Terence. *Eshkol: The Man and the Nation*. New York: Pitman, 1969.
Rabin, Yitzhak. *The Rabin Memoirs*. Boston: Little, Brown, 1979.
Reinharz, Judah. *Chaim Weizmann: The Making of a Zionist Leader*. New York: Oxford University Press, 1985.
Sharon, Ariel. *Warrior*. New York: Simon and Schuster, 1989.
Tamir, Avraham. *A Soldier in Search of Peace*. New York: Harper and Row, 1988.
Teveth, Shabtai. *Ben-Gurion: The Burning Ground, 1886–1948*. New York: Houghton Mifflin, 1987.
Weizmann, Chaim. *Trial and Error*. Philadelphia: Jewish Publication Society, 1949.
Weizmann, Ezer. *On Eagles' Wings*. New York: Macmillan, 1977.
————. *The Battle for Peace*. New York: Bantam, 1981.

Representative Fiction in English Translation

Bloch, Chana, and Mitchell, Stephen, eds. *Selected Poetry of Yehuda Amichai*. New York: Harper and Row, 1986.
Kaniuk, Yoram. *Confessions of a Good Arab*. New York: Braziller, 1988.
Kishon, Efraim. *The Baumalich Canal and Other Stories*. Tel Aviv: Oved, 1987.
Oz, Amos. *My Michael*. New York: Knopf, 1972.
Shammas, Anton. *Arabesques*. New York: Harper and Row, 1988.

Index*

* This is an abbreviated index in two ways. First, with a few exceptions, references to anything that occurs in the text only once, or that is referred to only in passing, have been omitted. Second, material in notes to the chapters is also not indexed since this material is tied by number directly to the text.

mamlakhtiyut (statism), 86, 117, 193
Mandate for Palestine; *see* British Mandate
  for Palestine
Mapai (*Mifleget Poalei Eretz Israel*, Land of
  Israel Workers Party), 79, 84, 179–
  181
Mapam (*Mifleget Poalim Ham'uehedet*,
  United Workers Party), 79, 179, 187
Marx, Karl, 40, 135
Marxism, 47, 80
media, 16, 30, 115, 150, 187–190
Meir, Golda, 59, 126, 160, 204–205, 222
Meretz, 161, 179–180, 195, 197, 257, 275
messiah, messianism, 25–28, 30, 34, 88,
  103, 144, 221, 255
military courts, 65, 171–173
military doctrine, 67–69, 206–207, 211–
  212, 284
military industry, 133–135
miluim (reserve duty), 15, 68, 271
Ministry of Absorption, 140
Ministry of Agriculture, 132
Ministry of Defense, 111–112, 252
Ministry of Foreign Affairs, 110, 203–205,
  252
Ministry of Health, 127–128, 191
Ministry of the Interior, 140, 190
Ministry of Religious Affairs, 140
Mixed Armistice Commission, 62, 207, 241
Mizrahi, 76–78, 185
Mohilever, Rabbi Samuel, 76
Moledet (political party), 88, 110, 166, 184,
  275
Montagu, Edwin, 45
Morocco, 63, 89, 98, 104, 185, 195, 243,
  272
Mossad, 94, 204–205
municipal government, 107, 155, 190–192
Mussolini, Benito, 47, 49, 52

nachtasyl (night shelter), 102
al-Nasir, Gamal Abd, 208–217
National Religious Party (*HaMafdal*,
  Hamiflaga Hadatit Haleumit), 79,
  161–162, 185–186, 188, 217, 221
National Water Carrier, 71, 91, 212–213
nationalism, 21–22, 34–35, 37–39, 42–43,
  47, 105, 152–154, 214, 215, 218,
  241, 253
Nazism, 47, 49–51, 66, 237
Negev Desert, 53, 67, 71, 107, 210, 272
Netanyahu, Benyamin, 100, 164, 167–169,
  171, 183–184, 194, 233, 246, 257–
  269, 271, 291

Neturei Karta (Guardians of the City), 79
New Zionist Organization; *see* Zionism,
  Revisionist
newspapers; *see* media
Nixon, Richard, 222, 224, 230
Nordau, Max, 40, 46
nuclear weapons, 147, 211, 215, 231, 235,
  238–239, 245, 283–284

October (1973) War, 127, 204, 222–226,
  230, 243, 248
Orthodox Judaism, 78–79, 139–141, 145,
  284, 288
Osirak raid, 116, 204
Oslo II, 254–255, 257, 261, 269
Oslo track, 205, 247, 252–254, 261, 266, 273
Ottoman Turkey, 6, 26, 28–29, 37, 44, 76,
  140, 237

Pakistan, 93, 208
Palestine (Palestina), 27, 29, 36, 39–40, 44–
  45, 53, 61, 65–66, 69
Palestine Authority (PA), 89, 171, 256, 260,
  264, 269–270
Palestine Conciliation Committee, 62–63
Palestine Liberation Organization (PLO),
  79, 199, 212–213, 220–221, 225,
  228, 248–255, 277
Palestinian Arabs, 51–52, 54–55, 61, 83, 93,
  184, 215, 218–219. 245–246, 248–
  249, 276
Palestinian autonomy, 249, 254, 258–259
Palmah, 92, 110, 205
Peres, Shimon, 105, 127, 163, 166–167, 169,
  182–183, 204–206, 211, 228, 246,
  252–253, 256–257, 259–262, 276
peripheral strategy, 93
Persia; *see* Iran
Pogrom, 35
Poland, 29, 37, 47, 89, 101, 202, 237
political culture, 9–11, 80, 95–96, 154–157,
  291
political Zionism, 40–41, 44
Pollard, Jonathan, 231–232
population; *see* Jewish population of Eretz
  Israel
practical Zionism, 40–41, 44
Presidency, 169–171
price controls, 131–132
Prime Ministry, 111, 159–162, 165–167,
  198–199
Privatization, 100, 118, 128
projection state, 4–5
Provisional National Council, 57–58, 156

Adam Garfinkle has taught Middle East politics at the University of Pennsylvania and Haverford College, and his essays on the Middle East have appeared in such journals as *Middle Eastern Studies*, *The National Interest*, *Political Science Quarterly*, *The Jerusalem Quarterly*, *Current History*, and *Orbis*. He is the author of *Israel and Jordan in the Shadow of War* (1992), and of *Western Europe's Middle East Diplomacy and the United States* (1982). He is presently completing *Deep and Wide*, a book on the historical relationship between high politics and water in the Jordan Valley from 1916 to the present. Dr. Garfinkle is now an adjunct faculty member of the School of Advanced International Studies, the Johns Hopkins University. He is the former executive editor of *The National Interest*, and former director of the Middle East Council at the Foreign Policy Research Institute in Philadelphia.